96

FIRE
ON
THE
RIM

FIRE
ON
THE
RIM

A Firefighter's Season at the Grand Canyon

Stephen J. Pyne

With a New Preface by the Author

University of Washington Press

Seattle and London

Library of Congress Cataloging-in-Publication Data
Pyne, Stephen J., 1949–
    Fire on the rim : a firefighter's season at the Grand Canyon / Stephen J. Pyne
      p.   cm.
    ISBN 0-295-97483-4 (pbk. : alk. paper)
    1. Wildfires—Arizona—Grand Canyon National Park—Prevention and
control. 2. Wildfire fighters—Arizona—Grand Canyon National Park. 3. Pyne,
Stephen J., 1949-   . I. Title.
[SD421.P93 1995]   95-4726
363.37'9—dc20   CIP

To Sonja,
who shared most of it.
and the memory of Joseph R. Pyne,
who made it possible.

Contents

Reburn

FIRE ON THE RIM was a book I wanted to write for a long time but didn't know how and to some extent didn't know why. There were really three problems, related of course, but also autonomous.

The first was technical. How do you make a profoundly seasonal experience into a coherent narrative? Fire season has a beginning, middle, and end, and so do fire careers, but how to reconcile an annual cycle with a secular one baffled me for many years. The typical solution is to imitate a diary and highlight the bigger events of the chronology or to collapse the whole into a single, composite year. Neither, I decided, was good enough, but in pursuit of an alternative I chased a lot of waterdogs. Eventually I hammered out a format around the idea of a "great season," framed by initiating and valedictory years, that allowed me to say what I wanted to say. That decision led to the use of the historical present, the creation of composite events, and inevitable distortions as to who did what when. Not least it committed me to a narrative persona more or less fixed at a particular, and timeless, stage in his career. Accordingly I even found it necessary to invent one character to convey certain of my experiences without forcing the narrator to claim them. Still, all this gave coherence to the prose.

The second, more daunting problem was a coherence of purpose. Was this a collection of beer-fogged anecdotes, or did the experience, and through it, fire, acquire a larger significance? If so then the story needed the discipline of literature (with a small "l"). It needed, at its core, some moral drama.

As I read it, the literature of fire falls into three genres, a kind of conceptual fire triangle. One exploits fire as a narrative driver. The chronicle of a fire carries the other plots along with it, and fire illuminates, literally and symbolically, that larger narrative. Probably the classic expression is George Stewart's novel, *Fire.* That book captured most of the possibilities of fire as narrative, which is why, despite its technological anachronisms, the book continues to find an audience. The second genre hovers over the central existential drama of firefighting, the tragedy of the burned-over crew. Here is the trying fire, the fire of judgment, the fire that sorts out the living from the dead. It is the prospect of death by fire that, in practice, moves the experience of firefighting beyond the domain of outdoor recreation and that, in principle, elevates its literature beyond juvenile sports stories. But until Norman Maclean wrote *Young Men and Fire* the genre had few serious practitioners. Possibly Maclean has exhausted the literary prospects. It is difficult to imagine anyone revisting the subject without quoting his vision if not his words.

That leaves the third genre, firefighting as a rite of passage, fire season as a coming-of-age story. This is, by far, the most common experience of wildland firefighting, linked as it is to the seasonal employment of young people. Fire season becomes a time in one's life, the passage from adolescence to adulthood. What added rebars to the narrative concrete, however, is the fact that the year after I began at the North Rim the National Park Service changed its policy toward fire. An emerging wilderness ideology proposed that firefighting might be fundamentally wrong. So as fire became more important to the crew it became less so to the park, and the crew—the self-mocking Longshots—had to decide for themselves just what it was they were being initiated into. The park would have liked to dismiss them. What made us indispensable was that, whether Grand Canyon National Park cared or not, the fires kept coming.

Still, the transition is there, and it is that life passage to which the title *Fire on the Rim* refers, attempting to capture the moment through a geographic metaphor. (But while this was, from the beginning, the central metaphor of the book; it became the book's title only after Weidenfeld & Nicolson's marketing department flatly refused to promote a book called *Flame and Fortune*, which had been my working title from the beginning and which remains, to this day, the real title of the book in my mind. In the end I plucked "fire on the rim" from a subhead in the book's plotted center, the fire on The Dragon, and exchanged it for "flame and fortune.") Regardless, it was fire-season-as-coming-of-age that I wanted to get into something like formal literature. My barely voiced hope was that *Fire on the Rim* might become an archetype of its subgenre.

There remained one final conundrum. What did the experience mean to me personally? I hadn't wanted to leave. I left because the time had become undeniable, because wrenched knees, a bad back, a warped wrist, a growing family, and the burden of an unemployable Ph.D. forced me to leave. Leaving, I knew abstractly, was always a question of when, not whether. I left at the right time. But I wanted the possibility of returning, wanted to search Swamp Ridge once more for its elusive smokes, wanted to wander through the fire cache from time to time in a glow of comraderly nostalgia. I could do that if I left quietly. If I wrote a book like *Fire on the Rim*, I could not. I, and perhaps by implication the rest of the North Rim Longshots, would be forever persona non grata.

The rangers, in fact, did have their revenge. I interviewed on the *Today* show to promote the book until I was cut off in mid-sentence by an NBC news bulletin announcing the death of Lucille Ball. (I never did love Lucy.) A few days later the Glendale police staked out my house and nabbed me while, in gym shorts and baseball hat, I was pedaling my bicycle along the Arizona Canal and Diversion Channel. It seems there was another Steve Pyne, different middle name, different social security number, eighteen years younger in age, but this one was wanted on felony charges in Linn County, Iowa. The Iowa authorities cleverly tracked down and arrested (while away from his Uzi-armed bodyguards) the Steve Pyne who appeared on the *Today* show, not the one named in the warrant. I spent the night in the Madison Street jail with twenty low-lifes, watching my own life swirl down a toilet. Fortunately a MacArthur Fellowship check arrived and we used that to post bail. The episode left me with an arrest record and several thousand dollars poorer (after legal fees), and furthered my conviction that fire had been the right choice. As a postscript I learned that I could not inspect the warrant under which Linn County had ordered my arrest because its provisions were covered by privacy statutes, and not being the person named therein I had no right to see it. The Iowa authorities have not yet unsealed their files.

Closely related to the question of my future relationship to the Rim was the matter of my on-going one. If I was reluctant to distance myself physically from the Rim, I needed to distance myself emotionally. The kind of book that *Fire on the Rim* would become depended keenly on whether I wrote it while I still worked on the crew, or after I had left the Rim for a few years, or if I told the stories to my grandchildren. *When* I wrote would influence *what* I wrote. I thought the ideal time was while the sensory memories, the excitement and tedium both, were still fresh, but after a little distance had helped sort out the vicious from the merely irritating and the juvenile from the enduring. In September 1985, with the help of Jim Olson of the Rocky Mountain Regional Office, I returned for a two-week tour of duty to the North Rim as a grunt firefighter—this after a forlorn summer at Yellowstone trying to rewrite that park's fire plan. At midpoint during my tour the Longshots gathered for a reunion. The mixture of details reflects my furious notetaking during that brief reimmersion.

Not least, I crashed through the first draft after I had completed manuscript revisions for *The Ice*, a historical and philosophical meditation on Antarctica. Writing that book had utterly drained me. I had nothing left, not a phrase, not the scrapwood of an idea, not even a stray nail or two in the dirt. I was ravenous for sense impressions, data, details, all the minutiae of place and time and person that Antarctica had leached away. *Fire on the Rim* was for me an affirmation, the triumph of the senses over abstraction, the reclamation of fire over ice. Probably that accounts for the book's obsessive detail. Some of what I had gained from distance, I thus lost through reaction.

Nothing—not arrests, not ice, not official displeasure—has in the least dampened my satisfaction at having seen the book through as best I could or in revisiting the North Rim. I return often. I'm never disappointed. For me—for all of us—the North Rim remains the best of places and our seasons there the best of times.

The rekindling of *Fire on the Rim* is largely due to Bill Cronon, friend, colleague, and editor-in-waiting for the series of histories I have come to call Cycle of Fire. Without his pointed prompting I would never have overcome the implacable inertia of two publishers whose corporate indifference covered the book like a mudslide. Thanks go as well to Gerry McCauley, who skillfully exhumed the copyright, and to Don Ellegood and Julidta Tarver, who have given the book as good a home as an author could ask for. And not least, thanks go to the far-scattered Longshots who from time to time remind me of what it all meant and why it still matters.

Steve Pyne
Alpine, Arizona
April 1995

Fire Call

A FEW MONTHS after I turned eighteen, a day after I graduated from high school, I reported for work as a common laborer to the South Rim of Grand Canyon. Even as I signed my papers, an opening appeared on the fire crew at the North Rim. Because I was on the scene, I was offered the job. I accepted.

I returned to the North Rim every summer for the next fifteen years. In my fourth season, I became foreman.

I saw the North Rim through fire and smoke. I saw it as a seasonal employee. I knew no one on the crew outside of fire season. Sonja and I dated each other for six summers before marrying. Our individual lives and our collective character were contoured by the geography and the rhythms of fire on the Rim and by the structure and cadences of Park Service bureaucracy.

Each year I lived twice. I knew two springs and two autumns. I knew one life on the Rim and one apart from it. It was a wonderfully schizophrenic existence. It was then, and it remains, an eternal present, lived and remembered.

This is a story of that place, those times, and the fires—those marvelous fires—that made it all possible.

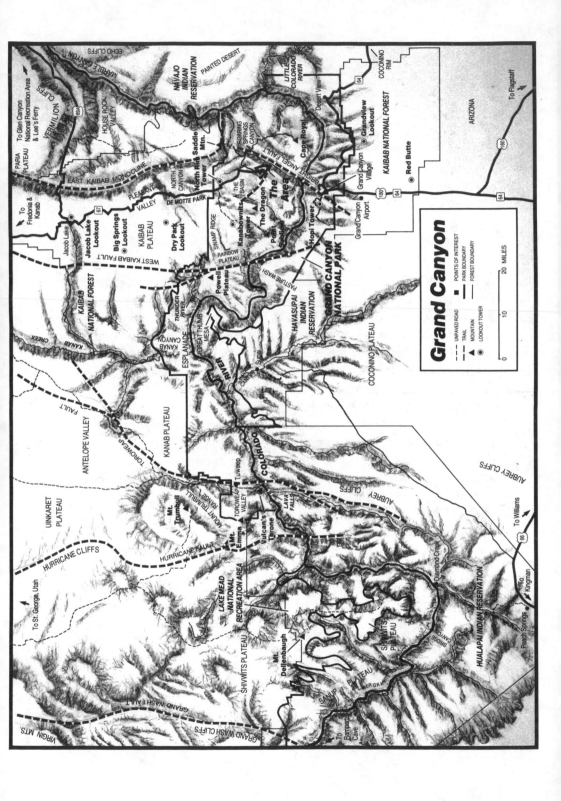

Grand Canyon

- - - - UNPAVED ROAD   ■ POINTS OF INTEREST
  ———— TRAIL   PARK BOUNDARY
  ▲ MOUNTAIN   FOREST BOUNDARY
  ◉ LOOKOUT TOWER

0   10   20   MILES

ECHO CLIFFS

MARBLE CANYON

NAVAJO INDIAN RESERVATION

PAINTED DESERT

To Glen Canyon National Recreation Area & Lee's Ferry

VERMILION CLIFFS

HOUSE ROCK VALLEY

PARIA PLATEAU

EAST KAIBAB MONOCLINE

To Fredonia & Kanab

89A

Saddle Mtn.

ROARING SPRINGS CANYON

LITTLE COLORADO RIVER

COCONINO RIM

64

KAIBAB NATIONAL FOREST

ARIZONA

Desert View

●Grandview Lookout

180

North Rim Tower

NORTH RIM

DE MOTTE PARK

THE BASIN

Cape Royal

●Red Butte

67

Big Springs Lookout

PLEASANT VALLEY

BRIGHT ANGEL FAULT

Grand Canyon Village

180

Jacob Lake Lookout

KAIBAB PLATEAU

Dry Park Lookout

SWAMP RIDGE

The Dragon

Kanabownits Tower

The Walhalla Area

Grand Canyon Airport.

64

64

Jacob Lake

WEST KAIBAB FAULT

RAINBOW PLATEAU

Point Sublime

Hopi Tower

GRAND CANYON NATIONAL PARK

Powell Plateau

FASTURE WASH

HAVASUPAI INDIAN RESERVATION

KAIBAB NATIONAL FOREST

THUNDER RIVER

ESPLANADE

KANAB CANYON

GREAT THUMB MESA

COLORADO RIVER

TAPEATS CANYON

COCONINO PLATEAU

KANAB CREEK

ANTELOPE VALLEY

TOROWEAP FAULT

KANAB PLATEAU

Tuweep

COLORADO

AUBREY CLIFFS

UINKARET PLATEAU

Mt. Trumbull

MOUNT TRUMBULL RANGE

TOROWEAP VALLEY

LAVA FALLS

CLIFFS

AUBREY CLIFFS

To Williams

66

HURRICANE CLIFFS

HURRICANE FAULT

Mt. Emma

Vulcan's Throne

LAKE MEAD NATIONAL RECREATION AREA

Diamond Creek

To Kingman

To St. George, Utah

SHIVWITS PLATEAU

Mt. Dellenbaugh

SHIVWITS PLATEAU

BRIDGE CANYON

HUALAPAI INDIAN RESERVATION

Peach Springs

VIRGIN MTS.

GRAND WASH FAULT

GRAND WASH CLIFFS

SANUP PLATEAU

To Rampart Cave

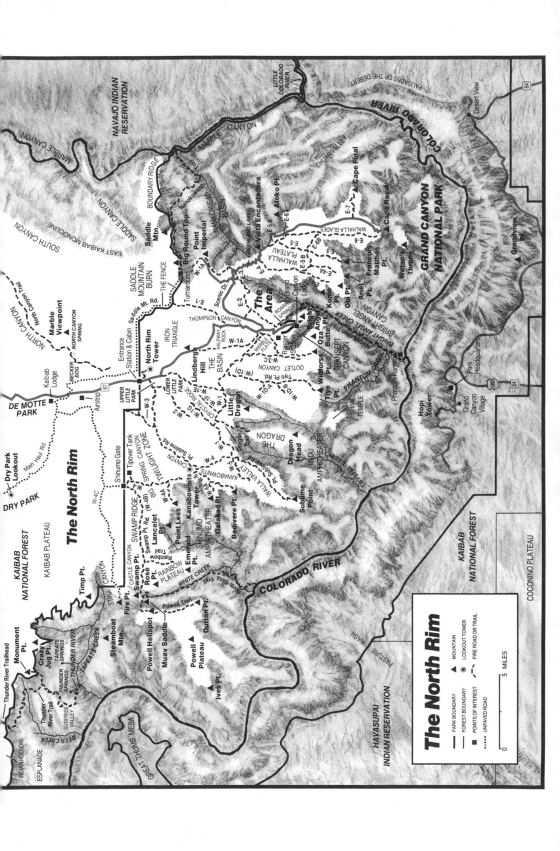

The North Rim

NAVAJO INDIAN RESERVATION

MARBLE CANYON

SADDLE CANYON

EAST KAIBAB MONOCLINE

SOUTH CANYON

PALISADES OF THE DESERT

LITTLE COLORADO RIVER

COLORADO RIVER

Desert View

64

CHUAR VALLEY

Cape Final
E-7
E-6
Atoko Pt.
E-5-A
Vista Encantadora
Cape Royal
Wotan's Throne
Grandview Pt.
E-6
Francois
Matthes
Pt.
E-5-B
E-4-A
E-3
Ariel
Pt.
Obi Pt.
Komo
Pt.
GRAND CANYON NATIONAL PARK
WALHALLA GLADES
WALHALLA PLATEAU
WALHALLA FLATS
GREENLAND LAKES
ROARING SPRINGS
Grand Canyon Lodge
Oza Angry
Butte Pt.
Widforss
Pt.
BRIGHT ANGEL CANYON
Ranger Station
Park Headquarters
Phantom Ranch
Grand Canyon Village
180
64
Hopi Tower
Hopi Point

MARBLE CANYON

BOUNDARY RIDGE

NANKOWEAP BASIN

Saddle Mtn.
Big Round Top
Point Imperial
Nankoweap Trail
SADDLE MOUNTAIN BURN
THE FENCE
Tumaround
W-1A
E-1
E-2
Scenic Dr.
The Basin Area
THOMPSON CANYON
HALFWAY ROCK
W-1A
Lindbergh Hill
IRON TRIANGLE
North Rim Tower
Entrance Station & Cabin
Saddle Mt. Rd.
NORTH CANYON SPRING
Marble Viewpoint
North Canyon Trail
BECKER BOG
Kaibab Lodge
DE MOTTE PARK
Airstrip
67
Main Haul Rd.
UPPER LITTLE PARK
LOWER LITTLE PARK
W-3
THE BASIN
W-1D
MARBLE FLATS
OUTLET CANYON
Tiyo Pt. Rd.
W-1D-B
W-10-A
Tiyo Pt.
TRANSEPT CANYON
SHIVA TEMPLE
PHANTOM CREEK
W-4
Dragon Spring
THE DRAGON
Dragon Head
INDU AMPHITHEATER
CRYSTAL CANYON

Dry Park Lookout
DRY PARK
Kaibab Lodge
Shinumo Gate
Tipover Tank
W-4C
SWAMP RIDGE
Swamp Pt. Rd.
CASTLE CANYON
Pt. Sublime Rd.
BIG SPRING CANYON
TWILIGHT ZONE
W-2
W-1G
CRYSTAL RIDGE
W-1F
W-1E
Little Dragon
W-1
W-5
Dragon Trail
Pt. Sublime
KANABOWNITS
KANABOWNITS CANYON
WALLA VALLEY
Sublime Point

Timp Pt.
KAIBAB NATIONAL FOREST
KAIBAB PLATEAU
STINA CANYON
Fire Pt.
Swamp Pt.
Lancelot Pt.
Point Less
Rainbow Trail
Rose Pt.
RAINBOW PLATEAU
Emerald Pt.
SHINUMO AMPHITHEATER
Galahad Pt.
Kanabownits Tower
Bedivere Pt.
WHITE CREEK
North Bass Trail
COLORADO RIVER

Monument Pt.
Crazy Jug Pt.
TAPEATS SPRINGS
THUNDER SPRINGS
THUNDER RIVER
TAPEATS CREEK
SURPRISE VALLEY
DEER CREEK
Thunder River Trail
Thunder River Trailhead
INDIAN HOLLOW
ESPLANADE
GREAT THUMB MESA
Steamboat Mtn.
Powell Hellspot
Muav Saddle
Powell Trail
Powell Plateau
Dutton Pt.
Ives Pt.
COCONINO PLATEAU
KAIBAB NATIONAL FOREST
PASTURE WASH
HAVASUPAI INDIAN RESERVATION

The North Rim

——	PARK BOUNDARY
— —	FOREST BOUNDARY
■	POINTS OF INTEREST
.....	UNPAVED ROAD

▲	MOUNTAIN
◉	LOOKOUT TOWER
○-◉	FIRE ROAD OR TRAIL

0   5
MILES

... and he told the truth, mainly. There was things which he stretched, but mainly he told the truth.

—HUCKLEBERRY FINN, ON MARK TWAIN

... and after the fire a still small voice.

—1 KINGS 19:12

Part One

EOD

WHEN THE CLOUDS PART, there are disjointed colors and shadows and fragments of more cloud. Lou's eyes bulge and dart like a chameleon's. Clouds close and strike the Rim like surf. The storm seals off the Canyon in slow swirls of black and white. To the west there is lightning; clouds billow like wet smoke.

Lou flies the Cessna northward. We circle and wait for the clouds to break. They lift, suddenly lightening, and reveal a great bowl of a meadow; Lou plunges the plane through the cloud deck. Across the meadow runs a plowed brown scar. An orange wind sock identifies the site as a landing strip, and we are soon bouncing over mud and cobbles on the ground. Two men and a green Park Service station wagon are waiting for us. Stan wears a ranger uniform, complete with Stetson. Harry—much older—is outfitted with a cowboy shirt, a cowboy hat, and boots. Lou declines to fly back to the South Rim. He will wait out the storm.

We drive to a paved highway, U.S. 67, and turn south toward the North Rim. The road runs along a vast grassy plain, green and yellow, grey and brown. Around the edge of the swollen meadows there is an impenetrable forest. Some patches of snow collect along the perimeter. Under the darkening sky white clouds scud across the meadow, and fog streams through the woods. Occasionally there are bursts of hail. After a few miles the meadow narrows, pinched off by a portal of trees. A wooden sign, heavy as a boulder, announces GRAND CANYON NATIONAL PARK. Beyond is a small log cabin that serves as an entrance station. It is vacant, dreary with winter. We

3

drive through another large meadow. The clouds break momentarily, sunlight streaks to the road, and steam rises from the pavement.

Harry, half deaf, shouts, "How do you like this country?" "It's all new," I reply. Stan nods. Stan, Harry, and Lou talk about the road. It is narrow and full of potholes, "disgraceful," "unsafe." Replacement of the entrance road, they agree, should be the Park's highest priority. I stare out the window at the fog and trees. "Those aren't smokes," Harry yells, laughing. "If you're going to be a smokechaser, you'll have to tell the real smokes from the waterdogs"—he points out the window—"like them. That's only fog. Remember Smokey's First Rule of Firefighting: You can't fight a fire you can't find."

When we reach the ranger station, I hand over my papers, and they send me to my quarters with the rest of the fire crew in the Sheep Shed. The crew is out now, I am told. When they return I can get a bunk, clothes, and firepack. I am to report for work in the morning at 0800 hours.

No one says much to me when the crew returns. Bill, the foreman, gives me a hard hat and a firepack from the fire cache. The Sheep Shed is a dilapidated wooden bunkhouse, and I take the only unclaimed bunk. It has about six inches of clearance from the ceiling. Someone motions me to join them for dinner. We walk through the woods to a cafeteria called the North Rim Inn. The next morning, having mis-set my alarm clock, I am dressed and ready at 6:00 A.M. A few groggy eyes blink incredulously. I don't know what to do. I sit in a chair, fully dressed with a Levi's jacket and hard hat, and read for two hours, while the rest of the crew, several of them hung over, rouse themselves about fifteen minutes before work. No one more than glances my way. No one needs to.

Pete is driving a red Dodge powerwagon outfitted with a slip-on unit, tools, saws, and firepacks. We turn off the paved road for two muddy ruts ("E-1," he calls it) across a short meadow, then enter a dark woods. Pete insists on being called by his nickname, The Ape, which he earned by virtue of a huge barrel chest and a passion for climbing trees. His car is known as the Apemobile; his bed is the Ape's Nest. He wears a Levi's jacket over an orange fireshirt. An orange metal hard hat, slightly too small, sits incongruously on his head. His facility with language is astonishing. He can make even four-syllable words sound like four-letter words.

We roll from one rut to another. A fallen aspen blocks the road. I climb out and look for an ax. "Break it," The Ape grunts. I stare blankly. Disgusted, he leaves the vehicle, picks up the short end of the aspen, swings it against some trees, and pushes until the log snaps. We drive to where a large tree bristling with branches has fallen lengthwise down the road. The branches spin across the road like a spider web. The Ape selects an enormous black and yellow chain saw and begins cutting. I pull branches away. Together we roll the large chunks out of the road, sometimes using a long pole with a floppy hook, a peavey. The rain starts, followed by hail and fog. We slide along portions of the road; in places the truck splashes sheets of mud past the window. When the road bends and The Ape slows, the powerwagon sticks in a mud puddle the consistency of brown tar. The Ape runs a winch cable out to a tree. The cable tightens, then springs loose. "Fuckin' goddamn clutch popped," mutters Ape. We gather some wood and surround the left-side tires. Still no luck. Ape dumps the water out of the tank, all one hundred fifty gallons, and with winch and engine operating together, we lumber out of the puddle. We drive for what seems like hours. More trees, more mud, more hail. Then the forest abruptly opens; our keys undo the lock at the gate, and The Ape drives onto a logging road.

The clouds are still too thick to see much. Dense pockets of fog sweep across the road like gentle brooms. When the scene lightens, it is filled with charred black stalks and dense brush. Alongside the road are rotting piles of roots and logs. The ground is rocky and grassy. "The Saddle Mountain fire," The Ape explains. "Started in 1960, on Park lands. Fuckin' Reusch sent out two smokechasers to find it. They couldn't locate fuckin' anything—too dark and no goddamn roads. They came back to the Area and agreed to return the next day. Jesus H. Christ, it happens all the time. But this fuckin' fire burned through the night, forty acres in the Park, then wiped out nine thousand fuckin' acres in the Forest. The fire crew made buckets of overtime just on patrol. Lucky bastards. The ranger station has a photo of the crew that the Park sent to the fire. The Forest Service built this road to log off what they could of the burn. If you ever want to get them fuckin' mad, just say 'Saddle Mountain.' "

Another truck is at the end of the road, with another smokechaser. The Ape goes to the other truck and talks. I stare at my fire map. I unfold and refold it. The Ape returns and we eat lunch in the powerwagon. The Ape warms up a small can on the truck manifold. The steam in the cab is so thick he turns on the defroster. I now see a group of Indians huddled under a small tarp off under some trees. When the rain and hail let up, The Ape says, we will begin work on the boundary fence.

Booby jogs toward me as best he can while stepping over the heavy windfall and balancing a chain saw. "A smoke on Powell Plateau!" he yells. "Meet me at the truck."

Booby, one of the Indians, and I ride in the cab. The other Indians—"SWFFs," Booby calls them, short for "Southwest Forest Firefighters"—climb onto the back of the slip-on. "How do we find the smoke?" I ask. Booby replies that we have a good location for this fire, that we usually smell a fire before we actually see it. I have no idea where Powell Plateau is, and every ten minutes or so I stick my nose out the window to sniff for smoke. The drive lasts nearly an hour and a half. When it ends, at Swamp Point, we are at the rim of the Canyon. On a mesa across from the Point there is a column of smoke.

Booby hands me two canteens, which he drapes around my fire-pack, and some tools and tells me to take off. There is a trail of sorts across to Powell. "Just follow it." A couple of SWFFs are outfitted in the same way. From the slip-on he fills up fedcos—rubber bladder bags that hold five gallons each and can be carried like backpacks—and hands them to the remaining SWFFs. The trail is easy going down; we descend for maybe a thousand feet. The trip up staggers us, however, and I pass one reeling SWFF, then a second. We are strung out over maybe a quarter mile. The sun blasts off exposed rocks as though Muav Saddle were a reflector oven. Near the top I realize that there is no trail to the fire. I wander around for a few minutes, trying to orient myself, then slump down a little ways from the trail and wait.

Eventually one of the SWFFs appears, then another. They talk in gasping, hushed Hopi, and finally leave the trail to bushwhack cross-country. I follow. We come to the fire—the smoldering stump of a tree and a burning log. There are now three SWFFs and myself on the scene. I am a seasonal employee, they are temporaries; I have a government driver's license, they do not; I am a fire control aid, an FCA, they are SWFFs. I am the fire boss. They wait for me to say something. I fumble with my pack and canteens, buying time. "All right," I say. "You guys know what to do. Get to work." They nod and pick up tools. One grabs a shovel and begins to throw dirt on the log. I copy his every gesture. By the time Booby arrives we have most of the log covered.

We cut and dig some more before Booby decides that he will spend the night on the fire with Hugh, crew boss of the SWFFs. Booby and Hugh have each brought a sleeping bag. I am to return to the Area with the rest of the SWFFs. If we leave shortly, we should reach Swamp Point before sunset. The SWFFs who carried fedcos go back empty-handed; I have to carry my firepack across the Saddle again. I am exhausted when we get to the powerwagon, and it is apparent that it will soon rain and that we all must ride in the cab.

I am the only one with a license, but I have never driven a standard transmission truck. The SWFFs sit on one another's laps. One straddles the gearshift; he will shift for me if I will work the clutch. We lurch forward. The ride lasts several hours. I have not the slightest idea where we are. When we come to forks in the road, the SWFFs debate in Hopi about the proper road to take, then point and say in English, "This way." One of the Hopis is quite old, probably sixty, and he chants in a low voice, almost in harmony with the engine whine. At last we come out to Highway 67. The remainder of the drive should be easy. It is nearly midnight when we run out of gas about a half mile from the Area.

Booby and Hugh come back the next day. Gummer drives out to pick them up, and Booby announces that it was a nice fire. There wasn't much mop-up left, he says; they slept well, and Hugh got up early and made coffee. "That's why," he explains, "I wanted Hugh to stay the night."

*   *   *

There are four smokechasers on the crew: The Ape, Gummer, Booby, and I. We have a foreman, Bill ("Wee Willie"), who is married and lives in a cabin. He hangs around the Area, never participates in fire crew parties, and dispatches himself immediately to every fire. We are supervised by a permanent Park Service ranger, Chuck, who reports to the unit manager. There is one patrol ranger (Weird Harold), a Park Service permanent, and one seasonal ranger. There are four or five ranger naturalists; it is hard to know exactly. The maintenance crews—Buildings and Utilities (B&U) and Roads and Trails (R&T) both—have fewer than ten people. The B&U group calls itself the Rare Breed. There are no fee collectors; there is no visitor center. The ranger station is a slightly refurbished mess hall constructed by the Civilian Conservation Corps (CCC) in the 1930s. Almost everyone who is single eats at the North Rim Inn. The fire crew and the SWFFs always go as a group.

What makes the fire crew the largest collective entity on the North Rim are the SWFFs. Each summer a squad of six is requested out of the Southwest Forest Firefighter program for a tour of duty that lasts most of the summer. Our group consists of Hopis. The SWFFs live in the east bunk room of the Sheep Shed, the fire crew in the west. Separating (or binding) the two bunk rooms are a common shower and a toilet. The fire crew used to reside in a cabin, another relic of CCC days, and wishes to return. There are rumors of trouble among the SWFFs.

We are returning from the Grand Lodge when we notice flashing lights outside the Sheep Shed. The rangers are present and there is yelling. I am told to watch our bunk room. There is more screaming and the sound of tires on gravel. After a while Booby comes in. "Butch has been drinking," he says. He assaulted Albert and nearly kicked his ear off with the pointed toe of his cowboy boot. Albert is on his way to the Kanab clinic in the back of the ranger station wagon, but the SWFF crew refuses to bed down in the Sheep Shed until Butch sobers up. Booby says that I am to stay in the Sheep Shed and watch Butch. I can hear Butch stalking across the floor and chanting on the other side of the shower stall. "I have to go now," says Booby. "And, yeah, Butch may have a knife."

I dress in my fire gear and drag my blankets outside. The moon is nearly full. Forest and Rim are bathed in silver light, and the Canyon is a black abyss. There are large ponderosa outside the Sheep Shed and some aspen. I stumble over to the aspen. Light streams out of the Sheep Shed, but there are no screams. I hear only the wind, and under the trees I cannot feel it.

Two days later we move to a cabin.

The lightning storm comes late in the day. Early the next morning Chuck sends me to Kanabownits tower with three SWFFs. We man Kanabownits only on special occasions. Chuck says he is sending Hugh with me because Hugh has a lot of fire experience; I should seek his advice. If there is a smoke in the western portion of the North Rim, we will be dispatched. He hands me a pair of binoculars from the ranger station safe.

Hugh struggles up the steps to the tower. He is breathing irregularly, his eyes are bloodshot, and his speech is a little slurred. He is unusually talkative and eager to please; after the episode with Butch, he fears that the whole crew will be sent home. I scan the horizon with the binoculars, trying to see more of the landscape with them than without. I can see the Rim and Canyon clearly. Powell Plateau stands out in bold relief. There are bluish mountains to the south, southwest, and west. I can't name any of them.

Hugh and I sit down in the lookout booth and open the windows; the other two SWFFs stay with the truck. I begin to read a book and plan to survey the scene every half hour or so. Hugh chatters away. He tells me about the biggest fires he has worked, how long he has been with the SWFF program. He asks for the binoculars. I return to my book.

After a while Hugh points to a bluish haze hanging around a point on the Rim and declares that it is a fire. "I can't tell," I say. I have seen only one forest fire in my life. It is still early morning, Hugh explains, and the fire is only smoldering; now is the time to attack it. I take a bearing with the firefinder and watch the smoke some more with the binoculars. The haze is unquestionably dense, like the air in a campground during the early morning. On the other side of the point the bands of the Canyon are visible. The fire must be right on the Rim. I radio the information to Chuck. "The fire is at Rose Point, on

Rainbow Plateau." "Good," he says. "Start to it and we'll send up Recon 1 to guide you."

With Hugh's help I stop the powerwagon just north of Rainbow. There are no roads or trails, and Rose Point is more than a mile away. We load up with firepacks, chain saw, fedcos, handtools, and extra canteens. I flag our route by tearing off pieces of plastic surveying tape from a roll and tying them to tree branches. The drive takes an hour, and we walk for more than another hour before we hear that 211 has departed from the South Rim airport. We have found nothing, though several times I am sure that I can smell the odor of something burning. Hugh is enthusiastic. I want to traverse along the Rim, but Hugh points out that if we do that, we must cross several steep ravines. Better to follow deer paths, he cautions. So we do. We can always retrace our flagging back to the truck.

We hear the plane but we cannot see it, so we work our way to the Rim. The plane is circling far to our north. I get on the radio and ask the observer if he can help us reach the fire at Rose Point. He says that he is at Rose Point. "No," I reply, "you are much too far north." No, he replies, he is at Rose Point, and we must be somewhere else. After some maneuvering he locates us at Violet Point, the southern extremity of Rainbow Plateau and maybe an air mile from Rose Point. He cannot see any smoke. Are we sure there is a fire? "I guess not," I reply, wondering if my nose has led me to anything more than the memory of a morning breakfast of bacon and burned toast. After Recon 1 surveys the rest of the North Rim, he heads for the airport.

The day is late, so we stagger back to the powerwagon by the most direct route we can imagine. The fedcos and extra canteens, useless, are drained to lighten the load. The next day we return and pick up our flagging.

It is a slow season for fires.

So it is, but there is still much to do. There are fireroads to open: the SWFFs clear brush, while we cut and move logs with chain saws and winches. We work with the R&T crew in rebuilding the Sublime Road. Two days a week we cut wood for the campground. We cut down snags—hazardous trees—along the main road, and buck and split the wood for the campground bins. We work in the fire cache:

there are tools to sharpen, paint, rehandle; there are signs to rout and paint. If there is nothing else to do, we go to the Fence. The north boundary fence is a great sink for labor; usually one smokechaser will take the entire SWFF crew to the Fence for the day. If you drive slowly, this means only five and a half hours of real repair work. And we overhaul the network of tree towers.

When the CCC was in force, they moved North Rim tower to its present location, built Kanabownits tower to provide additional coverage, and constructed a dozen tree towers by attaching metal ladders to the trunks of prominent trees around the North Rim. The idea was that smokechasers could climb a nearby tree tower to get a better fix on a fire. The ladders were secured by lag bolts and joined by a heavy copper wire to conduct lightning to ground. The best tree tower (TT-1) scales a giant white fir behind the ranger station and ends in a small crow's nest. The tree is topped, there is a small platform on which to stand, and a metal pipe encircles the affair in imitation of a handrail. The other towers end in branches, which have to be climbed to acquire a view. Over the course of thirty years, the system has decayed. Some trees have died, and others have been weakened by lightning. Some have been so overtaken by surrounding trees that nothing can be seen from their tops. In some cases, the tree has grown so much that bark overlaps the rungs of the ladder, making it all but useless. The Ape wants to restore the whole network.

The work goes slowly. It may take us an entire day to drop a useless tree and remove its ladders; locating a new tree may require that we climb half a dozen. Ape instructs us in the use of spikes and ropes. Many of the trees selected are ponderosa and have no branches for the first forty feet or more of trunk. Someone has to spike up to the nearest large branch in order to position the ladders. The tree must be wired to protect it against lightning. The crown jewel is TT-15, which The Ape personally selects along fireroad E-1. This is a new tower, not simply a replacement, and it is intended to prevent the kind of disorientation that brought about the Saddle Mountain debacle. Gummer does the climbing, while The Ape puffs thoughtfully on his pipe. The tree is a ponderosa pine with a diameter of nearly five feet. The bark seems thin, like an orange balloon ready to burst, as though the tree has been stretched and exceeded its natural dimensions. Gummer proceeds slowly. The tree is almost too wide and the bark too thin for him to grip. We work late to get two ladders (each about twelve feet long) up the first day. Gummer leaves his rope on the branch in such a way that we can pull him up the next day without spiking. Cutting branches is slow work; at thirty-five pounds and over three feet long our chain saws are too cumbersome to use so we cut with handsaws. When the ladders give out, there are large branches to climb. The Ape is content with the view. It is the most difficult climb of the summer, and with it the rehabilitation of the tree towers is complete. Within three years, however, the great ponderosa at TT-15 dies, is declared a hazard, and is felled.

We do odd jobs as assigned, although much of the work is dismissed, fairly or unfairly, as make-work. There is never enough work when there are not enough fires, and there are never too many fires. To kill time, we drive out to Point Imperial to check on the progress of the diseased trees at the overlook, drive through the campground, or make a quick visit to the store. When times are slow, the horseplay begins. To skirt a bad washout on the Sublime Road, Gummer carefully eases a powerwagon through an aspen grove and over a couple of aspen saplings. The Ape is impressed. When The Ape next passes the site, he stops the powerwagon, puts it into four-wheel drive, turns his hard hat backward, and proceeds to level the entire grove of aspen. About a week later Chuck comes down to the fire cache to inquire if we know anything about this aspen grove on the Sublime Road, the one with tire tracks all over it. No one knows anything, but Chuck understands everything.

The Ape is convinced that there is a fire near The Basin. Twice in the past week Red Butte lookout has reported a smoke at fifteen degrees on the North Rim. No one has found anything, and the bearing runs suspiciously close to the dump and to the campground—both sources of smoke—but The Ape trusts the lookout at Red Butte. Red Butte itself is a strange, camelback-shaped monadnock between the South Rim and the San Francisco Peaks. The Forest Service has done nothing more than erect a small shack at its summit. The lookout's name is Barbara, otherwise known as Barbara Red Butte. When Barbara Red Butte is not sighting smokes, she shoots rattlesnakes. The inside of the shack is plastered with snakeskins and coils. The Ape drives to Lindbergh Hill, site of TT-7, climbs it, and returns with the compass bearing of a possible smoke. He plots his bearing along with the azimuth reported by Red Butte. They cross near Hades Spring in Upper Thompson Canyon. He insists that it has to be a fire.

We drive down fireroad W-1A, a former entrance road for the Park. When the new road was paved, it followed Lower Thompson Canyon; the old road skirts Upper Thompson Canyon. The Ape studies his map. We don our firepacks and begin to walk. When we come to a long meadow, Ape says he smells smoke. He reconstructs the flow of evening air, cooler and heavier, as it spilled like gentle rain over the contours of hill and ravine before emptying into the meadow-lake. Back in the woods he comes upon a smoldering fir. It has been burning for days and would probably smoke for several more. The Ape is triumphant. He announces the location of the Hades fire over the Park radio. Then he tells me that we will bring the powerwagon into the fire.

We mark the route from the meadow to the fire with flagging tape. Getting the truck from W-1A to the meadow is awkward, but The Ape is determined. It will complete his coup. Ape walks ahead with a pulaski, cutting downed aspen logs with its ax end and pulling debris away with the hoe half. There is no vestige of a road present, no prospect of a road in the future. We wind around the forest, our route like oxbow lakes. Eventually we come to the meadow and the fire. The fir is hollow and burns on the inside. Ground fire smokes stubbornly in deep duff. We use up all the water in the slip-on. Ape volunteers— insists upon—taking the powerwagon back to the Area for another load of water, while I scratch a fireline and mop up. He is gone for almost two hours; it is dark when he reappears. We dump the load on the fire, stir the sizzling coals and duff, and prepare to leave. We will return tomorrow before we declare the fire out. The Ape drives back to the Area.

The next morning, however, Stan and Chuck call us into their offices to discuss the "serious," dents and destroyed side mirror on the red powerwagon. They believe I was driving when the accident occurred. From The Ape's account it must have happened when I

*drove the powerwagon through the woods. I don't know when it
happened; I didn't know anything had happened. A vehicle accident
is a serious matter, they remind me. Later, they inspect the scene and
discover red paint on the bark of a tree and find splinters of the mirror
on the ground nearby. The arrangement of debris makes it clear that
impact occurred on the way out. Knowing nothing of this, I approach
Stan and Chuck after work. "I don't know what is going on," I say,
"but I did not smash the pumper." "Don't worry, son," says Stan
kindly. "We just figure Pete had a little accident."*

The fire crew does everything collectively: we eat together, work
together, play together. Our social world is as compressed as our
housing, Building 155, a small cabin constructed during CCC days
as temporary officers' quarters. There is one large room, big enough
for two sets of bunk beds along one wall. The wall does not presently
exist because a new room is being added to the cabin; in its place is a
canvas sheet. On the opposite wall there is a closet and a small
bathroom. There are four chests of drawers, two stacked on the other
two. The double-decker dressers block the closet. For entertainment
we have a battery-operated phonograph and three albums. By the end
of the summer I despise every song.

There is a small kitchen that is never used. Instead we eat nearly
every meal at the North Rim Inn. We are issued discount cards that
entitle us to breakfast for $.50, lunch for $.75, and dinner (except
steak) for $1.00. When we work outside the Area, we order box
lunches from the Inn at the same discounted price. A rookie smokechaser at pay grade GS-3 makes $2.05 per hour, so it is possible to eat
very well on little more than one hour's pay. We occupy a table at the
Inn; the SWFFs take one also, and so do the maintenance crews and
the rangers. After dinner we all sit around the table and BS. Everyone
has a pipe. I do not smoke, but it becomes apparent that a pipe is
mandatory, so I get one and chew on the stem determinedly. We talk
about work and money; about girls and parties at the Lodge; about
the Park Service and our bosses. We talk about the fire crew.

There are endless discussions about life in the "old days," generally last year or the year before. A fire crew turns over rapidly. Rare is
the seasonal who stays with fire for four summers. Crew traditions

are oral, incessantly refashioned, and made ancient by the brevity of seasonal life. In the old days the fire crew ruled the North Rim. They were crazy and hardworking and had lots of fires. They restrung the Fence clad only in hard hats, Jockey shorts, and boots. They cut fireline faster than the Forest Service fire plow. They were living legends. "Call me Shane," one insisted when he first arrived, so they did. He spent most of his free time on a motorcycle. Drunk, he drove the whole fire crew to the Lodge on his cycle. There was brawny Tim, reckless and roguish, an inventor of rough sport and censor of fire crew morals—which meant, in perverse inversion, that he oversaw a certain level of "corruption." Tim organized endless parties with girls from the Lodge, Inn, or campground. Above all, there was Reusch. Reusch had been district ranger for a decade, had weathered the Saddle Mountain Burn, and had passed his rough benediction over the fire crew. Reusch was built like a grizzly. One night he picked up Tim, who had the bulk of a tree stump, and placed him on the fireplace mantel. Reusch, it is said, constructed W-6 fireroad while en route to a fire, driving a Jeep with one hand and swinging an ax with the other. He pampered and ruthlessly worked the fire crews, invited them to his house for drinking and general hell-raising. After the Saddle Mountain fire, Reusch made it a policy not to pay for overtime unless his crews found a fire. In disgust, Tim and Shane located a snag with a catface, started a fire in the basal cavity, and extinguished it. We found a fire and we put it out, they solemnly swore.

Now, of course, the new regime is less colorful and less sensitive to fire crew needs. The cautious Chuck has replaced the reckless Reusch, and I have replaced Tim. Chuck's manifold fire credentials are dismissed. The crewmembers blink with incredulity when they learn that Tim and I attended the same high school in Phoenix.

They are determined to corrupt me. There is hope. I carry a pipe, though I have yet to smoke it. I drink a beer from time to time. I have learned to use simple swear words, not in fluent fire crew idiom but as a halting, second language. But I do not party. Gummer finally proposes that we organize a "book party." The Ape reluctantly agrees. We each find a book and go to the Lodge. For half an hour or so we variously read or, more commonly, prowl restlessly around the

Lodge. The book party is a failure. Books will not substitute for girls. My initiation becomes a matter of some importance. It will not be easily solved, but there have been stubborn rookies before: Gummer got his nickname because Tim thought he acted like a bubble-gummer. There is hope; there will be fires.

The crew is cutting and splitting wood on Lindbergh Hill when the smoke report comes in. North Rim tower sites the fire just south of the Sublime Road "in a grove of aspen." The Ape and I depart imme-diately. We exit the Sublime Road at W-2 and, with pack and tools, begin walking. We walk for an hour. No smoke. Ape radios the tower and asks if he still sees smoke. "Yes," Rick replies. "It is in a small grove of aspen." "Christ!" mutters Ape. "Does he know how many fuckin' groves of fuckin' aspen there are on the North Rim?" We walk for another hour. It rained last night, and the sky remains largely overcast. It is difficult to spot smoke against that kind of backdrop. We climb another hill. The spruce branches are still wet; we brush against them as we trudge, loaded like pack mules, through the woods, and we both are soaked. At last we stop. Something bounces off Ape's hard hat. He picks up a piece of charcoal. Some more charcoal falls nearby. We stare at each other and look up. Imme-diately there is a thunderous crack; awkward in our firepacks, we stagger as fast as we can away from the noise, while the top of a large fir crashes to the ground. It is the lost smoke.

The Ape grins. The tree has broken far below where it has been burning. The entire burning section is now on the ground. Ape tells me to dig a fireline. He hacks off branches with a pulaski, then stacks the green branches on the quiescent flames. The smoke thickens. He radios North Rim tower that we have arrived at the fire. I complete the line, and Ape continues to pile on more branches. The fire, which was nearly out, now flares and smokes heavily. North Rim tower calls to ask if there is a problem. The Park fire officer, Clyde, asks if we need an air tanker, some slurry, some advice. "No," says The Ape. "We're holding our own." The fire rushes through the branches in sudden, gulping flames and sends up dense pockets of black-and-white smoke. The Ape lights his pipe. "Good fuckin' work," he says to me. Clyde has personally gone to Hopi tower to observe the smoke column puffing malignantly from the North Rim. He can have an air tanker up in minutes, he reminds us. It is now after 1700 hours, the start of overtime.

The Ape decides we should eat. In digging for my C rations, I unearth a bag of marshmallows. The Ape sees it and goes bananas. "It's just a gag," I explain. He insists that we cut some sticks. He squeezes a marshmallow down the point, locates a bed of red coals, and turns his hard hat around. We are just browning up the first batch when we hear a voice.

Rick trudges past our last flag. He is carrying a coffeepot, has carried it all the way from North Rim tower along our flagging. "After that fire flared up, I thought you boys could use some help," he explains. "Thanks," we say. "We're doing just fine. Would you like a marshmallow?" Blankly, alternately staring at the smoking log and the pot, Rick shakes his head no. The fire has nearly expired; the large wood is much too wet to sustain combustion; only the oily branches, carefully prepared, could torch. We begin serious mop-up. It does not take long. Before he leaves we ask Rick to take a picture of our marshmallow toast. Trying to juggle coffeepot and camera, he quietly obliges.

When I return in early June the next summer, Ape asks me how the winter went.

I am driving the red powerwagon to the Inn. School had gone OK, but for months all I had thought about was the North Rim. For an instant I am caught between polysyllables and swearing and can't say anything. "At least you learned to drive," The Ape shouts. "Christ, you were fuckin' awful." "Yeah," I say lamely, glancing out the open window. "It's great to be back."

But it doesn't matter what I say or how I say it. The wind gusts, and my words vanish in its thundering rush through the pines.

Part Two

TOURS OF DUTY

CHAPTER ONE

The Area

COME EARLY.

When you stand at Little Park, it does not matter how far, or for how long, or for what reasons you have been away. Everything outside the North Rim vanishes instantly. The cold air shakes you awake; your skin feels as if it has plunged into a mountain stream; lungs ache for breath at the high elevation; trees in the crystal air look as if they have been etched on glass. The scene shocks with recognition. The great, many-boled ponderosa, dead for centuries, still guards the Sublime Road. Every sinkhole in the swelling meadow has a story. Every cavity in the old road revives an instinct. Eight months seem like a weekend. The sense of freshness and familiarity is overpowering. There is only the North Rim.

And fire. Scan the snowpack at Little Park. If it is deep and furrowed, there will be no spring fire season, and fires will be coincidental, spasmodic, ignited peripherally around the points that outline the Canyon. But if, by mid-May, the snowpack is broken into floes and the meadow is braided with briskly running streams, the fires may come early, and they can enter into the interior. They will go to the heart. This year the ground is raw with dead grass, mud, and duff. There will be fires.

So come early. There is no feeling like it. There are ample jobs; there is a promise—a wild hope—that can leap chasms; there is an animal thrill as the crew builds and the fire danger escalates. The Rim erases the outside world. Snow gives way to smoke. Nothing else matters.

* * *

The fire is at Deer Creek, and there is not much that can be done. Jim and I greet 210—the Park helicopter—with a firepack, some handtools, canteens, sleeping bags, and a Mark III pump with accessories, all ransacked from the fire cache. It's the best we can manage on short notice. The cache is in disarray. Unopened boxes, heaped late in the fall, collect like snowdrifts in corners; slip-on units hang from the ceiling like monstrous beeves; packs are scattered, rifled, and incomplete from winter pilfering; saws are unassembled and pulaskis unsharpened. Jim hastily tests the Mark III while the 210 is a distant speck over Oza Butte. We barely complete our enter-on-duty (EOD) papers before climbing into the helo. The fire will probably expire before we reach it. If not, the pump should give us an edge, and there are few occasions to use it properly on the waterless Rim. At least we have a fire.

We fly over Tiyo, The Dragon, Sublime, Rainbow Plateau, Powell Plateau, a topographic fugue of Rim peninsulas and Canyon gorges. Then we cross beyond the edge of our fire maps. Deer Creek is a narrow gorge, like an opened coffin, with springs gushing out of limestone and a creek that debouches into the Colorado River itself. The fire is below the springs in a floodplain of grass, rushes, mesquite, and cottonwoods—ignited by yet another river party, conscientiously burning its toilet paper. We land at a small knoll, an Indian ruin overlooking the creek, and agree to a pickup the next morning at 1000 hours. A handful of cottonwoods, probably hollow, puffs with sad smokes. The hot air of the Canyon cloys and suffocates.

The Mark III, lugged painfully to the creek, proves worthless, full of sinister, hopeless sputters. Methodically we attack the cottonwoods with pulaskis and shovels, until we suddenly realize that the fire— from somewhere, somehow—has crossed the stream. The scene explodes. Within minutes the fire races through reeds, shrubs, cacti, cottonwoods and across the narrow floodplain and up the rocky slopes. The rush and crackle of flame echo off the cliffs. The box canyon concentrates a convective column black with roiling smoke; fire lookouts from Flagstaff to the Arizona Strip report the towering column, rising angrily like a thunderhead; Dick Johnston, fire officer for the North Kaibab National Forest, sights the smoke while taking out the trash at his Fredonia home; two hikers, who just minutes

*previously painfully staggered down from Surprise Valley, scramble
back up the trail with the agility of bighorn sheep. Then it ends. Within
thirty minutes the fire has run its course. The head dies out amid the
Tapeats sandstone, and there is nothing left but flaming trees and
smoldering pack rat middens stuffed under boulders. A group of river
rafters appears, also drawn by the awesome smoke, and wonders if
the Park Service knows about the fire. "We are the Park Service," Jim
informs them.*

*Nightfall creeps over the gorge, and we retire to our camp at the
ruins for a fitful sleep. The evening is oppressively hot, filled with the
obnoxious odors of tamarisk and sour woodsmoke, and when we rise
at dawn, haze hangs in the gorge like a prehistoric smog. We mop up
scattered pockets of flame and smoke, more to keep ourselves busy
than to control another outbreak. Jim surreptitiously tries, without
the least success, to start the Mark III.*

*At 1000 hours, the helo has failed to show; at noon we eat the last
of our rations; at 1400 hours, we slink off the knoll for the timid shade
of a mesquite. Deep within Canyon gorges our radio is worthless. We
are dead to the Park. Not until 1600 hours does 210 appear, delayed,
the pilot explains, by assorted "river emergencies." The helo rises,
like a fluttering raven, out of the Canyon. The snowbanks under
spruce and fir shock us back to life.*

*At the cache I grab some C rations for dinner, while Jim, readying
the Mark III for storage, tries the starter rope once more. The pump
coughs, rocks the cache with noise, and roars with a cacophony that
could fill Transept Canyon. "Dammit," he mutters. "Nothing at this
place works except at this place."*

*The smoke column rises from southeast of Cape Royal, near Lava
Canyon, where the Colorado River makes its great bend to the west.
Flames move briskly through desert grasses, shrubs, and scattered
pinyons. The fire burns in a narrow canyon but will soon crest onto a
broad terrace. If it continues it may spread through one of several
brush-covered debris cones that span the vertical cliffs of the Redwall
limestone; it could, conceivably, continue all the way to the Rim.
Winds gust upslope in slow coughs.*

Park fire officer McLaren orders fire retardant and requests a small crew from the North Rim. The "crew" will be an ad hoc group—a handful of recent regular fire crew arrivals, but mostly reserves, curious and untrained, who have been impressed into service from duties as garbage and fee collectors, a carpenter and plumber, even a ranger. The reserves are unenthused, and everyone is unacclimated. Even the regulars have only just arrived, and they have not yet un-packed their gear, which clusters on bunks like lichen-backed stones.

We begin arriving by helicopter around 0900 hours, store our firepacks amid a large rock outcrop, and throw dirt along the advanc-ing flaming front. The grasses have the kindling temperature of Kleenex; even the prickly pears burn hot. No fireline needed here, only a vigorous perimeter of hot-spotting and cold-trailing—knock-ing down flames and using burned-out patches as a surrogate fireline. But the fire moves upslope through the rugged terrain much faster than we do. We will be saved only by the slurry. For nearly an hour a B-26 and a PB-4Y2 drop retardant, operating out of the retardant base at the South Rim airport. McLaren directs the drops from the Park helicopter. We follow behind the slimy trail of slurry, extinguish-ing flames that escape it or that burn under its pink patina. The helo brings in more firefighters and removes one, overcome by heat, back to the North Rim. When the B-26 shortens its return time and suddenly appears on a drop run directly over us, Wil and Dave take refuge behind some large sandstone boulders; the retardant cloud, in a slow, graceful vortex, swirls around the boulder and paints them pink. When finally contained, the fire totals 350 acres—a quarter mile wide and a mile and a half long.

Dave and Wil establish a small helispot, where 210 can land, then we fly the perimeter. At areas that need mop-up we drop off two-man teams, each with at least one regular fire crewman, along with shovels, saws, and fedcos. The chief problems are pack rat middens tucked around giant boulders and hollow-trunked junipers that can smolder for days and in a high wind throw sparks outside the old burn. While the scenery is spectacular—great fault blocks, bands of ancient lava, a topography of terrace and ravine, an unblinking desert sun—the heat is oppressive. Then 210 is called away to other Park duties, and, fully equipped, we climb on foot through the colossal silence. Mop-up slows. The reserves tire quickly; they have

long since sweated away the flush of excitement; they want to go
home. Around 1700 hours we fly them off the line and reposition a
handful of fire crew regulars at another trouble spot. Two hours later
the only smokes are safely within the deep interior of the burn. As the
last crew departs, the Chuar fire—in the lee of a Canyon sunset—is
engulfed by deep, cool shadows from the Rim.

Building 176 echoes with emptiness. Its screen door flaps in the
evening winds. One by one we shower, open cans of beans, peaches,
and beer, and throw sleeping bags on bunks. Dave searches for a
fresh shirt and socks. I clean and oil my boots; the heat has baked
them as stiff as sheet metal; ash, once wet, then fired, congeals like
concrete. My left foot is blistered. Wil moves with studied deliberate-
ness, his muscles as stiff as two-by-fours. Ralph and Joe should EOD
tomorrow. We can unpack our gear tomorrow. Outside, winds from
Rim and Canyon mix in black, noisy gusts.

Tomorrow we will open the fire cache.

THE CACHE

The great double doors draw open. Chilled morning air seeps
through all four stalls. A winter's mustiness rises, like an invisible
steam, out of the cache.

The grime looks wonderful. I have come home. We all have. We
are what we do, and the fire cache is where we do it—or where we
start to do it. Fire season ends when, in the late fall, the cache is
stuffed with the residue of one summer and the ordered goods for
another, and fire season begins when, the next spring, the cache is
again exhumed and revived. As often as not, we are dispatched to
fires from within the cache or its annex, the Fire Pit. All backcountry
roads (and all the roads of winter) lead to the cache. After fires are
out, we clean up our gear in the cache. We begin workdays in the
cache, and as often as not we go to the cache on our days off as well.
We can live without a ranger station, without a resource management
office, without Building 176, without a Grand Lodge, a North Rim
Inn, a saloon; but we cannot survive without the cache.

There is a rough logic to excavating the fire cache. We take the bulk items first: oversize cartons of paper sleeping bags, cases of canteens, cotton hoses, twelve-packs of shovels and pulaskis, a small warehouse of postseason fire orders. Kent, The Kid, Gilbert, and I dump them willy-nilly on the asphalt outside the cache. The fitness trail paraphernalia goes next. We carry the stations—like miniature dinosaurs constructed of two-by-fours—behind the road shed until they can be set up in proper sequence. Next to them, under a white fir and a looming ponderosa, we stash the slatted sections of the hose drying rack; it will not be assembled until the snows melt. Right now our need is access to the cache; it has to be opened, emptied, and refilled.

So, after a winter away, do we. The cache is an exchange as much as a warehouse. Step across its threshold, and its crowded exhilaration will overwhelm whatever else you bring to it. The cache is inexhaustible and infinitely renewable. This is ritual as much as logic, and to make the renewal work, every item has to be touched, pondered, moved, reshelved, and allowed to crowd out a winter of remote experiences, distant thoughts, and abstract emotions. Rookie or returning veteran—the effect is the same. Already, as the day progresses, I begin to slough off one existence and take on another. Shovels replace pencils; firepacks displace books; chain saws and fedcos suppress lectures, television, magazines, malls, libraries. The fire cache is made for access: its bank of doors opens half the building at once. Through them we pass into the North Rim.

After the bulk items have been removed, we start on the smaller boxes. Each goes to one of the four stalls or bays that make up the cache. The tool stall on the north end is reworked first. Our firepacks hang on one wall, each pack framed by a wooden nameplate; racks of shovels, pulaskis, McLeods, flanked by sledges, peaveys, picks, and axes fill up another wall; on the third are spare tool handles, wedges, a vial of linseed oil, cans of black and red spray paint, stencils, hand files, sandpaper. Sprouting from the floor are a wood box, bristling with worn tools ready for conditioning; a tool jig, with grinder, leather apron, ear protectors, vises for securing tools while they are sharpened; a black box, now cold, that emits steam like a witch's brew when it warms a green plastic goo that coats the sharpened edges of shovels and McLeods. Above are three flail trenchers liberated from the fire cache at Yellowstone. Progress is slow. We must re-equip each firepack and individually sort the usable tools from the unusable. On the floor, dominating nearly the whole of the stall, sit two slip-on pumper units of two hundred gallons each. As soon as the trucks are available, we will hoist the slip-ons using a chain block and tackle, back a truck underneath, and lower and bolt a slip-on to each bed. With the fireroads blockaded by snowbanks and mudholes, there is no urgency. We walk around and climb over the slip-ons. The logic of opening the fire cache is the logic of fire season: handtools and firepacks precede slip-ons; crewmen come before roads; fires, before project work.

It is hard to realize that the cache has a history. Its instincts are to rework and homogenize on an annual cycle, and it thus fits well the life cycle of a seasonal firefighter for whom two, perhaps three fire seasons may constitute a lifetime. That is one of the things that made my tenure at the North Rim anomalous: I returned for fifteen seasons. I came to the Rim when I was eighteen, shortly after graduating from high school. I spent four years at Stanford, returning to the Rim each summer, and in my fourth season—the youngest member of the crew—I was made foreman. I skipped my graduation ceremony to help open the cache and the fireroads, worked late into the fall to capture some prescribed burning, then started graduate school in January 1972 at the University of Texas in Austin. The ceremonies for master's and doctoral degrees I bypassed, too; better to open a summer than to close a winter. I took my doctoral orals with my fire boots on and my car packed outside Garrison Hall, ready—win, lose, or draw—to hurry to the Rim and begin fire season. In the spring of 1977, amid a dizzying snowstorm on the North Rim, Sonja and I married. Meanwhile, I landed a cooperative agreement, a sort of bastard grant, from the History Office of the Forest Service in Washington, D.C., and set about researching a history of wildland fire in America. For the academic year 1979–1980 I went to the National Humanities Center in North Carolina on a fellowship and wrote up a draft of my fire history; there our first child, Lydia, was born. Through it all I returned each summer to fire and the Rim. But finally I just got too broken down to haul my ass, a big saw, a firepack, and assorted handtools and canteens up the ridges. If I wanted to stay in fire, I would have to write; I would have to stock the fire cache with books. During my last season, 1981, as my first fire book inched toward publication, my back was a mess. By then I had accepted an appointment with the History Department at the University of Iowa and a fellowship from the National Endowment for the Humanities that would send me for a season to Antarctica. I always knew that the question was never whether I would leave but when. Now it was decided. I had stayed as long as I could; I would trade fire for ice.

Kent and The Kid move to the next bay. The cache is a rectangular building originally constructed by the CCC as a temporary warehouse for storing road equipment. The lumber is rough, the lighting poor; a corrugated tin roof reverberates during thunder and hailstorms. Small, murky windows rim three sides, and the bank of double doors frames the fourth. Only after the fire crew was assigned the structure, during a forced relocation from the indigenous cache, did the Park pour a cement floor. The interior design is our own. The north bay houses the tool stall. Here we concentrate the daily tasks, firepacks, and handtools. But the smell and noise during midsummer are too fierce not to quarantine the bay partially with a wall, and it is accessible only from the double-doored front or a doorway to the adjacent stall—the less frequently used project fire stall. We want daily access, but we also want isolation.

In the project fire stall we store matériel not destined for daily use. The bay thus acts as a buffer between the tool stall and the rest of the cache. Scores of canteens fill elevated racks. Five-gallon cubitainers climb one wall like cardboard ivy. Fedcos and project firepacks for first aid, heliport management, and saw repair festoon the other. Army pack frames crowd a corner. Old fireroad signs decorate the doorway like a collage. As we open the winter deliveries, we substitute new for old, and a pile of discards grows outside the heavy double door. Gilbert and I move some new rations and sleeping bags to an enclosed room, mouse-proofed and locked, in the back. I toss paper sleeping bags into a small attic above the room. Everything goes; we will sort the good from the bad as needed. Later that afternoon The Kid and I will visit the ancient root cellar, accessed by a trapdoor, below the bedroom of the supervisory ranger's house, where old rations, batteries, and other perishables (including hand-tools, which have a tendency to disappear) are stored over the winter. Some new crew mess kits are discovered, along with gas lantern mantles, long-range patrol rations, and fire shelters. But enough. The project fire stall can be straightened out on a rainy day. Kent and The Kid move to the primary work areas.

No wall segregates the two last bays from each other. Only a short shelf juts out like a jetty, and together the two bays make an all-purpose great room. Along one wall there is a workbench with wood and machine tools. Along another are storage shelves for assorted bulky items: the Mark III pumps and accessories, jerry cans for gas, GI surplus webbing harnesses for carrying canteens, saw supplies, whatever. There are cases of hard hats. One corner holds a chain saw bench; another, a wooden cabinet with flagging tape, headlamps, batteries, hydraulic appliances, assorted firepack necessities; a third, a ceiling-high rack for hoses; the last, a four-shelf cabinet for chain saws. The saw shop is more elaborate and self-contained—our concession to high tech—but it is far from functional. Boxes of winter-ordered parts pile around the dark workbench like mushrooms pushing through pine litter. On the bench are an electric grinder and a chain breaker and a can of oil with several seasoning chains; other chains hang in clusters from pegs like mistletoe; individual saw kits, destined for firepacks, are scattered across the bench like windfall. A surplus military field desk holds endless screws, spare parts, instruction manuals, specialty repair tools. Overhead dangles a fluorescent light, constantly bumped and swaying.

Steadily we unburden the great room of its congestion. The miscellaneous residue finds its way to shelves, or to other sheds, or to the asphalt outside until we can determine what it is and why we have it. A few bulky items are hoisted to planks crossing the joists that make a surrogate attic. A case of back-firing flares—fusees—goes to the flammables shed, a flimsy metal structure behind the warehouse that houses gas, saw mix, oil, drip torches, and flamethrowers. The outside saw bench, where we clean saws after daily use before storing them in the saw cabinet, is buried under old and new snow. We will dig it out later. The structural fire cache in another building we ignore. Kent plugs in a coffeepot, and Gilbert scrounges some spare packets of "Coffee, Instant, Type II" from the rations.

Yet there is more. A fire cache abhors a vacuum. Everything, it seems, sinks to the Lower Area and eventually finds its way, deliberately or coincidentally, to the fire cache, the great mandala of the Rim. Everything comes and goes in a grand recycling. The great room acquires quasi-permanent furnishings. Two metal lockers discarded by maintenance are eagerly scavenged and installed; a weight lifting bench appears alongside the saw cabinet; a punching bag hangs from a rafter. Some trash we haul to the Boneyard, some to the warehouse on CCC Hill. The cache is thus eclectic and plentiful; everything almost—but not quite—fits its purpose. For all its congestion it is profoundly utilitarian. A good fire cache learns everything and forgets everything. And all of it is grimy with oil and dust, coated with memory like pine pollen.

Coated, not stored. Unlike the tools and packs and fedcos, memories cannot be kept in steady state, removed like rations or restocked like shovels. The fire cache does not save the past. It reworks it, and by using the past, it continually converts past into present. But the rhythm of the cache—the cycle of fire season—is only one of several rhythms that affect us. There is also the cycle of a seasonal career, and it imposes a slightly larger rhythm upon the rhythm of annual renewal. To these I have added a third.

My longevity as a smokechaser on the North Rim was unprecedented. I even predated the existing fire cache. It is not uncommon for someone to remain somewhere in the fire community for as long as I did, but it is rare to spend those years all in the field. I experienced the annual fire cycle fifteen times, and I passed through the career cycle perhaps five times. For me, season must play against history. The opening of the cache is the opening of a Great Season.

Now, even after a day of housecleaning, the air is rank and heavy and suffused with a faint, sour odor of old woodsmoke. Memory mixes with hope. It is as though I have never left.

*   *   *

As 210 lifts off, we see several large thunderheads. We skirt them, yet it is apparent that they are moving in the same direction we are, that they are marching to the northeast, to Nankoweap Basin. Overhead arcs a magnificent double rainbow.

The fire is about fifty acres in size, flaring up a very steep slope in typical Canyon desert fuels. The helo delicately deposits King and me upslope from the fire, not truly landing but hovering on a small terrace under full power, perched like a raven on an outcrop, then quickly lifts off. Even as we knock down some flames at the head, it is obvious that two firefighters with handtools will not contain the fire. But this early in the season—preseason, really, with only fires in the Canyon—two are all we are. Suddenly, however, as we throw dirt along the flaming front, I realize that the onrushing storm contains a solution. The rain will not reach the Canyon bottom—it will evaporate into virga long before then— but the cascading winds will pour down the Canyon. The lower flank of the fire perimeter, now quiet, will soon become a new head.

We scramble to the bottom of the ravine and extinguish every flame. No fireline here, just a chain of linked hot-spotting, made rapid by the loose, sandy soils. The scheme works. Winds blow down the Nankoweap like a flume; the upslope flames are driven back into the burned area and expire; the lower corner is already dead cold. In fewer than two minutes, the Rainbow fire is out.

King leads as we trudge up the talus and select a campsite not far from our landing site. The fiery flush is gone, and I feel heavy sweat build up under my fireshirt. A parade of thunderheads washes through Nankoweap Basin and sweeps out across the Painted Desert. Sun and storm mingle among buttes and gorges. We search through our firepacks, extract a double meal of C rations—leftovers from last autumn—and pluck out our headlamps. The clouds transfigure the sunset into a colossal alpenglow. King fashions two fusees into a makeshift stove. Cloud and sun glide by us in grand rhythms, until the Plateau casts a deepening shadow, a false night, and evening winds slough off the Rim and pass over us—two busy ants—on their way east.

The Pit

Kent wrestles with the lock, which is sluggish, perhaps rusted from the winter. The sky clouds, and without sun the day turns suddenly chilly. The Kid squirts some graphite into the lock, then Kent tries the key again. The door opens to a small room, part of the maintenance warehouse that stands next to (but some distance from) the fire cache. Above the door is a routed wooden sign that reads FIRE PIT.

Beyond the first doorway is a second—this one with the door removed—and beyond that is a small, narrow room, lighted from a bank of dingy windows. Here we do our paperwork, hold what pass for conferences, and congregate for dispatching. The managerial revolution demands that "managers," even if they are fire crew foremen, have offices, and the Fire Pit is our ambivalent response. It is an imperfect weld between fire and bureaucracy. As much of the outdoors as possible has been brought inside. Its interior is a bizarre syncretism of the utilitarian and the whimsical, informed by neither logic nor history, defiantly untamable. The double entryway makes an anteroom known as the Arm Pit, while to the rear is a mouse-proofed storage room, once used to house hardware for mountain rescue operations, but now dedicated to items like fireshirts and firepants, gloves, batteries, fire maps, and compasses. Between front and rear there is barely room to walk. Crowded into the Pit are an oil heater, forcibly joined to an ancient brick chimney, which rises through the middle of the room; a metal government-issue grey desk, squatting glumly in a corner and piled with soiled fireshirts and gloves; a chair from the Lodge, its wicker unraveling; a dilapidated wooden bench, irrationally salvaged from the Boneyard; milk cans stenciled with FIRE in red letters; a giant round of pine, the only remainder of a huge ponderosa that once glowered over the flight path of the North Rim heliport but is now known fondly as the Base of a Big Yellow Pine after a favorite expression of McLaren, the Park fire officer; some scraps of carpet discards on the floor. The Kid turns on the oil heater, without effect; the drum outside is empty. Kent searches for a coffeepot.

The walls are saturated with fire paraphernalia. There are dispatching maps for the North Rim and the North Kaibab Forest, and a Federal Aviation Administration flight map of the Grand Canyon, all covered with Plexiglas. A trellis of clipboards posts biweekly tours of duty, requisition needs, helicopter schedules, work projects. There are posters of Smokey Bear, lightning, a pinup advertising Husqvarna chain saws; there are photos of former crews, our Hall of Flame; a slab of aspen, sheared longitudinally and routed with red letters that read NEVER GIVE A INCH. Above the desk hangs a square sign constructed from scrap plywood, with a metal button (scavenged from a government-issue brown metal cabinet); a large arrow that points to the button has been routed out with the caption "Lightning Button. Press for Fire." Elsewhere, mounted on wood, are a pair of photos, one from 1936 when the fire cache was opened, and another, forty years later, with FCAs taking the place of CCC enrollees but with the vehicles and arrangements otherwise identical.

The Kid opens the windows, but the only effective fumigation is smoke. From the floor Kent picks up a ball of flagging tape—the "Dragon Flaggin'," recovered from the great Dragon fire—and places it on a shelf labeled FCA Musuem. There are other trophies: a pulaski coated with slurry on one side and charred on the other that Alston recovered from the Sublime fire; the lucky turkey feather that guided Rethlake across Powell Plateau; a memorial plaque, signed by Park and Forest crews after the Circus fire; a two-foot bronze nozzle, discovered in a dark corner of the structural fire cache, now the John Smokechaser Award; a metal Log Cabin syrup can; a Mickey Mouse hard hat; a motorcycle helmet with drip torch nozzle and fusees bristling out of it; and the wooden sign itself, FIRE MUSUEM, whose misspelling instantly qualified it for inclusion. Mementos flood the wall. For a seasonal crew—for a migrant folk society like ours whose collective memory is brutally short—this omnium-gatherum of artifacts is our surest record of the past. If the cache tells us who we are, the Pit tells us who we have been. Outside the window stands our fire totem, a fire-sculptured snag brought back from Walhalla and planted as a sentinel.

In a perfect world the Pit would be located in the cache, but the Pit has two items that the cache lacks—a base station radio and a telephone—and the need to connect with an audience other than the fire crew. Distance from the fire cache is part of the price we pay for communication with the outside world. The Pit must syncopate the rhythms of bureaucracy and fire, Rim and Park. Alienation from the cache is more annoying than dysfunctional. We can shout from the door of the Pit to the doors of the cache, but we can speak to the Park only through radios, phones, and official forms.

Its real distance from the cache lies in its bureaucratic role. With its great battery of double doors, it is the character of the cache to open, to let mounds of matériel and throngs of firefighters pass through, in and out, day and night, season after season. Not so with the Pit. Its double entryway emphasizes that this is a place where things stay in or stay out, that it exists outside the mainstream of real firefighting. If the cache is a portal to the Rim, the Pit is a portal to the Park.

The Pit is less an office than a way station. It is too transient, too empirical, too filled with the minutiae and trophies of life in the woods; it tries to build from the bottom up rather than from the top down. It expresses how a fire crew would connect to a parent bureaucracy, not how a bureaucracy would choose to connect to its fire crew. Supervisory rangers don't like to enter it. The Pit is cold, rudely fashioned, less comfortable than the woods; and that is how we like it. The Kid reads aloud a poem scrawled in longhand and posted over the desk.

> Sittin' in the Pit
> Feelin' like shit
> There's somethin' I'm supposed to do
> But I can't think of it.
>
> Sittin' in this chair
> Breathin' in the air
> There's somethin' I forgot to do
> And it's causin' me despair.
>
> Walk around the cache
> Pickin' up the trash
> There's something I just got to do . . .
> But fuck it.

Kent discovers the coffeepot under a soiled fireshirt and plugs it in.
I step out the door and yell to Gilbert to bring some ration coffee from
the cache. The air is damp and chilled, alien to fire. We find chairs or
chair surrogates and accept the nostalgia of fires remembered and the
more powerful nostrum of fires promised.

But already we feel the distance from the cache. "We gotta get out
on the roads," Kent says. "Yeah," The Kid agrees. "And when the
hell are we gonna get a fire?"

*Three times during the past week observers on the South Rim have
reported a smoke near Bright Angel Point. There are six inches of
fresh snow on the ground with one to two feet of old snow in the denser
woods. The reports are viewed with skepticism until a routine helicopter flight sees, then flies over, the source—a puffing, live white fir on
the Uncle Jim Point trail. Our own Uncle Jimmy and E.B. begin the
hike in. For more than an hour they crash through snowbanks. The
sky has glossed over with filmy cirrus; it is impossible to discriminate
between sky and smoke; they ask for assistance. Recon 1 guides them
painfully to the smoldering snag. The tree is huge, alive, hollow, and
rotten at the top. From the ground they can locate no smoke, much
less flame. Convinced that the fire can only go out, they leave it alone.
A week later the fire is still simmering and actually ignites some
freshly exposed fuel on the ground. Uncle Jimmy and E.B. return to
fell the tree.*

*The amount of sound wood in the interior bole is uncertain. They
assess the lean of the tree, determine the preponderance of branches
on each side, and check the wind, which fills the canopy like a sail.
Uncle Jimmy cuts, while E.B., flapping his arms to keep warm, spots,
ready to swat embers that might rain down. A few flakes of white ash
settle on snowbanks. Their feet are numb with cold. Clouds of smokey
snow billow upward as the tree brushes past others, then crashes to
the ground. They extinguish the fire by stuffing the hollow interior
with snow. The stump is composed wholly of sound heartwood—only
the top is rotten. Not for another week, when they can travel across
newly exposed rock and mud, do they return to the fire and officially
declare it out.*

Back at the Fire Pit, as they fill out their report, E.B. remarks that the coffeepot put out more heat than the Whoopie fire. "Yeah," agrees Uncle Jimmy, searching the DI-1530 for a code small enough to enter the estimated fire acreage. "But you don't get overtime for drinking coffee."

176

It is a short walk—no more than a hundred feet—from the Fire Pit to Skid Row.

We amble to Building 176 for lunch. The screen door hangs up on a rock, half open and half closed. The whole cabin has sunk since it was constructed in the mid-1930s as temporary officers' quarters for a CCC camp, and the doors cannot clear easily. Kent kicks the screen door open. The front door also sticks, this time on a bulge of ancient linoleum, which rests on a foundation stone. This door, too, can be neither closed nor opened completely.

The cabin is partitioned into three rooms. The front room combines a kitchen, a sofa, and an oil furnace into something slightly larger than a shoe box; a middle section houses a bathroom of sorts, while the hallway swells into an open bedroom; the rear room, added decades later, makes a larger bedroom. I live in the middle room, which is really a broad passageway to a shower and toilet that joins an overheated front room with a frozen rear room. When the rear room was occupied by three rookies, it was dubbed the Nursery. When the Cosmic Cowboys—Lenny, Dan, and Charlie—claimed the rear room, they converted it into a miniature Gilley's. To compensate for the front door, which won't close, the rear door won't open.

Once considered prime real estate in the Area, the string of cabins of which 176 is a constituent is unable to compete with the sleek modernism of giant house trailers trucked in by the Park Service. The cabins have become known as Skid Row and assume the role of a slum, fit only for seasonals. Four fire crewmen now live in 176, and another crewman resides next door in 175. The great virtue of 176 is that it is a stone's throw from the cache. In 176 we eat and sleep and do little else.

No one assumes the least responsibility for upkeep. The sink spills out dishes; it bubbles bad odors, grease, and cups like a mud geyser; our sink, a friendly visitor observes in midsummer, is getting "very ripe." Our bathroom, another notes, smells as if Ralph's pickup truck took a shower in it. The back bedroom begins to resemble the kitchen. From time to time we clean up. We will not allow the situation to deteriorate to the state that 155 reached one summer, when it was necessary at the end of the season to clean it out with road brooms and shovels.

Dominating the kitchen, which dominates the cabin, is its wooden table, three feet by two feet in size. Inevitably there is a problem with doors. On one side the front door opens into the table, and on the other, the refrigerator door does. The refrigerator, moreover, has a reverse handle so that it opens first along the wall, then into the table; this means that it can be opened fully only with effort and never when the table is occupied. The table is equally obstructive to both doors, but there is nowhere else to put it, and we cannot do without it. The table itself is constantly, indifferently littered with debris. A random inventory discovers a hammer, a pipe wrench, a can of shaving cream, crumpled aluminum foil, salt and pepper shakers liberated from the Inn, a bottle of Louisiana hot sauce, a pocketknife, a gas cap, a harmonica, a measuring cup, an apple, dirty dishes, granola, cartons of instant milk, a three-year-old copy of *Life* magazine, a box of Kleenex, *Scientific American,* napkins, dirty silverware, a pot-holder, an onion, a mostly empty pitcher of Kool-Aid, crackers, a can of beans, paper plates, homemade bread, and an indeterminate patch of sticky goo (probably honey and maple syrup). With appropriate shufflings, we eat on the table, play cards on it, and rebuild carburetors. On it I write the last two chapters of my doctoral dissertation.

The truth is that 176 is a bivouac, not a home. It is another place we move into and out of. Built on one pattern, then modified with ad hoc amendments; designed for one purpose, then applied for another; used, not lived in; and moved through, not truly inhabited—176 is the perfect residence for a fire crew. We don't work on the North Rim because we live here; we live here because there is work to do, and the nature of that work, firefighting, dictates every part of our existence. Our cabin is little more than a detached annex to the fire cache, and we could sooner do without it than without the cache. Even on lieu days a crewman is more likely, after sleeping in (if he can), to hang around the cache than the cabin. That is the way we want it, and we treasure 176 as much for what it is not—which would divert us from what really matters—as for what it is.

What improvements there are take place outdoors. Outside the front door stands a concrete and rebar fireplace extracted from the Boneyard. Beyond the back door a brick-lined pit designed to accommodate a Dutch oven, in which Lenny makes his exquisite peach cobbler, points to the Rim. A wooden picnic table oscillates between the front and rear of the cabin. With a chain saw Dan carves two five-foot trunks of ponderosa into mock thrones. Cars park on both sides of the cabin. The Rim of Transept Canyon breaks open no more than thirty yards behind us, and the sun sets routinely across the Canyon, our backyard. It is a point of honor—a moral imperative—that we have a campfire in the evening.

When Hopi tower reports the smoke, it is no more than a pencil-thin column that scatters above the tree canopy into a diffuse plume. Booby and Vic hurriedly outfit a pumper, grab some packs, and drive north. No fireroads have been opened within the Park, so they plot an elaborate detour through the Forest. They are the only regular fire personnel available so early on the Rim—Booby as a seasonal fire-fighter and Vic as the new ranger supervisor. It is the first fire of the season, and they can almost taste the adrenaline.

The smoke thickens, builds, and rises. As Park fire officer, Clyde struggles to organize a recon. Booby and Vic drive steadily onward. They veer around some logs, cut others, pause at signs stripped by the winter. They are still deep in the Forest. The fire is an acre in size. Everything is unusually dry; and Rainbow Plateau—a peninsula surrounded on three sides by canyon—is exceptionally dry. It is a fire to kill for. The fire torches some trees. Clyde requests the Park dispatcher to ask the Forest dispatcher for the location of the nearest air tanker. It is only noon, and the fire continues to escalate. Black smoke erupts like a gushing well as flame enters the oily crowns of ponderosa; surface fires flash through scrub oaks and heavy litter like surf striking a rocky shore. Clyde orders a retardant drop from an air tanker stationed at Prescott, while Booby and Vic, temporarily mired in a mud puddle on a stretch of Forest road just outside the Park boundary, stare with longing and frustration at the Shinumo Gate. They extricate themselves with a winch.

The fire is now about ten acres; with a long burning period ahead of it, the fire will probably proceed to the Rim and up the peninsula. Clyde requests a helicopter; Booby and Vic struggle with the rusted lock at the Shinumo, finally break the chain, and enter the Park. They continue to dodge trees where possible and cut them where they must. The helicopter locates a landing site not too far from the fire, but there is a much better helispot possible along the Rim if a few trees are dropped—a chore quickly done. Within an hour it is possible to begin ferrying firefighters from either North or South Rim to the fire. Booby and Vic stop the pumper near Swamp Lake. Rainbow Plateau is due south. They study their fire map, realize that the plateau tilts downward from east to west, and wisely elect to hike along the eastern Rim; even so, there are three substantial ravines to cross. They seize packs, tools, and canteens and begin to flag a route south. The fresh personnel landed by the helo work a flank of the fire. The air tanker, a B-17, arrives, drops its load along the most active perimeter, then departs for the retardant base at Grand Canyon airport for another tank of slurry. Many more people will be needed. The fire is twenty acres and growing as it wishes. The smoke column is visible to all the regional lookouts. Clyde orders three SWFF crews. The fire flashes over Emerald Point and expires in midair as it sweeps into the void of the Canyon. Booby and Vic thrash through vicious meadows of locust. Not yet acclimated to the high elevation of the Rim, panting from both exhaustion and anxiety, they listen helplessly to their radio, a constant buzz of voices, a flaming rush of shouts, chain saws, aircraft. Hopi tower reports another fire farther west.

Clyde makes a pointless recon, for it is discovered later that Hopi tower, manned for the summer by the music teacher from Grand Canyon High School, has reported the sunset over Mount Trumbull as a fire. Meanwhile, Booby and Vic catch whiffs of smoke. They can hear the helicopter, then chain saws, then voices, shouts. They tie their last flag at the helispot, now piled high with matériel. Within a couple of hours the SWFF crews—Hispanics from New Mexico, tough and regimented—will trample over their flagged route to the *helispot at Violet Point. The route will become a trail. When the SWFFs arrive, the local crews will be released.*

Booby and Vic grab canteens and shovels and wander in the direction of the noise. They want to find someone to report to before they are released. They would like to see the Emerald fire, and darkness is coming fast.

"IF YOU DON'T GET OUTTA HERE . . ."

Our sense of geography enlarges slowly and empirically. It begins with a nuclear core of work stations and gradually expands, like a tree branching outward, to encompass the Rim. Skid Row, the maintenance shops, the gas pumps, the mule barn, the galleria of mid-scale managerial shops are added to the Greater Cache to form the Lower Area. The ranger station (a.k.a. "the Office") and a cluster of upscale housing constitute the Upper Area. Here the administrators of the Rim congregate, and here there are frequent contacts with Park visitors.

The entrance road passes near the Office on its way to a terminus at Grand Lodge, somewhat over a mile distant. Between the Park Service Area and the Lodge are side roads that lead to the North Rim Inn, the campground, the garage, the wranglers' quarters and mule barn, the ball park. We know the fire cache well and the Area somewhat less well. We know the Rim only as we encounter it during the course of our work—which is to say, where fireroads and fires take us. We know the Canyon from scattered fires that occur within it. Our interest varies by a kind of inverse-proportion square law. The Lodge can be reconstructed—*is* reconstructed—and the Inn can be rededicated as a store, and the changes affect us hardly at all. But when Horace Wilson bulldozes the heliport into dust, when the fire cache is relocated, when the storage sheds where we used to park the pumpers are converted to a galleria of clapboard offices, we are outraged. This is sacred space. It is our connection to fire.

In the great room of the cache there is a routed sign that reads IF YOU DON'T GET OUTTA HERE, YOU DON'T GET OUTTA HERE. After a few weeks even rookies no longer have to ask what it means. At best the cache is a portal; at worst, a sink. "The Area" becomes an expression of opprobrium. Rangers work in the Area. Offices, not fires, populate the Area. The Area exists because there is a source of water (Roaring Springs) to exploit, not because there are fires. The Area is staffed to serve the visitor.

This is the dichotomy that divides the North Rim into two realms: you work either in the Area or out of the Area. Every job apart from ours relates directly or indirectly to the Park visitor, and that compels everyone else to stay in the Area because this is where the visitors cluster. If there were no visitors, there would be no Office, no Lodge, no Inn, no campground, no paved highway or overlooks, no saloon, no sewage treatment plant; there would be no park rangers, no ranger naturalists, maintenance laborers, carpenters, plumbers, road workers, no supervisors. But we could pass an entire summer and never contact a visitor in an official capacity. We could be stationed anywhere on the Rim. We are informed by fire—by fires that originate from lightning, not from people; by work that puts us in contact with the forest and the rolling ravines of the North Rim, not with visitors or with the Canyon to which they come to gaze; by events that cannot be forecast with managerial precision prior to their occurrence, that can only frustrate career tracks and budgets. Fire is eclectic, ineradicable, invasive, stochastic, opportunistic, fun—and its attributes become ours.

Our status within the Park Service, and our place within the Park, are extraordinary. No one knows exactly where to position us within the organizational geography of the Park, or where to place the cache and the Pit within the functional geography of the Area. No one knows what to call us, what kind of uniform (if any) we ought to wear, what we should do and how we ought to do it. We are creatures of the Rim at a time when the River, not the Rim, defines the political geography of the Park. We manage by opportunity, not by objective. We are at once irrelevant and irrefutable, the fire weeds of the Park Service, thorny locusts in an otherwise open glade of ponderosa. We fit nowhere, and if we stay in the Area, we cannot survive as a fire crew. If you don't get outta here, you don't survive.

*   *   *

"I can't write the report," says Mac.

"It's easy." I shrug. "You just look up the codes in the manual, fill in the blanks, and sign it. No report, no fire. No fire, no pay. That's just the way it is." Mac shakes his head. "The manual won't help. What happened isn't in the manual. I'll tell you what happened.

"The original smoke report came from the Forest Service. Their fire recon guy—Observer 1, they call him—well, he wasn't even close. He might as well have flown over the Dixie as the Kaibab. They don't know the Park. He mistakes Big Springs Canyon for Kanabownits Canyon. So Tim and I drive down W-4, which has not yet been opened, and we have to clear it as we go. Just enough to get through.

"The Forest Service guy says to go half a mile beyond W-6, then take a compass bearing of 97 degrees. I don't think he corrected for declination. I don't know. We walked for over an hour, all of it across ridges and ravines. There is nothing there to sight on. There's nothing—no placenames, no landmarks, no roads; maybe no fire. Nothing works. Typical early-season fire. Call it the Shakedown fire.

"So I request Recon 1, and we walk back and pull our flagging and wait at the pumper. Well, it's getting dark. Recon finally arrives and circles for what seems like hours and then gives us a mixed set of directions. Waste of time. You can't mix geography and mathematics. You follow a ravine or you take a bearing, but you don't do both. Anyway, you forget after a winter. So recon has us park the pumper at this drainage and then tells us to follow it east. OK. We are supposed to come to a bend, then another bend. At this second bend we are supposed to find a fallen log in a small meadow, and on the south slope there is a grove of aspen. At the aspen we are supposed to follow a bearing of 162 degrees. This should get us to a small clearing on the ridge. Then he wants us to climb up the ridgetop for another quarter mile. 'The fire is burning at the base of a big yellow pine.' We can't miss it.

"You can see this coming. It's dark by the time we reach the second bend. Or maybe it's the third. Or the fourth. The whole drainage is a tangle of bends and oxbows. There are logs in all of them. The whole south slope is covered with aspen. So I figure, 'Fuck it. The fire's somewhere on the ridge. We just hike up the slope and follow the ridgeline until we come to the smoke.' Besides, it's getting dark. We

*get out our headlamps. I'm hungry as hell, but I figure we can eat
when we get to the fire. I'm tired. I haven't been up on the Rim but
three days, and I got a bad case of Kaibab emphysema.*

*"So we climb up. Tim's heaving for air. We use our shovels as
walking sticks. The canteens hang below our chests and clang like
cowbells. What a comedy. We get to the ridge, and we walk up it. We
walk all the damn way to the summit. We don't see anything. It's
pitch-black. We're sweating like hogs. So we drop the gear, sit down
on a log, and eat rations. Haven't a clue where the fire is. But I reason
we can walk back down the ridge to W-4. If the fire is on the ridge, we
have to find it. Right?*

*"Forget it. It's about eleven when we reach the pumper. We drive
back to the Area. I still have my wash sitting in the laundromat, so I
dump the wet clothes in the dryer and eat, and in the morning we set
off at seven. This time we get a compass bearing, and we walk to the
fire. Ridgetop, my ass. Well, I knew—just knew—we'd be sent traips-
ing around the countryside again, so we didn't flag. The fire was a
mess. The snag had pretty much burned through, but there was quite
a patch of surface fire and a lot of mop-up. We could be there for
maybe a couple of days. You and Charlie were on the Preamble fire,
but there was nothing else going on, so I asked for some help with
mopping. Big Bob, the BI himself, and Holden, that new seasonal
ranger, came out.*

*"But how we gonna get them in to the fire? Neither one of them can
compass worth a damn. So I send them up a drainage just below the
fire; the ravine goes all the way to W-4. Or it seems to if I got the fire
located right. We had a lot of logs to buck up and figured to run the
saw pretty much continuously. Let 'em hike up the draw. If they don't
see the smoke from the morning inversion, they'll hear the saw. Well,
they don't see anything or hear anything. I think they took the wrong
draw. They get on the radio and ask us if the saw is running. Of
course it's running, which means we can't hear the radio. Well,
eventually we hear them, and they want us to run the saw. So I send
Tim up and down the ridge with the saw running—a complete waste
of time. These guys are lost. I mean, they're out in the Twilight Zone.
So I keep Tim revving up the Big Mac, and I run some flagging tape—
a continuous roll—across the ravine. There's no way they can miss it.*

The place is looking like a goddamn carnival. I run another set of flags over the ridgetop and down the ravine on the other side. Then I just sort of wander around. It's like a Brownian movement. Eventually we run into one another and collect at the fire. Big Bob nearly passes out under a tree. Holden is willing; he used to be a logger and got on some fires in the Sierras. Holden, Tim, and I mop up like mad the rest of the afternoon. We won't get it done, but it'll be good enough to leave at night. And it is night when we get ready to pack up. We leave the full canteens and a fedco and some handtools. Holden and the BI of course didn't bring any headlamps, and the batteries in mine are weak. Then the great debate. How we gonna get back?

"*I want to compass back to our pumper. But Tim doesn't trust the compass, and Holden and the BI want to go to their vehicle, not ours. We decide to follow a ravine out. We take the flagging to the south ravine. We can't see a fucking thing. I walk a little ahead of Tim, and Holden and the BI walk one to each side. The bottoms of the meadows are a mess, totally trashed—spruce, fir, aspen. The smoke hangs there, and the light from the headlamp scatters. It's nearly worthless. No moon. And it's wet. The damn inversion is forming. My headlamp gives out. Everything seems familiar and nothing seems familiar. Every place looks like every other place. We reach the road around midnight. So where's the pumper? Any pumper?*

"*We split up. Tim and I go north, and the two bozos go south. Sooner or later one of us will come to a vehicle. Whoever finds a pumper will drive back to pick up the other guys and look for the second pumper. We don't get back in the Area until 3:00 A.M. Holden and the BI parked their pumper somewhere; I don't know where, but it wasn't where it was supposed to be. Maybe their map was bad. We were lucky to find them. Now that I think about it maybe we were unlucky.*

"*So Tim and I hike in the next day—our basic compass bearing— and we mop up and carry everything out. I'll be damned if I'm going back in twenty-four hours to check for smokes. It's out. If it isn't out, I'll wait until it comes to find me. Anyway, the BI says his time is too valuable to waste on any more snag fires.*

"*Now how the hell do you put this in a report? Just where do you find all this stuff in the manual? Where are the codes for running up*

and down a ridge with a chain saw and flagging tape? I'm not even
sure I could draw a map. Where are the codes for wandering around
the goddamn woods all night? What the hell does it matter what fuel
model burned? 'Elapsed time,' my ass! You write the report. Find it in
the book. Try it. I'll give you a bearing.

"OK, OK, I'll fill out the forms. But you know what I think? I think
we need a new book. Our own book. A North Rim book."

TASTE OF ASHES

There is something wrong in the Pit.

We sense it as soon as we pry the winter lock open. There is
something missing; no, not just some *thing* but a feeling. Wil points
to a space where the Base of a Big Yellow Pine used to be. The bench
and milk cans are gone. The Musuem is gutted. Most of our photos
are stripped from the walls. The BI has cleaned out the Pit. Now that
the resource management office is complete—now that he has a
proper office with electric heaters, venetian blinds, fake paneling,
carpeting, a ritzy location within the new galleria of mid-level managers—the Fire Pit will be decommissioned. It is an act of bureaucratic vandalism.

For years our position within the Park has deteriorated, and the
winter gutting of the Pit is a culmination, not a novelty. When the
original fire cache was inaugurated in 1936, its double stalls—one
for forest fire and one for structural fire—opened onto the major
crossroads of the Area. Until the late 1960s, the fire crew remained
the largest in size, and its mission—with the exception of actual
lifesaving—the most vital to the Park. But that mission has been
abandoned, without establishing an adequate surrogate; the fire crew
diminishes in size, and other divisions increase dramatically in numbers; fire management is transferred from agency core to periphery.
The fire cache is relocated to its present site between the warehouse
and the mule barn. The old forest fire stall is reconditioned for an
ambulance and mountain rescue apparatus—ranger operations. And
rangers—the quintessential people managers—assume control over
the Rim. Rangers turn the fire cache into a logistical slush fund and

oversee a steady hemorrhage of tools, canteens, headlamps, hiking equipment.

What is fantastic is that this final act of vandalism has come from the top, not from the bottom. The brutality and cowardice and pettiness by which it has been perpetrated leave us speechless, then angry, then resigned, and finally indifferent. For us, fires are indispensable; the Pit is not. We need a future more than we need a past.

"OK, OK," Joe laughs, magnanimously, cunningly. "Forget it. They can't stop the fires from coming."

The storm rises in the South and begins depositing lightning everywhere. We watch, disgusted and unbelieving, as a smoke curls up from the South Rim. A recon is mounted. There is a fire on Powell, near Dutton Point. Kent and Tyson race off, oblivious to the knowledge that they face a long drive and a longer walk. A second smoke is sighted deep in the Iron Triangle, near the abandoned E-1 fireroad; Randy, eager for overtime, takes a rookie; the fire, he calculates, will be simple. A third smoke, faint and remote, rises out of the Poltergeist Forest south of the Sublime Road. Alston takes Johnny Begaye and Howard Tsotsie, two SWFFs.

Recon 1 circles lazily over the remainder of the Rim, dodging thunderheads, biding time and watching for smokes. Alston enters the Sublime Road. Recon 1 powers back to give him a bearing—187 degrees magnetic, 202 degrees corrected—before departing for the South Rim.

Loaded for bear, Randy hikes up E-1. "The fire is to the north, left, at the third large log across the old road. Just up a little hill from there," he remembers Recon saying.

Alston climbs into his firepack, while the SWFFs take a pack, a saw, and a fedco. Methodically, Alston adjusts his compass, smokes a cigarette, and begins to flag a route in. Two ridges. The compass hangs from a button on his fireshirt. Every twenty yards or so he takes a new reading, walks to an object in his line of sight, backsites his old flagging, and adds a new flag.

Kent and Tyson, another SWFF, reach Swamp Point. They see no smokes in the vicinity of Dutton Point. Since there are tools cached at the Powell helispot, they elect to take only firepacks and canteens across Muav Saddle. They check their map. The surface relief of Powell Plateau dips sharply from east to west; if they stay on the eastern Rim, they will cross the fewest ravines. There is no need to bring sleeping bags. They will work all day, all night if necessary.

Randy has reached the third log. The ridge is at least one hundred fifty feet above him, but he cannot see it through the dense forest. His crew hop and climb like enormous beetles over downed spruce, over branches, trunks, windfall; they move in slow motion, as though they have entered another planet whose gravity is twice, three times that of the earth. Branches tear their carefully balanced packs. Still, they climb on, blindly and always uphill.

The SWFFs follow Alston wordlessly. He halts, backsites, pulls out another cigarette. They have walked for more than a mile and a half, he estimates. Early in the season the large fuels are still wet. Plenty of time for a cigarette. May is a season for patience.

Kent and Tyson plunge down into Dutton Canyon, the great drainage, overgrown with scrub oak and locust, that segregates Dutton Point from the rest of Powell Plateau. There is no other route across the towering mesa. Overhead the midday sun glares tauntingly. Soon they will arrive at the fire; the narrowing geography of the Point will draw them irresistibly to any fire. There is no way the fire can escape them.

Randy concludes that they have reached the ridgetop. But there is no fire and no smoke; there is only an opaque forest of Engelmann spruce and white fir. Randy slumps down, crouching against a log to hold up his pack; he scans his map; he flips a coin. "Heads we go north," he announces to the uncomprehending forest. "Tails, south." The squad flounders north; after about fifty yards they see the fire—a flaming snag, half a dozen burning large logs, smoldering duff a foot thick, everything arranged to resemble the aftermath of a tornado. Maniacally, panicky, Randy scrambles around the site. Where, where, he screams, is the goddamn dirt?

So intent is Alston on his bearing that he hardly hears the SWFFs. "Kq'! Kq'! The fire!" He looks up from the compass. There, a mere ten yards away, is a pool of smoke. Cautiously he abandons his bearing and moves to the smoke. A dead aspen log—not more than eight inches in diameter and leaning against a white fir—is puffing furiously. There is virtually no ground fire; in fact, water oozes out of the duff as they tread. They trace the line of lightning down the furrowed trunk of the fir, untouched by fire, to the aspen. Alston sits down on a log, stuffs his compass into his pocket, and smokes another cigarette while he contemplates their incredible fortune. Had they arrived an hour later, the fire might have expired. The SWFFs want to extinguish the fire instantly, but Alston dampens their enthusiasm. He is sure there must be subtle complications in the scene. He is confident that he can extort at least an hour of overtime from the fire.

At Dutton Point the view of the inner gorge is spectacular. Kent climbs a tree, searches avidly for the smoke, and sees nothing. There is only one response possible. He requests another recon. Clyde obliges, and almost as soon as the plane leaves the airport, Clyde recognizes his error. "It looks like I gave you a bum steer," he admits to Kent and Tyson. "I meant to say Ives Point, not Dutton Point. When you get to Ives, you'll see the fire. There is nothing else around." He does not say—does not need to say—that Ives Point is the farthest possible extremity of Powell Plateau, that Kent and Tyson will have to recross Dutton Canyon, hike back almost to the helispot, then trace out the declining backbone of the plateau. They arrive well past sunset. The Bumsteer fire—a flaming pinyon—acts like a beacon. They slump beside an adjacent tree, packs still on, and stare at the fire for perhaps two hours. Occasionally they drink from a canteen. At some point they fall asleep. In the morning they mop up the quietly flaming stump and start the trek back. When they reach the truck at Swamp Point, they open the doors of the cab and, reaching across the seat, pull each other in.

Randy calls for reinforcements—for water, rations, saws, firefighters. Three of us trudge in. No one has found any dirt. It will be a difficult mop-up. Sitting despondently on a sawn log that evening, Randy names it the Rekup fire. " 'Rekup,' " he explains, "is 'puker' spelled backward."

Alston returns to the cache shortly after 1700 hours redolent of satisfaction. He has worked through his lunch hour; the Smoker fire was uncontrolled when he arrived; his crew will receive hazard duty pay.

CHAPTER TWO

Tipover

THE FIRE CACHE and the fireroads are symbiotic. The cache opens
to the roads, and the roads take us to the Rim. Without the fireroads
we are condemned to the Area. With them we can recapitulate the
ritual of renewal on a grand scale. The roads take us to fires.

It is good, tough work. We exploit every tool, test every vehicle,
initiate every crewman. Trees must be cut and hauled off, branches
and brush trimmed back, eroded sites repaired, new signs installed.
Milk Creek must be spanned with another corduroy bridge. Old
roads, abandoned and retained as foot trails, must be reflagged.
Every road and trail must be revisited and reopened. Hands toughen,
and muscles harden to the texture of Gambel oak. Mind concentrates—a chisel rather than a probe.

From the fireroads we learn (and relearn) the geography of the
North Rim. There are two geomorphic terranes: the Canyon and the
Plateau. They are incommensurable; they operate according to two
sets of geologic processes and represent two epochs of geologic
activity. The Plateau is a landscape without vantage points. There are
no peaks to which you can orient and from which you can look out.
Hydrology is no better guide, for the Plateau is karstified, its drainage subterranean and deranged. Where Canyon and Plateau meet,
along the Rim, their conjunction is startling, arbitrary, relic, violent.
Yet only there can you determine your location with any precision.

Gradually the days lengthen, the landscape sheds its winter snowbanks and dries, and the sky clears. Forest and meadow slough off
their dormancy but have yet to flower. The storm tracks have moved

too far north for weather systems to pass through routinely, yet the summer rainy season has not arrived. There is neither fire nor water, only the recession of the latter and a promise of the former.

On both time and place the fireroads impose a kind of order. They instill a functional integration on a topography that is otherwise at odds with itself. They establish reference points, and they give access. The only way to move from rim point to rim point along the surface is through the Plateau, and that makes the roads mandatory. Opening the roads likewise imposes a complementary temporal order. Clearing the roads marks a tumultuous, subtle change in season, between spring melt and summer rains, when the Kaibab exchanges mud for dust, when the sun streams through the dappled woods and the air is full and warm. It is a critical moment in the annual cycle of natural history at the North Rim—and in the life cycle of a seasonal fire crew.

Whatever the season holds, the fireroads open it to us.

The fire is reported along fireroad W-1, on the last ridge before The Basin. "Yes," Recon 1 reports, "right along the road." Kent is restless. Others have been sent to fires reported earlier in the day, yet he and two SWFFs have remained in the cache. It has not been an easy fire bust. Recon 1 has been flying unceasingly since late morning. There have been long, indecisive walks. No more than a fraction of the roads are open. The snowpack prevents access to Sublime and W-1; only the Walhalla fireroads are passable. None of the crews can see fire from their vehicles. Kent takes the white powerwagon and proceeds down W-1, about a twenty-minute drive from the fire cache.

Recon 1—with reliable, soft-voiced McLaren calling the shots—is right. The fire is adjacent to the road. The snag has been shattered by lightning into a thousand splinters; a gouged trunk flames on the ground like a candelabra. Kent fires up the pump on the slip-on. While he adjusts the throttle, the SWFFs pull out the hardline hose and drag it toward the fire. In two minutes the fire is out. Incredulous, they buck up the log, roll it over, search through the duff for smoldering cinders. They find nothing. The log steams and hisses. The slip-on chugs happily. They empty the rest of the tank on the log, roll up the hardline, abandon the Scorcher fire, and return to the cache.

The Kid has just cleared the Shinumo Gate, after a long detour through the Forest. His crew faces another forty-five-minute drive before they come to TT-2. From there they will have to compass at least a mile south cross-country. Kieffer's crew, meanwhile, has yet to locate their fire. They have hiked nearly two miles down W-1G, then bushwhacked into the woods on a compass bearing. Kieffer is gasping out his presumed location over the radio to Recon 1. His crew is trying to signal McLaren with compass mirrors. They can hear the plane but they cannot see it.

How the Fireroads Are Opened—and Closed

Aspen are easy. Ralph kicks most of the branches off the road. If the trunk is dry, he breaks it by snapping it like a whip or by wedging it against other trees and pushing. Bone sits in the truck and shouts friendly obscenities. There are so many branches and logs across the road that you can wear yourself out just getting in and out of the pumper. Ralph drags an aspen log across the road, then hefts another and throws it like a spear. A large bole remains, green and sweating. He motions for a chain saw. Two saws—Big Mac and a Stihl 045— are mounted for easy access onto the slip-on. Bone mocks disgust. "Use an ax," he shouts. Ralph chops where the trunk narrows; huge chips spray into the woods. Bone cinches his chaps, inserts plugs into his ears, and fires up the Stihl. He lops off the branches, then bucks the bole into sections while Ralph hauls the residue over the road berm. Another tree is visible about forty yards ahead. Bone hesitates before plodding forward, the saw perched on his shoulder. Ralph climbs into the cab and drives to meet him.

Spruce are dreaded. Some perverse instinct guides them, in their fall, down the center of the road. They descend in clumps; not one tree but several crash at any site. Although the trunks are not large, the branches are prickly; limbing them is like trimming a porcupine. The work goes steadily, but a clump may take half a day to clear. Worse than mop-up. Ralph spots a spruce cluster just beyond the next bend. Only an hour remains until noon; they will work through the maze, then eat. A warm sun streams down on the fireroad—powdery silt, scattered mudholes, and cobbles of buff limestone and hard, spangled chert.

It is worse than they anticipated. A white fir has crashed across the road and taken several smaller spruce down with it. The bole of the fir is enormous; the branches are large and messy; the tree is heavy with water. Limbing proceeds cautiously. The fir's weight rests on nearly buried branches, and one tree sits uneasily upon another. They limb cautiously. Almost always the trunk will bind when cut, and often roll to one side; wedges, a sledge, and a second saw are essential. As Bone trudges to the thicket, Ralph prepares another set of chaps, another saw.

The trunks of the several spruce are all green. Each section, once cut, will resist movement; everything will bind. Ralph and Bone wedge each section free, then wrestle the rounds off the road with peaveys. Too slow. Ralph sets up a chocker chain around a large pine and hooks a snatch block to it, while Bone pulls out the winch cable. Section by section the logs are disassembled, dragged in whining protest over the drainage ditch and across the berm. Ralph and Bone strip every branch from one final round and roll it down the road. The road bends, but the round continues and neatly caroms off into the woods. Finally they kick the littering branches off the road. Still in chaps, they eat lunch under another fir. The next logs down the road are aspen, easy stuff. "Bare hands," Bone yawns.

The road gradually descends to the Rim, and after another mile or so they will leave the trashy spruce-fir and enter the more open ponderosa forest. Here logs seem to fall perpendicular to the road; the trunks are round, clean of branches through self-pruning; wind-fall is less extensive; it is easy business to buck, roll, or winch. If the top of a ponderosa crashes across a road, it can throttle passage with large, cumbersome branches, but with pine only a few judicious cuts, a selective carving, are needed—not a shearing as with spruce and fir. Yet more is at stake than ease of sawing; large expanses of ponderosa coincide with the Rim, and the Rim with fire.

The Plateau and the Canyon are dichotomous. They meet with catastrophic suddenness along the Rim, a border that is profoundly irrational and immensely powerful. The Plateau is a great inverted dish, shallow and carved into ridges and ravines that radiate outward from a central axis like spokes in an oblong wheel. The hydrologic connection between Plateau and Canyon is subterranean; the Plateau absorbs moisture like a sponge, then discharges it at spectacular springs deep in the Canyon. The surface drainage of the Plateau is a relic of Pleistocene fluvialism, while the sidegorges of the Canyon expand along ancient, long-dormant faults laid down during the flexing of the Plateau. In some areas surface ravines drain away from the Canyon, in others, parallel to it; where a ravine does debouch into the Canyon, its contribution is negligible. The topography of the Plateau does not lead logically to the Canyon Rim; the fireroads do.

Fires are not limited to the Rim, but they have a peculiar relationship with it, as though snags were somehow ignited by the friction of Canyon against Plateau. To get from point to point along the Rim, however, you must pass back into the Plateau. That means that the fireroads want to go other than where the Plateau wants them to, and it means that the opening of the fireroads is slightly out of sync with the natural cycle of the fire season. The points dry first, and fires appear there earliest in the season; but to reach them, you have to pass into the Plateau, where the snowmelt is incomplete and the roads impassable. The incongruity of the fireroads is the incongruity of fire, Park, and Rim.

Superimposed on the annual cycle of road opening is a larger history by which the roads were installed, maintained, and abandoned. Clearing the fireroads opens questions of Park policy. Even as we labor to clear the system, there is a movement to shut them permanently. The fireroad grid was largely laid out during the CCC occupation of the Rim, and as a network it reached its apogee during the early 1960s. When fire policy is reformulated, the fireroads feel the impact quickly. Some of the roads are abandoned because they cannot be restored without extensive maintenance. All the roads that pass through meadows are closed for ecological reasons with the exception of those that, like Sublime and W-1 to The Basin, also carry tourists. The euphoria of closure is contagious. E-1, E-2, E-3, E-1A, E-6A, E-6B, E-7, W-2, W-1G, W-1C, W-1B, W-1D-A, W-1D-B, W-5, W-4A, W-4C, W-3, W-1E—the fireroad system of the North Rim is soon gutted.

We keep some old roads on our fire maps as trails and otherwise increase our reliance on helicopters, though the Park refuses to allow permanent helispots to be constructed and steadily downgrades our priority access to the Park helo. The old fireroad names become disjunctive, remembered by veterans and learned by rookies but without integration or purpose. As the roads close, we nail the old road signs to the fire cache wall and replace their alphanumeric nomenclature with geographic names. W-4B becomes the Swamp Point road; W-1D, E-6, and E-5 become, respectively, the Tiyo Point road, the Obi and Ariel Point roads, the Matthes Point road. But the old names persist, like fire-sculptured snags in green woods.

The operating principle seems to be that fireroads which are visible to the public but not opened for public travel are condemned, while those with public access, regardless of the terrain through which they pass, are retained. The Park will not deny public access in the face of public criticism, and it will not deny access to the heaviest user of all: itself. To close down all roads would shut off the backcountry not only to visitors and to the fire crew but to rangers, interpreters, and researchers. In fact, as the ranger division swells beyond the carrying capacity of the Rim, it is essential that some fireroads remain open so that excess rangers can undertake "backcountry road patrol." Thus for major fireroads the Park refuses to let them be either repaired or closed: it wants the roads without appearing to have the roads. Closing fireroads is a way to convey a new fire policy without having to support that policy overtly. It is not fire that the Park wants to manage but its fire establishment. Shutting down fireroads is a way to shut down activities that no longer seem relevant to the agency. The only road that truly concerns the Park is the entrance road, which it insists must be widened and rebuilt to accommodate the motor homes that swarm like tent caterpillars. The future reconstruction of the entrance road will keep the Park in a happy uproar for several seasons.

Bone mentally notes the indirect effects of the approaching Rim— the more open canopy, the gusts of warm wind, the drier forest. If Rich and Lenny move down from the Swamp Point road, they should meet Ralph and Bone by midafternoon. With two vehicles in tandem, they should be able to clear the Kanabownits tower road. There might even be time, on the way back to the cache, for a detour to Tipover.

* * *

Both fires are probably started by the same storm cell. The fire at Matthes Point is instantly reported by Scenic Airlines; the Rookie fire is a sleeper.

Jack and I race to Matthes in the red powerwagon. Unlike other Walhalla fireroads E-5 is rarely boggy. We pass rapidly through ponderosa forests interspersed with glades of rock and grass. The fire is at the end of the road, a snag exactly on the Rim, not ten yards from the road.

Jack drops the tree carefully inland, against the lean but away from the Canyon, a maneuver that exhausts our stock of wooden wedges. The active fire flickers in the lightning-gouged furrow around the trunk. Clouds darken the sky, and in the distance there is thunder. We limb and buck the snag, then prepare to start the slip-on. Easy money. As the slip-on coughs to life, however, the first raindrops strike. There are more and soon a deluge. We kill the slip-on and scramble into the cab of the truck. The rain lets up slightly, only to continue in a steady drizzle. We draw cards. I lose and dash out of the truck to turn over the bucked sections of snag. They sizzle in the rain. Before I reenter the cab, I grab my firepack. It contains enough rations for both of us.

Then it is Jack's turn, so he finishes his crackers and runs to turn over the logs. The rain falls steadily. For another two hours we dash to the fire in a weird minuet. Each run fogs up the cab, and we have to turn on the defroster. We stand a couple of logs upright, vertically, and let the rain drain into their rotten cores. We finish our rations, read, and talk; at about 1600 hours the rain lets up. We climb out of the cab and inspect the fire. The air outside is cold and damp; the Canyon is a rocking sea of clouds. The slip-on has a full tank. Jack wants to know whether or not we can claim that we worked during our lunch hour.

The Rookie fire is not reported for another three days. It probably survived the rains by retreating into a catface, a cavity at the base of a pine. The fire is two acres in size, spreading steadily but unspectacularly in all directions.

We send the Nursery from 176, and the rookies have a good time. They race around the fire with a pumper, knock down the flames, and return for a second load of water. They take the second pumper as well; Gilbert reminds them that there is also a small water tank along

E-5 from which they can draft. They return that night, serenade the saloon and Skid Row with exuberant beeriness, and the next morning announce ambitious plans for mop-up. They want both pumpers and the water truck. Everything returns empty late that afternoon, and Tom explains that they intend to return the next day for more. "More what?" Dave asks. No one has ever used this much water on a North Rim fire.

The next day we all turn out. The fire is a mess. There is a mediocre scratch line around the perimeter, no evidence of bucking on large logs; there are gouges in the ground where high-pressure hoses streamed through the soil, and puddles of standing water, in one of which a patch of duff still smokes. Disgusted, Dave issues shovels and fedcos, and we break up into two-man teams and section the fire off into blocks. By lunchtime the fire is out. Gilbert plucks a section of saturated duff, squashed and reshaped under a tire, for the FCA Musuem.

RALPH GOES TO BECKER BOG; OR,
LIVING WITH THE KANABOWNITS AXLE BUSTER

The mud is like a living ooze, and we are clogged in it.

It is axiomatic that there is no running water on the North Rim, only intermittent streams that appear during the spring melt. All of the ephemeral runoff, however, seems to be channeled into the fire-roads. The red pumper is now half submerged in a vat of mud where the Sublime Road veers into a meadow. I have emptied the slip-on and Wil and John Paul have attempted to dig out our right-side wheels. With the winch cable, we uproot a spruce, the only tree in the vicinity; one shovel is now stuck under our right rear tire. There is no other recourse than to radio for help. I tell Joe that our saw has broken and to bring out Big Mac. It is a code phrase that means "I'm-stuck-like-hell-so-get-your-ass-out-here-with-chains-and-a-block-and-tackle." Never publicly admit that you are stuck.

The mud is entirely seasonal. It is one of three hydrologic categories we recognize: no water, useful water, and mud. "No water" is the norm. It is why we dry-mop fires and pack in fedcos and wrestle with slip-ons and pumpers. "Useful water" is generally found in the Canyon and must be deliberately packed or pumped to the Plateau. The Area is sustained by an incredible pump and pipeline operation that taps Roaring Springs some thirty-nine hundred feet below the Rim. "Mud" occurs only seasonally but with devastating effectiveness. The mudholes tend to occur at the same sites each year, probably sustained by quasi-permanent springs and seeps—leaks in the karstified plumbing of the Plateau, an exposé on the inverted hydrology of the Kaibab. As the snowmelt disappears, so will the mud. Once it is gone, even the summer rains cannot restore it.

We learn all this empirically. It is enough to know where and when water and mud can be found. The springs are generally irrelevant, but where the subterranean hydrology bubbles to the surface by a fireroad, there is mud, and mud is always germane. The perennial sites have been named: the Elephant Trap, the Black Hole, the Kanabownits Axle Buster, Mogul Hill, the Little Grand Canyon, the Wallow Hollow. For each, too, there are regular procedures for extrication. The same trees, marked by collars of scraped bark, are used for winching; log fulcrums, commemorating previous disasters, decorate the berm like cairns along a trail; caches of rocks and branches flash an alert along roads, like river eddies that warn of submerged snags. But Wil and I have discovered a new site, and we will have to work out a new procedure. We sit to eat an early lunch and wait for Joe.

The crew mills around the fireline, waiting for the extra water to arrive. Though the forest brightens rapidly, the evening chill is slow to lift. There are wisps of fog in the Glades. A few sprouts of grass, tentative and thin, poke through old, dirty layers of pine needles.

There are misgivings about conducting a spring burn. The last spring fire flashed across an upper crust of duff like a flame through gasoline, fatally scorching even large trees, then expired suddenly without much total fuel consumption. The large fuels and the deeper duff are still too wet to burn. But the plans have been approved, the fireline and a large portable folding tank are in place, and when the water arrives, we will lay down a hose system within the line to protect the fire perimeter. The extra water, it is felt, should allow us to quell any unwanted flare-ups. But the water never arrives. Jonathan and the dump, with the old water tank attached to it like a turtle's shell, reach only the junction of E-6 and E-6A before he radios for someone to bring him the Big Mac and an extra chain.

The junction is located within a shallow draw, where E-6A doubles back on itself. The site is dense with young fir—curiously rank within an otherwise open ponderosa forest. One rear wheel of the dump has found a mudhole. The dump cannot move, there is nothing on hand that can pull it out, and the first hope of extrication is to lighten the load. That Jonathan and Rich attempt, using the Mark III. Water sloshes rapidly out of the tank and onto the hillsides, only to slide over the surface back into the hole. More moisture will enter the hole by seepage. A mud bog has become a mud moor. The mud now captures a second rear tire, and the skewed truck blocks the entire road.

We prepare a detour for our pumpers and report the incident to maintenance, which greets the news with its usual scowl. Yes, we agree, we will pay overtime for someone to get the dump. It takes several hours for the front-end loader to reach the scene, trailed most of the way by a covey of curious Winnebagos. At first Dane attempts to pull the dump out directly with heavy chains. Then he tries to dig out the rear wheels with the loader, to lift the rear of the dump out of the hole. The loader's tires spin; there is movement, a thrill of hope; then the thrust of the loader depresses its own wheels down through the surface crust. The dump has not been lifted; the loader has been sunk. Wildly Dane tries to free the loader, but each attempt only buries it more deeply. Water and mud ooze over its axles. The loader coughs to an ignominious death. It will take two weeks until the ground can dry sufficiently to liberate the vehicles. In the meantime, we so improve the detour that everyone agrees the temporary road is superior to the old one.

The prescribed fire is postponed indefinitely.

We open the roads in a traditional sequence—some for their importance, some for convenience, and always relative to the mud condition. The Walhalla roads are usually the first to dry out. Despite some notorious swamps, W-1 is usually drier sooner than Sublime

with its lengthy traverse of high meadows. For access to Swamp
Point and the Saddle Mountain Turnaround we simply rely on Forest
Service roads. E-1 is almost always opened last. When maintenance
brags that *it* can handle the Elephant Trap, the R&T crew promptly
sticks a road grader in the bog, then watches helplessly as a dump
truck, filled with gravel, sinks up to its axles. The Sublime Road is
closed for weeks.

Joe and Henry Goldtooth show up in the white powerwagon; they
have paused at the store to pick up some candy bars and Cokes. We
will be at the site all afternoon. After an hour of futile labor it is
apparent that we will not return by 1700. We debate whether to leave
the truck until tomorrow or stay with the project. Overhead the sun
bears down; mosquitoes germinate spontaneously out of the ooze;
the mud, like brown tar, washes over the axle; the doors can no longer
be opened. We pause for a break, chew on candy bars and tins of
crackers, and debate strategy.

Wil and Joe recall episodes from previous seasons. Nearly all the
worst mirings have been the result of administrative decrees that—
conditions be damned—such and such a road would be opened by
such and such a date. When Captain Zero, North Rim manager,
demands that W-1 be cleared within a day so that visitors can travel to
Point Sublime, we protest and are told to remember our place. Our
place, apparently, is in the mud. On Crystal Ridge we stick all three
vehicles within the space of thirty yards on a road that resembles a
slow stream of chocolate pudding. We work individually—each crew
to its vehicle—for an hour, then realize that our only hope is to treat
the problem collectively. We scratch out drainage ditches to carry
water off the road, dig out wheels, stuff rocks and logs into the
enveloping ooze, cut small green trees to make fulcrums and levers.
We free one truck, then another; the last we abandon for a week. The
ruts and drainage ditches are visible for years afterward.

I recall when Kent and I were sent to clear W-1E and had only to
cross Lower Little Park to finish when we sank up to our axles and
spent four hours winching and digging and plowing the pumper
around the perimeter of the meadow, a passage commemorated by a
line of scalped, plucked trees. When we finally arrived at the cache,
the white pumper had a swath of mud on each side halfway up the

doors. The winch was cluttered with grass and wildflowers. That night I woke abruptly, as from a nightmare, and stared around uncomprehending; the lights were on, and The Ape, Booby, and Swifter stood around my bunk and watched while in my sleep I furiously wrapped an imaginary winch cable around a bedpost.

The fire is a sleeper, about half an acre in size and no more than two hundred yards from W-1D-B. Alston, Achterman, and a SWFF, Billy Begaye, flag a route into the fire from their pumper.

It is nearly sunset. The fire spreads poorly, smoldering in deep pine duff and flaming in downed logs. Quickly the crew cuts a line around the fire; but dirt is scarce, and without water mop-up could last for days. The situation calls for water, lots of water. Alston proposes that they bring the pumper to the fire.

Already darkness grows around them, and towering pines cast shadows over nightfall. Achterman issues headlamps; the group spreads out and walks slowly back to the pumper. Alston drives, while Achterman and Billy swamp. Achterman drags away some downed logs; then he and Billy cut through a small sward of reproduction, while the pumper's headlights cast bold, eerie shadows through the woods. There is one moderately steep hill to negotiate—steeper than they anticipate—and they winch the pumper up the last thirty yards. No need to flag: the tire tracks will not last long, but they will survive the fire.

Late that evening Alston returns to the Area to refill the slip-on and announces slyly that the fire will be called the Double A fire in honor of him and Achterman. All three sleep on the fireline, happily supplied by the pumper. Early the next morning they leave a dead fire. They propose we keep their route open as fireroad W-1D-B-AA.

Then there was the time when Captain Zero decided that the stream at North Canyon on the Kaibab National Forest was the solution to the North Rim water crisis and arranged to meet Forest officials there. The Forest Service refused to drive across the Crystal Springs road. This was the Forest's road, but Captain Zero insisted that his boys would drive everyone to the trailhead. Becker does, and mires the vehicle up to its door handles on his way out. Because

Zero's party will rendezvous with another truck on the other side of the trail, Becker is on his own. So far from the Park, his radio does not work. He walks out to Highway 67 (about five miles), hitchhikes a ride to the entrance station, and calls for help. Our other engine promptly sticks next to his. Both vehicles are in a broad meadow where their winches are useless. We call for the water truck. Fully loaded, it can either pull us from the mud or act as an immovable object from which we can winch. With the mechanic for a driver, the water truck gets lost on Forest roads, and we have to arrange for another vehicle to help locate the water truck. By 1800 hours we have two terminally stuck pumpers, eight people, and a thousand-gallon war-surplus water truck ensconced in the mud at what has become known as Becker Bog. By winching one truck against another, we make a little progress. But much more collective power is needed. In desperation we decide upon a grand gesture, a do-or-die scheme that will either liberate the vehicles or terminate our careers in a quagmire of accident reports. With chains and cables we join all three vehicles into a single complex knot. The two pumpers face opposite directions. It is nearly 2200 hours; everything is done by headlight, headlamp, and not a little moonshine. The parade spins, tugs, sloshes. But at any time at least two vehicles have some traction, and the tiny convoy slides ungainly out of the mire. The next morning Captain Zero describes the wonderful meal he had at Jacob Lake Inn after his hike. He refuses to authorize overtime for the crew at Becker Bog. He refuses to reward what he dismisses as an error of judgment.

Farther west, it is not going so simply. A fire is burning in some snags near Lancelot Point, but the nearest fireroad, W-4A, is more than two miles away and ends at an unnamed point. Dana, Tim, and I are clearing roads when the smoke report comes in.

The forest is relatively open and will probably become more so as we approach the Canyon. I send Dana ahead with instructions to line the fire and wait for us. Then Tim and I plot a route. There is a shallow ravine separating us from the main peninsula to Lancelot Point, so we cross it and steer into the woods. The going is remarkably easy, and the clearing marginal; I walk ahead and select routes. Suddenly I halt, dead in my tracks. To Tim, blinking over the hood of the pumper,

I point out a log that has a center section neatly sawn out of it; the width of the cut is exactly the size of a truck. Later we discover another log, cut the same way; there is a blazed tree; crossing a shallow depression, we think we can detect the ruts of ancient wheels. We have uncovered an old fireroad. It is taking us to the Grail fire.

When Dana arrives at the fire, it is nearly dark, and the flames are subsiding. He corrals it with a scratch line, but mop-up will be a mess; there is more smoldering fire than Recon 1 reported. We decide to request an additional pumper, and today that means the Forest Service—always happy to oblige. One of its ground tankers, a model 20 commanded by General Tom, has been hovering around the Shinumo Gate like a turkey vulture. "Take W-4A to the orange flagging," Tim tells the General. "Then follow our tracks."

When they catch up with us, we are about a third of a mile from the fire and continuing to crawl delicately through the woods. Their swamper arrives clothed in brush turnout gear, more suitable for the chaparral of the Angeles National Forest than the North Rim. I point out the evidence of the ancient road. They are astonished at our labors. "We never go to this much work," the Angeleno remarks. "The Forest would never have abandoned the road," says General Tom. "The Forest would have built a real road," says the Angeleno. If this were a Forest Service fire, a Cat, not people, would be swamping, they declare. We walk by the glimmer of our headlamps, searching for evidence of the old road or new routes. Then we sight the fire, a huge orange glow against the Canyon.

Dana shouts a greeting, and Tim and I loudly congratulate ourselves on getting the pumper in to the fire. Never has anyone in the Park driven so far in to a fire. Never, the Angeleno confides, has he been to a Forest Service fire to which he has had to walk so long.

The problem is not the springs but the fact that they cross fireroads, which means that they intersect matters of policy. The fireroads are opportunistic, and often arbitrary. The Forest Service recognizes the character of the Plateau and constructs its roads along ridgetops, but the Park puts them wherever it can, mostly through or across ravines. Many Park "fireroads" are nothing more than easy routes through the woods during the dry season; some simply traverse meadows; nowhere are there provisions for drainage. But all the roads emanate from the crest line, and since the early-season fires gather at the points, which dry sooner than the interior, access by road demands that the higher, wetter elevations be breached first. The Plateau's geography of water will not be joined easily to the Rim's geography of fire. Where they intersect, there are bogs.

The fireroads are means that are no longer reconciled with ends. What may be opportune at one time, when the surface is dry, can become a bog at another. The fireroads cannot be repaired and they cannot be traversed with vehicles adequate to their state of disrepair and they must be crossed, as often as not, in defiance of the curious hydrology of the Plateau. Yet crossed they must be, by administrative decree. The Park will neither repair the roads nor close them. The reason the fireroads were constructed—access to fire—is no longer compelling to the Park, yet the Park does not want to give up access to the backcountry entirely. It wants the means, though it cannot decide to what ends they should be put.

Joe and I propose to try a double-winch arrangement, and Wil recommends that if that fails, we use the white powerwagon as a fixed point from which to attach a snatch block. The two SWFFs nod indifferently. Whatever happens we will be late for dinner.

MODEL 22

The primary fireroads are open, and we plan to spend the day in the Area, reconditioning tools and vehicles. Joe, our self-appointed Head Trucker, ponders the Slip-on Question.

The Park has acquired a set of Forest Service model 20 slip-on units, with two-hundred-gallon tanks and pumps positioned in a special cage to the rear of the truck. Unfortunately, the Park has not also acquired a set of Forest Service trucks to carry the slip-ons, and some adjustments to ours will be necessary, for the model 20s take up nearly the entire truck bed, add 420 pounds additional weight, and on decaying fireroads will cause the trucks to be torqued and battered in ways their designers could never have imagined. The new slip-ons are the beginning of the end for our old powerwagons. (The white powerwagon holds on grimly—Joe swears that he could drive it through Lava Rapids if the need arose—but its transmission failed when rookie Draper popped the clutch as the truck rolled backward down E-1A, and the rest of the vehicle tumbled into junk soon afterward.) The immediate conundrum is how to mount the model 20s to our old trucks, but the larger issue is how we get to fires at all—and whether the Park really wants us to get there.

Joe surveys our fleet—two Dodge powerwagons and a Three-quarter-Ton Chevy pickup. Nothing is left of the water truck—a 1943 war-surplus Chevy tanker—except the unbaffled one-thousand-gallon tank which has to be lifted onto the big dump with a backhoe and lashed down with heavy chains. The old truck blew a rod as Dana was whining down Lindbergh Hill. Dana later showed the truck to the Park mechanic, pointing out where the truck had a "problem." Staring at a hole the size of a softball in the engine block, Daddy Pat admitted through his half-chewed cigar that "that's a pretty good sign somethin's wrong."

Each pumper (or "ground tanker," according to Forest Service nomenclature, or "engine," to follow later National Interagency Incident Management System terminology) is a rolling fire cache. A pumper offers access, via fireroads; water, from a two-hundred-gallon tank, a pump, assorted hoses, and hydraulic fittings; handtools and accessories, from flagging tape to batteries to first aid; rations, drinking water, sleeping bags; chain saws, with extra chain oil, saw mix, chains, wedges, and sledge; and, of course, gear for vehicle repair and extrication. On the pumpers we hang our firepacks, and by means of pumpers we go for jobs out of the Area, at least two crewmen to a vehicle. Whatever else they are used for, the pumpers are fire vehicles first, and whatever jobs we may be assigned, fire has primacy. We take our firepacks everywhere; we gas and retool the pumpers nightly. And every week or so we inspect in detail those that are still functioning. The new slip-ons, and their advent at the opening of fire season, have complicated that chore.

The Head Trucker puzzles over the model 20s, while the fire crew—those working on the vehicles and those in the cache—drift off singly and in pairs for cups of coffee. There are serious design problems embedded in the Slip-on Question: there is no place to attach our saw racks, tools, or firepacks; there is nowhere to hang a spare tire; there is no way to enter the protective cage over the engine to work a starter rope. Joe feels a momentary thrill when he discovers that the pump is designed for an electric starter, yet the euphoria fades as he realizes that to install a cord will require that we drill a hole through the bed of a General Services Administration vehicle. GSA will not allow any holes, and the Park mechanic will not assist us with the wiring without a hole. Hot coffee in hand, Tom asks the Head Trucker how he proposes to stabilize the slip-on unit without drilling holes for machine bolts. Joe sighs and walks to the Fire Pit. Time for a phone call to GSA.

The General Services Administration is a bureaucracy that has moved beyond Kafka's nightmares. Joe knows what the response will be, but the query is for show, not substance. GSA will tell him not how to do something, only that he is not allowed to do what he needs to do. The agency is sublimely indifferent to any nuance of North Rim life and geography. It will not supply a vehicle adequate to the loads and wear to which it will be subjected; will not allow the Park mechanic to make repairs (that means repairs cannot be made because we are eighty-five miles and a tow truck away from the nearest authorized garage); will not even recognize that, on primitive fireroads, tires wear by spalling and gouging, not by a uniform attrition of tread, millimeter by millimeter. Joe is not even sure he wants to argue for a new vehicle. Last season ("only that long ago?") Harding flew to the South Rim and hitched a ride to the GSA motor pool at Holbrook and picked up a badly needed replacement truck. On the return trip he stopped for lunch at Jacob Lake, only to have the transmission freeze up. GSA towed the truck away, and we arranged to send Harding back for a second vehicle. This time he got no more than fifty miles out of Holbrook before he blew a rod; GSA had neglected to put oil in the engine block. Eventually we got from the Navajo Reservation a recycled pickup that died before the season ended. The phone rings, but Joe already knows what the reply will be. GSA will deny authorization for any modification in the vehicle. Joe calls the Park Service garage on the South Rim. Do not anger GSA, he is told; do not reinstate the old slip-ons; do not install the new slip-ons without securing them; do not call and complain anymore.

The crew returns. Joe watches them pass by the door of the Pit. The solution to the Slip-on Question ultimately resides with the Park, not with GSA. The problem is that we need water to fight fire. Water requires slip-on units because there are no sources of surface water on the North Rim. The slip-ons require special vehicles. The vehicles demand at least a minimal road system to be effective. Fireroads—their presence and maintenance—require a clear policy on fire. The Park will not solve the Slip-on Question because it will not address the fireroad question. "What do we do?" Tom asks.

"Drill the holes," says the Head Trucker. No one else, he reasons, will ever want or get stuck with these vehicles, so we might as well treat them as permanent acquisitions. Attaching the two slip-ons should occupy the crew for the remainder of the day. Joe walks to the fire cache. The first order of business will be to hoist the slip-ons with a block and tackle attached to the roof joists.

Ralph suggests that the new slip-on should be known as model 22.

THE TANK

The struggle to get to fires and to get water on fires is endless.

The CCC solved both difficulties by laying out a system of roads and by constructing water storage tanks. In effect, it brought to the surface and rationalized the subterranean drainage of the Kaibab and imposed a reference system for the surface topography. The roads had a logical nomenclature, complemented the network of permanent and temporary (tree) towers, and carried a truck to within a couple of miles of any site on the North Rim. A few additions were added during the Reusch era—E-1A, to improve access to Saddle Mountain, and W-6A, which improbably scales a ridge at right angles. A fire map dated 1955 shows the system at its apogee. The year also commemorates the first entry on the Tipover Tank by a smokechaser.

The origins of the Tank are obscure. But it (or the spring that feeds it) probably dates from CCC days. The corps erected a series of artificial springs, some no more than hollow logs fed by pipes jutting out of hillsides; it improved several old stockman ponds like Greenland Lake, Robber's Roost Spring, and Basin Spring; and it added some unnamed ponds and springs of its own. We suspect that Tipover Spring was developed to supply the CCC camp at Shinumo Gate with potable water. During the tree tower reconstruction program, we upgraded a few of the old CCC sites and erected several new tanks as water sources—the most elaborate being the one at Swamp Point. Within a couple of years, however, the pine to which the tank had been attached yellows, dies, falls over the Rim, and carries the tank with it. The only survivor of the system is Tipover.

The Tank seems, in fact, to be tipping over. The logs on which the Tank rests are decaying. The base of the log foundation itself is eroding. The tank—all three thousand gallons of it—sits at a junction of two ravines, where dark conifers and leafy aspen give way suddenly to meadow. The site is lovely, but the immediate, the overwhelming impression is that the Tank is about to topple downhill.

Words string across the Tank like vines. "Built by James Kennedy and C. E. Chamberlain." There is no date given. "Walter Lay. Smokechaser. 1955." The Tipover Tank is the Inscription Rock of the North Rim. New crewmen pencil in their names and dates, and veterans update their list of seasons. To formal names are added, willed or otherwise, occupational nicknames: Pinyonfoot, John-Boy, Greenback, The Dancing Pole. When Swift transfers to the rangers, "Rim Roach" is scrawled over "Smokechaser." When Stiegelmeyer decides to dedicate the Tank to himself in bold letters as the Stiegelmeyer Memorial Tank, an "S" is inserted before "Tank."

And not without reason. The Tank reeks. In its original design the Tank was apparently fed by a pipe from a spring located uphill, but the system fell into disrepair, and for most of its existence the Tank has been filled only by direct precipitation. The top is screened off by a two-by-four frame covered with chicken wire. It is only partially effective. Conifer needles collect in slumps. Dead birds float on the surface. The tank is filled with a vile green brew. In dry years a rookie is sometimes condemned to scour out the inside in the hopes that the plumbing can be activated. It never is. Still, there is a revival of sorts one season, and an ingenious construction project again brings water from the spring to the Tank along what is labeled the BOT Memorial Aqueduct, named for its builders, Brueck, Owen, and Tally. But this misses the point.

The Tank is not an effective reservoir of water. It taps a deeper watershed. It exists to record names, seasons, experiences. Signing the Tipover Tank is the final gesture in the opening of the fireroads. It is the mark of good planning that the fireroads can be opened with sufficient synchronization that all the crews converge at Tipover late one afternoon. Away from the Rim, the Tank is our one true reference point.

The fire is somewhere along the Park boundary, and Duane—laidback Duane with the stringy, long black hair—is determined to reach it before the Forest Service. The smoke lies within the mutual aid zone: it belongs to the vehicle that can reach it first. The odds are that we won't be able to get the pumper to the fire anyway, but Duane insists that we stop by the Tipover Tank while en route and try to fill our empty tank. The Tank is a fetid swamp of organic debris. It is full, however, and we draft water from its middle. Duane is galvanized by the thought that the Forest Service might beat us. "It's our fuckin' fire," he insists.

The area beyond the Shinumo Gate was logged late last autumn. Everything to the north of the boundary is a surreal jumble of torn earth and half-burnt slash; the roads are, if anything, confusingly abundant. Park fire maps show an old road, W-4C, that once reached out from the CCC camp at Shinumo, paralleled the boundary, and in a few places moved in and out of an otherwise impermeable aspen worm fence. The derelict road cannot be found. Instead, there are new logging roads, not yet numbered, and a tangle of skid trails. We pick our way as best we can among the wreckage. Duane steers by dead reckoning. There is no sense to the land: it is possible to drive everywhere and go nowhere. Yet we are at least driving, and we hope to maneuver as closely as possible before abandoning the truck, climbing the aspen fence, and walking into the fire. The ponderosa forest is open. Duane figures one of us can take a saw and a fedco, and the other, two fedcos. "And a couple of shovels, of course. And pulaskis."

But Recon 1 has become bored with our laborious maneuverings and has departed on a general survey of the Park. It will return only when we request it. We work our way to what we take as our best guess and call blindly into a dead radio for the plane to return. Duane is wild with apprehension. "Christ," he says through clenched teeth. "Let's drive." We traverse the boundary another quarter mile, bouncing over roots, stumps, rocks, then catch sight of some smoke drifting on southwesterly winds through the woods. Duane powers the truck to where the smoke intersects the fence. There in front of us—in all its wild improbability—is a gate, surely a relict of the old W-4C fireroad. We swing it open and drive forty yards through the open forest to the fire. We drop the snag, buck up the larger burning logs, douse them with water; the fire will be mopped up by evening.

A Forest Service engine crew, carefully following our tracks, appears near the old gate. Do we need help? they ask plaintively. "No," crows Duane. "We have a pumper on the fire." And yes, we have ample supplies of water. The gate, the skid roads, the Tank—it is like something out of a movie, and Duane names it the Hollywood fire. The drive back ensures that we will even pick up a few hours of overtime.

When asked later about its location, Duane replies evasively, "East of Swamp and west of the Twilight Zone. You know, the Tipover area."

KENNY SIGNS ON

When we arrive at the Tank, there is more graffiti, this time in bright red ink. Steadily, like a malevolent mistletoe, the names of people other than fire crew members have spread across the Tank. Rangers with no fire experience. Fee collectors. Interpreters. Vandals all. Even the road to Tipover is formally eliminated because it passes through a meadow. Official vandalism.

Closed or not, the walk from W-4 to the Tank is easy, and we make it often. During springtime the site is rank with greenery. In the autumn the deep hillsides of Tipover Canyon sway with the yellow and orange of aspen. Lunch at the Tank has a serene, bittersweet glow. The site is too remote from the Rim for there to be many fires— a fact for which we are grateful. Surrounding ravines are unusually steep, and the forest is satanically dense. One fire southeast of Tipover forced a party of smokechasers to cross three ridges, each steeper than the last. As they marched back and forth with fedcos, they named the ridges—Devastation, Desolation, Destruction. This is not a scene for fires, but it is an ineradicable part of the geography of fire. We travel here not for fires but for the Tank.

The Tank's status remains ambivalent. It will not be forcibly removed, yet it will never be integrated with the managed geography of the North Rim. Lenny and I add another year below our names. Dash tries, without success, to erase the name of a particularly obnoxious fee collector. The galvanized metal holds the ink like a brand. Kenny, a rookie, searches for an empty space on which to write. "Hey, what should I call myself?" he asks, almost shouting as the rest of us leave the Tank for lunch under the aspen. Smokechaser, FCA, fire guard, fireaid, fire management specialist—all have fallen into disuse. "Longshot," Donnie tells him. "We're Longshots now."

Dash marvels that the wonderful Tank has not yet toppled down.

CHAPTER THREE

Powell Plateau

THE DAYS LENGTHEN and dry under a crystal blue sky. Storms are infrequent, and lightning fires scarce. The mud recedes into a few stubborn holes. Snow vanishes from all but the darkest forest. The cache is fully operational; the fireroads are passable; the crews, the new and the old, are on board. For the veterans there is much to do, and for rookies, much to learn. Steadily we move out of the Area and even beyond the dendritic grid of fireroads. Through trails and heli-spots, through projects like the Fence, and through fires, we explore the boundaries of the North Rim.

The Rim—the Park—forms a ragged triangle shaped equally by geography and bureaucracy. The Colorado River makes a colossal, puzzling bend around and through the Kaibab. The River first proceeds southward along the east flank of the Kaibab Plateau; then it breaches the Plateau—the Grand Canyon proper—before returning northward along an old fault line that defines the western flank of the Kaibab. As the Canyon matured and expanded outward, the great bulge of Plateau caught in the looping triangle broke up into long peninsulas. On the South Rim it was reasonable to confine the Park proper to a roadway—a string of overlooks—along the Rim itself. But this was not possible on the North Rim, and a nearly straight boundary line was drawn across the Plateau with the result that large chunks of the interior were incorporated into the Park and an inter-agency DMZ was established between the U.S. Forest Service and the National Park Service. The larger result is that three points roughly demarcate the North Rim—Saddle Mountain, Powell Plateau, and The Dragon. Together they define the metageography of Rim and fire. Call them our fire triangle.

A Grand Tour of the Rim becomes a great vortex of places and experiences that all converge on fire. Not everyone makes the circuit in a season, and some could never make it regardless of time invested. Our life on the Rim is brief, usually ninety to one hundred days. We are annuals, not perennials. We are like an odd species of social insect that must hurriedly emerge from chrysalis to functioning adult before the season passes away. Fire is the catalyst, but in June fires can be scarce, and as surrogates we rely on an evening campfire program and on fire school. No event is more eagerly anticipated or more joyously concluded, because we don't need fire school, we need fires.

FIRE SCHOOL: BREAKING INTO THE FIRE TRIANGLE

Lenny is holding forth about the nuances of fireline location and construction. The room is gloomy; sleeping bag liners block off the windows, and light enters indirectly through the great double doors. No matter—after the written exercise there will be another short film. The ambulance has been pulled out, and its stall converted into a makeshift classroom. The setting is appropriate in a way, for S-190 is conceived as a first-aid course in fire and firefighter behavior. The students—fire crew rookies and reserves—read along in their workbooks, equally enlightened and confused.

The course is designed to teach very elementary fire behavior to firefighters in the Northern Rockies, the Pacific Northwest, Southern California—places that have large fires and a history of fatalities, places far removed from the daily routines of the North Rim. It will be a long, concentrated day. White-collar stuff—programmed fires; clean, well-set objectives; national standards; certificates of attendance. The Park Service loves it, and no one can be issued a red card without taking the course.

Rich hovers outside, trooping busily among the fire cache, the Fire Pit, and the old cache. Thumper and Jimbo rifle through the project fire stall. Sleeping bags, ration cases, camp stoves, lanterns, fedcos, canteens, cubitainers, project fire kits pile into a great mound. Tomorrow we will issue protective gear and small firepacks just as we would for a call-up. We will take everyone into the field, organize them into squads and crews; make them dig line with every handtool; start a practice fire; crank up the slip-ons; lay out pumps, hoses, portable tanks; demonstrate protective clothing; set up a small fire camp; spend the night. The prescribed fire site on Walhalla is a good locale. The scenic drive, blockaded by snowbanks on shaded road cuts, is not yet open, but we will issue shovels and tell the trainees to dig a route for the trucks. We call it S-130, Basic Fire-fighter—a national course whose contents can be established by local norms. Jimbo and Thump recheck their list. After the session Lenny will line up all the trainees and run them to the garage and back, a distance of a mile and a half, scorning the submaximal alternative, the ballyhooed step test, another white-collar surrogate for grime. In fewer than fifteen minutes he will know who passes and who does not. After the mock call-up and the real mop-up on a practice fire, the Longshots will know who likes to fight fire and who does not. All in all, basic training takes about three days.

For fire crew regulars there will be more. We offer special sessions on map reading, compassing, portable pumps and hydraulics, firing equipment, timekeeping, helicopter management, advanced fire behavior, the use of the Affirms terminal. Some years—years with good crews and few fires—there may be advanced national courses for crew boss (S230), fire business management (S230), air operations (S270), sector boss (S330), fire behavior (S390). Rainy-day stuff. The important things, like smokechasing, can't be taught in a classroom. There is no place to put those experiences on a red card—the official record of fire experience and qualifications.

Park officials hand out red cards like candy. The requirement that actual fire experience be kept current for each position is widely ignored. Park officials who have not seen a fire in a decade are allowed to keep ratings as fire bosses and sector bosses. A computer calculation based on national standards shows that when the Park's chief ranger assumed control over the Pistol fire, he rated no higher than tool manager. We certify the fire crew in everything we can, but the rate of inflation accelerates; rangers add shamelessly to bogus records; the Park administrative hierarchy cannot be violated, even during a fire. No one will deny his or her employees access to fire overtime. And a high rating looks good on a ranger résumé.

Some years fire school for the regular fire crew ends with a Fire Olympiad. A fusee is ignited at the fire cache and carried solemnly to the fire totem. There are a few team events—like a relay race with firepacks and shovels and a race to open ration cans with a P-38; but mostly there are individual contests, and each team contributes one person per event. There are contests of skill that test the ability to throw dirt with a shovel, to assemble a chain saw, to negotiate a pumper through a tortuous pattern of orange pylons, to cut logs with a pulaski, to put up flagging tape while burdened with firepack and handtools. There is an obstacle race through an opaque section of mixed conifer; there is a footrace to Harvey Meadow and back. The winning team takes home an ancient fire nozzle, recovered from the depths of the structural fire cache, known as the John Smokechaser Memorial Trophy. The whole affair absorbs an afternoon until Captain Zero declares the olympiad "an unsuitable use of government time." Dave suggests that fire school ought to be declared an unsuitable use of government time. Later a song, "The Twelve Days of Fire School," is composed, in which each day the foreman gives a new, worthless item of fire equipment to a rookie.

Lenny has concluded his session: the lecture; the film; the workbook exercises; the inane exam. To the standard crash course, however, he adds a slide-text presentation that illustrates the Ten Standard Firefighting Orders with historical examples of fires that have resulted in multiple fatalities. The narration thunders away; the disasters mount, as crew after crew is overrun; the eyes of the novices grow as big as shovels. They ask numerous questions—all obliquely stated—that want to know how dangerous the job really is. Lenny patiently explains that most fires are small, that the greatest hazards are associated with smokechasing, tree felling, helicopters, and vehicles. "Your biggest problem," Lenny suggests gently, "will be finding the fire." "You mean," says a fern feeler, hopeful for OT (overtime) and flushed with new insight, "that the trick is to find the fire before it gets big."

"He means," mutters Joe as he and Ralph slip out the partially closed double doors of the cache, "that the trick is to find the fire before it goes out."

I drive like a madman to Swamp Point. It is possible—just possible—that we will reach the Point before sunset. We do not. When we arrive the darkness is growing rapidly. Powell is rimmed with crimson, the final coals of sunset. The fire, we were told, is on the north side of Swamp Ridge, in Castle Canyon. I had hoped to reach Swamp Point and sight back on the fire and walk in with at least some daylight. It is not to be.

I climb the water tank, then scale the tree to which it is attached. Darkness envelops us like quiet smoke. Kent rummages through the pumper for some rations. I can see nothing, descend, then climb the tank and tree again. Clouds squeeze off the lingering light of the sunset and shield the night sky completely. The darkness in Castle Canyon is abyssal. The Canyon seems bottomless, but up the drainage I can see a pinprick of light that sharpens into the size of a small candle, a spot of flickering yellow on black velvet: the fire. There is no point in unpacking our fire maps; there are no points of reference; the fire could be anywhere or nowhere. Below, Kent has turned the tailgate of the pumper into a small cafeteria, with half a dozen rations, gallon canteens, even a quart canteen of instant lemonade; he discovers some pound cake and fudge, mislabeled in a B-2 unit. I yell down that my best guess is that the fire is about a mile away, that if we drive back on the fireroad, we can walk north, reach the Rim, and contour around it in a way that will bring us to the fire. Kent stuffs some extra cans of crackers into his pack. "It's all overtime," he says.

We drive, park, double-flag our embarcation point, and, fully loaded with fire gear, walk by compass and headlamp. The Rim is not well defined; instead of ending on a rocky point, which we could use as an observation platform, we find ourselves glissading down a steep slope of pine needles and shrubby locust. We follow our flagging back to the truck; I drive on another half mile and we repeat the expedition, again without result. From time to time Kent shifts his tools to one hand and reaches into his fireshirt for crackers or candy. The night is opaque, broken only feebly by the clanging of canteens and metal tools. The taunting flame was visible from Swamp Point. I reason that we should come upon it if we contour along the Rim. It is simply a matter of logic and smokechasing. We will get to it. We must get to it. I drive another half mile down the road. This time we will walk to the Rim and traverse along it back toward Swamp Point. Kent inserts a spare set of batteries into his headlamp.

We walk for an hour, confident that I have found the Rim—a high mound—and are contouring along it. Any moment now I expect to discover the eerie glow of the fire. Then Kent points. Ahead of us, caught in the beam of our headlamps, glare two yellow eyes. Too small for a coyote, they can belong only to a mountain lion. We drop to our knees and slide behind a tree. We turn off our headlamps and approach cautiously. As nearly as we can tell, the eyes, now dulled, watch our every move. We are stalked and stalking. Abruptly Kent stands up and flashes on his headlamp as we stare slack-jawed at the rear of our truck. Two yellow reflectors stare menacingly back at us. We have come full circle.

We drop our packs and spread out sleeping bags and listen to the Park radio. It is nearly midnight. Other crews have reached and controlled their fires and prepare to rack out for the night. "You're right," says Kent, as he tosses empty ration cans into a sack. "There is a fire out here, and I'm going to make it." He gathers needles and branches and starts a cooking fire and warms up a can of chili. The Park dispatcher tries to contact us; but we are in a dead zone and cannot reply. The radio is worthless. Everything is worthless. "How do you figure it?" Kent asks matter-of-factly. "Seven hours of OT, no hazard pay?"

I turn my pack away from Kent's fire and face Swamp. The next morning, with assistance from Recon 1, we will walk directly to the fire, by then no more than a collection of nearly burned-out snags. But not tonight. Tonight, when I close my eyes, I see it. The image of the Castle fire endures, a specter of flame on black velvet. Kent is snoring. My last thought before passing into sleep is the sight of flame dancing darkly across my hard hat.

INTRODUCING PYROMANTICISM! UNCLE JIMMY TALKS

"Good evening. Welcome to the North Rim. Our show tonight is titled 'Pyromanticism,' and it deals with a subject dear to our hearts and pocketbooks: fire." The screen at the campground amphitheater shows a huge fir torching upward to a smoke column. Uncle Jimmy, outfitted in Nomex and hard hat, paces restlessly on the proscenium.

"Nearly all of our fires are started by lightning. When lightning strikes a tree—like this ponderosa—it spirals around and gouges a furrow. Sometimes fire starts in the furrow; sometimes, on the ground. Sometimes it can burn for days in a cavity, like the catface at the base of this tree. We call this kind of fire a sleeper. Most of our larger fires are sleepers. We average about thirty-five fires a summer. The majority occur in July and August. But they come with enough rain that we can usually catch them before they get very large. You can see from this map that the Southwest has the heaviest concentration of lightning fire in the United States, perhaps in the world."

The audience squirms, unsure of what is happening. Why, at a national park campground talk, they wonder, is there no campfire? Uncle Jimmy struggles to keep his agitation under control, but his talk is punctuated with flurries of hand gestures and short, stabbing paces. He tosses out lines as though he were throwing shovelfuls of dirt. He does not elaborate on the curious status of the Kaibab Plateau, that it is a kind of off-shore island located between the High Plateaus of Utah and the great fire and ponderosa belt that sweeps across Arizona along the Mogollon Rim. "Are you fellows interpreters?" we are asked by an elderly man before the show. No, we reply, and before we can apologize, the man blurts out, "Good. I won't go to those stupid shows anymore." (Someone relays the story to the fern feelers. They couldn't care less. Because we might be called to a fire, they have someone formally scheduled for the program. If we proceed with the show, the ranger naturalist—or "interpreter," as they prefer—has a paid evening off, while we receive nothing. The fern feelers smile at the story. The joke is on us.)

"Once you have a fire, you have to find it. We have several methods." A photo appears of a one-hundred-foot tree, stripped except for a small platform at the top. "This was an approach that was tried in Oregon. I think if I were told that I would spend months in the top of that, I would consider summer school." A shot of a man with a plane table and horse appears. "This is another approach, if you have mountains. We don't have mountains. We do have two lookout towers, North Rim tower by the entrance and Kanabownits tower near the Sublime Road. We don't man either one continuously anymore. Sometimes we send someone up for a look after a lightning storm. We have tree towers, too. This one is by the ranger station." Uncle Jimmy does not elaborate. He has fifteen minutes to describe how fires occur, how we find them and fight them. He does not say, if he knows, how it is that North Rim tower reached its current state of disrepair.

The reason is Abner, the last person hired as a regular lookout. Early in 1970 he sighted the Desert View dump burning, and he became a momentary champion—at last we had a challenger to Barbara Red Butte. But it was the last smoke he ever reported; fire busts came and went with hardly a word from North Rim tower. Whether Abner was even in the tower, no one could say. He was a writer, and the only smokes he reported were the ones in his novels. He lived in a trailer behind the entrance cabin, but he was absent so often that he demonstrated that we did not need a lookout, because having Abner in the tower was the same as having no one. The position was abolished. Kanabownits tower has not been routinely manned since CCC days. "We use aerial detection now. All our fires are sighted by fixed-wing aircraft or helicopter. The fixed-wing is known as Recon 1. The helo we call by its radio sign, 210." Uncle Jimmy leaves unsaid the ambiguity of fire dispatching. Unlike normal fire operations, and unlike all Forest Service procedures, we dispatch ourselves. The Park Service dispatcher, located on the South Rim, deals only with ranger-related operations. We follow a dispatch rotation system that equalizes the number of fires each crewmember goes to, and we follow two rules: Go with what you know, and Go with the guy in the field. Translated they mean: "Don't second-guess nature," and "Don't second-guess the firefighter on the scene."

"Once you know you have a fire, you have to get to it." A grimacing fire guard is shown driving a 1914 Model A outfitted with fire tools over a deeply rutted road. "This is our principal means. Not much has changed. Same condition of roads, same kind of vehicles, same expression by the firefighter." There is a slide from the Pisgah National Forest, circa 1919, that shows four dour fire guards pumping a velocipede. "This is a method that works well where you have railroad tracks and people who are in good shape. We don't have either." We acquire a half hour of government time at the end of the day for formal exercise, but as often as not we return to the cache too late in the day to claim that time; no one considers endless rounds of softball, basketball, and volleyball exercise. "If we go by truck, we get a bearing from the recon plane and use it to reach the fire." The slide shows a 1919 Army Air Corps biplane flying fire patrol, a great public relations coup in the early history of fire control. "The problem with the planes," Uncle Jimmy notes, "was that they had to tell the ground crews where the fire was. They tied notes to rocks and dropped them to waiting messengers. I think this was when fire crews started wearing hard hats."

"More and more we use the helicopter. We can land in meadows and along the Rim. Before he departs, the pilot will give us a compass bearing from our helispot to the fire. Remember to correct for declination," Uncle Jimmy lectures. "Fifteen degrees east. Add fifteen degrees.

"We always flag our way into a fire. That way reinforcements can reach us quickly—and we can find our way back out." There are, in fact, three informal rules for initial attack: Always flag, always bring a saw, and always expect to climb at least one ridge. "When you reach the fire, the first thing you do is take a break." Nervous laughter from the crowd. They are unsure about the intent of the humor. There is enough fire displayed on the screen now that they have ceased to worry about the lack of a campfire next to the proscenium. "You scout out the fire. This is called size-up.

"If there are real problem areas, you hot-spot. You knock down those hot areas before they have a chance to cause trouble later. Sometimes we use air tankers." The specter of a B-17 rushes across the screen, pink slurry cascading out of its belly. "For six weeks each summer we have an air tanker stationed at the South Rim airport. The Forest Service runs a retardant base there all summer. We can get a turnaround drop in under fifteen minutes. Sometimes—for instance, if we have a long hike into a fire—the Park fire officer will call for retardant to hold the fire until we can get there. And sometimes we need slurry when we are working the fire." Air tankers are exotic, romantic to most of the audience. Uncle Jimmy shows a series of slides that capture in stills the sequence to a drop over the head of Transept Canyon made by a C-119J. "A B-17 can hold about two thousand gallons of slurry. The pilot can drop it all at one time or in quarter sections. A good practice is to drop half a load on one flank of the fire and the other half on the other flank. That pinches off the head of the fire.

"Then you build a fireline. The dimensions of the line will vary according to the fire and the fuels. The line goes to mineral soil." Several slides of crews digging line appear. In the last, taken at the Regeneration fire, everyone except one man is raking material to the same side. "That man facing the wrong way is a ranger." Some coughs and muffled laughs. Uncle Jimmy suspects that the laughter emanates from a contingent of fire crew hidden in the rear of the amphitheater. "Sometimes it is necessary to back off from the fire and burn out fuels that remain between the fire and the line. A flamethrower like this one is pretty dramatic, but it is awkward to carry and use. Better to use a fusee. To secure the line, we drop all snags that can throw spots across the line. The one in this slide is a white fir, completely hollow. It is throwing sparks like a Roman candle. We knock down other concentrations of fuel, too. Then we break for a meal. The lucky guys get to patrol the fire. The unlucky get the C rations.

"Now begins the fun part of firefighting: mop-up. We work at night when we can. Normally a fire will die down at night. You can do a lot of good mop-up. You can see—faintly—a man with a hose and headlamp in this picture. We start with the larger fuels and work down to the duff. You can see in this slide that a saw team is bucking up the burning logs. They will cool off each section, then roll it out of the embers into a boneyard. Yes, that man leaning on his shovel is a ranger.

"Well, nothing left but duff mop-up. We extinguish every smoke. The best way is to pick out a small section of the fire and work it over.

If everyone does that, the fire will be out. Instead, guys seem to wander aimlessly from smoke to smoke. Notice how the firefighter in this picture is stooped over. You will stay that way for hours, perhaps for days. We conduct a special training program for rookies to help them. We make them walk around the fire cache for two days without ever straightening out." Uncle Jimmy chuckles at the thought, and the audience, wishing to be polite, joins in. "That guy with a McLeod in this slide will be in the woods a long time if he wants to mop up the smokes in punky wood like that. He's an interpreter. Twenty-four hours after the last smoke we return to check the fire and pull our flagging." A slide shows two men immersed in smoke, crepuscular rays of sunlight streaming through the forest. A final slide shows what appears to be a team photo full of grinning firefighters against a backdrop of torching trees. The flames are probably eighty feet tall.

Alston is euphoric to have a smoke so soon after fire school and to have Henry John, crew boss of the SWFFs, for guidance. They park their truck near the junction with E-6 and load up. Recon 1 gives a compass bearing, which they ignore. The fire is at Atoko Point, about a mile and a half distant. They cannot fail to find it; they have only to cross an unnamed, apparently inconsequential drainage. They plunge into the woods. After an hour they admit, without exchanging a word, that they are lost. Alston looks confidently to the savvy Henry John. He will, of course, know all the tricks of smokechasing. Henry John returns a blank stare. "Well, John, which way to Atoko Point?" Alston asks, flashing an exaggerated grin. Henry John removes one of his boots and tosses it high in the air. The toe of the boot lands in a direction that Alston's compass says is north. Henry John points in that direction.

Archie and I find the Benchmark fire with only modest difficulty. The compass bearing is true, although the route is rugged. We pass by, but fail to locate, a U.S. Geological Survey bench mark shown on our fire map. We drop the tree, complete our line, and quickly buck up the snag before dark. I volunteer to return to the pumper for sleeping bags, water, and a fedco. A classic overnight snag fire. Archie, a SWFF, nods appreciatively. The trip back to the pumper is uneventful, and I conclude that I could eliminate two ridges by dropping into the first drainage and circling to the fourth.

There is no easy way to carry the big cloth bags, which hang from under my arms like broken wings. Since our saw was not working well, I decide to carry in a second. All the more reason for a shortcut. After about fifteen minutes, however, the drainage that should have graded down has moved up. I walk up the nearest ridge and follow the crest. Nothing looks familiar. A queasy feeling gnaws at my stomach. It is nearly midnight; the sky is salted with stars; there is no moon; the trees form India ink silhouettes, every needle traced against the sugary sky. A cool wind flows by, and each breeze seems to take a small portion of me, molecule by molecule, along with it.

I decide to retrace my steps to the last known flag and then follow my old route to the fire—or, in the worst case, back to the pumper.

When they reach their fire, Alston and Henry John instantly forget their miraculous methodology and congratulate themselves that they have put out no flagging tape that will embarrass them later. Flames are confined to the stump of a large fir. The main trunk has already toppled to the ground, where—hollow—it smokes contentedly. Then they realize that they have no saw; that to travel light, they brought only a firepack, fedco, pulaski, and shovel.

They chop at the log and are able to pry a few large splinters out but it is obvious that their choices are two: they can let the fire burn itself out or they can crawl in after it. With a shrug Henry John takes a pulaski and pulls the fedco behind him. Alston wonders what kind of accident report he will have to fill out. Surely the government, which has a form for everything, will have one to address crawling into smoking logs. He cuts some small holes in the top of the log for ventilation. Before the afternoon ends, the fire is out. Gleefully they collect their gear until they realize that they have no more idea where their truck is from the fire than they had where the fire was from their truck.

Wordlessly Alston asks Henry John. Henry points in one direction. Alston shakes his head and points in another, skewed nearly ninety degrees from Henry's. They split the difference and tramp off. At every junction, they repeat the process. Henry John knows in his gut where the truck is and points emphatically. Alston knows just as certainly that the truck is elsewhere. After an hour they come to the highway. They look to the right and see, not twenty yards away, the white powerwagon.

I cannot discover the old flags. Each drainage looks like every other. The flags are here, I know. They have to be here. I put down the sleeping bags and chain saw, and walk in widening circles around them, expecting to intercept a flag at any instant. I don't. The evening air, not quite a breeze, moves silently through the woods, and when I stop even momentarily, I chill. It is time to return to the bags. If worse comes to worst, I can always bed down wherever I choose and find Archie in the morning. But the bags, the saw, the canteens—the whole cairn of matériel has disappeared. "I think . . ." I say out loud, until the night swallows the sound, and I feel smaller for the outburst, and I attempt to walk a grid that will inevitably intersect either my pile of gear or a flag or that at least will keep me moving because something, something has to happen and I have to keep moving even though the grid becomes more and more arbitrary and this draw looks no different from that one. But I am moving, and my mind is empty, and I walk with headlamp flashing dimly among shadows, and after half an hour there is nothing—nothing—beyond a tightening circle of trees and an adamantine sky.

I come to a larger drainage and follow it down to a broad meadow shining silver in narrow moonlight. Already the night air is filling the valley and the tall grass is wet with dew. I hear a cry. If the moon were full, I would call it a coyote. But the moon is no more than a sliver, and it is only a cry, and I turn away from it. I fight down an urge to run. I try to remind myself that I will eventually come either to the Rim or to a fireroad, but the thought cannot get into my subconscious. The canopy of trees is gone. I stare up to the heavens, as hard as quartz.

The valley bends and bends again, and I catch in the corner of my eye what appears to be a flicker of light. Stuporously I walk up a slope. Another small bend. There, silhouetted against the flames, Archie rises hesitantly. The fire glows like an enormous hearth. Archie says nothing, asks nothing. We make some coffee and roll a few burning logs to the edge of the fire and sleep in the fireline.

THE RALPH AND KID SHOW

The stage lights come on, and Uncle Jimmy announces that two other crewmen will demonstrate some of our equipment. Ralph and The Kid, burdened like mules, trudge down the center aisle. Their gear fills the stage. The program is wholly voluntary. Our one rule is that no rookies can apply. We have no training in public speaking, and our message must be authentic to be believed. We offer Pyromanticism biweekly. It is probably the most popular program given at the North Rim.

The Kid explains our protective gear. "We wear a hard hat. It protects our head. The yellow shirt is made from Nomex. It won't burn. Actually it will burn, but it won't flash. They say it will resist a flame for six seconds. I'll take their word for it. We wear Nomex pants, too. And belts. You need a sturdy belt. The belt holds your radio, canteens, your Buck knife. And your pants. No cuffs on the pants; they can collect embers. Let's see . . . boots. Yes, we wear boots. Good Vibram soles with high tops. No cowboy boots. If you step in a stump hole, a cowboy boot will fill with ashes." The Kid is dancing on the stage, hopping on one leg while holding the other up to show his boot. The audience is mute, baffled, then breaks out in spasms of laughter. The Kid is eager to perform but unsure of how to do so. Each laugh evokes an immediate Pavlovian response to repeat the last gesture. "Oh, yeah, socks. You need socks." The Kid looks at Ralph. "A bandanna. We wear bandannas. They are handy in smoke. You can pull them over your nose like this."

He gropes around his shirt. "We keep our compass in our pockets." He pulls out his compass, a Silva ranger model. "They told us if we used this we would never get lost. I pulled mine out the other day and found north. I still didn't know where I was. You can use the mirror to signal the recon plane sometimes. When you are really lost, you can look in the mirror and see who it is who got you lost." It is a true joke. It is no easy matter to locate a single tree by a compass bearing across broken country devoid of vantage points. Consequently, for years the lengthiest session of fire school was the maps and compass course taught by Clyde, the Park fire officer. He liked the North Rim, and we liked Clyde, so his classroom course, which was wretched, was tolerated. The culmination of the training was a kind of obstacle course for compassing, laid out by The Ape. Clyde himself became lost on it once, only to be found tramping intently across the sewage spray field. Achterman was discovered halfway to Lindbergh Hill. Tim aroused Reusch's fury when he laid out the compass course so that it passed directly through the store, and the fire crew showed up licking Fudgsicles. We eventually design a barebones course that tells everyone how to take a bearing and how to follow a bearing, which are almost all we need to know.

"In the other pocket we keep a notebook and pencil. This"—The Kid waves a pad of lined paper for all to see—"is the most important item you carry into a fire. This is where you record your overtime and hazard pay. Ralph?" Ralph has been sitting to the side and climbs to his feet.

"I'm Ralph. This is our firepack. We carry it wherever we go." He opens it on a folding table that has been set up on the stage. "We carry jackets. It gets cold at night, and it rains sometimes when you go into fires. We have a fire map. It's marked off in sections and laminated in plastic." He plucks the items out of his pack one at a time, as though dimly unsure what he will find. "We carry some extra parachute cord. Wooden wedges, to help drop trees. Black tape. Extra batteries. These go with the headlamp. The headlamp attaches to your hard hat like this, and the battery case clips to your belt. The wire between them always seems to hang in your face. But the headlamp frees your arms for use with tools." He turns on the headlamp, which throws out a dim light, then expires. "What else? A mill bastard file for sharpening tools in the field. A saw kit—tools and parts useful for field repair of chain saws. Some fusees. This way, if your fire isn't big enough to suit you, you can enlarge it." Ralph speaks with an enforced, vague drawl applied to each word. He comes from a family of lawyers and will become a lawyer himself. "A good fire is nothing to waste. Always be sure you have marshmallows." The audience roars with approval as, magicianlike, he produces a smashed, half-melted bag from the pack. "Now this," he announces, holding up a pair of plastic goggles, "is a real useful tool. They are supposed to keep the smoke out of your eyes. But you see, they have all these holes for ventilation. The smoke pours through. If you seal off the holes, the glasses fog up. The government issues these. We all carry them.

"Flagging tape . . . we tear off sections from the roll like this and tie them to trees. Orange and yellow are the best colors." The Kid could remind him about the time Ralph asked for reinforcements and a group tramped along Upper Thompson Canyon until they came to some streamers and followed them, step by slogging step with fedcos, up five hundred feet of dense hillside only to emerge at the site of a long-dead burn and learn that the going fire was on the opposite ridge. "We carry two one-quart plastic canteens of water. We fill this same kind of canteen with saw mix and oil. The covers to the oil are black. The covers for the mix are red. We had a ranger on a fire recently who couldn't tell black from white and took a nice gulp of thirty-weight. He was pretty well lubed for the night.

"We carry some first-aid material. Some of us include amenities. Extra socks. Candy or gorp. When we are on a fire, we eat rations. Government-issue C rations. Which makes this tool"—he holds up a small metal object on his key chain—"the most important item you can take. This is a P-38. To people who don't know better it is a can opener. Some of the cans you might wish would stay closed. All the entrees taste like tuna fish. This one is labeled 'Chicken or Turkey, Boned.' I guess they couldn't tell which it was. It tastes like tuna fish." The pack is now empty, its contents scattered like embers around the table. Ralph plucks up an orange package from the floor.

"Oh, yeah, the fire shelter. This is an emergency fire tent. It's designed to protect you if you are trapped. You zip it out of its pack and crawl under it." Ralph pulls a much-used model from its pack and flings it out. Under the glaring spotlights it shines like a silver space blanket. "You are supposed to be able to do this in thirty seconds. The instructions are in Spanish. The shelter melts on contact with flame. Everyone is required to carry one of these to a fire. We call them turkey tents. What do you do with a Thanksgiving turkey? You make a tent of aluminum foil, put the turkey under it, and then place it in the oven to bake. Some of the local hotshot crews use them to roast pigs in.

"Speaking of tents, we use these"—he holds up a fluffy white tube—"for sleeping bags. Paper sleeping bags. That's right, paper.

It's like sleeping in a cardboard box that's been made into crepe paper. Not too large and not too warm. You have to get close to the fire to keep warm, but not too close because these things can burn. They're also loud. It sounds like you're sleeping in a bag of potato chips. Kid?"

The Kid, the straight man, returns to center stage. The routine so far has taken about fifteen minutes. The Kid launches into a dissertation about tools. He demonstrates the chain saws, lashed with cord to Army pack frames. In later years Army-surplus web gear will become abundant for carrying bottles of saw mix and oil and wedges. "Usually you will have to cut down at least one tree. You prepare a place for it to land, then drop the tree in that direction. A burning tree doesn't always give you much option. You put it where the tree wants to go. The dead branches are called widowmakers. The fire and vibrations can shake them loose. You form a team; one man spots while the other cuts. The spotter watches for widowmakers and swats embers that land on your shirt. You have to cool down the base of the tree with dirt or water before you can stand in the ashes long enough to complete the cut. If you drop the saw in the embers, it will catch fire.

"Two of us are usually sent to a fire initially. We carry two shovels, a pulaski, and a McLeod. This is"—he holds up a shovel—"well, if you don't know what this is, you're in the wrong damn business. Actually this is a special firefighting model. It has a short handle. The head is curved. The edges are sharpened. You can dig dirt, throw dirt, scrape dirt. Until the edge wears, you can actually trim branches or cut small trees." He scrambles in front of the stage, flinging dirt and gravel perilously close to the front row of seats. The audience is hushed. He drops the shovel and points to Ralph, who holds a funny-shaped rake. "This is a McLeod. The flat end is sharpened. You can cut with it and scrape with it. The rake end is extra-long for use in pine duff. This is the best tool for building a fireline."

Both pumpers, each with three crewmen, are on W-1 when the smoke reports come. Tom takes one pumper to The Basin and turns south to Tiyo Point. The smoke is along the west rim of the peninsula. I take the other pumper to Swamp Ridge; we will have to walk south to the Rim.

Tom reaches the end of W-1D-A quickly. Recon 1 gives him a bearing. The fire is among the rocks along the Rim. He can't miss it. They walk across a steep ravine, come to the Rim and see nothing, and for another half hour walk the Rim. It is open ponderosa pine forest. The drainage turns inland. The walk is easy, and the view of The Dragon marvelous.

Recon 1 locates us on the Swamp Point road, gives us a bearing, and, low on fuel, flies hurriedly back to the South Rim.

While Tom studies his map, his crew takes a break. Without knowing whether the fire is north or south of their location, the crew could walk for hours and each step could take it farther from the fire. The observer, however, also gave them a detailed cadastral location: the northwest quarter of the northwest quarter of section 19, township 33 north, range 3 east. Tom takes out his compass. He begins sighting on objects in the Canyon—The Dragon, the Dragon's Head, Grama Point—and plots their bearings on his map. They cross just south of the putative cadastral description of the fire. If they follow the Rim north, they should come quickly to the fire. If not, they can compass east to the Tiyo Point road. Fifty yards later they come to the Miss fire. There is less than an hour of daylight left, just enough time to fell the snag.

We check our gear carefully. We are all veterans, wary about trading a rush of adrenaline for a night of aimless walking. We combine our three firepacks into two and mount a saw on a pack frame. Then I double-check the bearing. Uncle Jimmy sights on Recon 1 as it flies overhead, and the observer's reading, adjusted for declination, agrees with ours. "You have three small ravines to cross," McLaren cautions. "The fire is burning at the base of a big yellow pine." We mount our headlamps and take extra batteries. Already twilight crowds upon us. Much of the terrain is dense with fir reproduction and downed ponderosa logs. I put up extra flagging, and after posting a few flags I backsite to confirm my line. We cross one ravine, a ridge, another ravine. We are immersed in darkness; even our three headlamps together cast only a dim cone of light. Our progress slows. We cross another ridge and ravine, hike for another forty-five minutes before Uncle Jimmy shouts. There it is, the Pathfinder fire, slightly to our right, perched directly on the rim of

Shinumo Amphitheater, now a moon-swept bowl of ghostly light, three snags, maybe a third of an acre of ground fire, one pitchy snag flaring like a blowtorch. I flag the last stretch—across yet another shallow ravine—by line of sight.

We cool off the base of the snags by flinging dirt, fell the torching snag—sacrificing a saw chain to rocks and debris embedded in the trunk—then scratch a line. No need to burn out interior fuels; the night is warm and windy along the Rim, and the surface fire spreads steadily and cleanly to our line.

Uncle Jimmy reaches into his firepack and produces an inflatable pillow, a newspaper, an orange, and, while deftly balancing a ration can full of water against a burning branch, a bag of Lipton tea. Within minutes he is reading his paper, sipping tea, and sampling slices of orange. I cough down a can of Beanie-Weenie and "White Bread, Packed," and then draw the short straw that will send me back to the pumpers to bring in our sleeping bags.

Pyromanticism Ends; or,
How Is a Pulaski Like a Fire Policy?

I scavenge a pulaski out of the wreckage. "This is a special tool," I explain, "unique to firefighting. It combines an ax with a grub hoe. Not very elegant, but practical and, in its way, powerful." After the skits the audience is restless. On cold nights they will slip away, singly or in family groups, reluctant to shiver for what they suspect is a disguised lecture. A solitary pulaski does not seem like much of a prop. "The pulaski is special, too," I continue, "because it encapsulates the history of forest firefighting. The history of fire policy parallels the history of this tool.

"The story begins in the summer of 1910. Drought gripped the northern states and fires broke out. Lots of fires. In the national forests alone some five million acres burned, over three million in the Northern Rockies. Firefighters then did not have the tools we have now. They didn't have the knowledge about fire behavior we now have. They didn't have organization and money. The Forest Service—which had only claimed jurisdiction over the national forests since 1905—thought they had put in place an adequate system of fire protection. They were wrong. The great fires ravaged everything.

"The Forest Service didn't withdraw, however. For the first time in American history, it attempted to fight, head-on, a major conflagration. Forest rangers rounded up crews from wherever they could get them and sent them to the fireline. The Army was called out. But the fires were too huge. Crews and towns were overrun. Some seventy-nine firefighters lost their lives. The scars from the fires are still visible in northern Idaho. They traumatized the Forest Service for decades.

"The saga of the 1910 fires, however, has condensed itself into the story of one man, Edward Pulaski. Pulaski—a direct descendant of Casimir Pulaski, Polish hero of the American Revolution—led a crew of forty-five men to the firelines outside Wallace, Idaho, where they became trapped by shifting winds and spotting firebrands. The wind rose so strong, they later claimed, that it could nearly lift a man off a horse. They were cut off from an escape to Wallace. But Pulaski kept his head. A longtime prospector in the region, he remembered the War Eagle Mine, abandoned but close by. He checked the route, then led his men in a wild race to an adit. One man lagged and perished beneath a flaming tree. The others reached the adit entrance, where Pulaski ordered them to retreat to the rear of the shaft, soak their clothes in a seep, and cover their mouths with wet cloth. Meanwhile, Pulaski stripped the saddles and blankets from the horses, soaked the blankets and filled his hat with water, and returned to the mineshaft entrance. The fire was soon upon them.

"When it came, it came with the noise of a thousand trains rushing over a thousand steel trestles. The flames roared like tornadoes. A thunderous din compounded darkness and heat and smoke. The sensations unhinged some of the men in the rear of the shaft, and they started to run out of the adit. Pulaski knew they had no chance outside the tunnel, and to let one man flee would invite a general panic. He pulled his pistol—there at the mine entrance, silhouetted by the flames of an approaching holocaust—and threatened to shoot the first man to leave. The men retreated. The fire passed over the cave.

"Everyone blanked out during its passage. When they came to in the early dawn, they discovered that five men had died from asphyxiation, but the rest were alive and they painfully worked their way to the adit entrance. There, crumpled on the ground, they found the body of Ranger Pulaski. One man looked down and said, 'The boss is dead.' A weak voice from the body replied, 'Like hell he is.' But he was temporarily blinded and prostrate with smoke inhalation, and he never recovered the full use of either lungs or eyes. He had enough left in him, however, to see that the crew was started back on the road to Wallace. Most of the town was saved.

"Sometime later, recognizing that firefighters lacked the tools to implement a policy of fire suppression, Pulaski went to his backyard forge and hammered out a prototype of this implement, the pulaski. It was a perfect tool for fire suppression. Tens of thousands are sent out to firelines each year. It was the heroic age of forest firefighting."

This is an occasion for saga-telling not scholarship. The story of Edward Pulaski is one of the informing legends of American fire-fighting, a triumph of faith over higher criticism. The episode is true to its times. Conservation had assumed the proportion of a national crusade, with the Forest Service in the vanguard. Pulaski acted out his high drama the same month that William James published his essay "On the Moral Equivalent of War," in which he urged a national conscription of youths to wage a war on nature as a surrogate for war on fellow humans. Eventually the Forest Service established a graveyard at St. Maries, Idaho, to receive the bodies of firefighters killed in the line of duty. The adit to the War Eagle Mine was declared a National Historic Site.

The need for heroism was there, the timing right. In California that same August the Forest Service policy of fire protection came under attack by advocates of "light burning," an alternative strategy that sought to make fire use, not fire control, the basis of fire management. The 1910 fires decided that debate and set American firefighting down a distinctive path. At the trailhead stood Ranger Pulaski.

Most of what is known about the episode comes from an article Pulaski wrote many years later for a contest sponsored by *American Forests* on the theme "My Most Exciting Experience as a Forest Ranger." Pulaski won, the only cash award he received. There was no worker's compensation law in effect at the time. His considerable medical expenses Pulaski had to absorb himself. At the urging of friends he appealed to the Carnegie Foundation for a hero award, but his application was rejected because, to the minds of the judges, he was only doing what his job required. Other documents have surfaced that corroborate the story in general, but dispute some critical details. The flight to the cave may have been a scramble, not an orderly retreat, and the lost man abandoned in the encroaching roar and gloom. What really happened at the cave entrance is unclear. Pulaski himself had mixed feelings about his exploits, and he became increasingly reluctant to discuss the 1910 drama. Instead, he contented himself with arranging for the burial of dead firefighters and tending their makeshift graves. Shortly after the fire, a photo was taken of his wife, Emma Pulaski, dressed in Sunday whites, standing incongruously, forlornly at the entrance of the cave.

The story of the pulaski tool is likewise complex. Combination tools were common in the West, and the Collins Tool Company apparently displayed a very modern-looking "pulaski" tool in its exhibit at the 1876 Philadelphia Centennial. The early work on the prototype was begun by Pulaski's supervisor, W. G. Weigle, as a device to help with replanting seedlings on the burns. Pulaski revised the rough implement, and it was officially adopted, with substantial revisions, in the early 1930s as a firefighting weapon. But the legend is more vital and enduring. It *was* the heroic age of forest firefighting, and nagging details could be swept aside in the bureaucratic drive for justification. Faith could suppress holocausts.

"Times change. Here at the Park our fire policy is no longer one of pure suppression. A natural area has to accommodate natural fire. In 1968 the National Park Service officially revised its management policies in a way that encourages the use of prescribed—that is, controlled—fire. Grand Canyon is responding to that opportunity. We have a research program in fire ecology under way. We are rewriting our fire plan to accept, at some point, in some form, natural fires. We are experimenting with prescribed burning as an ecologically benign way to reduce fuel and as a means to rectify decades of fire suppression. It is an awkward time, though we think—we hope—it will also be as exciting a time as those early years of firefighting. This mixed policy brings us back to the pulaski.

"The pulaski is, as you can see, an ungainly tool, neither fish nor fowl. Yet it has proved itself immensely practical. Our new policy is likewise a hybrid. Yet it is the tool we need to implement a new era of fire management. We all hope that it will serve us as well in our day as this venerable old tool has in its."

The reality here, too, is more tangled. Far more is involved than the restoration of a natural process to a natural environment. The problem is to reconcile one hybrid of nature and culture, fire, with another hybrid, wilderness. The philosophical complexities are bottomless. They are soon matched by the difficulty of trying to translate what is fundamentally a national creation myth—wilderness—into a program of field projects. From the mid-1970s to the mid-1980s most of the disastrous wildland fires in America were the result of breakdowns in prescribed fire programs. It will take decades to learn the techniques. The philosophical issues, as John Dewey suggested in another matter, will never be resolved, just "gotten over." The era needs its Pulaski. There is none. The nation is experiencing, then recovering from, the Vietnam War, not readying for the Great War.

"That's our show for tonight. Thanks for coming."

By now the audience is restless, unhappy to have a variety show perverted into a lecture. Sitting in the back of the amphitheater, Dan the Man, master of the malaprop, says sympathetically to a visitor that Ralph and The Kid are a "hard ax to follow." People advance to the stage to handle the equipment. They are intrigued by the pulaski, which they think would make an ideal garden tool. Everyone, it seems, tries out the fedco.

There are inevitable questions. Why don't you light a fire for the program? "Because we would have to put it out and we refuse to suppress fires on our own time. It's a matter of ethics." Why do you use equipment that doesn't work? "We don't, and regulations require it." What do you do when you are not fighting fires? "You don't want to know."

POWELL AND COMPANY

Earl chooses his gear patiently, full of the lessons of past hikes. There is no hurry. It is one thing to do without amenities on a fire

call, something else again when you know you will be out all night.
Wil hefts his pack, tests its weight, frowns, lowers it, then repacks.
The heaviest item is water. We calculate three gallons at a minimum:
one gallon for the hike to Powell; another gallon to cover losses from
clearing the helispots; another for the hike back tomorrow. Water in
the helispot caches—several years old—is putrid, fit only for fedcos.
From the caches, however, we can extract what tools we will need.
Earl wanders to the old water tank, now sprawled half over the Rim.
The dead snag to which it was attached, the logs that made a base, the
galvanized tank and pointed top—the tableau resembles the half-
decomposed carcass of some ancient forest creature, now extinct.
Wil, a rookie, searches for the unmarked trailhead. He is drawn,
irresistibly, to the panorama overlooking Muav Saddle. Directly
across, on the north peninsula of Powell Plateau, he can trace the trail
as it vanishes into the pines; to the south, there are snatches of the
old North Bass trail deep in Shinumo Amphitheater; to the north,
Steamboat Mountain, Crazy Jug Point, Monument Point, Thunder River, the ragged flank of the Kaibab Plateau. A warm wind
rises from the Saddle. The day promises to be hot and dry, the way we
like it.

The Powell trail simply sloughs off the helispot to the Saddle.
Swamp Point is a prized locale in the geography of the North Rim,
but as a point of departure, not as a viewpoint. We plod along through
the oak and locust, which fiercely, implacably reinvade the site.
Every year the helispot must be recleared, but we allow the brush to
overgrow the trailhead. We don't sign the trailhead. If you don't
know where it is, you don't need to know. The path improves into a
graded trail. At one time Swamp Point was joined to Muav Saddle by
a constructed trail, first established by William Bass, a miner, then
opened to tourists when he realized the true political economy of the
Grand Canyon. The descent to the Saddle goes rapidly.

At Muav Saddle the trail branches. Continue on the main trail and
you climb up to Powell Plateau. The early explorers to Powell probably followed an old Indian route. Later, when hunting mountain lions
on Powell became a fashionable sport, the trail was improved. The
present trail dates from 1927; there has been no apparent maintenance since the CCC departed. Take the south fork to scramble down

the old Bass trail; around the bend there are some seeps at the base of the Kaibab limestone. Early in the year they have enough flow to qualify as springs. Nearby is a small cave suitable for sleeping, so we name the site Mattress Springs. Unaware of any choice, Wil stalks past the junction. He and Earl head directly to a clapboard cabin on stilts nestled, here at the dead center of the Saddle, amid an incongruous grove of ponderosa.

We drop our packs and explore the cabin, which must be at least forty years old. In the arid Saddle, it is beautifully preserved, an architectural mummy. We could reoccupy it, if there were a reason to. With a little plumbing Mattress Springs could supply ample water. The shade from the ponderosa is delicious, and desert winds through the Saddle keep insects to a minimum. The character of the Saddle is dramatically apparent. We can readily identify the trace of the West Kaibab fault that segregates the Kaibab and Kanab plateaus. The fault passes directly through the Saddle, and giant strata of limestone, sandstone, and shale warp downward on both sides, all converging at the Saddle. The fault is a great mirror; the Saddle, a focal point in symmetry; and Powell, a miniature, detached Kaibab. The fault has been long dormant, and erosion along the old fault lines now shapes the region. We shoulder our packs and begin the ascent to Powell.

The climb is surprisingly brutal. Vegetation is scant; the mid-morning sun slams off white rock, unbroken; the trail meanders in frustrating detours as it searches for natural breaks in the tougher strata. We pass a thin grey horizon of sandy shale, bursting with Permian fossils—brachiopods, pelecypods, crinoids. Wil pauses for water, and Earl and I join him. At the top the trail follows the spine of a sloping ridge. Ponderosa reappear. There are some blazed trees and others marked with can lids painted orange and nailed to the bark. Animal paths radiate into the deeper brush and woods. Looking back, we realize that Powell is significantly higher than Swamp Point, that the ascent from the Saddle is much longer than the descent from Swamp. Wil sights a green structure—metal, about the size of a phone booth—and points.

It is an old tool cache. Earl is convinced that it dates at least from CCC days. We pause long enough to pry it open. The interior is infested with spider webs; there are some axes, a kortick, two paper sleeping bags yellow with age. On the back side is a sign warning that this is U.S. government property. We close the door, search for some evidence of a trail, and follow the Rim south. The ponderosa are magnificent. Duff is thick and fresh with needles. There is a scattered understory of shrubs, as ravines along the Rim allow the Canyon, with its brush, to penetrate the forest. We can sense everywhere the enormous potential for fire. It is held in check only by an aggressive program of suppression. After a short walk we come to an old aspen corral, the skeletal paw of a mountain lion nailed to a tree, two aluminum coffins, and the helispot. We drop our packs, grateful that we are not, as in the old days, required to replenish the helispot cache with fresh water and rations. It is nearly noon.

We grab lunches and wander to an open stretch along the Rim, a clearing used as a helispot. The West Kaibab fault becomes an enormous looking glass. Almost everywhere on the North Rim, the Rim is lower in elevation than the bulk of the Plateau; one looks out to lower rock shelves and down into the Canyon. On Powell Plateau, however, you can look equally to Plateau and Canyon; the Rim is reflected back. The Kaibab spreads to the east, a great green shadow. That view, and the latent power of its fires, make Powell one of the corners of the North Rim's fire triangle. From Powell you have to look back on the Rim. You look way back.

We extract a fire map from a pack and identify critical places. Swamp Ridge, Rainbow Plateau, Lancelot and Galahad, Point Sublime—some of the hottest sites for fire on the Rim. We point out a few of the classic fires. In the green penumbra of the Sublime peninsula we can detect The Dragon. Over the course of the next week other crews will reflag the trails to Rainbow and The Dragon and clear their helispots.

Wil traces out the distant features on his fire map. He blinks uncertainly when he discovers that the north peninsula of Powell Plateau, where we now sit, is unnamed. Everywhere else Powell is littered with names, remote and unrecognizable. Most of them commemorate geologic explorers to the region; the mesa itself honors John Wesley Powell, leader of the first expedition to run the Colorado River through the Canyon proper and author of the classic river adventure *Exploration of the Colorado River of the West* (1875); the south peninsula is named for Clarence Dutton, a Powell colleague and author of the greatest book about the Rim, *Tertiary History of the Grand Canyon District* (1882); the westernmost point remembers Lieutenant Joseph Christmas Ives, who first explored the western Canyon and whose 1861 report first incorporated it into Western art, science, and literature. In that spirit I propose to call the unnamed northern peninsula Gilbert Point, after G. K. Gilbert, chief geologist on the Powell and Wheeler surveys and later for the U.S. Geological Survey. The idea goes nowhere. Everyone on the fire crew has at least one geographic landmark on the Rim named after himself except Achterman, and he claims the feature. Besides, geologists no longer visit Powell Plateau, and the fire crew does. Achterman Point it becomes.

Earl lights his pipe. A local boy, homegrown in Fredonia, he wonders who constructed the old corral. Hunters, certainly; Powell has long been famous for its cougars. Theodore Roosevelt and Zane Grey both wrote books about hunting lions on Powell. Buffalo Jones chased lions up trees with dogs, then climbed and roped them. During his tenure on the North Rim, Uncle Jimmy Owens, a government hunter, cleaned out most of the lions on Powell and elsewhere, to be himself lionized in the children's story *Brighty of the Grand Canyon*. No one has seen a lion on Powell within living memory. Wil explores the two coffins and begins to pull out tools. "Still good," Earl notes with satisfaction. We grab pulaskis and peel the brush back from the helispot.

The route to Dutton is marked by orange can lids nailed to trees. We freshen them with a can of spray paint. The path traverses the Rim, nearly seventy-six hundred feet in elevation, as Shinumo Amphitheater falls away below us. With only pulaskis, headlamps, and canteens, our walk is brisk. Sometimes we abandon duff for rock. Passing a mound of chunky white limestone, we realize suddenly that we are walking across an Indian ruin. Probably Anasazi; there are dozens of Anasazi ruins on Powell. Paiutes came to Powell, too, for seasonal hunting trips. Before them big-game hunters, probably Folsom culture, visited the mesa and left split-twig figurines in

Redwall caves. We see deer and turkey, but no lions. At Dutton Canyon, the one major ravine that the trail must cross, the can lids disappear. They are not much missed. We bushwhack to the eastern Rim again and follow it to the point.

This is nothing like a prepared Park Service viewpoint, and we all scramble to locate a suitable perspective. The Rim is rocky, brushy, indeterminate—not a distinct point but a hummocky mound that faces everywhere and nowhere. When John Wesley Powell wanted to create publicity for his survey, he brought Thomas Moran to the North Rim in 1872, then took him to what was then known as Powell's Plateau. The view of the inner gorge that informs Moran's "Grand Chasm of the Colorado" (1873) is a composite of scenes from Muav Saddle to Dutton Point. But the painting never had the simple appeal of Moran's "Grand Canyon of the Yellowstone," to which it is a companion; there was no focal waterfall, no single sweeping gorge, no palette of pastels, no obvious vantage point. There were many gorges, many colors organized into rigid strata, a medley of incomplete platforms from which to view the scene; the painting is operatic, disjunctive; not the structural geology of the Canyon but clouds and storms in the gorges integrate the scene. Earl thrashes around just north of the Point and discovers some torn red flagging tape that leads to a small clearing, the lost Dutton helispot.

The first tremors of a Canyon sunset are felt. Shinumo Amphitheater sinks into shadow; the inner gorge softens into brilliant pastels; crepuscular rays of light and shadow stream down the River corridor; dust fills the gorge like old smoke; mountainous shapes dissolve into a fluid mosaic of color and shadow, Jackson Pollock as a cubist; an amorphous, colorful haze gathers and organizes into a twilight wedge. But the scene lacks the one feature that is present in every Canyon painting by Moran: there are no clouds, the one natural phenomenon that makes the Canyon compelling to view day after day, season after season. Without clouds the Canyon is too constant and rigid a feature to sustain interest for long. Without clouds the Canyon loses some of its continuity. We want, we miss that tie to Moran. Even as the drama at Dutton Point reaches its crescendo, we are attaching headlamps to our hard hats. The hike back will be a race with darkness.

Sunset reds and oranges fill the forest. The deepening twilight causes a roll call of old fires to flash through the mind. This is where Kent and Tyson left the Dutton trail to bushwhack into the Bumsteer fire. Here is where Seeliger masterfully mismanaged the Porker fire, blithely helicoptering into his fire, having forgotten handtools but stocked with double *cases* of rations and cubitainers of water, forcing his reserves to scratch lines with branches and rocks, and burning the snag down and smothering it with dirt while they otherwise whiled away the hours eating triple rations. Not far away is the notorious Wander fire, where B. Gray and Bad Bob the L.A. Pimp got lost, spent the entire night tramping in circles and whining to the Park dispatcher, and eventually were led to their fire by the hand—literally—when McLaren returned the next morning. (Not long afterward, when Bad Bob, a fern feeler, refused to evacuate the cabin he shared with Alston and Hulett, they sat down one afternoon and ate every scrap of his food and piled his belongings on the hood of his car.) Over there Tim and I attended, as "monitors," the North Rim's first "prescribed natural fire," the crew's initiation into the new regime.

For most of that day there was no problem. We dutifully watched the fire smolder through damp duff and gnaw at the lightning scar in the snag; we took weather readings religiously on the hour; we mapped fuels; the stack of forms for recording data, if ignited, could probably have put out more BTUs than the fire. We munched on rations and tossed rocks over the Rim. "You know," Tim mused, "we could put out this fire in two hours, max." Then, as evening approached, we requested a decision. Do we stay on Powell or return to the Area? There was a panic: we could not leave the fire, and we could not suppress it. Tim and I compromised by estimating the probable natural dimensions of the fire if it were left unattended, then cut a fireline outside that perimeter and flew back to the cache. There was no hazard pay because, by definition, the fire was never wild.

When the smoke is reported by Scenic Airlines, we are halfway through the second day of S260 (Fire Business Management Principles), immersed in the care and use of property receipts. If it is a fire, it is a sleeper, for we have not had a storm for more than a week. McLaren is at Ramparts Cave along with 210 and the South Rim fire crew, all staring in stupefied outrage at the ugly smoke puffing out of the burning dung left by Shasta ground sloths extinct since the Pleistocene. Recon 1 will be delayed. I check the dispatch chart in the Fire Pit.

Within ten minutes Red Butte reports a smoke on Powell Plateau; Kendricks Peak follows; then Dry Park, on the North Kaibab, gives a bearing; another Scenic flight through Muav Saddle confirms the initial report. The fire is near Dutton Point. Recon 1 hurries off the tarmac, instantly sights the smoke, and estimates the fire at more than an acre and building rapidly. The Forest Service dispatcher at Williams informs us that the Kaibab helitack crew can land its Hughes 500 at the North Rim heliport within thirty minutes, and we place a formal fire order and quickly begin a massive transfer of matériel from the fire cache to the heliport and start to round up interested reserves. Two of the Kaibab helitack crewmen stay at the North Rim to supervise the shuttle. One remains with Tim and me as we fly to Powell. The sky is clear. A creamy smoke column is visible as soon as we lift off.

We circle the fire, now about five acres, and land at a clearing along the Rim. Tim and I drop our packs, double-loop canteens over our shoulders, grab shovels, and head for the fire. The flames are two to three feet high. The Kaibab helitack crewman—we never learn his name—remains at the helispot to receive the next shuttles and improve the site as best he can. It is obvious that the site, which is downwind, will be overrun by the fire. We circle the fire at a trot and determine, first, to relocate the helispot. When the Hughes next arrives, we send Dana and a chain saw with the Kaibab helitacker to a new site. Every few minutes the fire encounters and torches a patch of reproduction or an oak thicket.

We try cutting line ahead of the flaming front, lose it (and nearly a saw), and ask for retardant. The nearest tanker is at Coolidge, the West Zone dispatcher informs us, over an hour distant. All the Longshots have arrived, and the Park has begun to ship out raw reserves. As each batch comes in, we assign them to a squad, each squad headed by a Longshot. The fire will burn to the Rim.

There is no choice but to back off and burn out. The Kaibab helitacker is sent off to locate yet another site; the present one will be consumed by our backfires. When the air tanker arrives, we apply retardant along the Rim to keep the fire from spilling over the rimrock and into the Canyon brush below, where it would burn uncontrollably. I flag a route for the fireline along a ridgetop between the burn and Dutton Canyon. We have to keep the fire out of the deep ravine, and we will try to contain it within the peninsula that terminates at Dutton Point. But the work goes slowly; the reserves are almost worthless; we could make better time with the Longshots alone. I order food, headlamps, extra water, and spare tools, but no sleeping bags; we will work all night. Before the Hughes departs for the night, we have it deposit Tim and me directly at Dutton Point. We intend to scout the perimeter of the fire, upwind, and return to camp. The view from Dutton, scoured bare by the fire, has never looked better. Smoke assumes the role normally taken by clouds; it scatters and refracts sunlight even better than rock.

The line along the shallow ridge is complete by the time we return, and everyone breaks for dinner. There is a choice of C rations or box lunches from the Lodge. The box lunches contain orange drinks and bologna sandwiches. The fire crew, wily in the ways of rations, unscrupulously swaps with the reserves—B-1 for B-2 units, white bread for crackers, fruitcake for pound cake. There are a few apples and oranges, and the fire crew exchanges them for sandwiches. Ignorant, if not blissful, the reserves chew silently on their cold bologna sandwiches. We brief everyone on the strategy: one squad will burn out from our line with fusees while the remainder, organized into holding squads, stake out a portion of the perimeter. A spot weather forecast from Phoenix predicts normal evening inversion winds—just what we need to carry our burnout gently away from the line.

It doesn't happen that way. The winds reverse themselves shortly after midnight and rage savagely from the southwest, and the fire, which had been slowly quieting, flares into activity. Our line is breached at one spot, and thick smoke drives the holding squad away in pandemonium. We reorganize, contain the slop-over within a new line, and prepare for a long, bitter night of smoke and vigilance. For breaks there are cold bologna sandwiches and coffee; for breakfast there is more of the same.

At last, at dawn—the eastern horizon outlined by thin stripes of red and orange under a yellow glow, the Canyon a pool of grey shadow—we hear the whine and whop of the Kaibab helicopter. It circles the fire and explains that we will be shuttled from the fire to Swamp Point and fresh hotshot crews will be shuttled in. We reconvene at the helispot; I go first since as fire boss I have to brief the new overhead team. But as the Hughes lifts off the knob, it is spun violently in ferocious, squirrelly winds along the Rim, before righting itself and heading for Swamp Point. There will be no more helicopter operations until conditions settle down. The hotshot crew prepares to walk across Muav Saddle, and the Dutton fire crew, Longshots and reserves both, fortify themselves for a difficult hike out.

I do not, in fact, brief anyone; I am briefed. Gonzo Gilliam, North Rim manager, has assumed responsibilities as service chief for the fire. Over the night he has assembled a Class II fire team, two Forest Service hotshot crews at Swamp Point and two SWFF crews in the Area, two helicopters, an air tanker, and a National Guard unit with a small fleet of troop trucks for transport between Swamp Point and the Area. When the initial attack crew staggers across Muav Saddle, we are released from the fire—now about three hundred acres, the largest fire of the decade on the North Rim.

It is no longer our fire. While we sleep, the day belongs to the reinforcements. The hotshots complete the line across the peninsula and burn it out; the big shots, led by Gilliam, strut around the Area and pose for special photos. By the end of the next burning period the fire has been declared controlled and demobilization begins. Groggy, we wander to the fire cache to hear the latest news. But the cache has become extraneous: Gonzo has established a GHQ at the ranger station, and the overhead team controls all information and all decisions; the Boise Interagency Fire Center (BIFC) and the West Zone cache, not the North Rim fire cache, supply the logistical needs of the fire. The supplies are sumptuous, almost sybaritic by our standards. No one seems to know what is happening at Dutton. For the new crews it is a generic fire, all overtime and action and nothing more.

We work for three more days and a night on the Dutton fire. The first day we return as a saw team, and for our whole tour we drop and *buck up snags. The Blue Ridge Hotshots work the north side of the burn; we work the south. That night we remain on the fire with a crew of Apaches who sit along the fireline, immobile as sphinxes, nursing small cooking fires and cups of ration coffee. The night air is cold, and the smoke thin. We remain on the fire a second day in mop-up, and a third day we spend slinging out assorted camp matériel by helo.*

The supplies accumulated during the fire are unbelievable. When yet another a tractor-trailer stocked with sleeping bags, rations, shovels, and other paraphernalia—all ordered from BIFC and charged to the fire—appears outside the fire cache a couple of days later, we help unload it. But Gonzo has aroused even the suspicions of BIFC; the next day the semi returns, and we help load everything, as yet unpacked, back into it. Still, there is enough to keep the cache stocked for years.

That afternoon Randy contributes a stale bologna sandwich to the FCA Musuem.

FIRELIGHT, STARLIGHT

When we return to the helispot, we make camp. The great shadow of Powell has spread relentlessly across the Kaibab. Wil paws through the coffins. Many of the ration cans have rusted, good bets for botulism. The crackers are sound. Coffee is abundant. We snack on scraps, then browse around the helispot for the right kind of firewood. A fire can make or break an expedition. It is unthinkable to come to Powell and not have a fire. Earl clears off a patch of needles near the Rim, and we pile our wood next to it and wonder, silently, how many others have camped here before us. It has been a good day. Sometime, we agree, we would like to walk out to Ives Point. Earl estimates that we should cross Muav Saddle before much sun gets on it tomorrow morning and be back at the fire cache by noon. "Early afternoon, tops." Wil suggests that on our return we try to locate the hunting cabin rumored to be near Swamp Point. It is said that Teddy Roosevelt used it when he came to Powell.

No one comes to Powell to hunt lions anymore. In fact, almost no one other than the Longshots comes to Powell, and we come less often than in the past. There are fewer reasons for trail patrols by the fire crew. Money for helicopter use is freer, so that there is less need to stock remote caches; there is little interest in a network of semipermanent helispots so removed from visitation; Roads and Trails claims jurisdiction over the maintenance of public trails such as Widforss, formerly cleared by the fire crew as part of opening the fireroads; the explosive growth in the number of Park rangers compels them to assume control over "backcountry" duties and to substitute trail patrols that end at the River, where they can hitch rides on the Park patrol boat, for trail patrols that end at fires. Not only the old Powell firetrail but the trails to Rainbow, The Dragon, and Saddle Mountain fall into disuse; our only trail assignment that excites the Park is our layout and construction of the Bawgd Pass trail from the Area to Point Imperial. The trail, however, is renamed for a ranger killed at Point Reyes, and, as a public-use site, its maintenance is handed over to R&T. Even the future of fire management at Powell Plateau is itself uncertain. The mesa is an ideal site for a natural fire program, and someday the Park will establish one that works.

For now we look forward to a good meal, with real food and real mess gear. We even have real (our own) sleeping bags, reserving the paper bags from the coffins for pads. Earl arranges some firewood, and Rich starts it with a fusee. It is a clean, sharp fire. Flames dance across the textured, black-and-orange bark of the ponderosa. Flickering lights reveal a great catface, jet black, in the base of one old ponderosa. Wil nods silently at a fire-sculptured snag just beyond the helispot. To the distant west, through a grove of trees, we can make out a sliver of moon above the collapsing twilight wedge. Then the stars materialize.

We heat some water for coffee. The stars arc over the plateau in thick strata, echoing the ghostly texture of the Kaibab limestone. Wil selects a large, pitchy knot that he tore out of a decomposing ponderosa and places it on the fire. For a minute it sizzles, then flares, then leaps into flame. All of the world we can see is illuminated by fire. Above the forest canopy the smoke momentarily vanishes into darkness, until the stars, now in thick swirls, carry the embers away.

CHAPTER FOUR

Saddle Mountain

JUNE GOES ON FOREVER. The forest dries. The air fills with the musky smell of warm pine, and yellow-green clouds of pollen swirl through the woods in languorous streamers. At damper sites mosquitoes gather into darkening swarms. Dust spirals up from the fireroads and clothes adjacent meadows. Ghostly smokes, like steam out of fumaroles, rise from land-clearing fires on the Hualapai Reservation, erupt from time to time into billowing columns, then settle into sheets like a blanketing fog. Dark smoke from a wildfire on the Coconino envelops the San Francisco Peaks. Hot, dry, windy—it is the time for big fires. The absence of storms, however, means that nearly all the big fires are started by people, and since we don't have tourists in the backcountry of the North Rim, we don't have big fires. There are large fires, it seems, everywhere except the Rim.

Work continues but changes in character. Projects—busy work—supersede true preparations for fire. Calling it "presuppression" doesn't change the reality. The crew becomes restless, anxious; tension builds like a developing thunderstorm; the air is electric with rumor; it rings with false alarms. We need fires. Many small fires are better than a few big fires. Fires make a fire crew. A good fire season can make a mediocre crew into a good crew, and only more fires can make a good crew into a great one.

So we wait, and we keep busy. We sweep the nature trail by the Lodge; check leaky hydrants; remove trees fallen across the scenic drive; replace broken windows in North Rim tower; cut wood for the entrance station; clear Vista Encantadora; sharpen tools; fill in a

105

sump on E-4; fell a tree tower splintered by lightning; pour a new concrete pad for the heliport; install check dams; conduct a search for a missing child, and cut an emergency helispot during the evacuation of an injured motorist; wash and rewash vehicles; paint, paint, paint. If small projects play out, there is always the Fence—the tangible equivalent of damnation, work without purpose and reward, the bad end of a poor fire season.

We keep busy because we are on the Rim, but we are not on the Rim to keep busy. So we wait for the fires—the big fires, fires for which we will have to leave the Park, fires to which we can get access only through the Forest Service. We have, in fact, a closer relationship with the Forest than with the Park, and with the fire crews of the Kaibab than with those on the South Rim. Until the fires appear routinely, however, fire season is disorganized, and the crew, ill formed and apprehensive.

June lasts forever.

Between Park Service recons the Forest Service reports a smoke at Coffee Lake. I take two SWFFs and drive down the Sublime Road until I find the limestone cairn; then I set my compass for one hundred eighty degrees, and begin flagging. We travel light. I carry my firepack; Henry John hefts a saw; Johnny Begaye, a knot of canteens and handtools. The route takes us up a prominent ridge, which becomes relatively broad and flat at the summit. Henry John points wordlessly to some torn, decrepit flagging beneath a white fir.

Coffee Lake, a sinkhole, has a thin coating of water in its bottom; otherwise it is as rank as the grasses over a septic tank. We walk around the perimeter. I look for a tree to climb, then decide against it. Recon 1 is breaking in a new observer and asks if we would like another flight. "Sure," I say.

We place our packs against some aspen, lean back, and wait. The SWFFs close their eyes. I read from a novel in my pack. Eventually I hear the drone of Recon 1, see it circle around and around us, and after twenty minutes or so he informs us that he can find no smokes around Coffee Lake. The Phantom fire. I shake the SWFFs awake, and we pull our flagging as we walk out. The rock cairn we leave.

The outcome surprises no one. Every spring the Forest Service ritualistically reports a smoke at Coffee Lake. Every year we send out a crew. Every year it returns without discovering a fire. When the report comes in, veterans otherwise fanatic to be sent to a fire slip silently away. We are convinced that it is all a practical joke, that it is another way the Forest has to remind us of the Saddle Mountain fire. But we always send someone.

Something There Is That Doesn't Love a Fence

Donnie saws, while Thumper stands by with wedge and sledge. The cut begins to close. Donnie slides the saw out. Thumper gingerly positions a wedge, then slams it with the sledge; the log cracks. Donnie reinserts the saw into the widened kerf and cuts, while the log breaks cleanly away. Shouldering the saw, Donnie studies the emerging tangle of barbed wire and debris, trying to decipher where new trees have crossed and crushed the Fence, but so many have fallen for so long that it is impossible to tell new from old. He sights back from where he and Thump have come but can see nothing of the splicing crew. The forest is dense, dark, moldy with half-decomposed spruce. They are no longer near the road; for the next few miles they will be nowhere in particular; they will be at the Fence. Donnie swipes at a mosquito, then trudges ahead. Thumper collects their paraphernalia—a can of mix, some oil, a spare chain, a saw kit, a sledge, and wooden wedges, glad that they have some web gear—and follows behind. He knows that they are the lucky ones.

Lenny, Bruce, and Rich remain within sight of the pumper. The Fence is a shambles. Nowhere are the strands up, and nearly everywhere most of the strands are broken. In places they appear to be cut—hunters, we muse—elsewhere, they have snapped from fatigue or failed beneath crashing trees. The metal strands must be pulled up, like the runners of weeds, from beneath duff and windfall.

Rich begins with the top strand. He forms a loop at the end and holds it with one pair of fencing pliers while he twists the loose end around with a second pair. Then he makes another loop with the other end of the break. He cuts a piece of splicing wire off a spool which is mounted on an Army pack frame, threads one end through one of the loops, holds it with one pair of pliers, and twirls the loose end with his second pair of pliers. The free end he threads through the second loop. Now he pulls it taut and repeats the loop-forming and loop-sealing process. The splice is complete. He attaches the wire to the metal post with a clip and closes the clip by squeezing with the pliers. Now he advances to the second strand and repeats the procedure. Then to the third strand, and the fourth. The mosquitoes and deerflies collect in hordes. If the break is too great or if the wire already holds too many old splices, Rich will cut out the bad section completely, replace it with new barbed wire, and splice the new barbed wire into the gap. In places the metal posts are twisted into knots by crashing trees; they will have to be replaced. Broken wooden stays litter the Fence right-of-way like the crushed bones of deer. Rich moves on to the next break. At every quarter mile there is a set of wooden posts, which can be used for stretching. A special fence-stretching tool is roped to the post at one end and clipped to the wire at the other; between the ends is a rope-and-pulley arrangement so that each wire can be pulled more or less taut and nailed into the wooden post with horseshoe staples. On a good day a full crew may make one or two quarter-mile posts. Today will not be a good day. The whole splicing crew shuffles along like a spasmodic caterpillar. They move everything as they go—the spool, the tools, the clips and staples. Everything moves except time.

Lenny, a rookie, asks if it is all like this. "No," Rich tells him, "only the part that the Park wants us to fix. Got to keep those cattle out." Dan explains that the older sections of the boundary—the stretches laid down by the CCC—are made of aspen and are indestructible; when trees come down, the fallen trees simply become part of the Fence. "Most of the western boundary fence is aspen," Dan explains. "That's why there was a camp at the Shinumo Gate." The eastern boundary fence, anchored at Saddle Mountain, is composed wholly of barbed wire. It was constructed in 1963, part of the cleanup after the Burn. It failed to survive the first winter. The following summer the fire crew and SWFFs were sent out to repair it. It was immediately obvious to those with eyes to see that rehabilitation was hopeless. This is not the place for a fence, and barbed wire is utterly inadequate.

Why a fence at all? The official Park Service reply is that we are
preserving the integrity of the Park, that we are defining the boundary between two philosophies of land management, that we are
excluding exotic intruders like hunters, loggers, and the occasional
Hereford steer which sometimes crosses the old Burn and follows the
shallow ravine that becomes Bright Angel Canyon and eventually
appears along the scenic drive, where an excited tourist reports it.
("Yes, sir, ranger. A buffalo. I know a buffalo when I see one.") But
we know it is all retribution for the Saddle Mountain Burn. The
origins trace to the old fire. If the Park had caught the fire, the Forest
would not have salvage-logged the site and reseeded it to grass and
introduced cattle; deer would not muster each fall to feast on the
browse and aspen that flourished on the Burn; and there would be no
hunters. Without the Burn there would be no need for the Fence.

The Park interprets the Fence as a symbol of its purity in contrast
with the Forest's commitment to commodity production; the Forest
sees the Fence as an emblem of Park incompetence and regal discour-
tesy. We know the Fence as the Black Legend of the North Rim, as
the embodiment of everything that can go wrong with a fire season,
of everything bad that can happen to a fire crew. "Fence" becomes a
generic adjective for "bad." There are Fence days, Fence fires, Fence
jobs; Fence face becomes a recognized occupational disease along
with North Rim eye, Kaibab emphysema, and the dread mahoakus (a
common syndrome on lieu days, caused by unspecified viruses and a
hangover).

As much as anything, the Fence, too, underscores the chasm
between those who work in the field and those who sit at desks and
manage. Every new fire crew supervisor—white-collar rangers all—
decides that he can succeed where others have failed and devises a
new strategy of Fencing. The principles are self-evident; the solutions demand only the proper sequence of reports and forms. None
of the schemers ever performs so much as a single splice, and some of
the proposals approach megalomania. When Hulick determines that
the solution is to install two wooden stays between each metal fence
post, some 14,500 stays are ordered. Each stay must be clipped to
four strands, and the strands are so deteriorated that it is simpler to
restring the whole Fence from Saddle Mountain to the entrance

station by hand. Incredibly, powered by SWFF crews and a Fence fanaticism, the project is accomplished and in late August a final, "golden stay" is attached. By the following May the entire Fence is in disarray. It is obvious to all, though admitted only by the fire crew, that the problem is one not of technique but of purpose. If the Park wants a real fence, it should build one. If it wants a fire crew, it should not dissipate crew enthusiasm by assigning members to tasks for which they are ill suited and, in fact, to which the Park is not truly committed. The BI has never even visited the site.

Rich wonders about tomorrow. Two consecutive days of Fencing is considered cruel and unusual punishment. Three days is cause for mutiny. Critical tools and spools of splicing wire mysteriously disappear; Fence face becomes epidemic; even the SWFFs rebel. In the last year of the SWFF program, after two consecutive weeks of Fencing, the SWFFs complained about their box lunches. "No-Tabasco-sauce," they whined. "But you had tuna fish sandwiches," Kent replied in exasperation. "No-Tabasco-sauce," they repeated. "No-good. Lunches-no-good. Fence-no-good." They left, and another SWFF crew was hired and sent Fencing. Within two weeks this SWFF crew, too, had gone, vanished in the night.

"SEE HIM WASTED BY THAT FENCE POST . . ."

"Takin' it off here, boss," Dan shouts.

He slowly unbuttons his fire shirt, slops his exposed skin with insect repellent, and returns to a splice. "Need some more staples," mutters Lenny as he inches back to the pumper. If he sustains his pace, it will take him a good twenty minutes to reach the pumper and return. The longer, the better. Rich drops out for a lengthy swallow of water. The mosquitoes and deerflies are thick and fierce; the forest is dense and disorienting; the air is heavy with moisture, and it will probably rain, maybe hail, by midafternoon, here at the highest point on the Kaibab. But there will be no fires, just rain. The Fence. Dan lavishly douses his hard hat with government-issue insect repellent and watches the orange paint slide off. Only forty-five minutes until lunch. Rich haltingly hums a few bars of "Big Bob."

The crew rouse themselves. Lenny joins in with an appropriate phrase. Then Dan. Rich sings the main verses, while the others, in a mock chorus, crowd around in feeble harmony.

Every morning at the cache you could see him arrive.
He stood five foot six and weighed two-forty-five,
Kind of narrow at the shoulder and broad at the hips.
Everybody knew there was nothing but lip to Big Bob.

[refrain] Big Bob . . . Big Bad Bob . . .

Nobody seemed to know what Bob called work.
He'd just sit in his office and unbutton his shirt.
He didn't say much, kind of stupid and shy,
And if you spoke at all, you just said, "Bye," to Big Bob.

Then came that day on the Fence line,
When a stay cracked and men started crying.
Fireaids were praying and hearts beat fast.
Everybody hoped that it'd fall at last, 'cept Bob.

Past the wire and the duff of that man-made hell
Walked a runt of a man the fire crew knew well,
Grabbed that sagging stay, and gave out with a groan
And like a quaking aspen just stood there and moaned. Big Bob.

With all of his strength he gave a mighty shove
And a fireaid yelled out, "There's a break up above!"
Twenty men scrambled from that would-be job.
Now there's no one left to stay and sob for Big Bob.

With wires and pliers they went their rounds.
Then came that rumble way down in the ground.
The needles and duff belched out of that stay,
And everybody knew it was the end of the day for Big Bob.

Well, they never rebuilt that worthless Fence.
They just placed a wooden stool up against it.
These few words are written on that stool:
"At the bottom of this stay lies a big, big fool. Big Bob."

The gang proceeds to other favorite Fence songs. "On the Crew Again," to the tune of Willie Nelson's "On the Road Again"; "Fire and Slurry," after James Taylor's "Fire and Rain" ("I've seen fire and I've seen slurry./I've seen crownin' trees that made me sort of worry . . ."); "Up, Up, With Beer," to the tune of "Up With People"; "Fireaid," to the tune of "Rawhide" ("Roll 'em, roll 'em, roll 'em;/Keep them hoses rollin' . . . Fireaid!"); "The Twelve Days of Fire School"; "I Wish I Was a Kaibab Squirrel," after the Simon and Garfunkel song "Punky's Dilemma"; "Overtime," from the Paul Simon song "Kodachrome" ("When I think back on all the crap I learned in fire school,/It's a wonder I can work at all . . . /Please, don't take my overtime away"); "Mr. Mop-up," to the tune of "Mr. Touchdown" ("They always call him Mr. Mop-up . . ./He can squirt and throw the dirt./Give him a fedco and look at him go"); "The FCA," a broadside of Kris Kristofferson's "The Pilgrim":

> See him wasted by that fence post
> In his jacket and his jeans,
> Stringing yesterday's misfortunes with a smile.
> Once he had a future full of money, love, and dreams,
> Till he started stretching fence wires for a while.
> But he keeps right on a-splicing, for the better or the worse,
> Stretching for an end he's never found,
> Never knowing if restringing was a blessing or a curse,
> Or if its going up was worth its coming down.
>
> [refrain] He's a fireman, he's a stringer.
> He's a ranger, he's a ringer.
> He's a money-hungry fireaid who's a problem when he's bored.
> He's a walking fabrication, both a fact and hallucination.
> Taking every wrong direction when he's driving home that Ford.
>
> He has tasted good and evil
> In your backwoods and your bars,
> And he's traded in tomorrow for a stay.
> Running from mosquitoes, reaching for those fires,
> Losing all his mind along the way.
> From the roaring of the chain saw to the stitches of the nurse,
> Its going up was worse than coming down.
>
> [refrain] He's a fireman. . . .

Everyone volunteers a favorite Fence song. Dan contributes "To Join the Devil" and Rich, "Hulick's Fence," both Kristofferson parodies. Then come two classics—"The Ballad of Ted Burke" ("Come listen to my story 'bout a man named Ted . . .") and "The Ballad of Joe Alston."

It is nearly noon when the chorus breaks up in a scramble for lunches. Should they eat at the Fence or wander back to the Turn-around? They elect to return to the pumper. Lenny announces that he will eat on Little Round Top. The songs are over. It will be a long afternoon, and they will be back tomorrow.

"Where are the SWFFs when we need them?" mutters Dan. "Forget the SWFFs," replies Rich. "Where are the fires?"

Recon 1 reports the smoke casually; it is more than ten miles north of the Park where a neck of mixed conifer woods separates Pleasant Valley from V. T. Park. But we drive a pumper to the entrance station and listen to the Forest Service radio there. Too often in the past we have missed the big fires outside the Rim. The Forest ignored us during the Moquitch Canyon fire, and we watched with dismay from TT-1 as the smoke rose like billowing thunderheads to the north. We missed the Quarry fire on the South Rim, ostensibly because the winds were too strong to ferry us across the Canyon by helicopter but in reality because the North Rim would not release us and the South Rim would not request us. We went to the Pistol fire there, and the South Rim recoiled at the spectacle of real firefighting, of real fire-lines cut through thickets of pinyon-juniper, of real fire crew disci-pline; when the Park chief ranger idiotically ordered crews to abandon their flank attack and to proceed to the head of the fire, John-Boy and Pferd politely told him to buzz off, and when he insisted, they ignored him.

There is then at least a vicarious curiosity to the DeMotte fire, and we listen to the traffic with a mixture of desire and anxiety. Initial attack crews are overwhelmed; the fire burns ferociously in dried slash. An air tanker is ordered, and within minutes a B-17 flies directly over us en route to the fire from the South Rim airport. More retardant is requested, more crews, some overhead. We break into the flow and announce that the Park has an engine, available for dis-patch, at the north entrance. Within half an hour we are proceeding to the fire.

A quiet pandemonium reigns everywhere. The Forest hierarchy has not yet arrived, and without regimentation there is entropy; Marcus has assumed the role as fire boss because as a sawyer he has been granted powers not available to other Forest crewmen. When we catch up to him, he is wandering openmouthed along a skid road slightly downwind of the burn. Flames reach fifty feet high, standing timber is torching like a chain reaction of firecrackers, and flames—twisting like fiery dust devils—spiral over the forest canopy. Marcus numbly tells us to put out spot fires. The air is charged with embers, and there are spots the size of cigarette ashes by the hundreds all around us. The fire whooshes through another cluster of trees, and squads of Forest firefighters rush to their vehicles. It is obvious that the main fire will overrun our position within minutes. Smoke sweeps across us in thick clouds, a dry enervating fog. One engine pulls out. Another, overloaded, sticks in a rut, then breaks free as a squad piles off and pushes. Jeff pulls wildly at the rope starter on a third, the last. The slip-on will not turn over. Jeff swears and rewinds and pulls and rewinds; the engine itself is flooded, stalled; we rush past Jeff—a Forest Service brat and former Green Beret, previously a crewman on the South Rim, now on the Kaibab, black mucus pouring from his nose—still swearing and pulling and coaxing the unit as it coughs and sputters, ever pampering the choke, until at last it catches and Jeff sprays the entire vehicle and the crews hanging to it with water as spot fires flare nearby in piles of branches and a fir torches with a clamor like a rocket. The engine, too, comes to life, and the vehicle crawls like a tortoise clad with barnacles away from the pulsing flames, spouting water recklessly, while we jog alongside and breathe through bandannas. Another tanker drop, worthless on the rising column of fire, but welcome—we only hear it—then green and open space and cold, clear air. We dive into the Park pumper and drive it to the highway, where we are separated from the fire by better than a hundred yards of insurmountable meadow and two lanes of macadam.

The Forest Service begins to gather. From everywhere appear crews and machines—TSI crews, surveying crews, office workers, logging crews, engines, water trucks, bulldozers—and a hierarchy of authority begins to shape it. The Forest is mobilizing for a cam-

paign fire, and nothing else matters. The two powers, fire and Forest, will collide. Even the Park Service has become engaged. Every forest in Arizona has a major fire, and the Forest requests additional hand-crews from the Park. Gonzo Gilliam is wild with anticipation. Surely, he reasons, if the Park sends enough support, he will be granted a position of honor on the overhead team. Dazzled perhaps by the parade of air tankers now flying rhythmically from the airport over the rims, the Park agrees to commit its two pumpers, one handcrew from the North Rim, and another from the South Rim. The Park wants to play in the big leagues. Then the spot fire is discovered.

The slash has lofted brands high above the forest canopy, and the ambient winds, steadily gusting and swirling from the southwest, have carried them across the meadows of Pleasant Valley, across Highway 67, across the lower slopes of Telephone Ridge, and near the ridgetop itself. Smoke curls up, tentative and insulting. We are the only organized handcrew at the site, and the order goes to us to "get that spot." No matter really that the main fire is uncontrollable; it is contained by its forested isthmus. The spot, if it escalates, can burn unimpeded to the East Kaibab monocline. But even as we cross the highway, what was one spot becomes two, and two become four, and the four become dozens. We divide, then redivide, then attempt to corral clusters of spots with handlines; but more fall, and those we attack with shovels and dirt escape easily. The fire crests over the top of Telephone Ridge. A conflagration is in progress.

For a while we retire below the treeline, reorganize, and scrape out a line through the meadowed slope. The Forest ignores us, then orders us to the southern flank of the spreading fire. We drive for half an hour with Forest guides. For another hour we dig line through tough mixed conifer before a dozer appears and within minutes passes over our handline, quadrupling it in size. The Forest will not allow us to burn out. "Just hold and patrol." We manage to work one of our pumpers into the site, but, overloaded and ill-designed, it is quickly disabled trying to drive down the cat line. The Forest will not allow us to fell snags either. We plod along a quarter-mile stretch of line, tossing dirt at encroaching flames and otherwise steeped of our energies and adrenaline by the monotony of patrol. Eventually we realize that it is evening, that we are overwhelmed by fatigue, that we have nothing to look forward to but a long, smokey night. Whatever is happening elsewhere on the DeMotte fire is too remote for concern. We know only our sector. We have no responsibilities and no sources of information. The Forest assigns a sector boss, a former hotshot now in timber management on the South Kaibab, and he is polite but silent. We huddle around small warming fires and wait for dawn. The night is long and inky black. The smoke pall is heavy and stagnant and blocks out even the stars. There is only the flicker of flaming logs, impenetrable thickets of dense shadow, C rats, and coffee.

A crew of hotshots drives up in the predawn and spills out of their bus full of horseplay and grabass until their foreman, perched on top and tossing down packs and tools, roars into the morning darkness, "All right! Line up, shut up, and go look for smokes!" The effect is instantaneous. We search out our sector boss and inform him that we are ready to be released. He hesitates, but he can find no good reason to keep us, and he cannot deny us the request. We walk down the fireline, down Telephone Ridge, and see sprawled across Pleasant Valley the tent city of a major fire camp; there must be four hundred firefighters, a Class I fire team, a caterer, a heliport, a fleet of vehicles; overhead, in the early light, air tankers swoop like circling hawks. It is an unsettling, Oz-like scene. We dress up our line and march into camp, where we report our times and eat a hot breakfast before returning to the North Rim to collapse into sleep.

The South Rim crewmen—many of them older maintenance workers caught up in the excitement of foreign duty and overtime— never understand the mechanics of a large fire. Not until the second night are they released from their sector on the north flank, apparently forgotten by the Forest Service overhead team ("Another Park Service crew? You mean we had to call two Park crews here? Damn"), unable to tap the flow of information and authority, hungry, overwhelmed with thirst and blisters. Some are nearly cyanotic; all vow never to return to another North Rim fire. Gonzo Gilliam spends the day strutting furiously back and forth in his office, unlit cigar in mouth, waiting for a call that never comes. The DeMotte fire consumes more than eleven hundred acres.

From the Grand Lodge at sunset, after a long sleep and a few beers, we gather contentedly on the veranda to watch the smoke

column thrown up by a sister burn to the south, the Radio fire
sweeping over Mount Elden at the base of the San Francisco Peaks.

THE BURN

The Fencing crew scatter like field mice. Each grabs a canteen
from the pumper and disappears to a favorite viewpoint. It is a warm
day; a miasma of lethargy descends on the Turnaround, where the
Saddle Mountain road loops back upon itself. Bruce climbs down the
slope just north of the Turnaround, finds some shade, and peers
across the Nankoweap Basin, beyond which stretch the Little Colorado River gorge, the Painted Desert, the Hopi mesas. Uncle Jimmy
and Ralph shuffle down the Nankoweap trail to the base of Little
Round Top, then ascend the mound. Duane opens the door to the
pumper and eats in the cab. Wil forages randomly to the north of the
Turnaround, the scene of the Burn, where elderberries, raspberries,
and strawberries compete with aspen, grass, locust, and stumps.

A Forest Service road leads to the Burn, and to reach it, we drive
outside the Park. The road was constructed in order to salvage-log
the Burn and not incidentally to create a firebreak along the boundary
with the Park. For miles the logging road and feeble Fence run in
parallel until they meet, in dramatic contrast, at the Turnaround. The
dichotomy persists in other forms: monocline and Forest to the
north, Canyon and Park to the south; no one can mistake the difference, and there are no gradations between one and the other. It is not
an equal partnership.

The Burn was fought by the Forest Service, and the road and
fuelbreak were constructed by the Forest on Forest lands; the Park
responds with its laughable Fence. In an era devoted to wilderness,
however, the Forest knows that it cannot win any contest with the
Park. Historically the national parks have expanded at the expense of
neighboring national forests, and the Kaibab fears that the North Rim
will enlarge in the future, as it did originally, out of national forest
lands. The Forest knows that it exists, for the traveling public, only as
a way station for the North Rim; that the splendors of the Kaibab
Plateau are irrelevant to tourists hungry to see the Grand Canyon.

The public will not allow the Park Service to fail; so important is the *idea* of the parks that the public will not tolerate any serious criticism of the Park. All failures are, by definition, outside the control of the Park Service. In the deepest sense it is not held responsible or accountable. The Saddle Mountain Burn is only an especially vivid reminder, but it is one that is appropriately hidden from public view. That the Park can walk away from the fire with its public image untarnished is, to the mind and morals of the Forest, incredible and unjust.

Forest fears about Park aggression would be comical if they were not consistently reinforced by Park behavior. Affronts are endless. After the Park acquires an ambulance, it appoints itself as the responsible agent for all medical emergencies along Highway 67 from Jacob Lake south. When an airplane crashes into V. T. Ridge on takeoff from DeMotte Park, the Park sends rangers, an ambulance, and an engine, even though there is no fire and everyone on board is dead. No one bothers to tell the Forest, which learns about it when curious tourists ask a "ranger" about all the hoopla across the meadow. One predawn June NORAD telephones the Park dispatcher with information that it has sighted a large explosion and fire along the north Park boundary. Only a few weeks before, a Soviet satellite with an atomic power plant crashed near Yellowknife, Canada, and Gonzo Gilliam is convinced that another secret satellite has plummeted to the North Rim. In fact, the Forest has ignited a large prescribed fire in sagebrush along the flank of the Kaibab; NORAD is probably sixty air miles off target, and the whole question could have been resolved by a courtesy call to the Forest. But such a thought never occurs to the Park. Within an hour the Park has a helicopter, a recon plane, two pumpers, and a ranger patrol car prowling along the boundary— mostly outside the Park because there are no access roads within the Park. When they find nothing, the search widens and intensifies into an armada of Park vehicles swarming northward; Gonzo telephones about sources for procuring protective gear suitable for working around radioactive materials; the comedy continues through the morning until the fire crew finally contacts Big Springs and asks if its lookouts have seen anything. When Captain Zero wants a more reliable and inexpensive source of water for the Area than Roaring

Springs, he organizes an expedition to North Canyon, wholly within the Forest, to investigate the possibility of constructing a pipeline to bring the water south. That North Canyon holds the only flowing stream on the entire Kaibab, and that the Forest manages the stream as a protected site are irrelevant. The important facts are that the Park needs water and is prepared to construct a pipeline through the Park and suck North Canyon dry to get it. If more water is removed from Bright Angel Creek, visitors might complain, but no one will ever know about North Canyon or a pipeline. And with more water, the Park can accommodate more visitors.

The visitor is, of course, the key. Every Park Service program is designed to please the visitor and encourage good feelings about the Park Service. The actual natural resources of the Park are only a means to this end. If people feel good about the Canyon, then they will feel good about the Park Service, and if they feel good about the Park Service, then there will be more money for road chips and rangers. The Park Service knows that people come to the Park wanting to feel good. Thus the highest priority on the North Rim for years has been to upgrade the entrance road, which is the source of the greatest visitor irritation. Any visitor-related service is claimed by the Park Service as a source of goodwill, except, of course, those—like lodging and food—that are, almost by nature, destined for complaints. Those are left to capitalist concessionaires, outside the Park's control. But medical emergencies, law enforcement, interpretation all are points of positive contact, and the Park Service seizes on them. The Forest leaves law enforcement to the sheriff, ambulance services to the local medical establishment, and interpretation to the Park.

Instead, the Forest focuses on the natural scene. Its staff knows trees, forage, cattle, rocks, water. The Forest ranger evolved out of a professional class, foresters, educated to understand and deal with natural resources. The Park ranger has never had an equivalent professional stature—or deserved one; the job of a Park ranger is to project the image of a Park ranger. Unlike the Park ranger, too, the Forest ranger knows fire. Fire experience saturates the Forest, fire is a part of the genetic heritage of the Forest Service, and upon the national infrastructure created by the Forest Service all the other federal agencies, including the Park Service, depend. When a large fire breaks, our first request for assistance outside the North Rim is to the Kaibab Forest dispatcher, then to the West Zone dispatcher for Forest Service Region Three, then to the Boise Interagency Fire Center, most of whose matériels depend on the Forest Service. Locally we send late crew arrivals to the Forest fire school at Big Springs; share some fire courses; participate in collective prescribed burns; meet at Jacob Lake for season introductions; try to work out methodologies for mutual assistance on fires; meet at the saloon or Kaibab Lodge for raucous reunions after burns. Increasingly our new recruits come with Forest Service experience, and more and more we request assistance from the Forest on the theory that real Forest Service firefighters are preferable to amateur Park Service reserves. They always respond. While both agencies function, in reality, by crisis management, for the Park, a fire is a crisis of omission, and for the Forest, a crisis of opportunity. The one visitor-contact program the Forest routinely funds is for fire prevention.

Forest incursions into the Park almost never involve anything except fire. When in the late 1960s the Park elects to leave a lightning fire on the Dragon's Head to burn out, the Forest fire management officer (FMO) threatens to put the fire out himself if the Park does nothing, and the Park is compelled to send in an air tanker. Along the north boundary, a mutual aid zone, the Forest is aggressive in dispatching its engines. Its superiority as a fire organization is indisputable. Even after a national obsession with wilderness fire thrusts the Park Service into the limelight of national fire policy, its advantage is only philosophical; the Forest Service, not the Park Service, has the expertise to translate concept into field operations. The Forest Service is soon light-years ahead in the management of natural fires and, except for special sites within selected parks, in prescribed burning. But the inequality persists. When the Park moves into the Forest, invited or not, it performs an act visible to a welcoming public. When the Forest assists the Park in fire, its aid is invisible, and to the vision that informs the political economy of the Park, contemptibly misguided.

There are formal agreements between Park and Forest. The most important is the designation of a mutual aid zone for fire suppression one mile to each side of the Fence. A fire in this DMZ belongs to whichever unit reaches it. But our relationships, if they are to work, are personal. In fact, we often feel greater rapport with the Forest, which values fire, than with the Park, which is confused about fire management. We more admire the Forest FMO, who has spent a lifetime in fire, than the BI, a ranger whom the Park assigns to supervise the crew despite the fact that he has never been to a fire. Such behavior is, to the Forest, an act of criminal negligence. Our differences in firefighting, too, are more personal than matters of policy. There are a few formal distinctions, primarily the prohibition (after 1967) against the use of bulldozers on Park fires without approval from the Secretary of the Interior. Forest crews crowd a fire, a foot away from the flames, inhaling smoke by the shovelful; Park crews back off a few feet, stay out of the smoke, burn out. Forest crews will ignite sagebrush while walking downwind, trailing fire from drip torches behind them; Park crews always ignite upwind. Smokechasing means, for the Park, that we compass into fires, that we carry everything vital with us. Forest crews, never far removed from a road, either drive directly to the fire or dash into it with hoses and handtools and flag their way out. The Forest has a dedicated fire dispatcher; the Park allows us more or less to dispatch ourselves. Our individual discretion is, to Forest crews, unfathomable. We insist that every Longshot be trained in every fire job; we place a premium on versatility and individual resourcefulness. Recruits drawn from Forest Service ranks welcome and marvel at our freedom of movement.

But as a system, with a national presence and support, we are retarded. Like our pumpers and slip-ons, our fire operation is nonstandard, an eclectic assembly of compromises. The Forest is much more specialized and regimented. It knows and respects the power of organization; it trades the strength of the whole for the versatility of its individual parts; if power is required for a job—machine power, bureaucratic power, manual power—it is prepared to send it. Once we assisted the North Kaibab with some prescribed burns in sagebrush. The experience was equally disorienting and enlightening. No one, apparently, told the string of engines at Big Springs to drive to the site, or, once there, to fill up with torch mix, or to ignite in any particular pattern, or to contain the spots that from time to time flashed across the bulldozed lines. It all just happened, and we were content to follow the example of the Forest's engines. Burning crews walked nonchalantly downwind of their ignitions, swallowing smoke by the gallon; holding crews stood impassively in pockets of smoke, waiting for the flaming front to pass; engines rolled and banged over catlines as though swept along by flash floods. Then, as suddenly as it began, it all ended. As if guided by some mechanical instinct, the engines and dozers and crews and helitack crew massed into a great pack and worked back to Big Springs. The fire was a success, and our pumper was disabled for weeks.

The national parks are, in truth, not a system so much as an aggregate of baronies; the political philosophy is feudal, with each park administered by a superintendent possessed of great latitude; the director of the National Park Service is no more than a medieval monarch, accepting symbolic expressions of fealty and offering thaumaturgical services in return. Superintendents can ignore national directives with relative impunity. By contrast, the national forests are a federal system, and no amount of local discretion is allowed to defy a national policy.

Park Service fire programs reflect these distinctions. They are highly sensitive to personalities and chance, and no less than superintendents, we are reluctant to abdicate our freedom. The Forest Service does everything by the book; if you violate the rules, you can expect to suffer the consequences. The Park Service has no books; it puts a premium on the individual. Its collective behavior is tribal, and it protects its permanent ranks. There is a saying commonly heard on the South Rim that there are two organizations you don't leave: the Mafia and the Park Service. We envy the Forest its fire expertise and respect its power, but we relish, too, our discretion and mobility, and we wouldn't want to be anywhere but where we are.

Duane rouses himself and stares at the cloud of dirt spilling off the Turnaround. A fire prevention technician from the Forest climbs out of his vehicle. Wil and Bruce wander over. "Great view," grins the tech. "Yeah," says Wil. "We like it. Good elderberries, too." The tech informs us that the permittee will be bringing his cattle up next week. He eyes the Fence. It is obvious that cows will cross at will, and then, he knows, the Park will loudly demand that the Forest remove its offensive beasts from the sanctuary and the Forest will dispatch folks to haul them back to Saddle Mountain, where they can cross through the porous Fence again. The tech surveys the panorama, its vistas shaped by the Burn, then nods a good-bye.

Wil recalls how, in the old days, the Forest used to joke about itself, how it once volunteered to host a softball game and when Jack expressed surprise that they had a field, one Forest foreman piped up, "No problem. We cut it this morning!" Now they no longer laugh about such matters. Now they politely shake hands at annual meetings and quietly proceed to log and lay down roads along the boundary. They have not forgotten the Saddle Mountain fire. They do not wish to forget.

We trail behind the Forest Service engine, impatient and slightly embarrassed. The smoke was reported by Recon 1 more than an hour ago; when it grew steadily, McLaren suggested a backup crew and ordered an air tanker from the Forest dispatcher. Because the fire is within the mutual aid zone, we request Forest assistance, and because we must reach the Swamp Point road by way of the Forest, a Forest engine crew actually arrives first. They cannot hear the Park radio. We honk when recon tells us to stop and gives us a bearing.

We climb into our packs, think through our tool needs, water, headlamps. But the Forest crew instantly dashes into the woods— though the fire is more than a mile away, invisible—without flagging, with nothing more than a quart canteen, shovels, and pulaskis. More crews have been ordered; the air tanker will arrive within the hour. Wil lags behind with instructions to flag a route in, one that we can see at night on our way out, that even later Forest crews could follow in. We hasten ahead on a loose compass bearing, catch up with the engine crew, and advance through the woods like a swarm of bees.

At the fire, two other Forest Service crewmen—from where, we have no idea—are already scraping a line along the active front of the fire, one foot figuratively in the burn, wrapped with smoke. A PB-4Y2 circles overhead. Two passes—two salvos of slurry—knock down the head of the fire, now about two acres in size. While the fire smolders and fumes, we organize into two squads. The Forest crew takes the east flank, and the Park the west, and new arrivals are shunted to one or the other. It is a fire for grunts. There is a carnival atmosphere, as Forest crews chant across the burn that the Forest Circus has arrived, and we race, friendly rivals, to put down the most fireline. The air tanker, however, forces us to a decision that we normally delay until the fire is declared out. The Forest dispatcher demands a fire number and a fire name. McLaren softly relays the number and asks us for our choice of a name. Too early, I think. From the Forest crews rises the cry "The Circus fire! Call it the Circus fire!" And when I do, the Forest crews are momentarily stunned into silence. They cannot believe that we have such discretion, that what they offered in jest we would accept out of politeness. The name is providential.

Until nightfall Forest and Park work shoulder to shoulder; we trade jokes and insults; we drop a few burning snags and let the Forest crew drop a few. It is unusual for the Park crews to have so much skilled manpower massed on a fire; it is unusual for the Forest crews not to have engines working along the perimeter or to have a fire Cat plowing line. We break for dinner, share C rations—ours are the only firepacks on the site—and loan headlamps to get them back to their vehicles. Someone discovers turkey feathers near the north fireline, and emplaced on hard hats, they become a sign of solidarity. The fire is controlled. The Forest crews are released, and the Park crews depart soon afterward in heavy darkness. We will mop up tomorrow.

Mop-up, however, is a catastrophe, a study in cross-cultural confusion. Scot decides that it is futile to extinguish a fire of this size with dirt alone; the Forest would bring in pumpers or burn it out with torches or just patrol it. Dana submits the observation that the South Rim fire crew never mops up fires to the final smoke. Only the North Rim, it seems, insists that every smoke be extinguished with dirt and water, fedco by fedco, shovel by shovel. They stare across the smoldering acres. The retardant has complicated matters by allowing the fire to burn beneath the slurried crust in such a way that the fire neither expires nor burns up. Scot half-heartedly rakes up swaths of smoking needles into mounds, then ignites them with fusees. Dana marches fretfully across the terrain, pondering a strategy—any strategy—other than antlike spading in duff; perhaps, he pleads, it will just burn itself out? Disdaining to mount the fedco on a pack frame, with the result that it hangs around her knees, Fran crouches down to investigate smoke puffing from a catface, loses her balance, and falls backward on the bladder, rocking like an overturned turtle on its shell. The day concludes with the conviction that, if the fire must be extinguished completely, nothing less than a pumper will do it. The Forest wouldn't settle for anything less.

The pumper experiment, too, ends with near disaster. Overloaded, it cannot climb a shallow ravine; even with a winch, it stalls near the top, the cable snaps, and the truck slides diagonally down the needle-slickened slope. We drain the water from the slip-on. Gasoline splashes out of the fuel tank. The truck cannot be moved without pushing into a huge ponderosa, and the tree cannot be felled without the trunk likely crashing into the side of the pumper. In desperation we begin carving sections lengthwise out of the tree with our saw as though we were slicing pan fries from a potato. We cut away perhaps a third of the tree. The ploy works, and we slide the truck downslope and return to the cache with nothing to show for the day but a slice of ponderosa and a fistful of unused accident reports.

The next morning we all—the whole crew—leave for the fire, and we depart the cache with everything we have. "We will stay on the fire with fedcos and dirt—with fingernails and spit, if necessary—until every last smoke is out," I tell the crew during our briefing at the Pit. "We will stay all day today. All night tonight. All day tomorrow. We will stay if we have to dip every goddamn smoking pine needle in water, if we have to pack in that water with quart canteens. I don't care if the nearest dirt is at Tipover and we have to carry it in our hard hats. This time we do it our way, and we do it once. No overtime, no grabass. Understand?" That night, when we pull our flagging, the fire is out.

Scot rolls up the orange and yellow flagging into balls, inserts them into holes in the pine sliver, and routes out "Circus fire." Then he commits the rough plaque to the FCA Musuem.

WILDERNESS AND THE ELIHU ROOT; OR,
BACK IN THE SADDLE AGAIN

We huddle in the pumpers, three to a cab. The rain descends in sheets. From time to time bursts of hail rattle off the hood, while for brief interludes the scene clears sufficiently to reveal a mysterious palette of opaque white and grey clouds, like fluid marble, dense as the surface of Saturn. Occasionally we hear thunder. But this is Saddle Mountain, the Fence; there will be rain without fire. Just the way we remember it. When the storm passes, the forest will reek of moisture, and mosquitoes will be thick as pine needles. Another hour must pass until we can leave for the Area. "At least it cleans the air," Ralph says plaintively.

We have heard rumors that the Park Service is concerned about air pollution over the Canyon. For the North Rim in particular, where sky dominates the field of vision, the prospect is alarming. Yet the North Rim is obsessed with the North Rim. While the controversy over proposed dams at Marble Canyon and Bridge Canyon raged across national headlines, we worried about homemade check dams in Fuller Canyon. When congressional legislation proposed to expand Grand Canyon National Park, we worried about which side— North Rim or South—would respond to an Inner Canyon fire. When maintenance bulldozes the heliport into a mound of dust, the scent of scandal permeates the Rim. "Pollution" refers to the smell of sewage wafting from a chronically defective treatment plant.

The clouds part fitfully, then in great gulps; they rise like sullen whales out of the depths of Nankoweap Canyon; sunlight crackles off puddles on the cobbled road. Before us, emerging out of the fog, appear the succession of mounded features—Little Round Top, Big Round Top, and Saddle Mountain itself. They form a ragged peninsula that separates Marble Canyon from Grand Canyon, Park from Forest, Burn from nonburn. There is almost no gradation in geomorphic terranes: the Canyon eats across the south-facing flanks of Big Round Top and Saddle Mountain from top to bottom, shearing it as Yosemite glaciers sheared Half Dome. The scene is dramatic and comprehensive, a thesaurus of landforms. But it is also disconcerting. What makes it unusual is not the abrupt conjunction of Plateau and Canyon but Saddle Mountain, which projects this intersection out before you so that the dichotomy is undeniable. Elsewhere you see the Rim sideways, as it were. You see it obliquely from the Plateau or the Canyon. At Saddle Mountain it is as though a piece of Rim were cut out and placed on display.

There is an uncanny symmetry to the scene. Each feature to one side of the Saddle has a counterpart on the other. Each contributes to an eerily balanced dichotomy. They are parallel but dissimilar universes—Park and Forest, Plateau and Canyon. Saddle Canyon to the north is matched by Nankoweap Canyon to the south; Marble Canyon by the Grand Canyon; upwarp by downcutting, monocline by canyon. Saddle Mountain exactly divides them. It compresses the entire geographic ensemble of the region into one tableau. From the Turn-around there is no end in sight. Only if you move to the Canyon or the Plateau and look back can you see the end of Saddle Mountain, but when you relocate your vantage point, the dichotomy is lost, and so is the unsettling dynamism of the scene.

The view north is the more expansive and complete. It features a double set of vanishing points: one, in the foreground, focuses on Saddle Canyon; another, at mid-ground, gathers together the Vermilion Cliffs, the Echo Cliffs, and Marble Gorge. The eye cascades from one to the other. The gorge and the luminous lump of Navajo Mountain suggestively interrupt the powerful horizontal planes that otherwise dominate the scene. The sky effects are wonderful: deep, swelling cloud shadows cross the red rock platforms like spiders. Virga forms a translucent veil, and the entire panorama is enhanced by sunsets: shadows boldly silhouette landforms and cliff facades; the refracted light ripens the reds and purples of the cliffs, the greens and yellows of Houserock Valley. By contrast, the view south to Nankoweap Canyon is crowded and confined, a view downward and cross-grained to the movement of the Plateau and the Painted Desert beyond. It is a vignette of the Grand Canyon that requires, for its best effects, a linkage with the simultaneous view north to Marble Canyon.

But that double vision is the essence of Saddle Mountain. Go north to Marble Overlook, and you can see Marble Canyon and the Kaibab

Plateau, but the Grand Canyon is obscured by Saddle Mountain. Go south to Point Imperial, and you can see Nankoweap Canyon and Grand, but Saddle Mountain blocks off Marble Canyon and the Kaibab Plateau. Only at the Turnaround can you see both, and the eye moves from one side to the other, sliding off the ridge, unable to settle on either, in a restless, unbounded dialectic.

A comparison with Powell Plateau is inevitable. At Powell you look back, and at Saddle Mountain you look out. Yet it is not just the geology—the peculiar, binocular perspective—that is disconcerting: it is the Burn, too. There is nothing else like it on the North Rim. It hardly seems to be a part of the Park at all, and most of it in fact is not. It is as though its baptism by fire transferred the region to the Forest and then into wilderness. The Burn is the only part of the Kaibab that is included within the National Wilderness Preservation System. None of Grand Canyon belongs; the Park Service will not deny access to the visitor, will not condemn motor transport on the Colorado River, will not close the Point Sublime Road despite its decrepitude. It is a matter of principle: the Park will not alienate its constituency. Cynics may note that the Forest Service transferred to wilderness a site that, because of the fire, would have no commercial logging potential for at least a century—and they would be right. But they should also note in the same breath that the transfer saved North Canyon from the Park, that it will unburden the Park from the Fence, that in a few years the aspen at Saddle Mountain will become a major tourist attraction. The wonderful view from the Turnaround is made possible by the Burn. The Burn is special.

Still, it is hard for us to imagine Saddle Mountain as wilderness. Wilderness is distant, exotic, metaphysical, and no place on the North Rim has those qualities. No one goes "to the backcountry"; they go "out of the Area." Saddle Mountain is not wild land. It is twisted metal posts, wooden stays, buried barbed wire, deerflies, hailstorms, aspen jungles, the Burn, the gate at E-1A, sawing logs, Fence songs, elderberries, and wait-a-minute bushes. The Burn, not the Fence, defines and segregates Park from Forest. The North Rim is not a heritage of past wilderness adventures, to be preserved inviolate and savored vicariously; it is something we have created, out of our relationship to fire, by tramping over and naming it.

Unlike the Forest Service, which names fires only after existing geographic places, we name fires for any reason. We name fires after girlfriends. There is a Carol, a Lynn, a Kate fire. When Tom receives a "Dear John" letter, the Shauna fire is redesignated the Disappointment fire. When Stone wants to name a second, larger fire after Carol, we name it after the great Carolinian, Charlemagne. We name fires for events or natural phenomena. There are Morning, Sunrise, Evening, Star, Sandy, and Rainbow fires. When everyone from 176 goes to a fire, it becomes the 176 fire. When the Cosmic Cowboys vow to "return by 7:00 P.M." that evening, they hurry to the BB7 (Back By 7) fire. A fire on the Fourth of July becomes the Independence fire. The first fires of the year take names like Shakedown, Preamble, Prologue, Kickoff, Inauguration. When the season opener, long delayed, appears at Cape Final, it becomes the Finally fire. Closing fires take names like Farewell, Epilogue, So Long, 10-7, Adiós. A crew birder names fires after grosbeaks, flickers, and owls; a physicist names them for high-energy accelerators like SLAC and CERN; a Mexican-food devotee gives us the Taco, Frijole, and Enchilada fires. No one has ever found the Phantom fire. The Poltergeist fire withstands three attempts before it is ultimately located. The Phoenix fire occurs on the site of an old burn. A wrong compass bearing leads to the Miss fire. A crewman whose last name is DeForrest gives us the DeForrest fire. The punning impulse yields the Sure fire, Cross fire, Cease fire, Balza fire. A fire that has cases of rations but no tools becomes the Porker fire. When Sonja and Tim smell smoke while driving to a project near Cape Royal, then follow the odor to an unreported fire, we have a Sniffer fire. A reeking burn in deep duff becomes the Odoriferous fire. A fire north of Point Imperial evolves into the Emperor fire. When Dave and Ralph have to share a single sleeping bag, we have a Honeymoon fire. The growth rings on a burning fir date it to 1687, the year of Newton's *Principia Mathematica,* so we have a Principia fire. Since it looks as if it could be the start of something, a fire in the Iron Triangle becomes the Genesis fire. Sonja and Fran have a Femme Fatale fire; Becker and Stiegelmeyer, a BS fire; a second trip to Atoko Point by Alston yields the Atokotwo fire. There are Funky, Whoopie, Pits, Booga Booga, and Far Out fires. The Dancing Pole fire results when Lenny—a

Polish kid from Syracuse—tries to make a Sterno burner out of saw mix and a hot ration can, only to have the mix ignite and spread to his plastic quart canteen; when he is unable to blow it out, he drops it to the ground and tries to stomp on it, misses the flaming head, and strikes the canteen, which shoots out a ten-foot flame and sets fire to his boot, which he tries to beat out with his other boot, resulting in a jig that sends the remainder of the crew into hysterics. The named fires become geodetic points in our collective map of the Rim.

From naming fires it is an easy transition to naming places. On USGS topos, Canyon features are wholly named, Rim features are fairly well named, and interior features of the Plateau poorly named. Most of the Canyon placenames occur in clusters and according to themes. Clarence Dutton named most of the Canyon buttes, whose shape reminded him of pagodas and whose inspirational qualities recalled Eastern religions. Buttes he transfigured into "temples" with names like Deva, Shiva, Vishnu, Brahma, Buddha, Zoroaster. Features closer to the Colorado River were named principally by the Powell Survey. For the North Rim the naming of Bright Angel Creek was probably its most important contribution because it led to Bright Angel Canyon and Bright Angel Point, which have spawned a host of placename clones. The numbering of rapids by mile from Lee's Ferry was the work of engineers on the Birdseye Expedition. Major indentations into the plateau were imagined to form "amphitheaters" like Shinumo, Hindu, Ottoman. The points of Powell Plateau were named for prominent geologic explorers to the Canyon. A few points were named for artists like Thomas Moran and Gunnar Widforss. The Dragon looks like a dragon; The Basin, drained by Outlet Canyon, functions as a hydrographic basin; Transept Canyon crosses Bright Angel Canyon below its nave. When he prepared his gorgeous topographic map of the Canyon, François Matthes countered Dutton's Oriental allusions with Nordic mythology—Thor's Hammer, Wotan's Throne, Walhalla Plateau. Richard Evans plastered names from the Arthurian legends over Shinumo Amphitheater—Galahad, Bedivere, Lancelot points; King Arthur Castle; Holy Grail Temple; Excalibur. A few Indian names survive in the form of Tiyo, Kanabownits, Kanab, and Komo. The placenamers inserted their own names on their maps, too, so that there is a Dutton Point, a Powell

Plateau, a Matthes Point. A. H. Thompson, Powell's brother-in-law
and chief topographer, gave his name to Thompson Canyon. Harvey
DeMotte, a surveyor with Thompson, bestowed his in DeMotte Park.
Cowboys called Walhalla "Greenland," and the name survives in
Greenland Lake. Government hunter Uncle Jim Owens lent his name
to Uncle Jim Point.

The official names are far from adequate either in descriptive
power or in sheer number. We need many, many more; ours is a fire
geography, and we need a gazetteer of fire names based on fire crew
experiences. We name relevant (and not a few irrelevant) features
after ourselves: Alston Point, Achterman Point, Stiegelmeyer Ridge,
Kid Saddle, McGann Window, Pyne Forest. From Rethlake comes
the name for a pond, Reth Lake. From Tom Gross comes the name for
a new sinkhole, Gross' Hole. When Ralph informs everyone that his
impossible middle name, Elihu, refers to the American statesman
Elihu Root, the large root that encumbers the trail to the store
becomes the Elihu Root. At Cape Royal there is an Eisenstadter-
Stiegelmeyer Natural Balancing Rock—or Stiegelmeyer-Eisenstadter
Natural Balancing Rock, depending on which faction you support.
There is Bum Steer Arch, Badger Meadow, the Asbestos Forest. The
Iron Triangle denotes a region in which the forest is unusually dense
and fires are impossibly difficult. The area between the Sublime
Road and the north boundary, where fires are rare and access is
lacking, is known as the Twilight Zone. An unnamed point where a
helispot is hastily cut becomes Point Blank. The warped aspen grove
by North Rim Tower is the Crooked Forest. The site where we
reconstruct and repaint some trees damaged by a vehicle accident
becomes the Magic Forest, and where we clearcut a grove of pole
aspen to lay across an exposed roadcut and hold grass seed becomes
Hayseed Hill. Walhalla evolves into Waller Holler. The fireroads are
heavily endowed with names to commemorate hazards: the Black
Hole, the Little Grand Canyon, Mogul Hill, the Kanabownits Axle
Buster, the Elephant Trap, the Dragon Turnout, the Turnaround, The
Narrows. Lifesaver Rock testifies to a small boulder on Forest road
223 that bounced Kieffer's pumper back onto the road after he lost
control on a curve. Halfway Rock is a large limestone slab midway
between the entrance station and the Area.

Yet what we celebrate as a mark of our special relationship to the Rim, our distinctiveness within the Park Service, is also a symbol of our isolation, even our irrelevance. No one outside the fire crew has the slightest idea where such names belong or from what events the names derive. Outside the Area, beyond the paved roads and vistas, there is virtually no visitation. Our placenames will never be entered onto public maps. When two crewmen erect a small rock cairn on an unnamed, minor point, they place within the cairn a Prince Albert tobacco can with a note formally christening the site as Point Less, a designation the Board of Geographical Names will never accept. When the crew digs a trail from Point Imperial to the Kaibab trailhead, we name it the Bawgd Pass trail, an acronym for all the crewmen who work on it. When asked how the name came about, we reply that it refers to Pete Bawgd, an old trapper in these parts. It is not surprising that the Park Service renames the trail, but it is symptomatic that it is renamed after a ranger. When Stiegelmeyer is asked his location by the Park dispatcher, he starts to answer, "Stiegelmeyer Ridge," then hesitates. No one outside the fire crew has the slightest inkling where Stiegelmeyer Ridge is located. "Thompson Canyon," he replies dejectedly.

The sky clears to the north, and clouds continue to excavate Nankoweap Canyon. Here, at the binocular Turnaround, we step outside into damp, breezy air, swept by sunlight as clouds race overhead. Dana stretches, and E.B. points out the site of the Wait-a-Minute fire, buried deep in a locust patch in Saddle Canyon, now a part of the American wilderness. Of course, we want to save such places, but it is difficult to think of them as anything exotic or abstract. It is impossible to imagine Lifesaver Rock or the Elihu Root within the context of a pristine, fragile, remote wilderness. It is where we work. It is what we are.

"Hey," says Dana, his hand sweeping the panorama, "it's not much, but it's home."

It is a confused, disorganized storm. Cells pop up at random around the plateau. There is no pattern to the smoke reports. The Park picks up two smokes, but the Forest, we learn, has many. The Kaibab helitack crew, normally stationed at Williams, is reassigned to the

North Kaibab district. Even so the Forest dispatcher asks the Park for help with a smoke at Saddle Mountain. "Half an acre. White smoke. Heavy fuels," he says. "Request a handcrew to hold it until our helitack can arrive later this afternoon. We'll fly your boys out after they are released."

We can see the smoke from the Turnaround—concentrated, apparently not spreading, probably in heavy slash left from the Burn and salvage. The smoke appears to be on the opposite side of Big Round Top. We only have to get there; no need to flag, or pick a route for resupply, or even worry about getting back; just get there and sit on it until the helitack arrives. The view is breathtaking, scoured clear of all obscuring vegetation by the old Burn. We load up heavily and trek down to Little Round Top. It is unbelievable that we will actually be able to hike to a fire by sight, that we will be able to participate in a regional fire bust that has otherwise missed the North Rim. We take the direct route, cross-country, and plunge down what once was the trailhead for the Nankoweap trail.

But the hillside is a tangle of charred logs, clinging aspen saplings, and sharp-needled locust ("wait-a-minute bushes," the Forest calls them) that clutch at everything. The legacy of the Burn and logging is not a desert but an embryonic jungle. There is nothing to do but thrash along. We string out, each convinced that he can select a better route than the nominal leader; no one stares much beyond his feet. Rich hacks at some bushes with a pulaski—a futile gesture. We cross the saddle between Little and Big Round Top and contour around the hillside to a large rock outcrop. There the truth comes to us, like the rasp of a raven. The fire is not on Big Round Top at all but on the extended mesa far beyond it. More submerged black logs, more aspen vines, more locust, more hiking. We are not halfway, and there is nothing to do but keep on. At least, we congratulate ourselves as we crash into the scene, we have reached the fire before the helitack crew.

The fire flames in old heavy fuels, spreading from log to log, reburning charred trees, consuming snags and trees killed but not burned up during the original fire. Without an interstitial carpet of needles, there is no ground fire, and there are no standing trees to cast needles. Between the logs sprout lush swards of grass, still flush from spring greenup. We construct a fireline by sawing out sections from interlocking logs. We make a few more cuts, throw some dirt—which is sparse in this rock pile—onto flames, and squirt water from our fedco. Enough; there is only an hour of daylight left and the helo will appear imminently; let the Forest do its own mop-up; left alone, the fire will expire in another day. We pluck out some rations from our packs, and we wait for the helo. Rich spots a grouse fluttering stupidly around one of the burning logs and speculates that it may be protecting a nest nearby. Jimbo is less concerned with the noise of the grouse than with that of aircraft.

The sound, however, comes from a fixed wing, not a rotor. The Forest recon, Observer 1, flies overhead and contacts us on the Park radio net to inform us that there are fires all around the margins of the Kaibab, that the helitack crew is still making initial attacks. "You're in our mutual aid zone," he says. "Just sit on that thing until morning." A mutual aid zone between two land masses or two agencies we can understand, but here everything is compressed into a peninsula no wider than the zone itself. There is nothing to do, however, but accede. We count our rations and canteens. To hurry our march, we combined four packs into two. Of our rations, two each, we have already eaten one; two one-gallon canteens and four one-quart belt canteens remain; and there is enough saw mix and oil to cut for perhaps another half hour. We have no sleeping bags, not even on the pumper. We buck up several logs and rearrange them into the shape of a large U, then move into the U for a camp, sheltered from the wind, and construct a small fire. The sun has set, drab and shadowy; a large moon hangs over the red desert Echo Cliffs; evening winds rush past, concentrated by the saddle, full of raw bluster from their descent down the Kaibab. We can see neither Canyon nor Plateau. The grouse appears again, just outside our firelight. Someone wonders out loud how you cook a grouse. Wil notes hypothetically that we could flatten it with a single swing of a shovel. We are not on the Rim, and only an act of faith in our fire maps allows us to believe we are even on the Kaibab. It is a long, fitful night, a hard sleep.

When we are relieved the next morning, a helitack crewman mutters something that sounds like an apology. It cannot be about the Grouse fire; anything the Park suffers at Saddle Mountain is considered just punishment. We learn later that instead of picking us up late last afternoon, the helitack crew suppressed a fire near Cape Royal, that the continued production of smokes did include some on the Rim. As the foreman directed the pilot south, the pilot hesitated, pointing out that the fire was within the Park, while the foreman only shrugged. They landed in a ponderosa glade, dropped a couple of troublesome trees, and attacked the fire. When the Forest FMO learned of the location, he was livid. "Why, why," he asked, "did you go into the Park?" "Because," replied the foreman, "that is where the fire was." The FMO softened. "How many trees did you cut?" "Six," replied the foreman. "Damn, damn," stammered the FMO. "The Park Service will be out there counting them stumps."

The Park fire crew, however, is counting its overtime. "These Forest Service fires are always the pits," says Eric. "You know," says Rich moodily, "I'll bet we could have made a spit out of chain saw files and roasted that grouse."

THE TURNAROUND

The sky clears incompletely.

Saddle Mountain straddles the lifting clouds. Clouds still slosh within the gorges, like a white-capped lake. Disintegrating thunderheads cast giant, racing shadows across the Painted Desert. Ralph mutters about the smudge around Navajo Mountain. Wil escapes to a thicket of elderberry; Dana, to raspberry; some years ago Joe, we recall, discovered strawberries near the Turnaround. Returning from Little Round Top, Tim turns and kicks a loose rock with his boots, and something catches his eye. He reaches down to pick up a fossil brachiopod. The Kaibab limestone is, in places, rich in Permian fossils. Most of the loose rock on the surface of the Plateau is chert and fossil, and the fireroads are cobbled with fossil shards. Tim asks if here, beyond the last Fence stay, we are in the Park. No one is sure. Both Park and Forest avoid ambiguities by allowing the road to double back upon itself. Only with fire is there a need to go farther.

Fire forces the eye to look. What gives the overall setting its compelling quality is the unstable linkage of the two panoramas by Saddle Mountain, but what makes that dialectic possible at all is the

Burn. Fire is the agency that made the Turnaround, that animated geology into metageography. The creative Burn began in the Park but worked its magic in the Forest; the Forest has legal wilderness, the Park does not; wilderness status will eliminate the coupled panorama; and so on, back and forth, lost in an infinite regression of cause and consequence, irony and purpose. Now the sky, storm and clouds, adds new motions and new complications and new balances. Some clouds are active; some, dissipating. At last the feet follow the mind. We walk to one side, then another, then down into the lesser of the saddles that make up the peninsula. We know intuitively why the road ends here.

It is difficult to go on without choosing one side or the other, but to return means to go back to the Fence. As new seasonals are hired by the truckful for maintenance, the rangers, and interpretation, we are phased out of general project work until only the Fence remains. Parks are for people. As national policy changes to restrict fire suppression, we abandon old patterns of wildfires but never successfully replace them with the promised designs of prescribed fires. Sadly, shamefully, we are even disengaged from fires in the Forest. For long seasons we request assistance from the Forest, which it always provides, but are never asked to help in return. At last we learn why. Every request from the Kaibab dispatcher, meticulously processed according to Forest protocol, is routed through Big Bob. He never releases us from the Rim, and he never explains to us why or even that he has refused. Access to Saddle Mountain remains through Forest road 420, however, and the site always seems more of the Forest than of the Park anyway. The Park may not care, but the Forest will not allow the road to close. So we come. Road or no road, Fence or no Fence, Burn or no Burn, fires still start in the Saddle, and willingly or not, we still come. We have to come.

Tim holds up the fossil, and the effect is contagious. Suddenly we all begin to collect. There are brachiopods, pelecypods, crinoids—crinoid necklaces have become the fashion rage of the summer. Yet there are doubts—are we in the Park or the Forest?—and they are not relieved until Uncle Jimmy points out that crinoids are far more abundant at Marble Viewpoint to the northwest, a site indisputably within the Kaibab National Forest. We abandon our small mound of fossils and decide to organize a trip to Marble after work. Wil urges another expedition in August to gather berries. Dana asks if anyone else would like to hike the old Nankoweap trail, the upper few miles of which traverse the devastation of the Burn before breaking down into the Canyon all the way to the River. Ralph comments again on the haze near Glen Canyon, which he is sure comes from the coal-fired Four Corners power plant at Page. "That's OK," Tim says. "In the fall it will be our turn." In the fall the Forest will ignite its slash piles and the Park may conduct its prescribed burns, and the prevailing winds will carry Kaibab smoke to Page.

Uncle Jimmy estimates that the monsoon can't be more than two weeks away. Dana calculates that we have less than two and a half hours of Fencing left before we can pack it in for the day. We can delay no longer. We turn around and go back the way we came.

CHAPTER FIVE

The Dragon

JULY SPROUTS RUMORS like wildflowers: it is time for the monsoon. On the daily fire weather reports, there are hints of an approaching surge of moisture, and images of a huge crescent of boiling clouds arcing from the Gulf of Mexico up along the summit of the Sierra Madres of Mexico and into the American Southwest. There are reports of sprawling lightning-fire busts in the mountains to the south.

We can trace the monsoon by its clouds. After days of empty skies, puffs of cumulus appear around the San Francisco Peaks, the Aubrey Cliffs, the Hopi Mesas; torn cumuli collect around the highest bulge of the Kaibab; more clouds move up from the south, more gather at the summit, and the two cloud banks spread and meet along the Canyon Rim. The ferocity of the first fully developed storms is unbelievable. Rain and hail descend in torrents. Then the moisture vanishes, sopped up like a giant sponge by the cracked karst landscape of the Kaibab or quickly shed over the surface. Rainfall, though intense, is spotty. Individual storm cells mature eclectically along the turbulent edge of the Rim. The air is electric with lightning. Bolts come down in sheets. Singularly hot cells track their progress across the Rim with a trail of fires.

There is no escape from the paradox that rain and fire have a common origin. A spark can survive the wettest storm, and fires set by the sharpest lightning may be suppressed by its complement of rains. The greatest fire loads seek out those times and those places that balance the two, that attract storms but dry them in some way. Now is that time, and the Rim is that place.

The mix is right. The advent of the monsoon is the fulcrum of fire season, and the metageography of the Rim approaches the apex of the fire triangle. The whole season—and the lives of seasonals—are funneled to the fires on the Rim. Throughout the rest of July and most of August the pattern of afternoon thunderstorms will repeat itself, and every few days the Rim will be submerged in rain, hail, and lightning.

It is time to fight fire.

UNDER THE MONSOON SKY

Tom opens the lock, then pushes the trapdoor up with his head, pleasantly surprised to find a use for his hard hat. Ralph follows. North Rim tower has survived another winter. Inside, there is not even much dust, just pine pollen and the dry, musty odor of disuse. The west window is boarded up with plywood; but the board is hinged, and they open it. The telephone still does not work—somewhere between the entrance and the tower, trees have fallen across the line—and the cross-hairs on the firefinder are broken. But the chair, and the small dais on which it stands, have a full set of insulators on their legs, without which no one would dare sit through a lightning storm.

Ralph points to the south. North Rim tower is the highest point on the Rim, but its panorama is only marginally useful. To the north the scene is blocked by a ridge of trees. The nature of the Kaibab, an inverted saucer, mitigates against dramatic perspectives. Because the North Rim is so much higher than the South, you cannot even see the Canyon, which appears as no more than a hazy chasm. But you can see long distances to the south, and it is there Ralph points. The San Francisco Peaks are congealing clouds. Already at midmorning there are distinct, shocking white puffs along Humphreys, Kendricks, Sitgreaves, and Bill Williams. Tom studies them intently through binoculars. They are good, solid clouds. The monsoon is on its way.

*　*　*

We gather on the Lodge veranda and peer south into the darkness. There is no moon; the Canyon is a black box, silent and invisible. Tourists glide past, with drinks and ice cream cones, then leave, disappointed that there is nothing to see. We occupy almost the whole line of chairs. The scene is spectacular.

Lightning blasts the Peaks like an artillery barrage. Bolt follows bolt with barely a pause. The Peaks are etched in jet and glow with an orange and yellow aura. There is an eerie remoteness to the scene. We see it all yet hear nothing. Some storm cells drift northward, perhaps to Red Butte. Cloud-to-cloud bolts illuminate great banks of cloud like ghostly X rays. If the moisture surge continues north, there will be storms on the Kaibab. If not, the clouds will recede south and the Coconino and South Kaibab forests will have sleepers pop up for several days, until the monsoon strengthens and again sweeps across the region. Tomorrow's situation report will make interesting reading. In the morning we will inspect our hygrothermograph. It will tell us if there has been much humidity recovery over the evening. If humidity persists, there will probably be enough moisture to support thunderstorms; if not, we must wait. The scene both soothes and excites. A dry forest is a dead forest.

We watch for an hour, two hours. Occasionally someone gets up and strolls to the saloon for a beer, then returns. The veranda belongs to us. All the tourists have retreated inside the Lodge. Some go to the saloon; some, to the interpretive slide show that the naturalists are offering inside the recreation hall. The lights from the rec hall cast the veranda in an unpleasant yellow light. Now the lights go off; except for starlight on limestone, the veranda is filled with darkness. We hear broken sounds from inside as a fern feeler describes the splendor of the Grand Canyon.

Relentlessly, ceaselessly, lightning rains down on the Peaks. "There! There!" Dash whispers as he points to a ground strike that hangs, as though suspended, for two, maybe three seconds. It is the kind of hot lightning likely to start fires. Clouds smear across the stars, blotting out the sky ever closer to the Rim. A few strikes approach nearer, but the spectacle cannot endure for long. It will not reach the North Rim. From inside the rec hall, there is a dim peal of

clapping as the slide show ends, the lights flash on, and the door to
the veranda opens. Some tourists pause at the door, blinking and
yawning, before shuffling off to their cabins. It is time to leave.

We rise, then hesitate. For a second we think we can hear a distant
burst of thunder, like a muffled drumroll, reverberating through the
rocky echo chamber of the Canyon.

Pferd, Wil, John-Boy, Bone, and I—we all cling to rocks and look
south. The sky over the Kaibab is empty, but there is good buildup at
the Peaks, and a few embryonic cumuli have marched north to Red
Butte. Komo Point is a good place for lunch. We can clear the
helispot after we eat.

The clouds over the Peaks thicken. Altocumuli gather and grow
between Red Butte and the South Rim, dappling the great tablelands
with massive, rolling shadows. Pferd nods toward the crest of the
Kaibab, over which some sharp wisps of altocumulus cas-
tellatus have appeared—progenitors of thunderstorms; fire clouds.
Strands and flakes thicken into dense puffs; isolated clouds mass into
banks; damp greys mingle with sun whites. The contrast between
blue sky and white cloud is razor-sharp. Clouds splash upward. They
mass in piles along the Rim—at Tiyo, The Dragon, Powell, Swamp
Ridge, Bright Angel Point. They collect along the west flank of
Walhalla and at Saddle Mountain. To the south there is virga, dust,
and lightning. Winds from Canyon and cloud rush past us.

It is, for us, the great Canyon spectacle. The Canyon's geologic
structure creates a wonderful esthetic matrix of lines and masses, a
unique equilibrium of the vertical and the horizontal, of baroque
variety carved out of enormous symmetries. But it is a pattern that is
rigid, predictable, and incomplete. What thrills are the Canyon's
atmospherics: clouds and sunlights; the interaction of light and
shadow on gorge and cliff and butte; the interplay of white cloud
and colored rock; mountainous clouds, water-sky grey at the base and
sparkling white at the summit; the movement of wind, virga, rain,
blue and white.

The North Rim has its fabled mule deer, its exotic Kaibab squirrels, its grand meadows, but it is fundamentally an inorganic wilder-

ness. Its great spectacle is its sky. On the Plateau we know that sky indirectly. We know it through its temperature, its crystal brilliance, its dry or clammy feel. We know it through its shadows, striping the forest floor, imposing a double layer of shade, one from trees and another, more diffuse, from veiled clouds. We know it through its winds—warm and musty in the day, full of dark rushing through the canopy at night. The most welcome scenes are those that open up the forest to the sky, and this, not its biology, is what makes the meadows attractive. In the Canyon, too, the sky is obscured by the depth of the gorges, visible only in snatches. But on the Rim the sky is everywhere.

The two Rims, North and South, are unequal in this regard. Stand at the South Rim, and your natural horizon is at or below the plane of the North Rim. Look out and you see the Canyon, a receding amphitheater. The sky serves as a canopy to complement it. Stand at the North Rim, however, and the natural horizon lies far above the Canyon, above even the plane of the Colorado Plateau, the San Francisco Peaks, the Aubrey Cliffs. The horizon rests at the base of the clouds. What you see is sky, for which the Canyon is an intriguing substratum. Work on the North Rim, and you will learn to read the sky better than the forest. From the sky come lightning, water, and fire. Only one of the Rim's functions is to delineate the Canyon: it also announces the great, liberating sky.

By early afternoon the Rim will be plastered with rain and hail. The Canyon will be capped by a swirl of cloud, and if the moisture persists, the clouds may fill up the gorges, leaving only the Kaibab limestone of the Rim and the Canyon buttes to rise, like lost islands, out of the specter. The storm, not unlike fire, induces a reverie. We can almost hear the sharp crack of thunder, see the sudden greying, hear the rush of wind and rain—tentative at first, then torrential. The rain descends in sheets, while lightning crashes overhead in brilliant cracks and hail falls in rattles and abstracts the forest with thick, translucent veils. Then it ends. The sky lightens; a rip in the cloud deck reveals a fragment of blue, the rain falls in thin drizzles and tapers off. Trees shed their water in sudden shudders. Thunder recedes in distant drumrolls. Fog streamers and fog packs rush through dense woods. Clouds clear from the Canyon, rushing violently upward to dissipate. Clouds of steam rise hissing from meadow and road under the shock of sunlight. Smoke reports will pour in.

We scrap lunch and hurry to clear the helispot and return to the cache.

The sound of rain and hail drowns out any conversation. The pumpers, drenched, have been outfitted with saws and sleeping bags wrapped in plastic garbage bags. We sit in the Fire Pit and wait.

Lightning crashes to all sides. Wind drives hail against the windows. We turn on the oil heater. Joe sits on the Base of a Big Yellow Pine, Ralph and Tom are on the broken bench, and Dave straddles a metal milk can, a souvenir of an ancient fire camp. The rest sit on their firepacks, hunched as though in a bunker under artillery fire. Joe and Tom light cigarettes. The SWFFs have chosen to sit in the fire cache rather than the overcrowded Pit. We stare at the dispatch chart. The teams are made up: one veteran, one rookie, and one SWFF to a team. If it appears that there will be many fires, we will send a rookie and a SWFF and keep some veterans to form teams with reserves. Although the storm has plastered the Area, other portions of the Rim have been hit much more lightly, and still others, along the points, will dry out quickly. Recon 1 plans to leave shortly from the airport. Another bolt of lightning—its sound and light virtually simultaneous—causes the lights to flicker. Rain is falling so hard that it cannot flow off the asphalt roadway quickly enough and piles up an inch thick.

Recon 1 sights a smoke near Ten X, outside the Park on the South Kaibab. Grandview tower reports a possible smoke near Sinking Ship Overlook, and Recon 1 swings over to examine it. A smoke is confirmed, just over the Rim along the Grandview trail, and a pumper is dispatched from Desert View. Recon 1 dodges the largest storm cells and veers west. It will follow the Rim out to Pasture Wash, just south and across the gorge from Powell Plateau, then fly north to Powell and close the loop by moving southeast to Cape Royal and back to Grandview. There is a smoke at Pasture Wash, a single pinyon. The South Rim pumper departs its cache, the start of an hour-long drive.

There is nothing showing on Powell. A large cell hovers over Point Sublime. The plane flies along the north boundary. There is a smoke on Swamp Ridge—old, reliable Swamp Ridge. Tom and Duane roar approval, grab their packs, and shout for Henry Goldtooth to join them in the blue pumper. It will take them more than an hour to drive to the Shinumo Gate, plenty of time for Recon 1 to scout the remainder of the North Rim and return to guide them in. A smoke, very faint, is reported along the Sublime Road, on a south-facing slope near W-3, burning at the base of a big yellow pine. Joe rises from the stump. "I knew sitting here would be good luck," he grins. There is no chance that they can make an initial attack with a pumper, so he takes Ken and calls for Francis John to join them at the Three-quarter Ton. The storm cell at Point Sublime is matched by one over Tiyo. Recon 1 swings to Walhalla and discovers a smoke near Cliff Spring. There are too many smokes for us to hold to our dispatch plan. Kent will take two SWFFs and the pumper, and Ralph is told to find some reserves. "Try the rangers first, then maintenance. Hell, take fern feelers if necessary. And get the ranger patrol truck [RPT]. We're out of vehicles." A burst of hail sweeps into the Pit as Ralph dashes out the door.

Recon 1 has crossed the Canyon and gives some directions to the Desert View crew at Grandview. They will have to walk down the trail a couple of hundred yards, then traverse west. The fire is burning in a snag. Another smoke is sighted on the South Kaibab. Recon 1 calls Red Butte, who has already reported it, returns to Pasture Wash, ready to undertake a new circuit around the Park. The South Rim pumper has made good time and wants some directions. But Recon 1 searches vainly for the smoke. For perhaps ten minutes the plane circles the site of the reported fire before identifying a black and white splotch on the ground. The fire has burned out. The South Rim pumper turns back grimly, while the North Rim jeers. Tom reaches the Shinumo Gate. Recon 1 tells him to drive another two miles and stop. In the meantime, he will search the Sublime area. There is a smoke visible by Galahad Point and another, it seems, in the Walla Valley. We request a helicopter for the Galahad fire and send a crew in the RPT to W-5. Two reserves have reported to the cache. We hand them standard GSA firepacks, fireshirts, and hard hats. One of the reserves, a ranger with some fire experience, goes with Kent and Reuben Begaye in the RPT. The other will stay in the Pit. Ralph and Kee Yazzie organize their gear for helitack; 210 will arrive within half an hour. Overhead the sky has begun to clear. Recon 1 flies over Tiyo, over Bright Angel Point, and across Walhalla: there is a smoke near the Area, just over the Rim between the Park Service area and the Lodge. I take the last of the SWFFs, John Tsotsie, a fern feeler, and the structural fire truck. We can see the thin smoke from the road.

The Desert View crew asks for more help, and Recon 1 recrosses the Canyon. He gives some more directions, then flies back to the North Rim. Ralph and Kee Yazzie are en route to Galahad Point aboard the Park helo. Three crews want bearings. Recon gives directions to each: a compass bearing; an estimate of what kind of terrain must be crossed; a description of the fire. "Only ground fire," he informs Tom. Regardless of what any aerial observer says, we always bring a saw, and Tom is grateful he does. When he arrives a snag is fully involved. Joe discovers an enormous white fir, far larger than anything he has ever attempted to fell, and he elects to burn it through at the base. The rookie George is overwhelmed by a flaming, outsized pine and asks for help in felling it. Kent, when he arrives, wants another pumper. Ralph discovers an old helispot—the functional relic of an ancient fire—and lands within a hundred yards of the fire. "No problem," he laughs. Recon 1 asks if we need more help. "No," someone interrupts over the radio, "only more fires." I tell George and Kent that we can help them after we control the Angel fire. "Do what you can until then."

The Angel fire is not large—a single log and a stump—but it is awkward, about one hundred fifty feet down from the Rim. I park the fire truck on the Rim side of the road and we walk down with handtools, where we scrape a line, careful to sculpture a trench on the downhill side and pile up dirt against it; then we return to the fire truck, run out the hardline hose, and carry an extra fifty feet of softline. No need to pump. Once we establish a prime, gravity will carry water to the fire. We mop up the fire easily; I release the fern feeler, commandeer the stake truck from maintenance, and realize that the sun has set.

John and I share a ration while we drive to George's fire. Following *flagging by headlamp, we walk up a steep hill with a saw, peripheral equipment, and two sleeping bags. Most of the surface fire is out. The snag towers above us like an obelisk, its top invisible to our headlamps. There is a slight lean apparent at the trunk, however, and we tell George's crew to clear a path in that direction. We shatter two wooden wedges in driving the snag over; apparently there were counterweights, most likely branches, that opposed the lean of the trunk. When the snag crashes to the ground, the air is thick with dust and ash that swirl eerily in our headlamps. We leave George and one SWFF on the fire. The rest of us drive to the Swamp Point road and swap the stake truck for the pumper. Tom asks us to transfer some batteries, rations, and canteens from the pumper to the truck. We take the pumper to Kent's fire in the Walla Valley. With an extra slip-on, mop-up goes quickly. We leave at about 0100 hours. We would like to stay—there are ample sleeping bags—but it is likely that there will be more fires tomorrow, and we must prepare for them at the fire cache.*

"Mop up your fire to the point you can safely leave it in the morning," I tell everyone. "And get some sleep." The next day we have three more smokes, two in the morning and one in the afternoon. We dispatch crews directly from each of the old fires, and I join one crew to drop another tree. The dispatching strategy almost works, except that the rookie George abandons his first fire too soon. The tree, when it fell, landed on hot coals, and after another day the trunk ignites into a very messy reburn. We are so bone-weary by now that the reburn draws all of us, crew by crew, over the course of the next day. By late afternoon it is over.

The Desert View crew never discovers the snag, which burns to ash somewhere in the buff-white Kaibab limestone.

QUESTING THE DRAGON

It seems an odd place from which to depart. Yet here, on Crystal Ridge, amid dense mixed conifer, is the trailhead to The Dragon. The sign sags slightly with age. We have left one man in the Area, but the rest of us, including all the SWFFs, prepare our loads. We strap five-gallon cubitainers of water and cases of rations onto Army pack frames. We cram our lunches and some extra gallons of drinking water into a couple of emptied firepacks. Already it is hot. To hike to The Dragon, remark the trail with flagging tape, clear the helispot of brush, replenish the water and rations in the tool cache, and return in a single day is a tall order. The old trail—tagged by orange can lids and roller-coastering over several ridges—is for fools. Our best guess is that it was laid out by compassing from Crystal Ridge to the Rim sometime during a fire bust. Instead, we drop immediately into the first drainage, ignore the locust patches, and follow its sinuous meanders to the Rim. Suddenly the Canyon sweeps open at our feet. To the east the panorama is blocked by the Tiyo peninsula, and to the west, by Sublime. But right in the middle—a fractured peninsula, half Plateau, half Canyon, and all Rim—lies The Dragon.

It is probably no more than four miles from trailhead to helispot, but the terror of the trail lies not in its length or multiple ascents but in its sheer arbitrariness. It is little more than a flagged route by which to reach an isolated mesa within the Canyon. In places as many as three or four separate routes are flagged, each in the belief that it will reduce the burden slightly; the flags are no more than graffiti, names carved into trees and sprayed on rocks. As we clamber along The Dragon's tail, climbing from east flank to west and then back again, we discover a natural window, sight a golden eagle, and peer down into the precipice of Milk Creek and Hindu Amphitheater. The sun strikes full force, blasting off bare rock and brush; upslope winds, warm and desiccating, rise out of the Canyon like soaring hawks; broken routes of flagging crisscross the hillside like goat paths. We pause at a red rock saddle below The Dragon's body. This, the last ascent, is the hardest. The route is a scramble uphill through large rocks and loose soil; with a pack, the ascent must be done on all fours. Near the Rim you can grab shrubs and pull yourself up. The summit is not well defined. When you reach it, you are shoulder deep in scrub oak and locust. There is no route at all here. Simply thrash through the thickets, and when you come to a clearing, you have reached the Dragon helispot. Two aluminum coffins mark the LZ.

We drop our packs near the coffins and pause for breath. Dawson says he understands now why it is called the Draggin' trail. It will be another ten minutes or so before everyone completes the climb. The first arrivals pass around a canteen. There is time for a quick survey of The Dragon. Its appearance is both familiar and unsettling.

At one time The Dragon was a narrow peninsula, flanked on both sides by ancient faults that have allowed the Canyon to penetrate deeply into the Plateau. The thinness of the residual peninsula has encouraged its erosion into an uncanny approximation of a sleeping dragon. Its tail is a large isthmus that extends for about a mile and a half between the principal mesa (The Dragon's body) and the Rim. This portion of the peninsula is broken with rock buttes, as though the tail were slightly coiled and studded with spikes. A broader mesa constitutes the bulk of The Dragon's body. It is about one and a half miles long and perhaps half a mile at its widest. A slight ridge on the east flank of the mesa makes a backbone of sorts. The sides of the mesa are indented into a series of amphitheaters, marked like a rib cage by great columns of Kaibab limestone. On the mesa you are never really out of sight of the Rim; The Dragon's body is a mis-shapen oval of Rim. The mesa ends sharply to the south along cliffs. Here another isthmus develops, thin and sinuous—The Dragon's neck. After penetrating several miles farther into the Canyon the neck rises dramatically into a large, pyramid-shaped butte, The Dragon's head. From the gorge of Crystal Creek to the mesas of body and head, The Dragon is higher than any peak east of the Rockies. Its colossal bulk gives it a sphinx-like quality. But in a Canyon packed with gargantuan rock masses, the eccentricities of The Dragon are lost amid an overabundance of geologic and scenic exotica.

Its function, not its shape, informs The Dragon. Like mythical dragons, this one breathes fire. For its size The Dragon has a higher fire load than any other site on the North Rim. The signs of fire are everywhere. Most of the trees are scorched black on their lower trunks; the ground is burned in places to mineral soil and creamy limestone; charred stumps rise harshly out of the rocky soil like carved lances, and charcoal mantles the surfaces; in places the dense stands of young ponderosa look like black scales. On its south side The Dragon suffered an intense fire in the early 1960s which burned so fiercely that only brush came back, bristling like a thorny mane around The Dragon's neck. To supply that firefighting effort, the Park experimented with paracargo drops, and torn parachute shroud hangs from trees like the residue of some barbarous meal. On the north side, where The Dragon's tail joins its body, a helispot was cut as the mesa pinches off. It is not a good helispot, but no one is about to put in another.

The Dragon is the purest expression of fire on the North Rim, both its good and its dark side. You feel as though you are treading across the spine of some rough beast that may, at any moment, slouch eastward. But even more than Powell Plateau, Saddle Mountain, or Swamp Ridge, The Dragon belongs to the fire crew. No one else comes here; no one else has any reason to. The Dragon is defined uniquely by its fires. It offers no special geologic marvels, no biological anomalies, no singularly spectacular view of the Canyon; there are not even Anasazi ruins. There is nothing to intervene between us and fire. The Dragon has no history other than what we give it, and no one can really claim to have fought fire on the North Rim without at least one smoke on The Dragon. Far from being a peripheral feature, The Dragon is central—the apex of the fire triangle that inscribes the metageography of the Rim. At The Dragon the Plateau meets the Canyon in fiery dialectic. Here the place, the season, our lives are concentrated. Its history is our own.

Only John Paul, oldest of the SWFFs, still lags. Dave inspects the coffins. Henry John gawks at the parachute shroud in the pines. Canteen in hand, Ralph walks to the edge of the LZ and stares across the Canyon to the crisp white cumuli rapidly piling up along the Peaks.

Everyone is in the field when the smoke reports tumble in. Dispatching has its reasons without any rhymes. Kieffer, Draper, and Johnny Begaye, cleaning up Kanabownits tower, go first—a smoke sighted by Scenic Airlines down the Walla Valley, the Buckwheat fire. Stiegelmeyer and Howard Yazzie depart from Imperial into the dreaded Asbestos Forest, plunging down the abandoned E-1, up one enormous ridge, then up a second, and there find the Pits fire— burned-out stump holes, filled with ash, littering half an acre like minefields; the active fire limited to a hollowed tree, its top burned away, smoking furiously. They have nothing more than one firepack, a fedco, handtools, and the fresh memory of a gruesome cross-country hike. Already their pumper is gone from the entrance road; since they have no use for it, Mac, driving in with Robert John and John Tsotsie, has exchanged the Three-quarter Ton for it and hurried on to the cache. There will be more fires. By the time Mac arrives in the Area, there is a smoke reported on The Dragon; he and Robert John will helicopter in. Suddenly Alston interrupts the flow of radio traffic. He and I, he announces, have a flat tire at the Lindbergh Hill picnic area; our vehicle radio unit has apparently been broken all afternoon and he has turned on a handset to request a spare tire. "Just what the damned hell is happening?" Alston pleads. Clyde is calm. "Good," he says, reviewing his notes. "Yes, we have a fire on Lindbergh." Clyde is circling the fire on The Dragon, a flaming snag between the heliport and the neck. Mac and Robert John—"Yes, 'you two.' Who else is there?"—depart from the North Rim heliport. "We'll find it. Give us directions," snaps Alston, mortified and impatient at being effectively AWOL. Clyde reports a bearing of 165 degrees, corrected, from the old quarry. "Half a mile. No hills." We quickly gear up and hustle to the quarry, which is several hundred yards long, and march into the woods on a course of 165 degrees. There is no way to know from where in the quarry the bearing should come. "How far can we be off?" Joe reasons. We wander for nearly forty-five minutes, staggering under hurriedly constituted firepacks, through dripping spruce forests before smelling smoke and stumbling onto the burn; the 10-7 fire is nothing more than a snag and a log and smoldering damp needles. Mac and Robert John land on The Dragon after circling the U-2 fire and taking bearings in the helo between the helispot and the snag. Recon 1 swings south. There are smokes on the South Kaibab. Red Butte is requesting help.

Suppression proceeds rapidly. Most fuels are still wet from the storm, and there is little spread. Then the problems begin. After Kieffer and Draper burn down their snag—a torch, impossible to approach safely—the top half of an adjacent tree apparently damaged by lightning but not otherwise involved in the fire breaks loose and tumbles with an earsplitting crash onto the flames. Within minutes its green needles have erupted into flame, and a whole new round of mop-up is initiated. When it gets dark, Kieffer volunteers, he will return to the pumper for another fedco and rations.

On the advice of recon, Stiegelmeyer and Howard Yazzie have not brought a saw into the Pits fire and now discover that they have no effective way to extinguish the fire within the smoking stump, which rises perhaps fifteen feet. For a while they toss dirt into the hollow with shovels, as though they were winnowing the duff. The smoke lessens, and from within the stump they can hear the telltale popping of cooled embers. But the smoke persists. Unless it is extinguished, it is only a matter of time until the remainder of the stump is involved. At last Stiegelmeyer explains to John in mimicry what he plans. John nods. Then Stiegelmeyer climbs the stump, plucks his quart canteen from his belt, and, reaching over the top rim, blindly pours the water down the sides of the hollow interior. A cloud of steam crackles and hisses upward. Stiegelmeyer tosses the canteen to John, who fills it from the fedco and flings it back to Stiegelmeyer who dumps this one also. For half an hour they continue the procedure, and they conclude it only in an opaque darkness, illuminated by headlamps.

The lengthening shadows worry Mac. He and Robert John have flung dirt until their arms drop with fatigue, but the fire continues to creep and flare; even the snag burns with alarming stubbornness. There is no way they can abandon the fire and return the next day—it must be dead out—yet they have no provisions for an overnight stay. There was not room in the helo for a saw and fedco along with sleeping bags; they must either fly out before sunset or sleep in the fireline. That thought renews them, and Mac bucks up the snag with rhythmic fury, while Robert John submerges each section in water and dirt. At the last moment Mac requests 210 to pick them up at the Dragon helispot. A final spray of dirt; a quick survey for lingering smokes; a cross-country dash toward the helispot; a race between sunlight and the sound of the approaching helo, its whine-whop like a bugle call. Twilight winds rush like confused swifts around the Rim. Three times 210 approaches the site. Twice it is forced to back off, escaping under full power. Frantically Mac tosses shovelfuls of dirt to impregnate and define the squirrelly winds. One blows back into his face, and, cursing, he spits out a small stone. On the third pass, the helo feels its way cautiously, hesitates, then rushes forward, its skids on the ground but still under full power, as Mac and Robert John scramble to store their tools and climb in. The ship shudders, pauses, lifts bulkily; swiftly the pilot turns the ship around; catching a burst of upcanyon winds it climbs savagely away from the Rim, and with a graceful arc circles back to the Area. A sigh from Mac turns abruptly into a gasp. The stone he spit out was, in fact, a dental filling; his molar howls in pain.

Alston and I are eating rations in wet darkness when we hear singing, followed by a darting light, the tramp of boots, and the beaming face of Gross Tom swinging a six-pack of Budweiser. On his own the North Rim's first chief clerk cashier (aka The CCC) loaded a spare tire into his car and drove to our disabled pumper, then followed our rambling flags in to the fire. In that innocent year it is his position, not ours, that is anomalous. We have to balk at the beer. ("Later, Gross," Alston says, insistently. "Besides, we need more than that to do any good.") Gross Tom is agreeable and waves us away while he assumes mop-up and regales us with the stories of the bust. But it is too good to last. Draper requests someone to help mop up his fire and transport some extra supplies. I agree to go. Alston can return with Gross Tom.

I find Draper's pumper, load a pack frame with water, rations, and sleeping bags, then advance along their flags. The flagging is mediocre; flags are placed at inconsistent heights and at various locales— here on a branch, there on a log, there around an aspen. What can be seen from one direction cannot be seen from another. Some flags, placed on dead branches, have already dropped to the ground. The color selection is poor; there is no flutter to them in the evening winds. I put up copious new flags, then I lose the trail altogether. For perhaps fifteen minutes I try to locate another flag. The night is wet, dark, impenetrable; it swallows the dim light from my headlamp; it is difficult to say whether I stumble onto Kieffer or he onto me. He has been lost for hours. We organize, systematically search the woods, locate a flag, and follow it meticulously to the fire. There is nothing left beyond a huge campfire. Around it Draper and Johnny Begaye are seated, drinking coffee and staring with studied reverie into the flames. No, admits Draper, they didn't need any supplies; they needed help finding Kieffer.

The next day Stiegelmeyer and Howard Yazzie walk into the Buckwheat fire to inspect for smokes and pull the flagging. While they are driving through The Basin, however, Yazzie—who speaks no English—points emphatically at a white cloud along the perimeter of the meadow. "Yeah, yeah," says Stiegelmeyer. "It's a waterdog." Yazzie repeats his gestures. "You know, waterdog . . . W-A-T-E-R-D-O-G." Yazzie is not convinced. He points again. It has rained over the night, and the morning sun works over the moisture; The Basin glows with green and yellow and whitish haze. Oh, hell, why not? Stiegelmeyer decides. It is a good morning for a walk. When they arrive at the scene, a large, deformed ponderosa is burning steadily within a small clearing. They have only the shovel and canteen that Yazzie has carried. The tree is split longitudinally from the top down for perhaps thirty feet. Stiegelmeyer calls for a sawyer. Alston and I veer away from rechecking the 10-7 fire, but before we arrive, Recon 1 reports three smokes. Stiegelmeyer is already at one; Alston and I go to another, and Draper takes two SWFFs to the third. Stiegelmeyer renews his request for help, and Kieffer takes Robert John and commandeers the RPT. At least Robert John speaks English. Mac pauses to listen to fragments of radio traffic as he clears the entrance station en route to the dentist in Kanab, his tooth throbbing like an exposed ember. Please, please, he prays, let that fire on The Dragon be out.

FLAME AND FORTUNE: LIVES OF THE LONGSHOTS

Dawson opens the coffins and removes some pulaskis. We have brought a fresh box of files; with them we put a new edge on both the grub and ax sides and proceed to chop. The helispot on The Dragon is narrow, a swath running east and west across the point that joins body to tail, and the actual landing pad rests precariously on a narrow ridge. If the winds are not too strong and the brush does not inhibit the tail rotor, a landing is usually possible. The manzanita, so brittle that you can sweep it with a baseball bat, is cleared briskly. The locust is more annoyance than threat. The scrub oak, however, requires patience or skill, and after the Dragon trail we have neither. Each original shrub has become a coppice, sprouting several branches with hydralike tenacity; each successive brushing is thus slower than the one that precedes it. Since the ground is rock, not soil, tools dull and tempers sharpen. The morning's trek, however, inspires us to keep at the job: it reminds us that a helo ride is easier than a hike.

When we break for lunch, most of the crew wanders to the site of an old fire camp. A streamer of parachute hangs from a tree. We discover a rusted coffeepot and ration tins—probably from the big fire in the early 1960s, the one for which the helispot was first cut. Tim and I elect to walk the length of The Dragon's body to look at the site of the great burn itself. The map shows clearly that the east rim is relatively straight and level, although most of the fires have occurred on the west rim.

Our hike is a running roll call of past fires, until at last we come to the old Dragon Burn, a scab of brush and black snags. Tim pauses, not only because passage through the brush is nearly impossible but because the intensity of the fire was more savage than anything he is used to seeing. We crash through the burn and shortly afterward come to where The Dragon's neck joins its shoulders. I can see the scar of the Dragon Head fire, where at Forest Service insistence the Park ordered a B-17 to seal off the fire with slurry. The scene is haunted by voices and flames. I cannot see the land without seeing the fires and cannot recall fires without recalling fire crews.

Kent paces fitfully in the cache. Everyone has gone to a smoke except him and Tyson, the one remaining SWFF, and the only consolation is the thought that a couple of the crews will probably return this evening with a lot of work and little overtime to show for the day. Then the report comes in via Scenic Airlines: there is a snag fire on The Dragon, where the body joins the neck. Overtime. Kent and Tyson are instantly away in the Three-quarter Ton.

They hike the scrambled trail in the midafternoon heat, pause at the helispot for handtools, and push on across the central mesa. As they pass through the old Burn, they slow to a crawl. Dying thunderstorms enflame the western horizon and immerse Sublime and the

Hindu Amphitheater in shadow. At last they break out of the brush; the sun is setting with grim insistence, and they climb out on a rock at the end of the mesa, where the neck begins, just in time to watch a final puff of smoke rise from a single burned-out juniper a mile beyond them on the rocky neck. The Noose fire. Without ropes, pitons, carabiners, there is no way they can even reach the site. There can be no hazard pay. There is no longer a fire.

In darkness they fight their way back through the old Burn, recross the length of The Dragon, and stumble into the helispot, where they extract a couple of paper sleeping bags from the coffins. They are too tired to make even a cooking fire. They scavenge a handful of rations from the stores and selectively feed on fruit and double helpings of crackers. The salt, Kent thinks. I crave the salt.

For three or four months we will live, work, and talk together and fraternize with almost no one else. We are infatuated with our comradery, and it is exclusive to the North Rim. We know one another only as members of the fire crew. We acquire nontransferable nicknames. The North Rim is our world, and its concerns—and its concerns only—are ours. Anything else is, in a profound sense, metaphysics. The life cycle of a seasonal firefighter is so brief that there is little room for much else. Dana promised to rout the pattern in wood: "Your first year you learn. Your second year you gripe. Your third year you have fun." There is no fourth year.

Within limits, our identity is ours to make. We dispatch ourselves. We outfit ourselves. We train ourselves. We name ourselves. From the Park there is little leadership. What really defines us is fire. Fires solve all problems: fires make everything possible. Without fires our bravura seems ridiculous, the fire cache a ghetto, and outposts like The Dragon a kind of hallucinatory Ultima Thule of the North Rim. Yet our relationship to fire is far from simple or unmediated.

Nature can claim some of the responsibility. Our lives are regulated by the capriciousness of lightning. You can't program or manage lightning fire as you can reconstruct a road. For careerists fire is a dead end—or worse, a random potlatch of feast and famine. In desperation, one slow pre-monsoon day, Stiegelmeyer makes a lightning button out of a discarded sheet of plywood and a knob from a

junked chest of drawers and places it in the Fire Pit. Becker adds a
cord and plug. "Press for fire."

The Park Service, too, intervenes. It can assert values more important than our relationship to fire, and it can reform its fire policy. Both
happen. At Grand Canyon we are caught between the move to make
parks into "pleasant places for people" and the rush to restore natural
fire. We are unable to relate to the visitor and unable to control our
relationship to fire. We live in isolation, in a state of personal prerogative and political helplessness. What meaning we gain from our lives
as Longshots we give ourselves.

As we amble along the Rim, Tim, a rookie, hums a few bars from
"The Ballad of Joe Alston." It is one of the classic Fence songs, a
broadside of a Kristofferson song, "Billy Dee," about a drug addict
who overdoses.

> Joe Alston was just a kid when he turned FCA,
> Fooling with some foolish things he could have turned away.
> But he had to try to satisfy some debts he couldn't name,
> Driven into fires by his need for hazard pay.

It is a lively song, with a fun, hustling tune. Alston hovers around the
cache, "getting by on getting high by working overtime." His is a life
of flame and fortune. Ask any firefighter what he likes about the job
and he will say, "The money"—that and the action. Fires are rated by
the overtime they ring up, and no one on the crew would publicly
declare otherwise.

Yet "The Ballad of Joe Alston" is a cautionary tale, too. Alston's
greed was "bigger than a body's ought to be," and the fire he got was
"bigger than the one he hoped to find." Alston ODs on OT.

> Yesterday they found him underneath a fallen pine,
> Reaching for the shovel, Lord, he'd used to build his line.
> Some folks called it careless, Lord; others blamed the tree.
> We just shook our heads and gave poor Joe his HDP.

The truth, unsaid, is that no one would do this for the money alone.
An unskilled maintenance laborer makes a far greater hourly wage.
Fern feelers rack up overtime without spitting their lungs out in

smoke. Nor does the action translate into career advancement. A ranger, even a fee collector, has a brighter future in the National Park Service than anyone on the fire crew. The experience has to be valued for other reasons. Its real flame is the unique, the initiatory fire, and for a true Longshot it is burned into memory. Its fortune is the turn of fate that brought us here and prompted us, individually and as a crew, to see it through. In most lives, in most places, that flame is hidden. On The Dragon there is nowhere to hide.

Tim ends the song with a cheerful flourish, while I point south. There is no more time to gawk or chatter. Storm clouds are building rapidly. Tim and I double back and half-jog to the helispot as lightning and rain meet on the Rim.

FIRE ON THE RIM

The camp is under assault, and there is no particular safety at the helispot. Before leaving Crystal Ridge, the whole party emptied our firepacks of everything except our lunches and canteens, so no one has so much as a plastic garbage bag to make into a poncho. The SWFFs crawl under some low brush and ponderosa reproduction. Dawson scrambles over the Rim in a futile search for a rock overhang. Lightning forks like a lizard's tongue. Dave and The Kid run to the coffins, as bright as metal scales, dump out tools and cubitainers, and climb in. It is Dave's third season, and he is tired of working small fires for small pay on a Rim removed from everything. He sometimes joins the rangers on patrol, but there are no openings for new seasonals. He has developed a phobia about the helo and refuses to fly. A smoker, he runs the hill only under coercion. And now he is caught in a rainstorm on The God-forsaken Dragon. Before he climbs in Dave yells something to everyone and no one about waking him up when it's all over. The Kid whoops defiantly, and as the lids close, their muffled metallic laughter mixes with the rumblings of thunder.

The intersection of Canyon and Plateau is everywhere unexpected, unnatural, and violent. The Rim does not integrate two systems: it thrusts them together. Some accept that experience, some deny it, most draw back from the brink, relegating it to the status of a viewpoint not a point of view. On The Dragon that experience is magnified because The Dragon is pure Rim. Once there you can't retreat easily to Plateau or Canyon. Accordingly, some hide The Dragon in bureaucratic papers. Others avoid The Dragon altogether as meaningless, disturbing, eccentric. Most people have never heard of it—and will never hear of it. But as Longshots we have to come, because part of the violence of the Rim is fire. On The Dragon you cannot merely observe: you have to act.

The rain ends, and hail pummels the helispot. Hailstones crash mercilessly on the coffins with a roar that deafens. Dave and The Kid try to push open the lids, without success; in slamming shut, the outer latches have caught and held. They begin to shout and pound on the sides of the coffins. No one moves. Everyone is soaked and chilled, and earsplitting thunder still rings in our heads, but the spectacle has given us something to think about besides the storm. The SWFFs watch the drama intently. From time to time Henry John and John Paul exchange words.

After half an hour the storm lets up. Sunlight makes the air thick with moisture and the pungent smell of oak, locust, and cliff rose. Everyone returns to the open ridge of the helispot, bright with colored chert and ivory limestone rocks that have been washed by the rain. Dave and The Kid continue to bang and yell; after a while the sounds from the coffins cease. The SWFFs shake their heads. The storm has delayed our departure, and we will probably return very late to the fire cache. We gather our tools and packs and open the coffins. Someone jokes that the storm brought a couple of sleepers to The Dragon. Dave and The Kid, both pale, say nothing. We dump the wet tools and cubitainers back into the coffins.

Dave hoists his pack and says to everyone and to no one, "This place is fucked." Tim looks back to where he and I plunged into The Dragon and pauses. "You-know," Henry John confides, smiling. "This-place-pretty-good-all-right. This-place-have-fires. There-are-many-fires-on-Dragon."

Twice we approach and have to back away under full power. The helo returns to the Area, unloads Henry, and this time lands at the Dragon helispot. The fire is located along the western Rim, cross-

grained to the surface drainage; Joe and I flag a route at a half trot. Even as we reach the fire perimeter, 210 deposits another pair of Longshots and Kent directs a caravan of vehicles, crammed with reserves, to the Dragon trailhead. Adrenaline flashes through us like lightning.

The fire burns erratically in a shallow valley along the Rim. Joe and I dump our packs, grab shovels and loop canteens around our shoulders, and begin a recon of the fire. Within minutes the Longshots at the helispot will arrive; soon afterward the helo will shuttle others in furious rhythm. If the fire had not been reported so late—well after 1700 hours, the crew scattered and outfitted in everything from gym shorts to dress suits—we could have ferried a full complement of firefighters. But now there will be time only to transport the regulars before the twilight and squirrelly winds (downdrafts from lingering thunderheads) force a halt. Gilbert and The Kid reach our impromptu camp. Another shuttle is within sight of the helispot. Joe and I hurry to complete our circuit. (Joe has the stamina and build of a power-wagon, but he is more aquatic than terrestrial and walks like an elephant seal. From time to time, he pauses to search for the source tree and further slows our reconnaissance.) Henry John and Kieffer land. The fire front advances like surf, with winds occasionally whipping it into flaming whitecaps. Before 210 departs, I remind him to bring in supplies for the evening—headlamps and batteries, rations, sleeping bags, water and fedcos. The storm breaks up, and a lowering sun transforms cloud fragments into great tongues of flaming orange and yellow vapor. Over the Park radio Hulick and McLaren debate the value of sending overhead to The Dragon and decide against it. The fire is ours.

As new arrivals reach camp, they go into one of two crews— SWFFs to one sector, Longshots to the other. The two squads should converge to seal off the fire between two massive limestone outcrops, ribs from The Dragon's flanks. The work goes slowly. The first of Kent's irregulars straggles into camp. A fee collector collapses under a tree and refuses to rise. A thirsty ranger, on a lieu day from the Inner Canyon, grabs a quart canteen and swallows chain saw oil. A fern feeler stares openmouthed and paralyzed. For an instant the fire threatens to surge through the unsecured middle between the two *crews until Henry John rallies the SWFFs and the fireline is held. Gilbert reports that there is smoke over the Rim.*

The pace slacks. It is our largest fire of the summer and my first season as foreman. I reorganize the squads. The SWFFs retire to the north flank, where they tidy the scratch line and begin to chop at a burning snag; they share a single pulaski and let everyone take a few swings in turn. The south flank goes to the Longshots. They dabble in line improvement, but, the rush over—adrenaline draining away, the flames subsiding with the encroaching night—they tend to wander curiously about the fire. The quiet middle I assign to Kent's mob, who stand and sit in stuporous amazement. Two Longshots return to the helispot with instructions to haul the supplies that the last shuttle was scheduled to deliver. A handful of the reserves also retire to the helispot for paper sleeping bags and canteens; there is no point in countermanding the impulse. At 2200 hours Kieffer and The Kid return with steaks, salad, potatoes, fruit punch—a banquet prepared by the Lodge and raced to the North Rim heliport in time for the final ferry. When the meal is finished, the crews begin to sleep in shifts. Joe and I will remain awake and patrol the line.

The fire is about ten acres in size, more or less confined within a shallow bowl and anchored at the Rim by immense limestone pillars. There is some fire apparently over the Rim between them, but that should burn itself out in lighter fuels and rocks. Joe positions himself on the north pillar. I slump to the base of a ponderosa near the south corner. Cool air seeps into the valley. Suddenly my arms and legs ache; sweat chills; despite dinner my stomach feels hollow; my mouth is bitter with ash; my feet feel cold and clammy, too small for my boots; my gloves are stiff with sweat and grime. I've reached the edge, I think. There is nothing more. A preternatural stillness settles over the scene, as though here, at the Rim, geologic time has been arrested. An hour, maybe two, passes. Then Joe suggests quietly over the radio that I look at the Rim.

The horizon is aglow. Flame soars like miniature solar flares, and it seems as though the whole of Hindu Amphitheater has erupted into fire. The slop-over did not die out, but crept silently under the brush, desiccating the overstory, and now races upslope through the canopy. I wake the crews. If the fire comes over the Rim, it will pass right through fire camp. A surge of flame rushes toward the Rim, but it enters the burned area and expires. More will follow. Of its source I can see nothing, but I know that the fire emerges from the Canyon depths, full of an instinctive fury at once ancient and unquenchable. It is doubtful that the fireline on the Rim can, unaided, hold it back.

We gather for a quick conference. It is suicidal to attack directly the fire in the Canyon. The Dragon fire has become our worst-case scenario. True Canyon fires are uncontrollable but quickly burn themselves out in flashy fuels far distant from the Rim. Plateau fires are messy and uninteresting, their infrequent eruptions into crown fire an event equally of calculated rage and of improbability. But to have a Rim fire escape into the Canyon, where it can be renewed and from where it can rise time and again, this is a uniquely North Rim condition. It is the fire we dread yet anticipate, at once both a nightmare and a privilege. Sooner or later we will each of us have to confront it. Most of the irregulars want to pull back, strip the camp, relocate to another time, another place, but the veteran Longshots know that there is no real retreat except to abandon The Dragon altogether. The fire would then sweep the whole mesa. Kent, The Kid, Gilbert—all want to make a stand at the Rim. Joe will try anything. "OK," I decide. "The Rim it is."

For nearly an hour the Rim becomes a frenzy of men and noise. Saws whine and cough, trees fall in crashes, handtools scrape and chip in atonal splendor, radios and voices shout over the roar of flames. Not once but several times fire rushes out of the Canyon in long, impulsive streaks. We apply, in retaliation, every particle of our experience and training. Longshots and SWFFs stand along the Rim in macabre silhouette as flames flash from the depths. Our faces are flushed with light, our backs etched in black. There is no shadow zone. The line holds, and shortly before a false dawn most of the crew retire to sleep.

Yet the fire is far from over. So long as smoldering continues in the Canyon, the scene can be repeated. The fire could even creep around the limestone ribs and outflank our Rim firelines. The fire in the Canyon will have to be suppressed. When they wake, I release Kent's mob and send them back to Crystal Ridge. Then we begin the retardant. A B-17 tries to drop by passing over The Dragon, then releasing a salvo along the Rim. Its first drop is premature and drenches our fire camp with two thousand gallons of pink slurry. A few subsequent releases make their way into the Canyon, but coverage is spotty and selective, with much of the retardant dissipated before it reaches the burn. The fire cannot be controlled from above, certainly not by anything as abstract as an air tanker. We will have to descend from the Rim and attack it at its sources.

With fedcos and handtools we spend the afternoon over the edge— careful to travel within the burned-out swaths, wary of accidents as we try to pick our way across talus slopes made slick with slurry. That night we sleep on the Rim in slushy paper bags. The next morning there are still smokes visible below, and we descend again. We are all smoke-happy, half brain-dead from being whipsawed by adrenaline and exhaustion, fatigued by constant vigilance and decision. But then it ends, and I call for a helo to take us home.

The first flight is scheduled to arrive at 1800 hours. We collect our tools, burn what is left of the paper bags, gather garbage, and drag our gear to the helispot. I pause for a last survey. This is one fire on which none of us can afford to overlook any lingering smokes.

The SWFFs will go first; if a snafu develops, the Longshots are better suited for another night on The Dragon. When the helo arrives, it holds a surprise—a meal from the Lodge. We open containers and distribute the food in a free-for-all, even as parties continue their shuttle to the Area. We are ravenous, overwhelmed by appetite. There are french fries that we gobble in greedy fistfuls. There is a layer cake, which Joe cuts with a pulaski. The Kid discovers small steaks and a salad. We devour both with our hands. Then we realize that the containers have several compartments. Under the french fries are condiments. Under the steaks are rolls with which to make sandwiches. Under the salad are plates, plastic silverware, packets of salt and pepper. The order of discovery, however, has dictated the order of consumption. As the last of the SWFFs departs, we laugh at the thought of having to be resocialized.

Seated on his firepack, his cheeks crammed with cake, Joe asks if anyone ever located the source tree. I tell him no. The whine-whop of the helo approaches. I tell him that we'll probably never know, that it is most likely that the source tree burned out before we ever got to The

Dragon. The helo circles the LZ, and Gilbert tosses some dirt in the air to indicate wind direction. Besides, I think, we don't need a source tree to know what caused the fire. The Dragon caused the fire. Joe and Gilbert and Kent begin strapping tools to the side-baskets of the helo. The source didn't matter; only the fire on the Rim did.

FLIGHT OF THE SWFFs; OR, TOMMIE BEGAYE DID *WHAT?*

We requisition a SWFF crew from the Forest Service dispatcher with a fire order, just as we would a case of pulaskis or an air tanker. The SWFFs are hired as temporaries, a notch below seasonals, and they are paid a flat hourly rate. When we work projects, the SWFFs make more money than Park Service seasonals. On fires, lacking premium pay, they make less. They are not issued government driver's licenses and do not use power equipment like chain saws. A typical squad of six will range in age from the early twenties to the early sixties. At first the crews are Hopis recruited out of Second Mesa, until the Hopis withdraw completely from the SWFF program; we hear rumors that the last Hopi crew dissolved after they shot their crew boss in a Flagstaff bar. The proper explanation may be that it has become more profitable to work tourists than fires. The new SWFF crews are Navajos from Rock Point. The adjustment is not easy. The Hopis were accommodating. At lunch, if one of the crew told a funny story in Hopi, someone would translate it into English so we could join in the laughs. The Hopis consider the Navajos barbaric, and both look down on the Apaches. A few of the Navajo SWFFs will talk freely with us, but most will speak only when necessary. How much they know is uncertain—and at their discretion to reveal. Fortunately, project work and fires demand little dialogue; a shovel speaks a universal language. Gradually, we work out the terms of a treaty.

The SWFF crew is handled as a unit. If there is a serious infraction by one member, the entire crew is released. If a drinking problem develops, everyone is sent home. In return, we send SWFF crewmen to fires just as we do FCAs. We house them and feed them. There are only two other rules: all SWFF lunches include Tabasco sauce, and FCAs will not lend money to SWFFs.

The SWFF program is designed to support project fires, not projects like the Fence; but there are provisions for keeping crews on standby, and we retain a crew under those terms. The normal tour of duty is about two months. The assignment at first puzzles the SWFFs, who expect to be sent to a fire camp or fireline. Some feel vaguely swindled; there are few deeds worth bragging about when one splits wood or rakes up pine needles or splices the Fence. But the pay is good, most of the SWFF crews stay, and often robust friendships evolve between the FCAs and SWFFs. We are the only group with which the SWFFs interact. They are never assimilated into the North Rim except through their joint work with the fire crew. They have no uniform and usually look as if they just fell off a Brahman bull. One night they go to a dance at the Lodge still wearing their hard hats.

Misunderstandings are legendary. Nearly everyone, it seems, is named John, and last names seem to consist solely of Tsotsie, Yazzie, and Begaye. The distinction between the National Park Service and the U.S. Forest Service seems to be untranslatable, and confusions, real or contrived, are endless. We-want-a-fireshirt, they say. Forest-Service-gives-us-fireshirts. No, they don't, we reply. They-let-us-keep-shirts. No, they don't. They don't even issue them to you. They-give-cigarettes. Why-doesn't-Park-Service-give-cigarettes? Nobody gets cigarettes. It becomes apparent that the point of confusion is itself a bargaining ploy; in perverse ways the cultural disjunction is something to be exploited. When John Tsotsie and I are tossing garbage into the dry dump, he picks up an orange pylon kept permanently in the pickup and stares questioningly. I shake my head. "Keep it," I say. He nods and throws it into the pit. When Kent explains to John Peshtony how to get to the fire, John nods sagely in agreement, then crashes into the brush 180 degrees from where he is sent. A nodding head means a nodding head. The spectacle of an FCA and a SWFF—barely able to communicate, staggering through the woods with overburdened firepacks and fistfuls of shovels and pulaskis, trying to find a fire that Recon 1 has mislocated—is one of the enduring images of the North Rim.

We learn survival Navajo. We pick up expressions for "fire," "water," "hello," "fuck you," "bullshit," and "bread." *T'óó baa'ih,* "no good," becomes a universal antidote to "OK." The green pumper is *t'óó baa'ih,* the Sheep Shed is *t'óó baa'ih,* the box lunches are *t'óó baa'ih,* the Fence is *t'óó baa'ih,* Big Bob is *t'óó baa'ih.* We have a *t'óó baa'ih* fire. The SWFFs name Stone *Shash,* "bear." They call Draper *Gáagii,* "raven." They name Becker *Tsishch'ili,* "curly hair." The rangers are *bilagáana,* "white men." Williams, a Hopi hired for the regular fire crew, they call *Kiis'áanii,* which they refuse to translate. The expression for "asshole," *nijilchii',* is indistinguishable to Anglo ears from *ńdishchíí',* the word for "pine." It becomes the source for endless bilingual puns. There-are-ants-*ńdishchíí'.* He-is-lazy, he-has-no-*nijilchii'.* The confusion is especially useful in talking about their boss, and it is doubly diabolical because they get us to do their punning. We threaten to take away their Tabasco sauce if the puns do not end. When something is agreeable, the SWFFs say—accenting every syllable evenly—that it is pretty-good-all-right. A coffee break at the Inn is pretty-good-all-right. The last fire bust was pretty-good-all-right.

After a fire or two together, shared experiences partially overcome the unshared. I try to pair up those FCAs and SWFFs who have developed some comradery. One morning the SWFFs show up wearing cords around their waists. The crew boss, Johnny Begaye, tells us solemnly that there are ghosts and advises us to ward them off by wearing a charm. We cut strands of parachute cord, and for the next two days, until we are told that the danger has passed, we wear strands from our belt loops. At night the SWFFs sometimes sit stoically in chairs outside the Lodge front door. One evening Stiegelmeyer troops past them time and again on his way between the saloon and the men's room. With each pass the SWFFs jeer and twist his name into such contortions as "Sticklepickle" and "Stink-lemeyer." Finally Stiegelmeyer can stand it no more. He turns with mock ferocity on his tormentors. "You, me—no more friends!" he shouts, gesticulating wildly. "Broken arrow!" The SWFFs are silenced.

But SWFF stories are not. They flock around the Rim like ravens. They became an integral part of fire crew lore. Orange and yellow pickup trucks, oversized mirrors sprouting from the doors, reeking of Johnny Cash cassette tapes; John Paul, silent for weeks, walking up to Hulick at 1000 hours one morning, pointing at his watch, and announcing, "Fifteen-minute-break"; Kee Yazzie, champion Brahman bull rider, climbing atop the hardline hose reel in order to ride it like a mechanical bull along the fire roads; SWFF self-mockery of their presumed knowledge of natural phenomena—this-tree-has-thick-bark, there-will-be-a-long-winter; pour-water-on-a-horned-toad-and-it-will-bring-rain; follow-deer-trail-to-fire. No fire story is complete without a bizarre cross-cultural misunderstanding that reduces us all to parity.

But everything is not pretty-good-all-right. The dramatic expansion of Forest Service hotshot crews, the rapid increase in North Rim seasonals, prohibitions against keeping SWFFs on standby for more than two weeks, some slow fire seasons, logistical hassles when the North Rim Inn closes, the reformation in Park Service fire policy, and the subsidence of their sole allies, the fire crew—all cause the SWFF program to fall into disrepair. The association loses its charm as well as its practicality. For the FCAs the North Rim is home; for the SWFFs it is a remote and alien land, a stay justified only by the prospects for money and action. From the Rim they can see two of the four sacred mountains—the San Francisco Peaks and Navajo Mountain—but seeing is not believing. They never say they are homesick; they just begin to drink. At the second infraction the whole crew is sent back to Rock Point in presumed disgrace. Often they thank us.

The stories remain. Once, after they have left for the season, Alston decides to visit some of the old SWFF crew. He stops by the trading post at Rock Point and asks about Henry John and Tommie Deshennie Begaye. Why do you wish to find them? Who are you? "My name is Alston. I worked with these men on the North Rim. On a fire crew. They were SWFFs." Alston? The Alston who backed a pumper up a hill by double-winching from pine trees? The Alston who made a cigarette out of notebook paper and Prince Albert tobacco? A crowd gathers. Alston is besieged by questions. He is a celebrity. We are all celebrities. The SWFFs have carried to Rock Point stories about the crazy FCAs they worked with on the North Rim. Through long winters Rock Point comes to know every nuance of North Rim geography, every choice episode of fire history, every inscrutable quirk of FCA personality.

*   *   *

Joe and Tom are at the saloon when the patrol ranger finds them and tells them about the fire visible on Neal Hill. A tourist has reported it. "A hundred feet from the road. By the picnic area. I think it is only one tree." Slowly, as through parting clouds, Alston contemplates the situation. How many beers has he had? The equivalent of only a couple cans, he thinks. Who is available? Tom and Francis John, both of whom were with him this morning on the Atokotwo fire. And Hulett, an off-duty ranger, who had asked to be sent to a fire this summer. "Hulett," he calls across the saloon. "Want to come with us on a fire?" "Love to," says Hulett, staring back at him, his speech slightly slurred. "But I gotta wait for Joe. I promised I'd go with Joe next time." No matter. With beery magnanimity, Joe invites everyone in the saloon to join them—wranglers, tourists, the Lodge nurse.

They all are at the fire when I drive up, having returned from a small burn and suspicious about the rumored circumstances of the Neal fire. The fire groupies must go. With the pumper headlights glaring at the snag's furious trunk, I ask Joe if he is competent to handle the fire. "Piece of cake." He smiles. "Just drop the snag and hose it down. Be home before midnight."

They use the pumper to cool off the base sufficiently to put a saw into it. Joe cuts, Tom spots, and Francis John—resplendent in his famous Banana Hat, a deformed hard hat painted psychedelic yellow—watches from a distant side. But there is rotten wood in the bole; the tree suddenly cracks, splinters, and swings uncontrollably to one side. Joe scrambles to pull the saw out of the cut before the tree claims and crushes it. Like a flaming sword, the snag crashes against a leaner, hesitates, then rushes in a broad pivot to the ground. It heads directly for Francis John. The snag lights the scene with oranges and shadows. "Run, Francis! Run!" screams Tom. But Francis John is already running, hopping, vaulting across the wet forest debris. He pauses to look back at the accelerating snag. "Francis, run!" yell Joe and Tom together. Francis stumbles and falls to the ground. His hard hat bounces stonily among logs, while the snag, like a flaming meteor, sweeps past several feet above him and thunders into a grove of ponderosa. For an instant, darkness returns, sucked back like air in a vacuum, and they can see nothing. They peer with their head-

lamps. Francis John rises, while an enormous grin spreads across his face. "Francis, are you all right?"

Francis John picks up the Banana Hat, places it on his head, and with arms akimbo proclaims, "Faster-than-speeding-bullet!"

TRAIL'S END

When we return from the Dragon fire, we crash, fall, plummet, and just plain collapse into sleep. The next day we work in the fire cache. There are packs to replenish and tools to sharpen and stories to tell. It has been a good fire. When Dave returns with the Dragon flaggin', there is a roar of approval. Joe pushes the Lightning Button. Everyone adds up his overtime and makes plans for a raucous night at the Lodge.

This will be the last big fire fought on The Dragon. Even as the fire crew struggles to integrate The Dragon into the North Rim fire program, others—wilderness purists, amateur biologists, cracker-barrel philosophers of parks, managerial rangers—struggle to disengage it. Park Service policy and enlightened public opinion consider fire control on The Dragon not only unnecessary but immoral; they argue that fire suppression is an alien culture intruding into an area it cannot understand and arresting processes it cannot hope to defeat, that firefighting is not a gutsy job but a tragically misguided commitment. A bewildering confusion of moral energies concentrates into an activity that had always demanded, and got, unambiguous purposes.

None of the architects of the new policy has ever been to The Dragon; most have never worked in fire. The Dragon becomes the moral equivalent of the Fence. Its philosophers can conceive but cannot—or will not personally—execute it. They never learn the patience of mop-up, never complete the paperwork that would put The Dragon officially and finally into a natural fire zone. Instead, they philosophize and manipulate Park politics and they talk. As a result the trail deteriorates but must still be used for access; the helispot overgrows with brush but must still deliver crews; and every fire on The Dragon inspires a cacophony of philosophical discourse.

No matter how small its commitment to fire control, until it can translate belief into policy and policy into practice, the Park is compelled to suppress every ignition. Wilderness fire is an idea whose time has come, but Grand Canyon, it seems, is timeless. Signs of the unraveling are everywhere.

The SWFFs experience it first. There have been drinking problems with some of the crew, requests for mutton and fried bread, demands for less Fence and more fires. We try to salvage the last crew by reconstituting it, allowing the three SWFFs who want to stay to return with replacements from Rock Point. But the scheme falls through. Fire control is not critical to the goals of Grand Canyon National Park, and the advantages of a standby SWFF crew are not worth the blossoming managerial headaches. There will be no more SWFF crews. Somehow the word never reaches all the old SWFF crewmen, however, and two days later Robert John shows up outside 176 with his red pickup. No, we explain, the crew is not here. The program has ended. "But-I-am-here," he repeats. Yes, we reply, but you were not to come back. "But," he goes on, "I-am-here. I-have-mutton-and-fried-bread." We're sorry, we say. There is no SWFF crew. There will be no more SWFF crews.

None of that matters tonight. We have been to a fire on The Dragon, and all of us—FCAs and SWFFs—are headed to the saloon to celebrate. Most of the fire crew drive to the Lodge, but I decide to walk, on the theory that it will loosen some stiff joints. The winds huff, warm and dry, out of the Canyon. A deep twilight blue floods the sky. Moonlight transforms stringy stratus clouds into miniature Milky Ways. Roaring Springs Canyon becomes a cubist study of navy blue shadow and ghostly light. On the opposite side of the road walks Tommie Begaye, a moving shadow. We see each other—Tommie, tall at six feet two inches, forever showing photos of his Army tank unit, notorious for pulling a knife on an Inn cook and threatening to slit his throat if he put another cold cheese sandwich in their box lunches; Tommie, who vanished after a night in the saloon, only to be discovered the next morning hung over on the floor of a tour bus stationed in the parking lot. Joe half-jokingly wagers that Tommie will be found dead in an alley within the next five years.

The road is empty of cars. Tommie has missed the pickup that took the rest of the SWFFs to the Lodge and is irritated at having to walk. "This-road-*t'óó bad'ih,*" he yells. He crosses to my side and ostentatiously jogs ahead. I catch up. He runs ahead farther. The wind is dry and crisp. Black asphalt glistens in the moonlight like scales. We trot together along the road, then, where the road turns down a long hill, we dash hell-bent for leather down the slope. Along the Rim we run, shoulder to shoulder, past the ink-black trees, all the way to the Lodge.

CHAPTER SIX

The Basin

THE ARRIVAL OF THE MONSOON is the great divide of summer. Until it arrives the summer has the mounting drama of its anticipation; after it appears, the season must be reconstituted. The extraordinary becomes the expected, and what could only be anticipated now becomes routine. Fires come or don't, but they lack the glow of distant promise. The prospect for really big fires is slight.

Like a burning snag on the Rim, fire season is poised to fall one way or another. If there is too little moisture, there will be no storms and no lightning. If there is too much, fire season will wash away. But if the balance is right, the fire load continues to increase. In a normal year July has more fires than June, and August more than July. The fires move away from the Rim—the points—and test the interior. If they are viewed synoptically, there is a logic to the surges and retreats of the monsoon moisture. But the North Rim is so high and so strangely positioned between the Mogollon Rim (and San Francisco Peaks) to the south and the High Plateaus to the north that it is a local anomaly. Its weather is constantly unsettled.

So it is with the Longshots. We return to old jobs, like the fireroads, and rework them with more care. We settle into a dispatching routine for isolated fires and busts. Crewmen actually accept lieu days—take time to wash clothes; drive into Kanab, Cedar City, St. George, and Flagstaff and shop for groceries and clothes; travel to tourist overlooks, other parks, or Lake Powell; or just plain sleep. The curious begin to explore sites of the Rim, such as The Basin, not associated with fire. The fire triangle—rigorous and compelling—is momentarily broken.

* * *

They can barely discern the dilapidated sign, W-1F, and neither of them has ever journeyed up the old fireroad, now only a scrawl of blue ink on their fire maps; but a smoke has been reported two to three miles away, where the meadows are overrun by dense mixed conifer. Though Recon 1 still patrols the North Rim, dodging the remaining storm cells, they inwardly smirk in the knowledge that they were the first out of the cache, that they got the fire. As they drive over W-1, they listen to the radio while the others, two by two, are dispatched to new fires. Kent and Kee Yazzie practically drive to a fire on W-1D. The Kid and Tom can see their fire from the entrance road. Joe and Johnny Begaye steer a pumper through open forest off E-5 into a smoke.

They hurry to load their gear while late-afternoon shadows close in upon them. Dave hefts a chain saw over his shoulder, allowing it to rest partly on his firepack. Ralph has his firepack piled as high as a sherpa's with sleeping bags and canteens, two shovels inserted into special slots. They attach headlamps to their hard hats and set off down rutted traces of the old fireroad. Darkness crowds in upon them; a dense forest and residual ridges of storm cloud blot out a sunset; the storm has left everything wet, and the night will be cold. They walk up a narrowing ravine, part meadow, part forest. Over the radio they listen while Kent announces that his fire is out, that he will return to the cache within the hour. Then the radio goes blank; they have entered a hole and can neither hear nor call out. After tramping nearly an hour and a half, they smell smoke. Ralph spots a glimmer of light by the old ruts. They hurry to it. The active fire is about a yard in diameter, no more than a couple of branches and a deep mound of smoldering needles.

They are too far in to hike out. Dave locates a good campsite, then scoops up the flaming branches with his shovel and carries the entire fire to their camp. While Dave stokes the timid fire, Ralph tears into the plastic garbage bag that covers their sleeping bags. To their chagrin the two bags they brought are really one bag, a fur-lined military model used for casualty evacuations. For a moment they are stunned. They can take turns sleeping and keeping the fire alive, or they both can crawl into the bag. The fire is feeble—it flickers like a candle in the cold—and they decide to share the bag. Dave swallows the last of his canteen water and complains of its taste. Ralph smells the canteen and asks where Dave got the water. "From the pumper, of course," he replies. Disgusted, Ralph explains that before leaving the Area, he poured into the slip-on a bottle of Firewater, a wetting agent—soap. Dave will be lubed for the night.

When they return, the honeymoon bag is retired.

THE NORTH RIM TURKEY FARM

Kent flies out the door of the cab even as Tom struggles to brake the powerwagon. A routine drive along the Sublime Road has surprised a small flock of turkeys. Kent ignores the young turkeys, screeching crazily in the grass, and flings himself toward the adult. The bird utters its high-pitched scream and hurries into the trees. Tall and rawboned, Kent pursues the bird with giant strides. The turkey weaves skillfully through trees and understory, amazingly agile. Kent's step is longer, but the turkey has less weight to carry. No one has ever caught a turkey before. Kent charges the final few yards to the ridge top while the bird screams. Suddenly the turkey turns around and flies directly at Kent's face. The adrenaline drains out of him, and he collapses on his back. The turkey watches, now silent, from a tree branch. While he waits for Kent to return, Tom searches the road, then plucks out a round cobble and places it in the front seat. "Next time," he advises Kent, "use a turkey rock."

Before long each vehicle has a small nest of rounded stones. The idea is to conk a bird before it has the time to enter the woods or at least to scare it out into the open meadow, where perhaps it can be run down. No one has struck a bird, but the theory seems sound. Adding to and sorting out the piles of turkey rocks become an ongoing obsession. Not until autumn will turkeys congregate into major throngs; but small flocks are commonly surprised along those fire-roads which traverse meadows, and with the roads cleared, chasing turkeys becomes a source of entertainment during long drives.

After a while it is decided that a stone is too small and feeble an instrument. One rain-swept day, Stiegelmeyer uncovers in the Area an ancient box of replacement teeth for council tools, a kind of rake.

Each tooth has the shape of a triangle with the long point cut off. When the base of the tooth is bolted into the rake, three edges, all sharpened, are available for cutting and scraping. Each base has two holes; when four teeth are bolted one to another, a kind of Frisbee results, with a square hole in the middle and a perimeter of unbroken, deadly edges. It is promptly dubbed the Turkey Terrorizer, and a half dozen weapons are fashioned. Inspired, Stiegelmeyer raids the ranger weapons cache for silhouette targets. On the reverse side he draws the silhouette of a turkey, then surrounds it with concentric rings and attaches it to the butt of a log. Turkey Terrorizers fly through the air.

It is quickly apparent, however, that the Turkey Terrorizer is more of a menace to its user than to its intended victim. It is our best, our cleverest, weapon, but it cannot be used without risk. Since the Park will hardly condone them, it also becomes necessary to hide them in the back panels of the pumpers rather than on the front seat, thus removing them from instant access—without which they are worthless. For both reasons the crew bans Turkey Terrorizers, and middens of new turkey rocks reappear.

Against other varieties of turkey, however, we cannot protect ourselves. Within a few years the character and caliber of Park managers change dramatically. In the aftermath of Mission 66—a massive, ten-year construction program in the parks that concluded in 1966—rangers were hired off civil service rolls by the score, few with any experience in parks or natural resources. And, in keeping with the premise of the Leopold Report that the parks should be "vignettes of Primitive America," the Park Service sheds its foresters for wildlife biologists, its fire officers for resource "managers." The suddenness of the change is astounding and generation-specific. For a while all five mid-level managers on the North Rim have the same birth year, 1939.

Big Bob approaches the fire cache, flicking the red handle of a busted sledge that he uses as a swagger stick. It is apparent that he has decided, as he does from time to time, to assert his authority over the fire crew. He calls everyone to the Fire Pit, while he stands outside the door and fidgets with the stick. "You are getting sloppy," he informs us in a high-pitched voice. "A taut ship is a happy ship. A clean ship is a taut ship." We are to wash the vehicles regularly. We are to wear clean fireshirts. "Save one," he tells us, "as a dress shirt." He pauses, struggling to remember the rest of his litany of abuses. "And, oh, yes," he brightens. "Clean out the vehicles on the inside, too. Why, the other day I opened the cab of the blue pumper and a pile of rocks tumbled out." He rouses himself to loud indignation. "Why do we have rocks in the cabs anyway?" he shouts, reddening.

"Because," says Joe in a stage whisper, "you can never find a good rock when you need one."

The helo lands, picks up Dash and Pferd, then circles the fire and takes a bearing from the smoke to the sinkhole. The sinkhole is large, but old and shallow, deep within the Twilight Zone. The fire is about an acre in size, and it grows slowly outward along a ragged front through dense mixed conifer. Once they land, Pferd and Dash begin flagging up the ridge to the fire. We shuttle more men, two to a load, until everyone and everything we will need are on hand. The fire is quickly contained. Burning is patchy; the fire has gnawed through heavy duff, leapfrogged into punky logs, occasionally flared in thickets of young fir. Large logs and rocks mix with dense mats of humus. Our fireline requires that we dig small trenches through half-rotted debris, but otherwise the work proceeds quickly until mop-up. Mop-up will be unbearably tedious.

If we had slip-ons, we could extinguish the Twilight fire that evening. But we are probably one and a half air miles from the nearest road, and there is not the slightest prospect of driving an engine anywhere. We can't lay hose much beyond the Kanabownits meadows. If the sinkhole were a pond, we could draft from it. It is not, and there is nothing to haul from it except dirt and wildflowers.

With the fireline emplaced, we snack on rations and discuss the delay in helo availability, the tragicomic diversion of Simms buckets from fire suppression to sewage disposal, the priority airlift of raw sewage each week out of Phantom Ranch to the treatment plant on the South Rim. Surely, Dash reasons, the same techniques could bring water to the Twilight Zone. The scheme that develops requires a staging area (with the water truck) along the Sublime Road from which cubitainers can be filled, then loaded into cargo nets and slung into the fire. By using long leadlines, the nets can be deposited near the fire despite the tall timber. Three slings could build up a reservoir of water equivalent to the capacity of a slip-on unit.

The idea almost works. The pilot, however, is unfamiliar with the long leadline; the net of cubitainers sways precariously over the proposed drop zone until it snags in some trees, breaks free, and is finally punched off in near panic. That ends the sling loads. Still, we have water.

We fill fedcos, organize into two-man teams, and mop up. We dry-mop where possible and wet-mop where necessary. By midafternoon most of the smokes are gone and we stage a mock baseball game with a broken pulaski handle for a bat and pine cones for balls. There are no more smokes. We arrange for a helo pickup around 1800 hours and haul our gear to the sinkhole and munch on rations until 210 arrives.

We lie on the grass, using our packs and bags for pillows. Dash finds a long branch, ties some flagging to it, and plants it to the side of the sinkhole, a primitive wind sock. The sinkhole is dry, its bottom coated with a grey dust. Farther up the flaring sides, ground cover appears—grassy green and dirt yellow. Conifers fringe the depression in a kind of reverse treeline. It is an uncommon environment: there are few fires here and, other than the sinkhole, no access. Dean from Mars picks up another branch, attaches some parachute cord to the end, and pretends to fish in the pond.

At last, unannounced, we hear the whop and whine of a helo. It is, of course, late, diverted by new emergencies—more sewage outflow, a dragout from Roaring Springs, a distress call (a false alarm) from a boat party on the River.

WELLSPRINGS AND WATERSHEDS: THE BASIN

For weeks we have talked about a trip to The Basin. Gummer wants to run the whole distance, ridges and all. Dave is content just to get there. When we finally arrange common lieu days, we both jog and walk.

In the late morning clouds build up—dark, full, and moist. We are near the cabin at Basin Spring when we first hear thunder. Rain is imminent, and we hustle across the meadows and hills to where W-1 spills down the ridge. Rain reaches us as we touch the road, at first a few large drops, then torrents. The sky is black, illuminated spasmodically by lightning. Led by Gummer, we shun the largest trees and crowd under a fir the upper half of which has been blasted away by lightning. Hunched at the base we are reasonably dry. But the storm is a sockdolager; already water flows down W-1 like a sluice; we stare numbly across the grassy plains, flush with summer growth and flowers, now turning into mud.

Meadows, not the Canyon, introduce the North Rim. If you come by plane, you land on a dirt strip in V. T. Park. If you come by car, you drive through a great chain of meadows, or parks, that delineates the crest of the Kaibab—Pleasant Valley, V. T. Park, DeMotte Park, Little Park. A small isthmus of forest separates DeMotte Park from Little Park, and it is here, at the Sylvan Gate, that you officially enter Grand Canyon National Park. (Not for another thirteen miles will you reach the Rim—hence, perhaps the most common visitor question, "Where is the Grand Canyon?") Most North Rim roads, paved or dirt, pass through meadows. Where one would expect to find water in most mountain forests, on the North Rim you find meadow.

The Basin is the greatest of the North Rim parks. If The Dragon testifies to a geography of fire, The Basin speaks for a geography of water. The geologic column that constitutes the Kaibab Plateau consists disproportionately of limestone, and it is capped by a thick limestone crust. Cold temperatures, abundant moisture, and a plexus of cracks from the warping and fissuring of the Plateau have conspired to karstify the Kaibab. There are few surface springs, and they are little more than seeps. There are a few permanent ponds—sinkholes lined with clay. Small, intermittent streams drain the Plateau during spring melt when the saturated ground cannot absorb more moisture, but even these are intercepted before they reach the Rim. Everything is sucked underground into a subterranean plumbing system that discharges through springs deep into the Canyon. Some springs are feeble, fed only by a local watershed. Others drain large expanses of the Plateau and debouch in spectacular waterfalls like Roaring Springs, Thunder River, Tapeats. The potable water demanded by both Rims is largely dependent on these Inner Canyon springs. Roaring Springs is the principal reservoir for both North and South Rims, and the principal watershed for Roaring Springs is The Basin. The people gather where the water is—or where it can be pumped. The hydrologic connections between Plateau and Canyon, of which seeps and sinkholes are runic manifestations, are internal. They bypass the Rim.

Thus the Mountain-Lying-Down, as the Paiutes referred to the Kaibab, has an inverted hydrology to match its inverted topography. The desert Canyon is mountainous, punctuated with spectacular waterfalls and laced with flowing streams, while the forested Rim has a subdued topography of ridge and ravine, almost barren of surface water. The Plateau surface resembles corrugated sheet metal— sharply rounded, rhythmic, subdued. The intervening ravines are paved with meadows in the higher elevations and notched with a rocky flume in their ponderosa-dominated lower regions. The surface landforms of the Plateau are Pleistocene relics. Its hydrology is deranged. Its most expressive biota is grassy rather than forested.

The Basin concentrates this whole story. Yet even among parks, it is anomalous, offset somewhat from the axis of summit parks by a set of ancient, intersecting faults that together shape a broad depression. Over most of the Rim, drainages flow parallel to one another, like ribs from the domed backbone of the Kaibab, but at The Basin several small drainages coalesce; two prominent springs feed into it (Robber's Roost, Basin); and there is a single point of surface discharge, Outlet Canyon, which is seasonally significant and actually contributes to a degree of Canyon erosion along the Rim. The topography is not that of a smoothed bowl but is lumpish, a collapse feature. Interior hills are topped with trees and decorated with limestone outcrops. Grass is sparse and clumpy, more like tundra than prairie. The ground surface is in turmoil, pitted with burrows, grass, and frost-hove mounds.

There is an instant appeal to The Basin, a thrill of recognition. It appears, at first sight, to be the kind of scene that a forested wilderness ought to be. Open and windswept, it is visible in ways that the rest of the Rim forests are not. There are wildflowers in far-flung bouquets. There is wildlife: badgers, wildcats, coyotes, turkeys, and

deer all have been sighted; golden eagles and red-tailed hawks glide
over the grassland frequently. There are relics of a pioneer past: a
dilapidated cabin and an aspen corral at Basin Spring. There is a
seductive smoothness to the scene and, for the fire crew, a final
emptiness. For us water is a means, not an end.

The Basin is a delight and for a fire crew an irrelevancy. It is a place
to take a girlfriend, not a place to work. It is common for everyone to
return on his own for a day to walk around it; rare for anyone to return
thereafter. The Basin promises more than it delivers. It opens the
Plateau to the sky, and it introduces a contrast that is otherwise
lacking on the Plateau. There are precious few borders within the
Plateau, and apart from the meadows that ride the crest, few reference points within the Plateau. The Basin is one. The Basin is vital,
however, because it is a watershed for Roaring Springs and in this
way sustains the developments at Bright Angel Point—an otherwise
indifferent viewpoint, at which the sun rises and sets over the Plateau
rather than the Canyon. The Basin connects to the visitor.

Unlike the Rim, which looks outward and startles, The Basin looks
inward and calms. It shows the Plateau without the Canyon. Its
border is biologic, not geologic—informed by water, not by fire.
While The Basin identifies itself, it does not lead to anywhere else. It
is not the hub it at first appears to be. It is self-absorbed. It is a place
to withdraw to, a place to which one can retreat from the Rim. It
gives an illusion of revelation. It offers dichotomy without dialectic.

The real lesson of The Basin is its hidden hydrology. "You will
carry in all your water," Randy thunders during fire school. "All your
water for drinking. All your water for fedcos. Water for anything.
What water you don't bring in you don't have. So goddammit, don't
waste any. All our water—even here in the Area—comes from the
Canyon. It is pumped up nearly four thousand feet from Roaring
Springs. You won't find water in the woods. Don't waste a goddamn
drop." The audience of rookies and reserves is silenced, bludgeoned
by the metaphysics of Kaibab hydrology. Randy starts to speak
again, but Dan interrupts.

"Yeah," he says, "and remember Smokey's Second Rule of Firefighting: Always piss on your fire."

*   *   *

It was not supposed to be a fire recon, only an orientation flight for the new unit manager, Captain Zero, but they report two smokes. Within minutes the green pumper and the Three-quarter Ton, crammed with Longshots and SWFFs, dash toward The Basin. McLaren is surprised at the activity and at the location. The afternoon storm had lingered much longer than usual. That and the cumulative moisture of three weeks of monsoon had argued, in his mind, against a recon. And there are almost never smokes within The Basin. He asks over the radio for more details. He requests a legal description—by township, range, section.

Hulick, supervisory ranger in charge of the fire crew, surrenders Recon 1's radio to Zero. The plane circles over the smokes. McLaren asks again. The fire vehicles enter the east side of The Basin, and the crews watch the plane spiral overhead. The radio is silent. McLaren asks a third time, then from the green pumper Joe submits his own inquiry, diplomatically using radio channel 2, which spares the request from being rebroadcast through the Park repeater. "We've misplaced the fires," comes the reply. "Misplaced?" says McLaren. "How do you misplace a fire?" "It appears," begins Captain Zero with studied authority, "that the two fires have gone out. There has been a lot of rain, you know." "But where were they?" insists McLaren. There are records to be kept.

In the center of The Basin, fireroad W-1 brushes against a short ridge. Joe stops the pumper and climbs up to the ridgetop. The view, though broken, is as comprehensive as any in The Basin. He can see no smokes. But out of the fringe, where meadow borders forest, steam pours upward. Each streamer of setting sunlight ignites another cloud. He smiles and shakes his head. McLaren demands some legal descriptions of the smokes. Crews have been dispatched and must be paid. The fires must be numbered and named. Captain Zero reassigns the microphone back to Hulick. "We may have been overeager," Hulick reports quietly. "But where are the fires?" insists McLaren, relentless in his inquiry. Surely, he knows, thinks Joe. "The sunlight on the clouds . . . the angle of our perspective . . ." Hulick stammers. "We think . . . the smokes may have been . . . something . . . else." "Like what?" says McLaren. "Cloud," says Hulick. "Cloud? You

*mean a waterdog?" McLaren declares quietly, in a voice as soft as
fog. "These two smokes are waterdogs?"*

*The crews from the green pumper and the Three-quarter Ton have
joined Joe on the ridgetop. They pause to admire the sunset and add
up their overtime, then they run as a mob down the slope.*

Dampness seeps under the blasted fir, and Dave decides that we
need a fire. Gummer has some matches. We gather a handful of short
fir needles into a mound and try to ignite them. The match puffs out.
This time we sift the needles, fluff up the fuelbed, and stack small
branches around the mound. Nothing. Dave plucks a pocketknife
from his jeans and proceeds to fashion a fuzz stick—an "old Boy
Scout trick," he assures us. Water drips down and through the
canopy. It drops on us with thick, intermittent splashes. The fuzz
stick is worthless, and we are down to two matches. We watch in
fascination as lightning blasts a tree on a hill positioned centrally
within The Basin. A cascade of debris spills out, a boiling flash fire,
until the heavy rains pummel it to the ground. For an instant the tree
flares, then sizzles into a shattered, cold hulk. Our last two matches
fail. Dave reluctantly concludes that fir needles don't burn.

We rearrange our berths as comfortably as we can—not easy amid
the low, spidery branches. Gummer discovers a gouge from the old
lightning scar that nearly destroyed the tree. We sulk and grow wetter.
After about an hour the storm abates, and we walk back to the fire
cache.

*Gummer has already departed for the trailhead by the time Jack
and I reach Bright Angel Point and see it all. There is a fire at Roaring
Springs. Large flames intermix with waterfalls. Fire threatens the
pumphouse, and it menaces the pipeline. The Canyon fills with grey,
swirling smoke.*

*Gummer just knew there was a fire and headed directly for the
trailhead. Chuck told us to confirm the report, then rounded up the
rest of the crew and the SWFFs and ordered a helicopter. With
firepack, shovel, and pulaski, Gummer runs down the trail, pausing
only to step around mule trains, full of excited tourists. Swifter and I*

head down next. The helicopter will take Ape and Neidemyer and return for the rest. The trail is a little more than four miles long and descends about thirty-nine hundred feet. The flames are visible all the way down. Fire is burning upcanyon through the dense vegetation around the springs—through cottonwoods, brush, grasses—then out into the surrounding desert fuels. Some heads die out against rock overhangs. Others propagate in flashy fuels, favored by upcanyon winds and slope. The fire threatens the trail. If it damages the pipeline, the North Rim will be shut down. The helicopter lands near the pumphouse, but the pilot loses control in the squirrelly crosswinds where Roaring Springs Canyon joins Bright Angel Canyon; the machine makes a hard, unexpected landing; a door flies open and is damaged; the pilot refuses to fly out. Everyone else heads down the trail.

The Ape stands at the pumphouse, blustering and slightly confused. His great bulk is useless. In the crushing heat he sweats uncontrollably. Neidemyer has vanished. One by one we arrive; even the SWFFs are strung out. We work whatever section of the fire we encounter. Mostly we hot-spot, a swarm of Nomex beetles: attack a head near the source pipeline; another head above the springs, where the fire could leap over the cliffs into denser timber (Swifter, upset on the muddy, shaly soils, tumbles down the creek after his hard hat); another head by the campground and privies. We save the outhouses. But no one understands what is happening. Except perhaps Gummer.

Gummer is everywhere. First on the scene, he rushes upcanyon, through stream and boulders to the main head. He stops the worst lead single-handedly. Then it is all Gummer, the rest of that afternoon and all that evening. Gummer, at another head upcanyon; Gummer, at a spot thrown across the creek, below the trail; Gummer, filling metal backpack pumps at the springs and cooling down hollow cottonwoods that are throwing sparks into dry desert grasses; Gummer, his headlamp a shooting star across the twisted hillside, advancing from flame to flame. Chuck sends down rations and sleeping bags and additional tools by mule train. Gradually everyone except Gummer shows up. Even the long-lost Neidemyer appears, with spotless fireshirt and street shoes, no hard hat and no tools. Neidemyer thought he was applying for a lookout job, such as he had with the

Forest Service in southern Arizona; there he would point out the fires and drink coffee while convict crews dug fireline. But we see Gummer only through his blinking headlamp on the distant slopes.

We work late that evening. There is no fireline as such, and we thrash through the burned-out center, over spring and smoking stump, water and fire, until we are too tired to move. The hillside is broken with small cliffs and long, shaly slopes, and we fill up the metal pumps at the springs. From time to time a large tree burns through and tumbles down the slope, announced by bouncing rocks and wild shouts. Except for our headlamps, only flames illuminate the scene. Firelight dances off plunging water. Once, with two of the Hopis, I pause to fill a pump at a spring below a small cliff; we hear a horrible crack and the thunder of rolling debris, and small rocks bounce off our hard hats as we dive to the base of the cliff, one on top of the other, knowing that a cottonwood will crash upon us any instant. But the flaming log hangs up on standing trees above the cliff, and we look at one another sheepishly. At last Ape yodels, and Swifter joins the cry, and we gather to bed down. Gummer remains on the slope, and Ape leaves him to his obsessed sallies.

It is Gummer's third year on the crew. He is a relic of the Reusch days, an athletic Swede, blond as snow, son of a Forest Service supervisor, a "bubble-gummer" full of simple, physical action. The Park hierarchy knows he would look terrific as a Park ranger—he could model for a recruiting poster—and he accepts its counsel that he cannot remain in fire and transfers in midsummer to the rangers, then enters Albright Training Academy in the fall. But while Gummer can project the ranger image outward, he cannot project it inward. He is sent to recreation areas like Lake Amistad in Texas and Civil War parks in the South and given law enforcement training. He resigns.

In the morning the scene is unearthly. There are black slopes and white waters and burned-out snags and pockets of flaming brush. All day we mop up. Something is wrong with the rations, and the SWFF crew becomes diarrhetic. We sleep poorly that night. The Ape and Jack have blistered feet. Neidemyer disappears with regularity, and returns, always spotless. Gummer alone never wearies. The misery excites him; the location, which seems to disorient everyone else and frustrate our technique, he ignores or exploits. "This is," he tells me as we meet at a spring, "an unusual fire." It has everything. And it's simple. We'll never again have water next to a fire. The Ape says the same through a blistering curse. At last, on the third day, the fire is extinguished. Chuck refuses to use the helicopter to evacuate the crew. He sends down a mule string. Gummer declines and persuades me to join him on a hike out. "It'll be a lot faster than a mule," he says simply. "And more comfortable." Naively, happily, I agree.

"THE PURPOSE OF A PARK RANGER . . . IS TO PROJECT THE IMAGE OF A PARK RANGER"

Tom shows all the symptoms of the disease, and it is terminal. Radio syndrome. He speaks in a quiet yet urgent voice, as though slightly bored with the routine of emergency calls; he chatters; his speech is flooded with jargon, ten-codes, in-group intonation; he holds the radio at a slight angle when speaking into it. His hand radio is no longer a tool; it has become media. Tom is defining, for a Park audience, his functional personality in terms of the persona he projects over the radio. It is inevitable now. Tom will join the rangers.

Radio syndrome is only the first step. It will be quickly succeeded by a fascination with uniforms. In extreme cases FCAs will purchase at their own expense a set of ranger duds, complete with beaver hats. The aspirant will arrange to join rangers on patrol. Ranger slang will creep into fire-based radio traffic. On lieu days he will hang out by the ambulance instead of the fire cache, will join the climbing team, will participate in emergency medical services and make ambulance runs to Kanab, will practice with firearms. The final, confirming symptoms find the victim at Santa Rosa, California, usually again at his own expense, to take the special Park Service training course and receive a law enforcement commission. The process is not reversible. It never happens that someone leaves the rangers to become active in fire; no one surrenders a uniformed position for a non-uniformed position; no one exchanges a direct connection to the park visitor for the bureaucratic anomie that accompanies fire management. If the visitor makes the park, the ranger—who administers to visitor needs—makes the Park Service. The park ranger *is* the Park Service.

Smoke drifts across the Sublime Road, down a side ravine, and Rich follows it to the fire—a sleeper, several acres large, in relatively open ponderosa. The fire was sighted at sunrise by a commercial pilot and reported to the Grand Canyon airport. Leo brings up a second crew, this of reserves, and a PB-4Y2 drops retardant on the active west flank. Within an hour—before Recon 1 ever gets into the air— the Sunrise fire is contained.

Rich leaves the reserves to puzzle over their C rations while the fire crew inspects the perimeter, pausing here to improve a hasty scratch line; there, to break up a pile of heavy windfall near the line; here again, to fire out an island of unburned litter. Smoke hangs heavy, a dry fog. A handful of mighty snags; dozens of active catfaces in live trees; furious smokes under the veneer of retardant; incomplete burn-out between the many active fingers of the flaming front—there will be lots of mop-up, too. The reserves are in good spirits. For many this is their first fire, and Rich plans to use that eagerness to good effect. He and Leo patrol while the rest of us pause for breakfast and watch the sun stream through the smokey canopy. Then the BI arrives.

He has the brim of his hard hat pulled down to his eyebrows and consequently has to cock his head slightly backward to see. His lips hint at a sneer. He carries his firepack in his arms. When he sights Rich, he announces that he is assuming control over the fire. He walks past us and places his pack on the north perimeter, away from ours. He informs the reserves that he is now fire boss; that they report to him; that no, they won't have to do any mop-up. Then he tours the fireline.

A few minutes later Mitchell and Jan, both reserves, ask about the booms and thuds emanating from the fire. "Branches," Rich explains. Snags are burning and shedding their branches. "That's why you don't want to wander around in the burn." Then Leo hollers, "Here! Hurry!" We follow the fireline to his voice. There on a flat rock sits the smoking residue of the BI's firepack. The top flap had draped over the rock and into the unburned fuels within the fire. The fire had crept

*through those fuels and into the pack itself. The noises we heard
earlier were made by exploding ration cans of peanut butter and
cheese spread. The reserves are incredulous, the mystique of firefighting shattered by blasts of peanut butter. Before we depart the scene,
Leo pulls out a small camera from his own firepack and takes a
picture, and we rescue some charred canvas duck and an exploded
can for the FCA Musuem.*

*Shortly afterward, the BI—stammering and pale—announces that
he has secured the fire, that he no longer needs to direct operations
personally; then he leaves. Before he releases the reserves, Rich has
them haul in a healthy supply of fedcos. "Just pack in the water. We'll
mix it," Rich says with resignation. To Leo he adds, "The duff I can
mop up. It's the cheese spread I can't cope with."*

Our relationship to the rangers is complex. Technically we are part
of the same administrative unit, what in the old days was known as
the Protection Division and has since become Visitor Services and
Protection. A tour of duty with the fire crew for a season or two was a
common prerequisite for future park rangers, and a transfer to ranger
status was a normal expectation of ambitious FCAs. Many of the
seasonal park rangers on the North Rim are former fire crew members. Rangers, and even fee collectors, form part of the fire reserves.
Yet the gulf between rangers and fire crew grows larger each year.

The critical events occurred in the early 1970s. On several occasions the Park Service was acutely—that is, publicly—embarrassed
by an inability to control large crowds or a perceived epidemic of
minor crimes. Rangering was redefined on the basis of people management, not according to the management of natural phenomena.
The most prominent expressions were an interest in search and
rescue, in emergency medical services, and in law enforcement. Park
rangers began to emulate urban models, especially the National
Capital Parks Police. Rangers could thus be seen as protecting the
parks from threats, and the emphasis on people management ensured
that these activities *would* be widely seen by the public. Equally,
parks became arenas for rangering. When Desert View debated
whether or not park rangers could wear a particular boot with their
uniforms, the larger question quickly surfaced: Why do rangers need

to wear boots at all when they have become white-collar managers, cops in patrol cars, and ambulance attendants? It was decided that these daily chores were really incidental to the ranger's real purpose. The real purpose of a ranger was to project the Ranger Image. The public wants rangers; the parks need rangers to satisfy public expectations; the ranger image is of someone who wears boots.

The park ranger thus evolves in a diametrically different direction from the smokechaser. As fire management is redefined by the Park Service, it becomes a compromised and ambiguous job. Emergent philosophies of fire management demand not only a retreat from traditional fire suppression, but a complicated program of fire reintroduction that will, until the system is mastered, involve difficult decisions and a quota of public relations fiascos. Rangering is poised for bureaucratic growth; firefighting, for retrenchment. A divorce from firefighting is thus almost essential to the new definition of rangering.

On the North Rim the rise of the rangers comes at the expense of the fire crew. The old fire cache becomes an ambulance stall; our old parking stalls are reconditioned into ranger offices; rangers assume trail patrol duties, patrol the fireroads—now proclaimed a "backcountry"—with new vehicles, receive special training and pay-grade increases until the lowliest patrol ranger outranks every one of the fire crew except the foreman. North Rim unit managers are not surrogate superintendents but aggressive chief rangers who encourage interdivision competition when it can enhance ranger status. Fires become second-class emergencies, distant from immediate administrative concerns because they are distant from visitors and because they are polluted with managerial and philosophical ambiguities. Fee collectors swell the ranks of the uniformed and provide an alternative entrée for seasonals into ranger ranks. Supervision of the fire crew is turned over to mid-level managers without fire experience, who enjoy such other fast-track jobs as safety officer. There is nothing we have that the rangers want. Their keys open the fire cache. They have access to overtime pay without onerous fire duty by providing medical runs to the Kanab clinic and prisoner escort to the Fredonia jail. The low-water mark is reached when we are asked to fabricate a fire or two and charge enough overtime to the park rangers so that they can purchase the boots considered vital to their uniform. We refuse.

It is all pandemonium. New arrivals fling themselves on portions of the fireline; the older crews continue to extend their fragment of line or join the throng of newcomers in a stampede of hot-spotting. It has not been an orderly dispatch. Every crew has dispatched itself from whatever project it was working on. There is no staging area, no fireline organization, nothing but a wild melee of shovels, pulaskis, and fusees. It takes some time, and a good deal of heated yelling, but Mac gradually pulls everyone off the fire, holds a quick briefing, and divides the mob into two squads, one to each flank. Then, with Dean from Mars at his side, he flags a route through open areas so that no cutting will be required. "It's time you learned this," he tells Dean. The lost minutes are rapidly made up. Another half hour, and the fire, a sleeper perhaps three acres in size on the hot side of Walhalla, will be contained. Mac studies his fire map. The fire is apparently within a hundred yards of the Rim, and it will be useful, when the line is established, to locate a helispot. "I'll let you do that," he informs Dean. "You need to know more than how to use a McLeod." Dean from Mars smiles broadly if vacantly. He is, in some respects, a difficult rookie. He is spacey, friendly, eager, talkative, unambitious. For him torching thickets constantly recall an oil tank fire he witnessed at Danang; chain saws mounted on pack frames bring back Marine memories of mortars and automatic rifles; on his lieu days he rides around the region on a motorcycle searching for medicinal hot springs. But he is a Longshot, and he can learn, and Mac is patient.

Suddenly the fireline, nearly complete, slows, then appears to disintegrate. There is a chain saw to the west, another to the north; Mac can reach no one by radio; the roar of the saws drowns out all communications. Then, through the smoke, he sees unfamiliar bodies. Captain Zero and a companion named Paul, the son of an old Park Service buddy and a buck ranger in his own right, are stalking the fireline. Captain Zero is giving a tour of the fire to Ranger Paul, and along the way he exercises his prerogative, as North Rim unit manager, to redirect "the troops." One squad leader he has ordered to the

Rim to construct a helispot; another has been instructed to drop two snags somewhat inward from the line, near the rear of the fire. Both line squads have now been dispersed and are without radio communications. A retardant drop has been ordered, though heavy fire loads elsewhere in the region will mean a delay by at least two hours of any air tanker. It is midafternoon, and the head of the fire renews itself with the invigorated sunlight and winds. Captain Zero flashes a pasty smile as he passes by Mac and Dean, and continues to inform Ranger Paul about the nuances of firefighting. "It is," he explains, "a managerial problem."

There is nothing to do but smile back and quietly try to put radios where they are needed and to continue the fireline and burnout operations. The felling squad has independently removed itself from the interior of the fire; they can stand in the hot coals no longer. They sit on a log outside the line and remove their boots and pour water into them to cool them off. Mac catches up with Captain Zero, wandering emphatically somewhere between the fire and the Rim—his arms lecturing to this point and that—and tells him that everything looks good, thanks him for his example and instructions, and, nodding in wondrous appreciation, agrees that he is utterly right, that management is everything. "What's next?" asks Dean. He means the fire, but Captain Zero discourses about the value of a business degree in the "recreation business." Zero surveys the scene, forces an enormous smile, and decides that it is safe for him to depart. "Besides, Paul has other appointments. Got to manage our time, too, you know."

It is nearly sunset before we reestablish the line. The helispot is poorly sited and will have to be relocated in the morning. Mac manages to abort the air tanker. Duane, however, thinks he has located a route from E-4A that will bring the pumpers to within one hundred fifty yards of the fire—close enough to run hoses for mop-up. The winds are strong, and at least two men will have to remain all night to patrol. Dean from Mars volunteers. "Hey," he says slowly, "it's part of the job, isn't it?" "Yeah," says Mac wearily, as the first constellations appear above the deepening twilight wedge. Then he proposes to name this the Star fire.

*   *   *

Rangering becomes more than a job; it is a state of mind. The ranger mind is designed to function in crises, real or imagined. It delights in juggling many thoughts and decisions but within a context whose purpose is predetermined and whose context demands only a choice of techniques, not of philosophies. It is a mentality of triage; it works rapidly but shallowly; it detests contemplation and shuns moral or philosophical ambiguity. On the surface, it appears to be an odd state of mind for future park administrators to cultivate, but it explains the almost total absence of any kind of contemplative study within the agency. No park ranger has ever written an important statement of national parks values or purposes. Instead, the ranger reacts to crises, and if existing crises are not enough, new ones must be invented. The best bet is crime.

The emphasis on law enforcement is staggering. Riot control gear is purchased in sufficient quantities to outfit two platoons with helmets and batons. Undercover drug operations are organized to detect marijuana use at the Lodge. Special agents from the FBI give lectures on hostage negotiation. The Las Vegas SWAT team begins a cycle of annual appearances for intensive three-day training in "officer survival." Certification programs in law enforcement and firearms mean that there can no longer be any transfer between fire crew and rangers. Where the Fourth of July used to be associated with rumors of the monsoon, it now rings with rumblings about bikers. Motorcycle gangs are descending on the North Rim. The rangers organize us for riot control drills. The fire crew, outfitted with batons, will form a wedge, while rangers behind us wield shotguns and handcuffs. The strategy is for us to hide in the trees by the entrance station and, if trouble develops, to pour out of the woods, assume formation, and attack the bikers. We begin to refer to the rangers as Grey Shirts. But the drill is academic because a smoke is reported near Sublime, and the wedge is broken up to respond. It is apparent that the fire crew cannot serve two masters.

It is academic, too, because no confrontation occurs. The bikers—the Dirty Dozen—agree to set up camp along the main haul road on the national forest. When they enter the Park, they do so under escort. Quickly between them and the rangers a symbiosis develops. The bikers revel in their armed escort; the attention is intoxicating.

The rangers thrill no less to their status as public protectors. To prevent a real crisis from intervening, the rangers and the bikers hold preliminary conferences to work out a protocol. Before the bikers leave, they invite the rangers to a beer bust. They promise to return the next year. Gonzo orders T-shirts to be made with the inscription "Bikers, 35. Rangers, 5. Rangers Win."

And he is right. Physical conflict has metamorphosed into a media show, a drama acted out over the Park radio. The North Rim becomes part of an annual pilgrimage by the bikers, and their arrival evolves into a critical ceremony for the crisis-starved rangers. Social functions and training sessions are scheduled around the anticipated appearance of the bikers, a kind of latter-day mountain rendezvous. Gifts are exchanged. When, after many years, the bikers announce that they will not return the next summer, the gloom is palpable.

Tom concludes his lengthy radio message. The Longshots are hurriedly loading pumpers for jobs in the woods—any jobs, even the Fence. Today the rangers will conclude their SWAT training with mock maneuvers against a band of terrorists holed up in the fire cache. It is prime theater, and Tom asks to be left behind as our man-in-the-area; he wants to watch, perhaps to participate. "If you wish," I tell him. "Tom's got it pretty bad, huh?" says Randy.

By the time we reach the entrance road, the assault has begun. Tear gas, smoke grenades, automatic weapons—all burst into the outlaw bunker as first one stall, then another, and finally the Rim itself are swept clean of saboteurs and subversives.

The winds are ferocious. But the fire did not get into the expansive fir reproduction downwind, and the site along E-4 is miraculously accessible to vehicles. Dash, in fact, makes an initial attack with his pumper. Other crews soon arrive, and we cut line furiously around nearly five acres of fire. Our fear is spots. In such a wind nothing is safe. Eddies dance across the scene, threatening firewhirls and broadcasting embers. Again and again we break to grid the downwind sites for spot fires. Yet the wind has more promise than punch. The fire is controlled. I name the fire Mariah.

That is the status when Gonzo arrives, flanked by two ranger lieutenants and a guest ranger. Gonzo promptly announces that he is assuming control over the fire; orders replacement crews from the South Rim and a chartered bus to bring them around by morning; and pointing to Bryan—once an FCA, now a permanent park ranger and protégé—explains that Bryan is a trainee service chief, that Gonzo will demonstrate how to requisition matériel for a campaign fire. Already an account has been established with BIFC. "All right," he bellows. "What do you need? Speak up." A few hundred more feet of one-inch hose ("unlined, of course") would be nice, and some gated wyes are all we can think of—they'll help with mop-up. "Fine," says Gonzo. He turns to Bryan. "Order those supplies from the BIFC warehouse. Use a fire order form. Charter a King Air for transport from Boise. We'll ferry them across the Canyon by helicopter. Let's see, that means we'll need a helispot nearby. Yes, dangerous fuels around this fire, and a miserable wind. How the hell do you spell 'Mariah' anyway? Anything else?" His words are almost lost in the howl of wind through trees. "No," I tell him. But I am looking at Bryan, who carefully stares at his clipboard.

Only a few years ago Bryan was an FCA at the North Rim. He copied The Ape's every gesture and gave up chewing tobacco for a pipe; he and Ape would climb trees at opposite ends of the Area and give off weird cries while Chuck wondered what kind of animal could set up such a racket. We shared bunks in 155. In those days it was possible to move quickly from seasonal to permanent status, and Bryan made the move. The price was that he had to leave the fire crew in midseason. A few days before the transfer to the rangers, there was a good fire—a couple of acres—at Point Imperial. It was his last fire as an FCA, and we named it Bryan's fire.

"Good," Gonzo replies. "Work through the night. All of you. The South Rim crew will relieve you in the morning. Bryan and I will return to the Area and make all the necessary preparations. Christ, we'll show this Park how to manage a large fire."

There is one snag to fell, and Dash promptly drops it and hoses it down. The light surface fuels and abundant water make short work of mop-up. By 2300 hours the fire is out. We make one final pass around the perimeter for spots.

We set up a campfire and keep water boiling for coffee. The wind continues to blow, cold and strong. A full moon glares through the trees, too bright to stare at directly. It gleams like silver off the ashes. We huddle around the campfire. We can barely stay awake. "Just how do you spell 'Mariah'?" Randy asks.

The morning sky is ash grey and cold when the South Rim crew— composed wholly of reserves, no regular fire crew—finally arrives after a sleepless, all-night bus trip. The men stagger off the bus and wander aimlessly around the burn in a search for smokes. About 0900 hours a helicopter lands in the Walhalla Glades and deposits two hundred feet of unlined cotton hose and two gated wyes. Soon afterward a ranger patrol car drives up, and out step Gonzo with his cigar and Bryan with his clipboard. Bryan completes the receipts and satisfies the requirements for a service chief trainee. Gonzo congratulates him. Bryan is poised for promotion to mid-level management, and an acceleration in fire credentials might give him the edge he needs. It is a long way from Tucumcari, New Mexico, and snag fires on the Rim and peanut butter and sardines at Thunder River. Gonzo and Bryan leave in a patrol car, loudly planning to celebrate later at Gonzo's house.

"The Mariah fire," says Dash with glassy eyes. "I don't care how you spell it. I want to know how you spell us." The Longshots leave shortly afterward, and when we reach the Area, we fall out, one by one, still fully clothed, into our beds and sleep the sleep of the dead.

GIGS AND GAGS; OR, CLOSE ENCOUNTERS WITH THE BI

Uncle Jimmy's speech becomes increasingly animated. The sounds begin to leak out of the Fire Pit, and Ralph pokes his head out the door to see who might be within earshot. Uncle Jimmy ignores him; he is absorbed in his tale and presents it to his crowded audience with even greater vehemence. Ralph positions himself in the Arm Pit, with an eye to the outside and an ear to the inside. You can't be too careful, he reminds himself. The crew, nominally convened for a "tailgate safety meeting," is swapping stories about Big Bob and Captain Zero. In a way, he reasons, we *are* talking safety.

He has heard the story from its source, Mitchell, a fern feeler. Early in the spring, when the snows form great dunes along the entrance road, someone reported a bear sighting. One might as well report Big Foot. Then there was a second sighting. Big Bob was intrigued and recruited Mitchell to track down the beast. A confirmation would create a sensation. They were well outside the Park when they spotted it—a huddled brown mass bent over with its back to the road, obviously mesmerized by something in its paws. Big Bob was cautious. In the spring, he declared, bears are hungry and unpredictable. He instructed Mitchell to circle the meadow widely, always staying downwind. Meanwhile, Big Bob would remain in the pickup, with the engine running, in case the bear charged and they had to make a hasty retreat. Stealthily, step by circumspect step, crouching low to the snow, Mitchell maneuvered around the meadow toward the bear. Suddenly he stood upright. Big Bob throttled the engine. Mitchell's words were lost in the roar of the truck. "My God, it's a cow! A dead cow." But Big Bob could not hear him. Big Bob could hear only the wildly racing engine. The pickup crept down the highway, as Bob unconsciously feathered the clutch.

Once the fire crew told stories about fires and SWFFs and devil-may-care bosses like Reusch. But the general reorientation of Park Service philosophy and the disassembling of its fire policy lessen the bravura of fire stories outside the confines of the cache and magnify the significance of intrapark politics and personalities. Now we tell stories about the absurdity of supervisors. "BI" stories are so abundant that they lose their charm and become bitter. The freshest stories concern Captain Zero, who created a minor sensation after his arrival by announcing that his "management goal" was to have the "cleanest unit in the National Park Service." "Yes," he assured us. "We're going to *zero in* on neatness." His nickname quickly followed. Immediately there are massive, unit-wide cleanup days; vehicle washing acquires a talismanic significance; roadsides and overlooks are scoured to a polish; select buildings are repainted. But then the story gets weird. Neatness is equated with grass. We are instructed to plant a lawn around the ranger station, to reseed the raw road cuts along the entrance road, to remove the unsightly veneer of pine needles that layers the Area, and to advance a program of prescribed burning on the theory that more fire means more grass. When the ranger station is transformed into the Office, a special green carpet is installed.

Captain Zero himself directs the Office reseeding project and orders Kentucky bluegrass, an exotic. It turns out that all the grass seed is bad, but we don't know that and fertilize it and water it daily with the pumpers. The road cuts are more troublesome because we are low on dead seed, and the real problem is not to seed but to stabilize. Our chief gardener won't hear of matting such as the highway department uses and orders us instead to cut aspen and lay them across the cuts. Meanwhile, he instructs maintenance to mow Harvey Meadow (and if necessary The Basin) to collect grass seed. Again we water the cuts—the largest is now known as Hayseed Hill—daily with our pumpers. But still the grass does not grow, and Captain Zero darkly broods over imagined conspiracies.

He concludes that the seed needs more water—and fertilizer. Several times each summer maintenance cleans out the accumulated muleshit in the corral with a front-end loader and transports it to an old barrow pit on the road to Marble Flats. He instructs us to bring back suitable bags of manure from the pit and spread it over all the seeded areas, beginning with his front yard. That morning we fortify ourselves with extra cups of coffee, pick up a wire-mesh screen and a case of plastic garbage bags, and drive out to the dump. Ralph shovels shit onto the screen, while Dave and I shake the fine, dry manure through and into the bags. "Hey, man," drawls Ralph. "This is pretty good shit." "Yeah," Dave agrees, as he knots another bag. "If the rangers catch us with all this shit, they'll probably bust us." The manure cannot raise dead seed to life. But there is no turning back. Captain Zero orders us to rake up and carry away all the pine needles in the Area.

New crises in Park cleanliness appear. One predawn an intoxicated Lodge employee loses control of his pickup, crashes into the huge sign at the Kaibab trailhead, and is pinned under the steering wheel as the truck spins over, slides into some aspen, and lands in the bar ditch. Gas drips on him, and dehydration burns his skin. After several hours we manage to extricate him by cutting away the seat with a hacksaw blade. Halfway into the proceedings, Captain Zero appears dressed in an old orange, untucked fireshirt. It is the first and only time anyone ever sees him with his hair uncombed. He studies the scene meticulously. While the rangers hustle the injured driver to

Kanab, he drafts a memo instructing the fire crew to rebuild the sign. Later, we receive an official letter of commendation for our skill in reconstructing it.

That success story inspires others. One of maintenance's large dump trucks spins out on a wet curve on Lindbergh Hill and crashes down the slope. No one is injured, but the accident and the recovery of the dump disturb the forest, especially the younger conifers. We are ordered to make the scene appear natural again. Joe and Ralph make stands for some uprooted trees with stones and prop up others with two-by-fours, while Dave and a cabful of SWFFs carry a load of pine needles from the needle mountains behind Skid Row and spread them around the scene. The dying trees, however, are far more visible propped up than they are half buried. There is nothing to do, Joe concludes, but paint the trees green. The site becomes known as the Magic Forest.

Ralph rises from the chair and waves us into silence. Someone is coming. "Now for the ceremonies," I announce, and we troop across the street to the line of fire vehicles. The official reason for the tailgate session is to reprimand Wil for a vehicle accident and to impress upon the crew the need to improve our safety record. It is useless to point out that most of the dents, spalled tires, and general wear are the result of inadequate vehicles and deteriorating fireroads; no good to point out that most of the damages inflicted on fire vehicles and charged to the fire accounts occur outside fire season, when fire vehicles are used by other divisions and for other purposes; worthless to argue that mandated defensive driving courses, with workbooks that describe how to merge smoothly on an interstate freeway, are meaningless. The fact remains that the accidents are charged to our account, and our own record is not as good as it should be. Wil's accident, in particular, was potentially serious. He nearly collided head-on with another vehicle on the Sublime Road. Wil was bringing in a load of reserves to a fire, while the other vehicle was returning to the Area, and neither anticipated any opposing traffic on the narrow road. A good scare and few dents, as Wil veered into the berm and brush, are the final results—that and the peculiar punishments the fire crew has evolved.

Anyone involved in an accident is required to complete virtually all the paperwork himself. If that is not deterrent enough, we schedule a small ceremony, like that now in progress; before the assembled crew, the perpetrator must describe the accident and then light up a cigar from our special stock—a box of cigars left by the abdicating Abner and subsequently donated by Ingrid to the fire crew. The cigars are stale, and they reek. They smell as though made from ingredients swept off the Brooklyn Bridge and stuffed into butcher paper. Between the endless government forms and an endless cigar we have a sufficient response to the problem of accidents. Or so we think.

Wil is called front and center. All the fire vehicles have been lined up across from the Fire Pit. The fire crew, also in a line, faces them. I pace back and forth between the crew and the vehicles, point out the cumulative dents in the vehicles, and lecture about the seriousness of Wil's accident. I hand Wil a sheath of accident forms. Then I give him a cigar. Duane steps forward with a fusee to light it. This is a time for firmness. I posture a bit further, then notice the widening eyes along the line of FCAs. "What . . .?" Wordlessly, with eyes the size of steering wheels, Duane points. The Three-quarter Ton has begun to roll downhill. Apparently it has been left in neutral and the parking brake is unset. The truck picks up momentum. Tim tries to open the door and get to the brake, but without success. The truck rolls past the fire crew, past the Fire Pit, past the fire totem before smashing into a one-way sign and grinding to a stop. Wil asks if the Three-quarter Ton will have to smoke a cigar.

We call it the Genesis fire because it appears, when first reported, that it might be the start of something. It burns deep in the Iron Triangle, the first fire ever reported in Section 12. The fuels of the Asbestos Forest are unimaginably dense; the wind, while moderate, is persistent; and there seems to be no reasonable way into the fire.

It is miles from any kind of road, embedded deep amid corrugated ridges and ravines, impenetrable forests, and endless, sinuous meadows. At the suggestion of Recon 1, the first crew breaks a trail from the mixing table on Lindbergh Hill. They compass down the hill through mixed conifer, then follow meadows to Thompson Canyon, then proceed updrainage; Recon 1 guides them through the tangle of ravines. The meadows are soft, their surface irregular and tiring.

Stringers of forest cross them from time to time like an abatis. The fire is up a shallow ridge, and it takes only one look for Tom to request help. The remainder of the fire crew follow the flagged route and sluggishly pack in everything. The last stragglers do not appear until nearly evening.

All night the wind blows. If the fuelbed were more porous, if the tree canopy were less dense, if the heaps of downed wood and duff were slightly drier, the fire might have raged across the ridge and propagated, unbroken, all the way to Saddle Mountain. Instead, it has spotted miserably into thickets of semi-decomposed fir and mounds of short-needle duff. Dave recalls that on the Booga Booga fire, not far from here, he and Gilbert walked for nearly half a mile without ever touching the ground. The Genesis fire is, in reality, not one fire but dozens of smoldering, episodically flaming fires—a large fire, not a great fire. A few spot fires have ignited thickets of fir reproduction, and several burn with constant flames in the natural slash heaps of jackstraw spruce. The Kid notes that this Genesis took only one day to start and will need six to mop up.

It might. There is no obvious pattern and certainly nothing that could be called glamorous. Only wind-borne firebrands have allowed the fire to spread. We proceed, spot by spot, with mop-up. There is little water and not much dirt. Tom locates a pocket of soil and begins to excavate it with a pulaski. Stone and Duane carry the dirt to burning patches and mix it with the smoking duff. The Kid quips that we need a dirt fedco. We find that we have brought in too many line tools—pulaskis and McLeods—and not enough shovels; Ralph tries, unsuccessfully, to stir dirt and duff with a McLeod. We sleep on the line—cold, remote, helpless. Mop-up continues throughout the next day. No play, no songs, no jokes, no allusions, no stories. The Genesis fire is disjunctive. The fire should not be here, no one at the fire wants to be on it, and no one in the Area or on the South Rim wants us to be here.

During lunch we study our fire maps. We are, we calculate, closer to the Saddle Mountain road than to Lindbergh Hill. If we follow the north meadow, we should be able to reach the Saddle Mountain road in perhaps half the distance of a reverse trip to Lindbergh Hill. But someone will have to return to Lindbergh and get a vehicle to meet us

*at the Fence. We draw straws—fir branches—and Tom loses. When
we evacuate, after dinner, some of us are uneasy. There are no smokes
showing, but fires in punk can smolder for days without visible
displays of smoke. No one volunteers to stay, however, and when we
leave, we leave nothing behind.*

The stories about Big Bob and Captain Zero are getting out of
hand. An impromptu safety meeting has been called for the purpose
of lecturing about hard hats, but it rapidly degenerates into burlesque.
Leo wears a 1950s logger-style hat with a circular brim, Dash sports
a child's plastic hard hat shaped like a turtle, Randy outfits a
standard-issue hard hat inserted with two round Mouseketeer ears cut
from sheet metal and painted black, and Charlie, outfitted with an old
fire shelter as a cape, wears a motorcycle helmet that bristles with two
fusees and a drip torch spout. "Captain Burnout, reporting for
firing," he announces. "Inside," I say.

The stories and gags have got to slow down. All the pranksters get
a gig. It is the best solution we can come up with. Every time
someone tells a "Big Bob story" during regular hours he gets a gig.
Whoever has the most gigs at the end of the week will be assigned to
the Area for the coming week. Thus the strategy is doubly diabolical:
not only will the loser miss the chance to get out of the Area, but by
remaining, he will acquire a host of new Captain Zero and Big Bob
stories—stories that he dare not recite or else risk repeating the
cycle. For several weeks the scheme works well. Stories are reserved
for the privacy of 176 and the entrance cabin.

"Is the BI coming?" asks Rich. Ralph shakes his head and recalls
how, as another protective device, the fire crew came to evolve a
special language to speak about Big Bob, even to his face, without
his knowledge. It began, accidentally, one morning when we had
convened in his office and he was suddenly inspired to demonstrate to
his "troops" that he was an assertive leader, with real stature within
the regional fire community. He decides to call up the North Kaibab
FMO, Lynn Thomas, and talk shop with him, man to man, while we
listen in. Unfortunately he consistently confuses Thomas's name with
that of a Phoenix newscaster. The Forest Service switchboard, which
has heard this all before, makes the transfer successfully, and sud-

denly Big Bob is speaking directly to "Len Thompson." He freezes. After a long, stammering pause he blurts out, without the slightest introduction, "How's your BI?" What Thomas's BI (burning index) was we never learn. But we soon adopt "BI" as a code name for Big Bob. "How's the BI?" is repeated a score of times during each day. ("Normal range. High ignition, low spread.")

Ralph waves everyone silent as the BI himself approaches the Fire Pit. Big Bob surveys the gathering and sights the gig sheet displayed over the foreman's desk. "What's this?" he asks. Think fast, think fast, I tell myself. "It's part of our safety program," I say. "Every time we catch someone doing an unsafe act he gets a mark. The man with the most marks must give a presentation at the weekly tailgate session. Like Uncle Jimmy today." Big Bob pulls his ranger hat low over his eyebrows and curls his lower lip. "Good idea," he stammers. "Damned good idea. But . . ." he pauses, studying the chart in detail. "Strange," he mumbles. "The old hands seem to have the poorest safety habits."

"Oh, we just have the most experiences," Uncle Jimmy reminds him.

Two days later a vigorous smoke column is sighted within the Iron Triangle—uncomfortably near the site of the Genesis fire. If this is not a reburn of the Genesis fire, it is so close that it may as well be. We name it the Regeneration fire, and this time we know what to do. Although helos are not routinely used in these years, we request one and get it. We ask for reserves and get them—a couple of rangers, a fern feeler, some laborers from maintenance. We get approval to take vehicles in from the Fence, if we can do so without damage. Maintenance agrees to drive the water truck out to the Saddle Mountain road. We establish a staging area in the old Burn and shuttle crews into the north-side meadow by helo.

We have been here before. This time there is a spark to the crew. The first crews in—regular fire crew—scout and hot-spot. As more firefighters arrive we organize for line construction. There are no impromptu lessons in handtool use, fireline protocol, or organization. A saw crew cuts a corridor through heavy downed timber and spruce thickets; a handcrew widens the cordon with pulaskis, then, bumping along, scrapes a line along its outside perimeter with McLeods and shovels. Down—all the way down—to mineral soil. The saw crew returns, breaks up a large concentration of crosshatched spruce near the line, and begins to drop snags; a hollow white fir shooting sparks high above the canopy is cautiously, accurately felled with fistfuls of wooden wedges. By late afternoon the fire is controlled. Ralph and Tom hike up the meadow toward the Fence, and before sunset they bring in both pumpers. In the meantime, we eat dinner—a rowdy round of rations, full of coarse humor. The BI arrives for his first fire duty, ever. We give him a shovel and tell him to patrol the line.

Between the water truck and the pumpers we have an abundance of water. Acres of embers glow like a mountain of candles. For hours into the night we mop up. The next morning there is nothing left but smoldering duff. We stay at it, all of us, until the last smoke expires. The BI wants to complain, to question, to investigate, but there is no one in charge. When the last smokes have vanished, we sit on bucked logs, split open earlier in the search for coals, and watch for the play of sunlight on tiny smokes. We grid the area outside the line, load the pumpers, and drive to Saddle Mountain.

Before we leave we take a crew picture. Once yellow fireshirts are grey with dirt and oil. The afternoon sun glistens smartly off our aluminum hard hats. Individual faces, blackened with soot, are indistinguishable, visible only by the flash of white teeth within large, loud grins.

Felling

The snag is large, and it has a noticeable lean over the powerlines. "It's on the west side, too. It will come down across the line for sure next spring. This one," says the man from Garkane Power, "has to go."

There is dry, rotten wood around the base. A bad tree, thinks Randy. "Why is there always something wrong with the trees we cut?" he mutters out loud. We have been felling hazard trees along the powerline for more than a week now, and we have had to use winches, ropes, jacks, wedges by the box, and even the Garkane cherry-picker to set cables—all in an attempt to drop trees in a direction other than their natural lean. Once, when a half-felled snag hung up, we had to clear it by dropping another tree across it. That time, we insisted, the power had to be off, but otherwise Garkane and the Park want no outages. "Because," answers Lenny, "if a snag isn't dead, rotten, or burning, or all three, we wouldn't be cutting it."

Think. Think again. Felling acquires a rhythm, and the rhythm can take command. Use it—and fight it. Size up the tree. Reckon the lean. If the trunk bows, calculate the average weight distribution. Count the limbs by their size and shape and the relative weight they contribute to each quadrant. That distribution affects the overall lean—the branches may even counterbalance the trunk lean—and they catch the wind. ("There," says Donnie, pointing north. "It wants to go there.") Watch for widowmakers. Test the trunk for good wood and rotten. (Kenny chips at the base of the snag with a pulaski, tearing away the bad wood in chunks.) Clear a work area wholly free of debris. Get good footing. Inspect the saw for oil and gas. ("Need more Gus and Earl," says Donnie, and Kenny obligingly fetches some saw mix and a canteen of chain oil.) Check your gear. Chaps protect your legs, particularly your knees, from chain kickback. Glasses protect your eyes from flying chips. Plugs, gloves, hard hat. Plot an escape path. If no route is suitable, cut one. Use the saw to inscribe the front cut lightly. Recheck the lean. Double-check that you and your spotter know the plan, know where the racing saw will be. (Kenny stands mute to the side, armed with pulaski, sledge, and wooden wedges.) Cut.

The front cut should be level, about a third of the way into the trunk, pointing in the direction of desired fall. (The chips fly in great roaring sprays; they splash off Donnie like hailstones.) The second cut joins it to form a hollow wedge. Loggers prefer to cut from below—it means more trunk wood—but they also cut as low to the ground as possible. We cut for safety, not lumber, so place your cut where it is comfortable, and finish your wedge from above. Clean it out so that the tree will fall free. If you need to make the tree pivot, insert one side of the wooden wedge back into the cut so that the trunk will strike it, and push away from it when the trunk fails and the tree breaks loose. (The front-cut wedge is hung up somewhere in the middle, and Donnie cannot seem to cut it free with the saw. Kenny knocks it out with a sledge and tosses it to the side.) Better still, use wooden wedges; manipulate the back cut, not the front. Double-check your line of fall. The front cut should point directly to where you want the tree to land. (Donnie inserts the sledge into the yawning front cut. He jams the metal head into the rear, so that the handle points away from the cut and toward the line of fall.)

Inscribe the backcut lightly. It should be nearly level and about two inches above the front cut. If you cut more heavily on one side, the tree will tend to pivot on the good wood left on the other side. If you cut evenly, the tree will fall as it leans. (Radiant in red cruiser vest, Kenny stands expectantly to one side, watching, a sledge in one hand and a stack of wooden wedges in the other.) Wait for a telltale sway like an ocean swell; a sudden crack like a cry in the night; a ponderous tug as the tree groans, twists, screams as the heartwood tears loose, snaps free, and sweeps like a gust of wind to the earth. The exhilaration is intense.

Never—don't even think about it—never cut through the heartwood completely. (Kenny watches the tip of the bar. The tree is too large for Donnie to see both ends of his cut at once. Kenny holds up his hand. "Stop.") If the tree fails to drop on its own, drive it over with wedges, jacks, winches. If the tree is cut through completely, you lose control over its line of fall. It will descend randomly; it may sit back on the saw; it may reverse its fall, coming back over the sawyer; it may rotate, hang up in nearby branches, and, if burning, drop fire into thickets of reproduction; it may bind the saw, twist it out of the operator's hands, spin it underneath the descending trunk, and crush it. (Donnie pauses, gently slides the bar out of the cut, and motions to Kenny, who inserts a wedge into the kerf and taps it expertly with the sledge. The tree rises a fraction of an inch. Kenny inserts two wedges, one on top of the other, and strikes them. The tree is held by good wood on the right side. Gingerly Donnie reinserts the saw and feathers the solid wood. Kenny watches intently for widowmakers, a diagnostic wobble, an unexpected jerk; then he slams the wedges. There is some slight movement, a coarse groan. Donnie removes the saw, shuts it off, and places another double wedge into the cut. Kenny pounds the wedges, which flake off in chunks.)

When the tree begins to fail, get away. Move to your escape route. A tree may barber-chair, hang up and rotate, or bounce madly off the stump. Branches broken loose during the descent may crash to the earth slightly later than the trunk. (The tree snaps, hesitates. Donnie catches his breath, his heart stops as he suddenly realizes that he did not check the canopy to see if the tree had a clear line of fall, so easy is it to let rhythm replace reason. The snag hangs up on an immense ponderosa branch, spins off and free, and crashes to the ground with a fury of screaming branches and a shower of needles and duff.)

Gather your gear, and size up the next tree. If the stump is someplace that the public might see it, cut the stump flush with the ground. And cover it with dirt. We are to disguise our work, not exhibit it. ("Your turn." Donnie grins.)

The Garkane project is our most concentrated hazard tree program, but there are others. We drop problem trees by the score along the highways. We fell a gigantic ponderosa that obscures part of the approach to the North Rim heliport. We drop some smaller snags, half rotten, by the Inn cabins. We circle the new water tank with a ring of fallen snags. We clean out the old sewage spray field of dead mixed conifer. When archaeologists excavate a ruin near Cape Royal for a public exhibit, we are told to drop the trees that have grown up within the walls without damaging the half-exposed walls. When a serious accident on Lindbergh Hill requires a helo evacuation, we drop two large ponderosas—missing the highway each time—to provide an exit. We drop a dead leaner by the gas pumps. And we routinely fell snags on fires.

There is not much chance to build up expertise on a seasonal crew, and most recruits have no experience in felling. We can teach principles, and we can point out obvious hazards—trees that, regardless of their fire status, ought to be left alone or burned down. But real skill demands practice. It can't be taught: it must be learned. In the Park, however, we haven't the luxury of a double set of trees, one for practice and one for performance; we must practice on the real thing. We use hazard tree projects to provide practice for burning snags, and burning snags to furnish practice for hazard trees. For a while, the Western Region of the Park Service sponsored a specially equipped tree crew that made a grand circuit among the parks and handled the worst cases. Lead time was long, however, and the crew was dissolved. At the North Rim the fire crew is the only group whose job requires felling, so when maintenance wants a dead tree removed in the campground, it asks us.

It is a modest-size ponderosa, utterly dead, hovering amid several campsites. We request the campground ranger to notify us when the site is vacated and to leave it open long enough for us to remove the tree. There is nothing especially complicated about the job, no apparent lean to the tree, no unbalanced distribution of large branches; the top, when fallen, just might reach a restroom, so we plan to drop it slightly to the south side. Two days later we are told that the site is ready.

Three of us go—Jimbo, Lenny, and I. We bring extra saws and sledges. Once the tree is down, we will buck it up into small sections, split it into quarters, and leave it for campers. The campsite due south, we notice, has not been vacated. But there is apparently no one there, only a tent. It is protected by two trees. It is nearly 90 degrees from our planned line of fall. I put on chaps, earplugs, gloves, goggles, and hard hat and fire up Big Mac. Jimbo, who will spot for me, grabs a fistful of wooden wedges and a sledge.

The front cut goes well. The heartwood is old but reasonably solid. The front-cut wedge comes out, and we toss it to Lenny. Jimbo inserts his sledge to test the direction of fall, while I idle the saw. Its noise attracts a small crowd, a rare chance for us to perform publicly. I plan nothing fancy for the backcut—just a straight cut. A little prematurely Jimbo slams in a wedge. It jams the bar. I give the saw some gas and cut through the tip of the wooden wedge and continue to cut in. The tree should go now. I pull the saw out.

Nothing. Jimbo strikes the wedge. Again, nothing. I insert the saw and cut some more. There should be a crack, a weaving, a point of free-fall adrenaline, then the accelerating momentum of the tree crashing smartly to the ground. But there is nothing. I cut some more, ever so lightly. The snag should be rocking minutely, even with the wedge in it, but there has been no movement at all. Now there is no real room for other wedges, and there seems to be no reason to force more wedges inside. Gingerly I cut further, and the tree snaps. I yank the saw out, kill the engine. Jimbo's mouth is open, and he strikes the wedge furiously.

It is no good. It is as though the snag has been blind-sided. It falls in the direction of the wedge, not away from it; it wavers; then, with a sickening snap, it falls toward the tent. A man shouts and rushes toward it. Not one of the trees that guard the tent like sentinels touches the snag. A branch strikes the man, and another, larger branch strikes a woman struggling to exit from the tent. We are stunned. There is no sound beyond the settling of debris, the delayed fall of branches broken off during the fall and momentarily suspended. As I rush to the tent, I know they are dead.

I call on the radio for help. "Send the ambulance. Get the helicopter from the South Rim with the Park EMS coordinator. Get some rangers down here. Hurry." The man groans. The woman is immobile. By the time the first wave of rangers arrives, she shows signs of consciousness. The rangers maneuver us—me—out of the action. It is their show now.

It is our worst moment and their best. They handle the scene perfectly. It is a genuine crisis—a true emergency—not one of their posturing make-believes, and they show how the ranger mind, when genuinely challenged, can respond. For all the apparent horror, the victims—two tourists from Belgium—are only badly bruised. They are flown directly to the Flagstaff hospital. The scene is cordoned off. A full-blown investigation begins immediately. Within hours there are questions from investigating rangers, from the Park safety committee, from a Forest Service team called upon to study the actual felling practices. Sy, the Park safety officer, recommends that I find a good lawyer.

If there is a rational explanation for the tree's behavior, we are never told it. No matter, the failure was in the decision to cut at all. If there had been regulations against felling in the campground during the summer season, as there are in the Forest, we would have been fired and probably would have been personally liable for a tort claim. But the Park Service has no such manual or policy for hazard tree removal. Had we cleared the vicinity entirely, not just the immediate site, our error would have been forgotten. We didn't—and it isn't. What becomes apparent is that the system, which has so often worked against us, now works in our favor. After years of occupational distance, after countless comic nights of pyromanticism, after all the institutional barriers that segregate us from tourists, we have at last established contact with the elusive Visitor. The Park knows how to respond. The first order of business is to get us away from the scene.

Later that afternoon I gather everyone—those who had been at the scene, those at the cache, those on lieu days—into the Fire Pit. I render an account and an apology. There is not much else to say. There is nothing that can be said that speaks louder than the deed. The act pollutes all of us. It is part of the price of a seasonal operation. We all share access to the saws, and we all share their failures. If one of us fells a tree badly, we all fall.

The rangers, we agree, performed splendidly.

When he flags down the ranger, the tourist is winded. "Fire!" he blurts out. "A fire! Back there." King relays the information to the Park dispatcher. Fire along the Widforss trail. The dispatcher is baffled. He does not dispatch crews to fires, only to visitor-related emergencies, so he relays the information to the North Rim patrol rangers, who put on fireshirts, drive to the trailhead, and, outfitted with canteens and shovels, begin walking along the trail. Two fern feelers, ostensibly assigned to nature walks, hurry to join them. Overhearing the exchanges—but only partly understanding their core—the BI directs two crews near The Basin to drive their pumpers down W-1C, then proceed on foot over the ridge to Widforss Point. "Yes," he asserts. "Initial attack, at Widforss."

It is Big Bob's big chance, and he knows the protocol; he knows that the fastest way to assert a public presence is to order a helicopter for personal use. Greer, Thumper, Phil, and Greenback reach the Widforss trail. "Which way?" Greer asks. "To the Point," shouts BI, intoxicated by the power of command, by the mystique of the machine. The rangers arrive at the fire, which is nearly an acre in size, adjacent to the trail, right at the head of Transept Canyon. The helo appears on the horizon. Gonzo radios that he is approaching the

Area; he is convinced that he should be able to see the smoke from the heliport. The helo lands, BI climbs in, and 210 lifts off. Gonzo reaches the heliport and immediately requests the Park dispatcher to contact the Forest dispatcher and order an air tanker. The smoke column rises in thick white and yellow puffs. Crowds gather at South Rim overlooks and point to it. Everyone in the Area strolls down to the rim of Transept and watches the spectacle.

BI orders 210 to circle the fire. "When will you arrive?" he asks Greer. "Soon, very soon," says Greer, who is clearly winded. "We're nearly at the Point. We can't see any smoke yet." The C-119J taxis off from the retardant base at Grand Canyon airport. Two fern feelers and a tourist appear at the fire and begin scratching a line along the east flank. When Rich and crew arrive at Widforss Point, the BI continues to circle the fire. Greer sends Thumper up a tree to scout, while he, Phil, and Greenback pant heavily beneath their burdens of firepacks, saws, and fedcos. "Where are you?" asks BI, panicky with anticipation. "We're at Widforss," declares Greer, gulping for air. "Where are you?" "Get that helicopter out of the drop zone," thunders Gonzo. "We're bringing this air tanker in for a run." Still perched in the tree, Thumper watches, in confusion, as the C-119 roars past the Point; watches, helplessly, as the tanker proceeds to the head of Transept Canyon; watches, unbelieving, as he sees the smoke column from the Transept fire spiral upward nearly three air miles from their location. Greer turns off his radio.

They retrace their steps back to the pumpers, drive the pumpers to the Widforss trailhead, and hike into the fire, now about two acres in size. There is a flimsy, but momentarily adequate, scratch line around the east flank; retardant has slowed fire spread to the north and west; and the trail itself, located right along the Rim, has halted spread to the south. The rangers, fern feelers, and tourist are released. During their drive to the Widforss trailhead, Gonzo continues to direct the air tanker operation from the North Rim heliport, an ideal command platform. Now he, too, goes home. The BI, still perched in 210, continues to ricochet between the fire, Widforss Point, and the heliport. At last, as darkness approaches, 210 lands. Leo meets it at the heliport.

It has been Leo's lieu day, and when he returned from Kanab during the height of the slurry drops, Gonzo told him to manage the heliport. Just as he is leaving the heliport, the Park dispatcher calls the BI with an urgent request from the Forest dispatcher. The Forest needs a name for the fire. It must have a name to place on the fire order for the air tanker. When he requested 210, BI announced that he was fire boss. Now the dispatcher wants a fire name. Big Bob is pale. The helo lifts off. Leo turns to walk back to Skid Row. The Park dispatcher demands an answer. "Wait, Leo! What'll I do?" he cries. "Wh-wh-what'll I call it?"

"Call it the Fuck-up fire," Leo says, walking away.

POINT OF PINE: DAN AND I AND BIG MAC

Dan and I bind the saws and gear to the side baskets with bungee cord, then climb in. We lift off from the construction camp located on what used to be the ballfield. We use the contractor's helo—a Llama—because we are to fulfill some Park obligations under the powerline contract, which will string new high-tension wires from Bright Angel Point to the rebuilt pump station at Roaring Springs. A major set of power poles must be erected on a promontory of Supai formation, high above the Kaibab trail. Though deep in the Canyon, the promontory is well shaded and heavily forested with ponderosa. We have to clearcut the site and do it in a way that cannot be seen by the public or endanger the trail below. The project has been on the books for weeks; the Park, the contractor, and the Bureau of Reclamation have important schedules that must be met; the project cannot be postponed or canceled.

Our first problem is to prepare a site for the helo. We land some distance from the promontory, bushwhack to the site with a saw and pulaski, and take down a tree and clear enough brush to make a helispot. When the Llama lands, we unload the rest of our gear, lunches, and canteens, and agree to a pickup time at 1600 hours. As the Llama departs, we have our first opportunity to study the site.

There is a geometry to the project. We can't drop trees in ways that might allow them to roll off the promontory or start landslides. We have to fell trees into an open area, which means that we cannot start at the center and work out but must proceed from one end or the other. There are at least a score of trees—some substantial—that must be felled. They will have to be bucked up and rolled away; the stumps must be flushed. We might use some pieces to build up and level off the helispot. Then we double-check our gear and I select the McCulloch 890, Big Mac. A ponderous, gear-driven machine, almost antiquated by the high-tech standards of recent engines, it is the most reliable of all our saws. It is also the saw I learned to cut with, the saw I always return to.

We begin slowly. Every gesture is exaggerated. We talk little. The morning sun bakes the red rocks. The sky is cloudless. The only sounds are the coughing saw, cracks and thuds of falling, crashing trees, the muted tread of boot on sand and rock. Initially we trade roles, sawyer and spotter, tree by tree, but gradually I find myself cutting more and more and finally almost exclusively. At noon we break for lunch and eat on the stumps. Everything smells of oil and gas; everything tastes like sawdust. In two hours the sun will vanish behind Bright Angel peninsula. The promontory deserves a name, and I suggest Point of Pines. "Not now you can't," Dan says with a laugh.

Stiffly we take up the saws again. The rest was welcome but it cooled us down, and it is hard to loosen up. Moreover, there is no cushion on the handle of Big Mac, and my hands become numb with the strain and vibration. Arms fatigue, then submit to new rhythms. Our ears fill with saw noises. Roaring Springs Canyon echoes with the scream of the saws. There is no one on Rim or trail who can see us. There is no effective radio communication with the Rim. There is only us. Shadows sweep over the promontory.

We refill the saws with oil and gas, install new chains, tighten and retighten the chains as they adjust to wear. Chips fly: the site is smothered with curling, feathery chips, the sign of a sharp chain. We drop the last tree, and hurry to flush stumps and buck up logs that litter the clearing. Too late we realize that we should have brought peaveys. We make a lever out of a cut pole pine and delicately use sledge handles to pry logs to suit us. The image of the returning Llama dominates our thoughts, and exhaustion mixes equally with exhilaration. We use two saws now, and continually we mistake the cough of the other saw for the whop of an incoming helicopter. Then we see it. The Llama hovers over our new helispot. The pilot nods, and we signal him to land. "Be right there. No need to shut down," Dan shouts into his radio. Quickly we gather our gear, lash it to the side baskets, and climb in, still outfitted with chaps, reeking of oil, sweat, and sawdust. As we lift off, the pilot backs slowly over the Canyon and turns the ship in an arc so that he can taxi across Roaring Springs Canyon.

The Point swings into view, a splendid havoc.

CHAPTER SEVEN

The Monument

SUMMER RAINS compete with summer drying. The season is inchoate; the weather, unsettled. Instead of well-defined patterns there is a chronic indeterminacy, a daily cycle of morning sun and afternoon shadow, a double gloom of cloud and shade, with sudden bursts of sweltering sunlight, dreary days in a rain-soaked cache, and hurried attacks on proliferating smokes. Take your fireshirt off, then put it back on as shade replaces sun. Then do it again.

The season can go several ways. The number of fires may increase while their average size diminishes; storms may be infrequent, with ample drying between them so that fires are larger and more difficult; or the season may be rained into oblivion. The fire frontier may roll back from the Rim and even leave the Kaibab altogether. Whatever the outcome the season gradually acquires a signature rhythm.

It lasts until the middle of August, then the monsoon falters. The established air flow from the south—monsoon moisture—is replaced by a flow from the west and north that is cooler and drier. Days shorten. Suddenly there is a nip in the air; even perennial grasses cure, pines prepare for needle cast, and the large fuels, whose drying is unpredictable in the short term, reach an annual low moisture content.

A crew becomes restless in August. If the rhythms of fire busts are regular, firefighting hedges into the routine. If not, we want to see more of the Rim—and less of it. We want more fires, different fires, fires off the Rim. Crewmen want to explore the Canyon, the plateaus of southern Utah, the Monument. We want to shop in St. George and Flagstaff, maybe watch the Shakespearean Festival in Cedar City. We want to spend a few days at Lake Powell or Las Vegas. We talk of Rim Rapture. One day, the crew, fully clothed in Nomex, tramps down to the Lodge for lunch; the maître d' points to the sweep of giant picture windows and asks where we would like to sit, and Dave replies, "Any place we don't have to look at the Canyon."

There is talk, too, about the Last Days. By the third week of August the crew begins to break up as collegians leave for fall semester. Everyone looks for something he can carry away from the summer. For a few crewmen money is enough. For the rest it will have to be something else, something even they probably won't recognize until it has long passed. Some look beyond the summer, because for them there will be no return. All of us look beyond the Rim, wanting, we think, more than the Rim can offer.

"But it's my birthday," protests Seal. "All the plans are made. Everything is set." "Yeah, so much the better," I say. "Come on. There's a smoke report, and we're up next on the dispatch chart, and besides, we're the only ones left. Recon says it's a burning snag. We'll be back by nightfall." Seal says nothing, his brow knotted in deep calculations. "Hey, you and me, buddy," I say, "just like the old days."

We take a pumper down the Sublime Road. The aerial observer, whose last name is Bell—known colloquially as Dumb Bell—says that the fire is just north of the Walla Valley, that we can reach it by foot easily from the Sublime Road. When she instructs us to stop on the road, she describes our route rather than give us a bearing. "Just climb up the ridge, then go to the Rim," she says vacantly. "You can't miss it."

We carry one pack, a saw, a fedco, handtools, extra canteens and climb up the ridge north of the Sublime Road, slowly, very slowly. There is some oak brush, but otherwise the forest is relatively open. At the ridgetop we scan the horizon for the grass and aspen scenery of the Walla Valley. It is nowhere to be seen. We look down not at the Walla Valley but at an unnamed side gorge of the Canyon itself; a conservative estimate places the gulf before us at fifteen hundred feet.

To cross it we would have to climb down to the Supai formation, bushwhack a traverse around to the head of the side canyon, and then ascend. From there we would have another mile of bushwhacking to the fire. It is midafternoon. "We can't cross here," I say. "This is crazy." "You got that right," says Seal.

I call for a helicopter. "Yes," I say, "land on the road by the old picnic area near Sublime. We'll meet you there." As we hustle down the ridge, Seal reminds me once again that this is his birthday, that there are other things in life besides fire. "No sweat," I say. "If we can take the helo in, we can take a helo out. We'll be back to the cache in plenty of time." "It's not the cache I'm thinking about," Seal murmurs. "You don't appreciate my situation. You're not hearing me. This is my thirty-first birthday. I've spent every birthday since my eighteenth with a woman." Since he is in the throes of a second divorce, I don't ask if the ritual requires a different woman each year. "Tomorrow's my lieu day," he continues. "I'm out of here, at first dawn, for Vegas. No piddling fire is going to stop me." "It's a lock," I tell him.

When 210 arrives, Dumb Bell acts as a heliport manager. She is irritated that we have questioned her judgment as an observer, and we are irritated that she presumes to escort us into a helicopter. There is no reason for her to come, and 210 will have to make an extra stop to pick her up on its return to the South Rim. Since the helo is relatively low on fuel, I suggest we bring along an extra fedco and, well, just in case—"strictly as an emergency precaution, you understand"—a couple of sleeping bags. We see the smoke shortly after liftoff. The fire is a solitary pinyon along the Rim. There is some ground fire, but not much spread. We land in a small clearing nearby, obviously the product of an ancient fire. There are fire signs everywhere, and the ground is baked to dust and rock. "Plan to pick us up at sunset," I tell the pilot.

The fire is less than a hundred yards from our helispot. The ground is full of pockets of loose buff and red soil. A snag fire in a near desert. No matter that we are over seven thousand feet high, the Canyon winds have turned forest to desert. We scratch a line around the surface fire, then start on the snag. We work quickly, carving it up, branch by branch. With water and dirt, mop-up progresses rapidly. Yet we must be thorough. We can't justify another helo flight just to

check the fire after we depart, and no one is about to hike in here after
we evacuate. The sun drops lower. The view to the west—almost
identical to the western panorama from Point Sublime—is stunning.
The geologic colors that stratify the Canyon are projected upward
into the yellowing light. As the Canyon fills with shadow, a twilight
wedge forms above Powell Plateau. The north lies hidden behind the
notch of Muav Saddle; south of Powell there are hints of the
Esplanade, Great Thumb Mesa, Sinyala Butte—all for the moment
buried in deepening shadows. The rest, apart from the sky, is blocked
by the mighty rock borders of the Kaibab. Above, the western sky
seems to be on fire. "Don't look," pleads Seal. "Work, just work."

But the sun drops lower faster. It is August; the sun sets a little
earlier each day. We buck the tree trunk into sections, spray them
with water, and smother them with loose dirt. The boneyard grows.
Not much left. Pilots are allowed to fly a half hour before sunrise and
a half hour after sunset. We are nearly at sunset now. I call for the
ship. The fire can be safely left, and we can tramp back to the helispot
quickly enough to meet the pilot. He can return us to our vehicle at
Sublime. There is just enough time.

No one can be reached: not the pilot, not the South Rim heliport
manager, not Dumb Bell. At last we call dispatch, who tracks the
pilot down to the El Tovar bar. "Hey, I didn't think you guys could get
done in time," he says. "I've had a couple of beers. I can't fly anymore
today. I'll pick you two up early tomorrow, first thing." "Yeah," I say.
"Sure thing."

We set up camp. The sunset deepens, and Seal's mood turns darker.
He adds up the cumulative losses, beginning with money. Now that
the fire is out, there will be no more overtime or hazard duty pay. We
will be penalized for our hard work. "Relax," I say. "We still got a
couple of hours OT. And that sunset—it looked like fire all the way to
the Monument." "Yeah," Seal replies, "but I can't spend anything out
here." "You got a fire," I continue. "You wanted some action tonight.
We'll name the fire for you: the Thirty-one fire." "Yeah, yeah," says
Seal, "this is some *action. I was thinking of something . . . else.*
Imagine, my thirty-first birthday. I thought I was gonna get off the
Rim for a few days. I could be in Vegas. You know what you do, first
thing, when you get to Vegas, if you're a real gambler? You know? You

fill up your car with gas so you can get home again. But I don't have to worry about getting back because I can't leave.

"I got news for you, buddy. This ain't Vegas. This is the middle of goddamn nowhere. Nothing to drink but water and ration coffee. Nothing to eat but"—he searches through the firepack—"Christ, haven't we got anything but fuckin B-1s? A paper sleeping bag for a bed. And you. 'You and me, the old days.' What a deal."

"Yeah," I admit. "You take your chances and you get paid your money."

MARKING TIME

Randy is arguing strenuously for a change of lieu days. Pferd and Jimbo are amenable but cannot agree on a new schedule. No one wants Sunday off because there is a 25 percent pay differential if you work. Rich has a question about his overtime on the Pistol fire. Ted and Fran insist on having overlapping lieu days so they can go to Lake Powell. Dan hasn't been paid for his OT on the Waller Holler fire. Everyone on the Poltergeist fire is convinced that his hazard pay has been miscalculated. They are right. When pressed, Randy admits that he has figured the probability distribution of historic fires by days of the week. Anyone with Tuesday and Wednesday off figures to make 20 percent more overtime. Since our dispatch chart considers only the number of fires each crewmember is dispatched to, not his premium pay, Randy wants his lieu days changed. No one can imagine the slightest reason why fires are not randomly distributed throughout the week. Rich agrees to have Sunday off, but only if he can have Friday-Saturday first, and then Sunday-Monday for the subsequent pay period; that will give him four consecutive days off when the pay period changes. "I could go to Vegas in style," he claims. "Maybe I could even get my wash done." Our published work schedules, organized into two-week increments, are still officially, archaically referred to as "tours of duty," but no one calls them anything but "pay periods" anymore.

Everyone proclaims that overtime (OT) and hazard duty pay (HDP) are their only compensations for fire—and their only motives.

For a fire crew money and action are complementary; both are catalyzed by fire. Money, not sex, is the routine topic of conversation. But anyone in fire solely for the money is a fool. There are moments of flashy wealth, but premium pay comes only through ass-busting labor, and the hourly rates for regular fire pay are less than those for almost any other group on the North Rim; even fee collectors draw salaries that match those of the fire crew. Every seasonal park ranger starts at a salary equivalent to that of the fire crew foreman. Maintenance laborers, on a different pay schedule altogether (set by union scales), command double the rates. A flagman on a paving project makes two and a half times as much as a fire crew foreman. Compared with many seasonal jobs—the more menial jobs at the Lodge, for example—that of the fire crew pays well, though it pays less well every year. When I began as a GS-3/1 rookie, I made $2.05 per hour; and $2.25 was enough to buy breakfast, lunch, and dinner at the Inn. When I left, as a GS-6/1 foreman with a family, I made $6.50 per hour, which had roughly the same buying power. And for anyone who truly dislikes firefighting no amount of pay is adequate compensation.

The incentive to fabricate the actual hours worked is omnipresent. No one resists it very well. It takes no great skill to claim on your report that you went to sleep at 0200 hours instead of midnight, that you worked through your lunch hour, that the half-hour break was really an hour. No one on a crew is likely to protest that the fire boss or crew boss has given him too much OT. Still, while we insist that everyone get every hour coming to him, we do not tolerate padding. There is no way really to check, however, and the only sensible approach is trust. By making each snag fire boss submit the times for himself and comrades, a kind of honor system develops. Outside the crew there are no such controls. Manipulation of the fire accounts becomes a badge of managerial skill.

The mechanisms for fire financing are complex, and they encourage some abuses. There are two sets of accounts: one is budgeted, and the other is not. The secret to creative financing is to transfer as many costs as possible from the budgeted account to the non-budgeted, "emergency" accounts, of which there are two. One, the emergency suppression account, covers expenses attributable to actual fires. The other, the emergency presuppression account, pays for personal services and rentals during selective periods of high fire danger. What happens, of course, is that everything imaginable is charged to fires, and the determination of "high fire danger" becomes more and more loosely interpreted. At its extreme the regular fire crew budget is actually abolished—expended for road chips and other visitor-dependent services—and all fire operations are charged to the emergency accounts. Short of this is the practice of over-ordering under the provision for "replacement" of materials used up or damaged during a fire. Though charged to a fire, the supplies often end up in the ranger caches. The allowable charges are apparently limited only by imagination and conscience.

Among ourselves we manipulate schedules, scrutinize pay statements, scheme for extra overtime assignments; hazard duty pay, in particular, is an endless conundrum, a Rubik's cube of timekeeping. We try to manipulate the system where some flexibility is possible. But the ultimate determinant is fire. If there are lots of fires, there will be lots of money for everyone. That others outside the crew siphon off some of that matters little; there is plenty of money—and plenty of action. If it is a slow season, queries about money become more intense, and we look beyond the Rim. The disparities become an issue of fairness, and the real status of the fire crew within the hierarchy of Park Service values cannot be disguised.

At times it appears that the only group that does not really gain from the fire accounts is the fire crew. Why does John-Boy make more money than Boone on the Hambone fire? Why does Terry, a garbage collector, make twice the overtime that Donnie, a Longshot, makes on the Morning fire? Why does maintenance make two, three times the regular salary of firefighters? Why does every seasonal ranger make more than any seasonal fire guard? How can the rangers order new holsters off the Wishful fire? Why is premium pay on fires deferred one additional pay period? Why can we put a fern feeler and a ranger on fire standby when they have no fire experience, just so their supervisor can direct a little premium pay to his favorites? How much program money is there to support those who want to work late in the season, or has it all been spent on road chips? There is no single answer—there are only individual solutions.

Subtly the conversation has shifted from lieu days to holidays. Randy broods over the nuances of holiday pay. The operative phrase is "double time." I try—once again, patiently, meticulously—to explain that the expression is misleading. "You are paid for working that day as you are for any other day you are scheduled to work in your tour of duty. In addition, you qualify for a paid day of vacation. If you are scheduled to work that holiday and don't have the day off, you still get paid for it. Thus you get paid for the day once because it is a regular workday and you get paid again for the day because it is a holiday." "Then," says Randy, "we get double time." "Well . . ." I hesitate. "Yes, in a way. You get paid twice for the same day." "OK, so if we get double time on a holiday," he says excitedly, "and we go to a fire and work overtime, does that mean our OT rate is three and a half times our regular rate? And what about hazard pay? What is 25 percent of three and a half times our base pay?"

Din fills the Fire Pit, and the meeting concludes in a riot of miscalculations.

Recon 1 is responding to an emergency signal from the River, whose cause is never found, when Scenic reports a smoke north of Swamp Point. We are out of radio contact and at Building 175, ready to feast on Jimbo's long-promised deep-dish pizza. The pizza party has been planned for weeks. A patrol ranger delivers the message. We snap on a radio just as Recon 1 circles a rich swirl of cream and black smoke from ten acres of burning brush deep in Stina Canyon. It is an odd setting, a mixture of borders between Park and Forest, below the Rim, in a symmetrical side canyon filled with the mixed brush and pinyon-juniper of the Esplanade, terminated along the West Kaibab fault zone. It is too late now to send anyone, and no one could reach the fire from the Rim anyway; yet there is too much to do to continue with the pizza. There is a project fire in the making, and at the farthest reaches of the Park.

For once there is time to plan—all night, if we wish—and we plot a strategy that will bring the full resources of the Rim to bear on the Deep Dish fire. Here is our chance to move out of the category of seasonal grunts, to manage a fire organization instead of knocking down a fire. We activate the Park's in-house project fire team, a new innovation of Gonzo's. We round up all the reserves on the Rim, painstakingly equip each one, and orchestrate the lot into careful squads. We plan a helispot at Swamp Point, a fire camp a short distance back from it, a radio relay station at Fire Point; arrange for transport to Swamp. McLaren informs us that he will direct an air tanker, so we request air closure around Muav Saddle from the FAA. For once, we can assume positions of importance within the hierarchy of a project fire. Regulars are assigned to jobs as crew bosses, camp bosses, communications officers, heliport managers. I assume the title of Fire Boss III.

But as the sun breaks into the shadows of Stina Canyon the next morning, that design falls to pieces. What is supposed to concentrate the suppression effort only diffuses it; instead of putting us on the fire, the machinery removes us from it. The team service chief, Gonzo, refuses to delay a scheduled vacation and leaves the Rim. The designated line boss, a South Rim ranger, confesses that he has no idea what he is doing and asks to be released. Swamp Point is a good heliport but a lousy staging area; no one has any direct connection with the fire, only with our interposed organization. The helispot in Stina Canyon is too far from the fire. Within an hour the reserves wilt from Canyon heat. Cramps, heat prostration, and disillusionment with the grimy realities of firefighting force us to ferry out as many crewmen as we bring in. Fire crew regulars perform logistics, not firefighting, and instead of inflating our credentials, the actual jobs degrade them. Without a crew Randy is not a crew boss but a scout; Leo is not a camp officer but a cook; Rich is not an air service officer for heliport II, but a gofer for an uninterested helo pilot; the ambidextrous Dan, probably the best natural athlete on the crew, spends the day lounging in the seat of a pumper with his fist wrapped around a radio mike; I am not Fire Boss III but a gadfly about our fire camp, the manager of a fire organization with decreasing relevance to the fire. When the Park project fire team was instigated as a concept, we were instructed over and over that the job of fire overhead is to manage the organization, not to work a shovel, and the design of this project reflects this principle perfectly. I can see nothing of the fire. Rather, I have to rely on the relay station at Fire Point even to communicate with crews on the fireline. Instead of expediting communications, the relay system inhibits it; McLaren is unable to penetrate Dan's thick New Hampshire brogue, concludes that he has a speech impediment, and proceeds to direct two air tankers without the slightest regard to our operations. By early afternoon the project fire organization is a shambles. The overhead team is dissolved, and the reserves are returned to the Area. Now that the organization has disintegrated, I join Randy and Lenny at Stina Canyon to look at the fire. It is a revelation.

The fire has advanced considerably upslope, and it has the potential to crest over the Rim within either the Park or the Forest or both. But the real spectacle is the air show. A B-17 and a B-26 make successive passes across the burning slope. One at a time they enter the head of Stina Canyon with a full load, follow the grade of the side canyon down to the fire, empty a full or half load on the fire, then, lightened dramatically, pull up and away from Steamboat Mountain on the west side of the fault zone. Together the planes shingle the slope, each streak of retardant overlaying the last along both active fronts of the fire. The amount of slurry dropped is astonishing. I try to communicate with McLaren, to agree on some chain of command, but he is indifferent to anything except more air tankers. He will agree to anything. "Yes. Do what you want," he advises, absentmindedly. And we will have to do something.

The fire continues to burn. We still need to put in a fireline, burn out, run a heliport, patrol—all the things that should have been done today. This time I admit that the fire is outside our control, and we place an order with the Forest dispatcher for two hotshot crews, a qualified burn boss, and a sector boss; we'll assign one crew to each flank and a smaller gang of Longshots to miscellaneous fireline chores. After the order is placed and rebroadcast over the Forest net, the FMO from the North Kaibab appears at Swamp and pleads with us to commit a crew from the Forest. But it is too late.

It is, in fact, doubly late, because the next morning there is not a whiff of smoke from the Deep Dish fire. The south slope of Stina Canyon fairly drips with fire retardant. We shuttle one IR crew down and put in a protective fireline—we can't afford a reburn—while the other crew sleeps. But the fire is out; only the fire organization continues. Everything apart from the air tankers has been irrelevant.

The crews are sent home, and a week later we travel to Timp Point for a formal critique of the fire.

Timp is itself an anomaly—along the Rim but within the Forest. Below it, Stina Canyon spreads out to the south in a magnificent amphitheater, revealed in every detail. Had the camp been here, we could have watched the fire firsthand; and with the Forest, we might have attacked it cooperatively and directly. Or we could have ignored it and let the air tankers bomb it into submission. Instead, even as it was suppressed, the fire was out of control. But we could not understand that from Swamp, much less from the Area. We saw it from the inside looking out. Too few of us saw the flames. The fire was only incidentally within the Park, beyond the grasp of a seasonal fire crew.

Now, as we munch on rations left from the Swamp Point fire camp, our eyes are drawn away from the Deep Dish fire. Timp Point offers a panorama beyond the Park. To the west spreads the marvelous terrain of the Esplanade, and in the distance, there is the lavender silhouette of the Trumbull Range, a hint of cinder cones shimmering like heat waves, the bold facades of sister plateaus. Lenny offers the only meaningful critique: "We should have eaten the damn pizza."

JOE AND I DESCEND TO THE RIVER

This time Joe and I agree that we are taking the shortcut.

We park the truck at Monument Point and in the early dawn stumble along the Rim, looking for a route down. There is no trail as such, only a way over the Rim and down some talus slopes, but compared with the traditional trailhead at Indian Hollow, it saves a good five miles of tramping through the red-rock corrugations of the Esplanade. Trapped at a short drop-off, we make a rope out of parachute cord and lower ourselves down. Once on the talus slopes we glissade. At the base of the talus cone we step onto the Esplanade. Nearby there is a dead horse, with a large cavity eaten into its side by scavengers. Beyond that we find cairns that delineate the Thunder River trail proper.

The sun strikes us full blast. The Esplanade glows with red and pink and orange. The terrain is eerie: sandstones and shales have been sculpted by intermittent waters into mounds, hills, and cliffs, like ocean swells of red rock; pockets of sandy silt gather into hollows, stocked by isolated pinyon and bunch grass; the entire shelf is gouged into deepening gorges that drain into Deer Creek. The trail follows an irregular route between cliff and gorge, circumambulating the entire drainage. Monument Point neatly sheers the Kaibab and Kanab plateaus. To one side there is the West Kaibab fault zone; to the other, the Thunder River region—a fragment, much fractured with faults, of the Kanab Plateau. Our view of the Rim is blocked completely. Our radios are worthless.

The old trail was designed to connect the natural breaks through the major cliff-forming strata. There are three breaks in all—one from the Rim to the Esplanade, a second from the Esplanade to Surprise Valley, and a third to Thunder Springs. From Rim to River each set of switchbacks becomes steeper; each intervening traverse shorter and more concentrated. It is not an elegant trail—more brutal than inspired—but the links between Rim and River are never easy. The breaks are the key: the Esplanade is included only because there is no other way to traverse between the switchbacks that descend the Coconino sandstone and those that pass through the Redwall limestone. The Monument Point shortcut, which exploits smaller fractures along the much-contorted border with the Kaibab Plateau, cuts that traverse in half. This is my third descent to Thunder.

The first time I hiked the trail, I did so alone. Chuck dropped me off in the early morning at Indian Hollow with instructions to rendezvous with a seasonal ranger, Maury, at Thunder River. Maury had elected to start at sunset the night previous, then to camp along the Esplanade and make his final descent at dawn. When I volunteered for a second trip the next summer, I explained that I couldn't believe what I remembered of the first. Swifter and I lumbered down, crawling the last few miles under a merciless July sun. Swifter had a fishing pole swinging from his pack, but at the river his answer to dinner was a package of sardines and a bottle of peanut butter. This time it is to be the shortcut, with Joe. We have probably two miles of Esplanade before we reach the break through the Redwall.

What we are supposed to do along the way is unclear. We are instructed to plant a Park Service boundary sign along the Rim at

Monument Point and another in the vicinity of Thunder Springs. The second sign, mounted on an aluminum pole, sprouts out of Joe's pack. Otherwise, we are there to display a Park Service presence and to clean up the campsite at Thunder. We reach the end of the Esplanade.

Below us the red rocks drop away at our feet. Surprise Valley spreads before us, a great bowl, green and yellow, vaguely mauve in the morning light. Surprise Valley is a colossal slump block, a collapse feature situated at an extraordinary concatenation of faults and subterranean springs. It is a geologic shock. Along its east flank are Thunder and Tapeats springs; along its west, Deer Creek Springs. As much as 40 percent of the discharge of the Kaibab Plateau is funneled through that geologic plumbing. We plod down the switchbacks that snake through the Redwall and enter Surprise Valley.

The heat and concentrated silence stun. With the sun overhead there is not a patch of shade anywhere. In the middle of the crucible, the trail forks. The west path goes to Deer Creek, the east, to Thunder River. The land is hummocky and grey, dry and rumpled as though warped by heat. The sun staggers us. When we reach the lip of the bowl, we make a small rock cairn in which to plant our boundary sign, though the concept of a defining "Rim" seems meaningless at this location. Then we survey the narrow gorge before us.

We can see where Tapeats Creek joins Thunder River, and we can hear Thunder Springs below us. The gorge is narrow and steeper than anything in the eastern Grand Canyon. We descend the final set of switchbacks. Mercifully they swing toward Thunder Springs—two eye-shaped cavities in a sheer cliff of limestone out of which rush cold crystal waters. The cascading water blossoms into an oasis, a swath of bright green against the red cliffs, overgrown with riverine shrubs and towering cottonwoods, loud with splashing waters. We pause at the springs, then complete the trip down to the campsite at the confluence of Thunder River and Tapeats Creek. There are an outhouse and a wooden picnic table. Under a rocky ledge nearby a Boy Scout troop from Utah has deposited a spiral notebook in which visitors scrawl observations. We soak our feet in the creek and read the entries.

The change in clientele is apparent. For decades Thunder Springs was a distant appendage of the North Rim, accessible only by the notorious Thunder River trail and its legendary shortcuts. But with the advent of mass-produced river running, Thunder River and Deer Creek Falls have become part of the routine spectacles of the Colorado River. After the controversy over Glen Canyon Dam and the proposed Marble and Bridge Canyon dams, the Canyon is equated with a free-flowing Colorado River. That is where the visitors want to go, and running rapids in a baloney boat is promoted as the supreme Canyon experience. Those portions of the Park which can establish solid connections to the River will prosper, part of the growth industry of environmentalism; those which cannot will shrivel. Thunder Springs survives; it is an easy walk to the springs from the River.

Our expedition is an anachronism, a relic of the time when access was by foot, not by boat, when locals traveled to Thunder River as part of a regional rite of passage, when the fire crew enjoyed the dubious perks of backcountry patrols. As more people flow into the area, however, people management takes precedent. Rangers replace fire crew; river trips, not off-Rim fire calls, become the highest reward the Park bestows on seasonals. Our travels to the Tapeats Amphitheater are restricted to occasional searches for lost hikers and to the fires that boat parties ignite—annual fires at Deer Creek and, once, at Thunder River. In the political economy of the Park, the Inner Canyon is where the action is, and Thunder Springs is absorbed into the routine of Park Service river patrols.

Until that transfer is complete, however, we patrol. Almost everyone asks for one assignment to Thunder River, and almost no one asks for a second. No amount of warning seems adequate. With reckless fatalism Duane and Uncle Jimmy drink themselves into near oblivion at Gonzo's annual mint julep party the night before their trek. The next morning—with Uncle Jimmy coughing violently to get the cotton out of his mouth, and Duane asking to be left on the sandstone as an act of euthanasia—they stagger across the Esplanade. "I'm dying. God, I'm dying," pleads Duane. "Leave me. You go on. You can make it. Call for a helicopter." "Forget it," coughs Uncle Jimmy. "They'll come if I slash my wrists," Duane continues. "They have to come. Christ, I forgot my knife." Uncle

Jimmy coughs, ineffectively. "Forget it. They can't even hear us." "Of course they'll come. I know they'll come. Give me your knife. God, it's fuckin' hot."

Joe and I spend the afternoon in the shade, shifting from one rock overhang to another as the sun moves across the sky. Although the Thunder River trail is famous for rattlesnakes, we have seen none. At last the sun sets behind Surprise Valley, and we walk to the Colorado. Already the path is better marked than the Thunder River trail. From the River we can see the sky again, and we observe fragments of thunderstorms. But the River dominates the scene. Our views of the River are so often from a distance—from the Rim or from a helicopter—that it comes as a shock to see it and feel it in all its size and vitality. Here the subterranean drainage of the Kaibab is gathered. Here the Park funnels its political agenda. It is a power that lies beyond our control. We can only watch.

The River's perspective is alien, without sky and without fire. To river runners and to those environmentalists who spared the Canyon from dams at Marble and Hualapi, the River is the great integrator of Canyon attributes. It informs the Grand Canyon. To those who live on the Rim, however, the sky integrates, the rhythm of storms takes the place of rapids, and the River is a remote scenic spectacle, like the San Francisco Peaks. It contributes but half the dialectic of the Rim. The River, moreover, obeys a different logic from the Rim. The River has a beginning, a middle, and an end. You go where the River takes you; its direction conveys its order. But the Rim simply appears. It lacks transitions, and it lacks the logic of a journey. It suspends you on the brink. Where you go is your choice, not its.

Yet Rim and River do share a common Canyon, to which they are complements. They share, too, a skewed relationship to the biocentric vision that increasingly animates the wilderness movement. The Canyon is peculiarly inorganic, almost elemental. It features earth, water, air, and fire—rock, rivers, sky, and flame. To be absorbed into the new ethos, the River was redefined into the "Living" Colorado. But no similar metamorphosis occurs on the Rim, and the fire program keenly feels that alienation. Nationally the reformation in fire policy showed a strong biological bias. Prescribed fire became not merely a defensive tactic, a means to protect against wildfire by reducing fuels, but a surrogate device by which to reestablish an important ecological process. It became a means to promote biological reform. Those parks that developed prescribed fire programs—places like Sequoia-Kings, Everglades, even Yellowstone—all had strong connections between fire and special biotas or organisms like sequoia groves, sawgrass, and elk. Through these relationships the parks established a constituency among visitors. At Grand Canyon, however, there are no unique biotas bonded to fire. There is essentially no relationship between fire and the Living Colorado River. The linkages between Rim and River are reduced until even trail patrols recede into insignificance.

Joe and I snap out of our trance. There is no more time for reverie. Bats already flap in the claustrophobic gloom. When we reach our camp, the roar of Thunder Springs is deafening.

The rain begins soon afterward. The sky darkens completely, lightning replaces the sunset, and rain pummels us, first in large, isolated drops, then in sheets. We search for shelter and decide that the picnic table is our best hope. We place our packs over it, to help plug the cracks, then crowd underneath. After a few minutes we admit that the table is hopeless; the area is crawling with thousands of ants. Joe retreats to the rock overhang by the creek that contains the hiker logbook. I scramble up a cliff to a narrow shelf and squeeze in. Lightning is ceaseless, and the pounding of thunder, relentless. Like great rocks breaking free from a cliff, lightning cracks into an avalanche of noise; a ghoulish light penetrates and bleaches into the gargoyle cliffs, then collapses; and thunder reverberates through the narrow gorge. It is impossible to sleep, to eat, to think. After what seems like hours the lightning at last abates, and the rain lightens but continues. Joe and I elect to stay where we are. "I've got our dinner in my pack," I yell in triumph. Joe grins. "OK. You've also got the snakes."

The next afternoon we begin our climb out. We pause for lunch at the springs. An animal got into Joe's pack and gnawed into our salami roll. "It's OK," says Joe. "We can split the roll in half." "Agreed," I say, and then cut the roll lengthwise so that all the chewed sections are in Joe's half. As we climb over the rim of Thunder Springs, we check our cairn and boundary sign. It is still there, still defining for anyone who might wander past just where we think the Forest ends and the Park begins, or, more properly, where the Rim ends and the River begins. In fact, it matters little. The region will be defined by its center, not by its periphery, and that means the River. The River is important: the Thunder River trail is not. Legislation will eventually expand the boundaries of the Park to include all of the Thunder River trail, the entire Esplanade, but that is beyond our concern. Our concern is to get back to the Rim.

Surprise Valley is deathly still. In the late afternoon it is a crucible of dying heat. The sun begins to set as we plod our way up the switchbacks through the Redwall. When we reach the Esplanade, the scene opens dramatically, and we pick up an extra half hour of daylight. We move briskly, and when the darkness makes it impossible to spot cairns anymore, we stop, locate pockets of sand, and make camp. Nights are warm, but mosquitoes are everywhere. We rise early, with the morning only a pale glow over the hidden bulk of the Kaibab.

We pass by the Monument Point cutoff with helpless shrugs. It is part of our arrangement—the price of an official trail patrol—that we must hike the full route to Indian Hollow on our return. Someone from the fire crew will meet us at the trailhead. As the sun crests over the cliffs, the Esplanade becomes a gigantic parabolic mirror made of red rock. It is obvious that the only real shortcut to Thunder Springs is the River. "Tell me," says Joe as we halt for water under the shadow of a mushroom-shaped boulder, "*please* tell me that we don't have fires here."

At Indian Hollow we arrive ahead of schedule. Joe turns on the Park radio, and we learn that the big storm the night before last has started a couple of fires and no one will return to the cache for hours. "Relax. We'll find someone—a backcountry ranger, if we have to— and pick you up."

We look around. The Esplanade of Deer Creek Amphitheater is bleached by sunlight, too washed out to be impressive under a cloudless sky. Sun replaces gloom, and the vision of smoke crowds out the memory of rising mists of water. We walk toward Indian Hollow and lie down in the shade of some ponderosa. Everywhere there is the smell of pines. From deep in the Kaibab comes the stir of a breeze.

The flight is brisk and dramatic, and Cone and I are the envy of the fire crew. We pass over The Dragon, Sublime, Powell Plateau. We pass Thunder Springs, hidden to the north; Great Thumb Mesa, Sinyala Butte, Havasu Canyon to the south; Kanab Creek, a meandering gorge that joins the Colorado to the Arizona Strip; to the fringe of the Kanab Plateau itself. The noise of the rotor thunders in our ears. Then we sight the smoke, rising thin and white, in the cold morning air. Behind it to the west loom Vulcan's Throne, the cinder cones of the Uinkaret Plateau, the Trumbull Range, Toroweap Valley. We land on a small peninsula of the Esplanade. The fire burns in desert shrub and grass up a steep talus slope. We will be out of radio communication and so arrange for a preset afternoon pickup.

We cache our gear at the helispot, take canteens and handtools, and hike up the slope. We build a line by spraying shovelfuls of dirt on flaming yuccas and bunchgrass. The sound of shovels on rocks echoes across the amphitheater. The grass is still damp from the storm, and Canyon winds have not matured for the day. Within an hour the fire is contained at eight acres. We mop up smoldering yuccas and pack rat middens tucked among large boulders. When the last smoke is extinguished, we trudge back to the helispot and decide to name the fire after ourselves: the Pyne-Cone fire. Cone locates some shade under an enormous boulder that has tumbled down from the Rim. The day is hot and clear.

Suddenly the silence is overpowering: it is as awesome a presence as the sun. Even our whimsy seems dim. Our words are lost in the immense emptiness. After a while we stop talking.

For hours we sit and stare at the unmoving landscape. The heat and silence intensify. Our vision of the fire fades, as though sweated out of our memory. Unusual, we think, for a fire to be so quiet; unusual, not to hurry away from mop-up; unusual, for a fire of eight acres to seem so small.

Searching for Ranger Riffey

The road to the Monument always seems longer than I remember it. I think that it is lucky for Dana and me that Riffey's pumper broke; it gives us two trips to the Monument—one to pick up the vehicle and one to return it—and it firms up a North Rim claim to the place, to a realm of fires beyond the district. The South Rim crew insist that they ought to respond to Monument fires because they are closer to an airport and run the Park's central heliport, but clearly the Monument belongs to the North Rim; we can drive there—even if it takes forever.

We have to go to Fredonia, then west toward Moccasin, then southwest again across the sage plains of Antelope Valley, the volcanic uplands of the Uinkaret, and into Toroweap Valley. There is no direct connection between the North Rim and the Monument, not even a connection by River; the whole Kanab Plateau, bisected by the gorge of Kanab Canyon, intervenes. The Monument, in turn, leads to nowhere else. You have to go to the Monument for its own sake. The road, such as it is, dead-ends at the Canyon Rim.

Toroweap Valley gradually broadens and deepens. On the east the Kanab Plateau ends with a sculpted facade of cliffs. On the west volcanic eruptions pile into the Trumbull Range. The valley floor is vegetated with desert sage, grass, brush, cactus, and dust. We pass a sign announcing GRAND CANYON NATIONAL MONUMENT. There is a primitive airstrip and a hangar for a light plane. Further on, nestled against some cliffs, there is a cluster of buildings made of native stone—Riffey's house, which doubles as ranger station; a garage and utility shed, which contains the diesel power generator—some road machinery, including a grader, and broad sheets of corrugated tin, blinding in the midday sun, which collect runoff for potable water.

There is no one at home. It's always a gamble whether you will actually find Riffey or not; there is no landline—no phone—to the Monument. Riffey has a large base-set radio that he uses when he needs to communicate with the Park dispatcher; otherwise he wisely shuts it off. The bustling affairs of the South Rim are only gibberish and chatter to the Monument. Technically the Monument is independent from the Park, established by presidential proclamation rather than an act of Congress, and everything looks very different. Dana is disappointed not to meet the legendary Ranger Riffey, "Old John Riffey," but we see his pumper by his garage, along with a note; then we continue on to the end of Toroweap Valley. We will pick up the pumper on our way out.

The view from the Rim is stunning—often reproduced in pictures, and distinctive from any other visible in the Park. The gorge drops an abrupt three thousand feet. Where the Valley meets the Canyon, a gigantic fault spans the gorge, dividing the Kanab from the Uinkaret Plateau. Along that fault volcanics have intruded, and atop the Rim they have erupted into a spectacular cinder cone, Vulcan's Throne, while at the River they are revealed as plugs like Vulcan's Forge and that most renowned of Canyon rapids, Lava Falls. There is a trail of sorts, marked by cairns, down Vulcan's Throne to the River, but it is rarely used. Below, in lumbering baloney boats, we can see a river party.

Unlike the eastern Canyon, where many geologic components contribute to a grand ensemble, Toroweap is composed of fewer parts and the linkage of those parts is more violent. The Uinkaret is the smallest of the plateaus that constitute the Grand Canyon. The Kaibab is the highest and the most elaborately carved. The Shivwits, on the far west, is the largest, the lowest, and the most subdued. The Kanab captures some of the features of the Kaibab where they collide along the West Kaibab fault zone, and it collects, on its border with the Uinkaret, some volcanism; but mostly it is dominated by its own marvelous sub-canyon, Kanab Creek. Each of the great plateaus has a distinctive geomorphic shelf, and their elevations relative to the River rise from the east to the west. For the Kaibab, this is the Tonto Platform, above the inner gorge; for the Kanab, it is the celebrated Esplanade, resting on the lumpy Supai formation; for the Shivwits, the higher, broader Sanup Plateau.

The Uinkaret Plateau is the odd man out. The great faults that define the borders of the Uinkaret sweep together into a bottleneck along Toroweap Valley. Everything is compressed and accentuated. The Esplanade vanishes into the mouth of Toroweap Valley exactly at the Rim. Everything seems to be glued by a volcanism that has squeezed through cracks and faults, oozed across, over, and down ancient cliffs, and exploded upward into cones and mountains. The geologic intensity seems oddly at variance with the stillness—too harsh to call a serenity—that hangs over the valley like the summer dust. We sit under a massive red sandstone boulder perched at the Rim and eat lunch, and Dana asks about fire.

There is not much to tell. What is known belongs to Ranger Riffey, and he reveals it at his discretion. He has been at the Monument since 1942, and he will die at the Monument. For most of us, Riffey *is* the Monument. It is said that Riffey handles fires, like everything else, by himself. He flies recon in his plane, *Pogo,* then puts out the fires with his pumper or asks his rancher neighbors or, occasionally, the Forest Service or the Bureau of Land Management for help. Sometimes he simply lets the fires expire of their accord. But every few years we get a fire call. One late autumn a forty-acre fire broke out in pinyon-juniper on Mount Emma, the southernmost peak of the Trumbull Range, and a couple of SWFF crews were flown in to suppress it. It was so cold at night that the fire nearly self-extinguished and the crews had little mop-up. Another time, on a summer fire—five acres on Mount Emma—we sent two pumpers and a dozen firefighters. Riffey and his wife, Mary Beth, treated the crews to a royal breakfast before they returned to the Rim. The fire established new standards for off-district hospitality. The crew named it the Mary Beth fire. We have coveted jurisdiction over fires at the Monument ever since.

It may be for the best that we have missed Riffey, I think. Better to leave him as a legend. Old Ranger Riffey—he has always been *old* to anyone at Grand Canyon—is a mixture of skills and attitudes that has no place in the Park Service. He does everything—road mainte-nance, rangering, mechanical repair, fire. It all looks wonderful from a distance, but life at the Monument is a bureaucratic dead end; its visitation will always be minuscule compared with that at the South Rim. Ranger Riffey could exist only at a place like the Monument, and the Monument will not be allowed to survive forever. Eventually the legislated expansion of the Park will incorporate the Monument within the domain of a Greater Grand Canyon, and the Park will retitle the area the Tuweep unit; but it will not be easy to assimilate, and as long as Riffey remains, it will always be identified with him and be known as the Monument.

It is sixty dirty, tedious, hot miles by dirt road back to Highway 389 and another ten paved miles to Fredonia. For an entire day we have been completely isolated from the life of the Rim. It is late evening when we reach the Area. The kitchen lights are on at 176, the front door is open, a desk light glows within the Fire Pit, lights from the tool stall flood out of the fire cache, and as the night winds swing the heavy double doors in and out, the cache flashes like a sem-aphore. A sickening feeling, a grasping anxiety, seizes us. "Fire," Dana says, sucking in his breath. "Yeah, I think so," I say. "It's the chance you always take when you leave the Rim."

"I don't believe it. A fucking fire," says Dana. "And we missed it."

Ramparts Cave was used extensively by the now-extinct Shasta ground sloth, and the floor is deep with deposits of sloth dung mummified over millennia in the dry desert air. The site has been known to archaeologists for decades; an exploratory trench divides the deposits, and a metal gate guards the cave entrance, located about five hundred feet above the River just before the Canyon ends at Grand Wash Cliffs. But someone has broken in and, deliberately or accidentally, has started a fire. The dung glows to life, and smoke from the cave is spotted by river trips.

The South Rim fire crew instantly claims jurisdiction on the grounds that they control the Park helicopter, that initial attack and resupply will require extensive helo use. We are powerless to protest. Stiegelmeyer, now foreman of the South Rim crew, gloats at his power over his former North Rim buddies.

When the initial crewmen arrive at Ramparts, they land on a ledge and walk into the smoking entrance, then abruptly turn around and walk out. So dense is the smoke that they can see absolutely nothing. The stench of smoldering sloth shit is excruciating. While scientists and administrators at Park headquarters debate what to do, the South Rimmers decide to treat the cave fire as they would a house fire and they return with structural fire equipment. They don breathing apparatus and turnout coats, set up a ventilating fan, even erect a portable tank and, using a helo bucket, fill it with water from the Colorado while a portable pump charges their lines. They enter the cave, spray wildly, and retreat again. Unlike in a structural fire, conditions in the cave make ventilation impossible. The heat turns the water instantly to steam, and huge chunks of the cave walls and roof threaten to spall off; the roof will have to be shored up before anyone can safely enter the cave again. And so it goes. Each solution only creates another problem.

It seems impossible to suppress the fire without trampling, decomposing, or otherwise destroying the deposits. Specialists from the Mine Enforcement and Safety Administration are called in for consultation. They float down the River on a Park Service boat and recommend that the fire be starved of oxygen. Accordingly the entrance to the cave is sealed off, and nitrogen is pumped in. But caves leak, and Ramparts Cave leaks in many places. The fire continues. When, after several months, the air lock is opened, smoke floods out. Again the cave is sealed. This time the Park waits a year, and when the entrance is unsealed, the air is stale but clear. The cave is free of smoke. It is also half free of sloth dung. The old trench, an accidental fireline, stopped the spread of the fire.

WESTWARD THE COURSE OF EMPIRE

Dust hangs pungently in the still morning air. Mile after mile the truck churns up clouds of dust, and it lingers in long serpentine stringers. We are in terra incognita, *Arizona deserta,* deep in the Arizona Strip. Fire season has lulled, and we are headed to the Shivwits Plateau, presently under the jurisdiction of Lake Mead National Recreation Area but possibly ripe for annexation by Grand Canyon if current legislation passes Congress. En route we stop by the BLM offices at St. George in what is billed as a courtesy call. It is just as well that there is no one in the office. Our connections with the BLM fire organization are mediated wholly by the Forest Service. Besides, fires in the desert range of the Strip have almost no socially redeeming value. A "Strip trip" ranks somewhere alongside litter collection as a preferred assignment; in the emerging hierarchy of the Park, rangers are rewarded with River trips, and firefighters with Strip trips. But if there is a land transfer, then the Park must learn to deal directly with the BLM, and we have been sent to Shivwits to ensure that the North Rim, not the South, will have primary jurisdiction.

The scene is vacant, a low, undulating tableland with great shadowy plateaus and mountains to its remote flanks. Nowhere is there any sign of the Canyon. We try to interpret the BLM road map and end up appealing to the sun for directions. We pass through a gate, and—miracle—the key we are given actually works. But there are lots of gates: private land is plentiful, even in the national recreation area. To the east we can see the Mount Trumbull Range, even Mount Emma within the Monument. To the far south, resembling a squashed monadnock, rises Mount Dellenbaugh. Beyond, the Shivwits Plateau extends in a series of narrowing peninsulas to the Canyon Rim. The road follows the longest of these peninsulas. Gradually, imperceptibly, the land rises; sagebrush is replaced by pockets of pinyon and juniper; and at the trailers, where Lake Mead maintains a small fire cache, there is actually a forest of ponderosa.

We set up camp at the trailers. Nearby there is a dirt landing strip, the one practical connection between the Shivwits and its administrating agency. We marvel that Lake Mud has the least interest in the Shivwits, then recall that Gonzo was chief law enforcement officer at Lake Mud before he became area manager of the North Rim. Rumors pass that the Shivwits once had a fire and Gonzo sent everything but the Seventh Fleet to fight it. We inspect the cache; most of the tools remain, unopened, in GSA boxes. There are rumors, too, of wild parties by NPS brass here, that a ranger broke his arm while climbing over the trailer during one such drunken blowout. The camp is about thirty-five miles from the Canyon, and there is enough time to watch the sun set over the endless Sanup, by far the largest of the Canyon terraces. The scene is yellow-grey and deceptively gentle, soothing after the raw, red Esplanade. Where the Shivwits ends—at Grand Wash Cliffs—the Grand Canyon, too, traditionally concludes.

The sun sets slowly, gracefully across the Sanup. The terrace is grassy, and ranchers winter cattle and horses under special-use permits issued by Lake Mud. Regardless of whether the new Park boundaries will incorporate the Shivwits as a whole or whether those boundaries will end at the Rim, they will almost certainly bring the Sanup into Grand Canyon. It is hard to imagine what kind of fire suppression will be required. Surely the sensible thing is to contract that responsibility to the BLM, as the Kaibab National Forest has done with Mount Trumbull, exchanging its Trumbull holdings for BLM land adjacent to the Kaibab. In turn, the BLM has transformed the old guard station at Trumbull into a helitack base. But we have not come to the Shivwits to abdicate a North Rim presence; we have been ordered to establish one. With a huge land addition, such as the Shivwits, the North Rim might become, as its more megalomaniacal supporters wish, North Rim National Park. If the only bureaucratic job that can be justified in such a place is fire suppression, so be it. Firefighting could become a first step. Fire might be recognized as important to intrapark politics—if, that is, there are enough fires on the Shivwits.

The next day we hike up Mount Dellenbaugh. Unlike the Uinkaret, which contracts as it approaches the Rim, the Shivwits expands. It is a marvelous panorama, but it is diffuse, and there is nothing on which to concentrate the eye. Somewhere on the hike I develop an allergic reaction unlike anything I have ever experienced; I sneeze uncontrollably, and my eyes water like a leaky fedco. We had planned to stay another night at the trailers but decide now to drive tonight to the Monument, maybe stop by the helitack base at Trumbull, stay with Riffey or camp along the Rim. But first we need to look.

There is no sign of fire anywhere. There are great swaths and stringers of pinyon-juniper among the sagebrush plains. We cannot see the Kaibab or even the Kanab, but we can see plainly enough over the Trumbull Range, and there are no smokes. There is no place to look but farther west.

There are fires everywhere in the West and Alaska, but the biggest are in California. The Park Service is asked to contribute personnel to a national mobilization, and it assembles a crew from the western parks; Grand Canyon is instructed to send four firefighters, two from the North Rim. Randy and I have less than an hour to ready our gear.

Our excitement mounts as 210 flies us to the South Rim, where we are to rendezvous with two rangers from Petrified Forest and catch a chartered plane to California. But nothing happens. For the remainder of that day and night we wait on the South Rim. We pass the hours pitching horseshoes beside the South Rim fire cache. One minute we are to be dispatched imminently; the next we are to be disbanded; the third we are to stand by. Hurry up and wait. Randy acquires the first injury of the campaign fire when, after forty consecutive games of horseshoes, a blister develops on his throwing hand.

At last we are taken to the airport and board a King Air for Fresno. Randy nearly promulgates a fistfight with a Petrified ranger when he casually insults the caliber of Big Ten football. A Park Service car from Sequoia-Kings picks us up and transports us to a motel. The next morning a bus arrives to take us to King City. We have no idea what fire we are going to—there are dozens. Along the way we are told how the crew will be organized. The designated crew boss is a seasonal from the Sequoia-Kings fire crew, flamboyantly mustachioed, hair parted down the middle of his head, wearing a ranger uniform. "Jeez," says Randy. "Him? He looks like Charles Manson." "Charlie" introduces himself. We ask about his experience. "Don't worry," he assures us. "No one has ever complained about my timekeeping."

It is late afternoon when we arrive at an enormous fire camp, which is spread over an entire valley. Smoke hangs in a thin veil across the surrounding mountains. The bus stops at a clearing. We pile out, collect our gear, and wait for orders. Charlie disappears for a few minutes, then rematerializes. He points out where to get paper sleeping bags. Randy and I get two each, one to use as a pad. When we return, Charlie, still in his ranger shirt, is playing cards with some of his Sequoia-Kings cronies, using an overturned box for a table. We have not yet seen him in a hard hat. The bus leaves. We set out our bags and wander to the mess line. "Bulk Up" is the byword, as rumors swarm like deerflies: tomorrow we ship out to the firelines; this may be our last good meal for days; stock up on carbohydrates;

squirrel away a few extra candy bars; swill all the liquids you can. Randy wants to know where the latrine is.

It is pitch-black when a terrifying roar startles us awake. There are headlights, the cough of Caterpillars, the rattle of truck engines. Vehicles are all around us. We have camped in the middle of the equipment yard. As we drag our gear to the comparative shelter of some large oaks, we congratulate ourselves that no one has been run over. Within a few hours we should be wakened, sent in predawn darkness to the lines; it is important to get as much sleep as we can. Instead, we wake to sunlight. "Must have pulled night shift," reasons Helitack Jack, another of the Sequoia clique. The hum revives: time once more to Bulk Up. "Just what fire is this anyway?" Randy asks.

Again, nothing happens. We locate the designated sleeping areas, eat lunch, snack on soda pop and candy bars, stuff ourselves at dinner. Bulk Up. The night passes without incident. Charlie plays cards. There are no orders. Randy and I visit the mess line again. The Palomar Hotshots are passing through the line like a scene from Night of the Living Dead. *"Watch it," warns a firefighter from Wyoming who stands next to Randy. "They'll roll you for your rations." Curious, Randy walks alongside, a strutting study in leisure with his Coors baseball hat, thongs, and gym shorts. He clutches a wad of grapes and a bottle of Gatorade and watches the hotshots intently. "We need something to do," he declares.*

We locate the camp boss, suggest that he let us go to town, bring back a few volleyballs and footballs, organize some games. We'll take over the camp bulletin board, we tell him. We'll put out a camp newspaper. Anything. He cannot understand why we are so energetic. "Well," he muses, "you are here for R and R. I guess you can do what you want." Suddenly all is clear. We have not been sent to the fire but to an R and R camp. We track down the source of the confusion to our name, Sequoia Number One. For the Park Service that was label enough, but there is also a Sequoia National Forest, and it has sent two crews, Sequoia Number One and Number Two, to the fire. Sequoia Number One was due for rotation out of the fireline and into the Arroyo Seco camp for a few days' rest. "Tomorrow," the plans chief promises. "You will go to the fire tomorrow."

When we arrive at the new site, Princes Camp, it is being evacu-
ated. The Marble-Cone fire has spilled over yet another ridge; burnout from the new lines will sweep across the present camp. We pack up
cots and stuff paper sleeping bags into garbage compactors. The
National Guard is supplying most of the transport trucks, the
showers, the mess line, so we help guardsmen load and pack. We are
the last to leave.

At the new new camp we are directed to sleep in a thicket of poison
oak. Randy and I refuse. We locate an open area and tell Charlie
where to find us. Charlie has still not removed his ranger shirt. What
we can't find, however, are folding cots. Shortly afterward a rumor
starts that rattlesnakes have been discovered near two sleeping bags,
so Randy and I wait until dark, then mosey over to the plans tent,
where there are several cots, and carry two back to our site. Before
racking out for the night, Charlie instructs us to report for breakfast
at 0430 hours. "Bulk Up. We're moving out."

Breakfast is surreal. There is not a shred of daylight. Bodies shuffle
through the mess line, then sit at tiny folding tables. The tables are
hinged and collapse into wooden suitcases for convenient storage
between project fires. Over the camp PA system comes the request for
the "following crews" to report to Transportation. Some ten crews are
named: Texas Number Two, Klamath Number One, Chilao Hotshots
. . . They are obviously being sent to the line. Not a body moves. The
kitchen is supposed to run two lines but can handle only one, and
the bottleneck grows with each minute. Perhaps ten minutes later the
camp PA system instructs the "following crews" to report to Communications: Texas Number Two, Klamath Number One, Chilao Hotshots . . . Again nothing happens. Randy and I have maneuvered
through the line and Randy opportunistically seizes a folding table.
Almost immediately he decides to get another cup of coffee. "You
want a second?" he asks. "No, thanks," I mutter. He rises, the folding
legs under my seat buckle, and the entire table flips over on me so that
I am covered with scrambled egg, bacon, and coffee. No one around
us bats an eye. "On second thought," I tell Randy, "I will have
another cup." The camp PA instructs the "following crews" to disre-
gard all previous instructions: Texas Number Two, Klamath Number
One, Chilao Hotshots. . . .

At the fireline we join a throng of yellow shirts marching along a bulldozed line that swings from ridgetop to ridgetop in the Ventana Wilderness. Never have we seen a fireline so huge. Never have we seen so many firefighters. There are crews by the score. Incredible as it seems there is almost not enough room for everyone on the line. The whole fire has been bulked up. We stake out a small stretch of fireline and wait. Two Hispanic SWFF crews perch on a rocky pinnacle. It looks like a seal rookery, and we call it Seal Rock. For the next eight hours we do nothing. We are not allowed to do anything. Shift plans call for crews to burn out from the ridgetop line, but only IR crews are allowed to touch any ignition device. We watch while the Lassen Hotshots shoot Véry pistols, toss fusees, and attempt to use flamethrowers to burn out the brush on the slope below us. There is hardly a whiff of smoke. I try to keep my squad from falling asleep. In desperation we volunteer to carry packs of fusees for Lassen.

The fire is far in the distance, deep in valleys. When it finally makes its run late in the afternoon, the flimsy efforts at burnout prove wholly inadequate. The flames roar over the ridge ahead of us, crest upon crest, like a stormy surf of fire. It is clear that the entire basin will burn out, that the bulldozed line will be hard pressed to contain it, that the firing operations have been too little too late. Air tankers are called upon to reinforce the line. We watch, numbly, as a succession of B-17s, B-26s, and C-119s fly overhead. It is obvious that the line will be lost. In a stage whisper, Stiegelmeyer muses, "You know, if only we could back this fire into a cave . . ."

We learn later that the fire overruns the entire line. The slop-over itself is now greater than five thousand acres. The Marble-Cone fire is growing by leaps and bounds, and the next projected fireline is beyond our camp. We will have to relocate the fire camp yet again. For reasons we cannot explain, we draw no assignment for the next two shifts. Charlie is nonplussed. "We get paid whether we work or not," he says with a shrug. Yes, we agree, but we are here to see fire. Randy and I wander over to the plans tent and casually ask why we are not being used. Plans informs us that we can begin night shift tomorrow. Charlie is irritated. When the crew hears that we are scheduled for night duty, the buzz begins: Bulk Up. Randy estimates that he has gained five pounds since we arrived at the Marble-Cone fire. One of the Sequoia-Kings clique, a man known as Lizard, proudly mentions a newspaper cartoon he saw posted on the camp bulletin board. The core of the picture is Mount Rushmore, and added to the gallery of presidents is the face of a "California firefighter," hard hat and all. "Oh, yeah?" sneers Randy. "Does he have a sandwich in his mouth?"

Our guardsman driver has never driven a deuce-and-a-half before; in fact, he wants to use the experience he gains on the fire to qualify for a license. The truck lurches up the hill, dies, slides back, leaps forward as the clutch pops, and the cycle begins anew. As we round a corner, there is fire to both sides of the road. The open back of the truck erupts in shouts. The driver inadvertently kills the engine. Another truck is ahead of us, and others follow, and we convene on the dirt road for a conference. The flames are relatively quiet. We decide it is better to proceed, at least to some place where we can turn around. Our driver will never negotiate a U turn on this narrow road.

At the top, at a place called Chews Ridge, the confusion multiplies. There are other crews somewhere in the darkness. There are flames, down and distant from us, like bubbling lava. Some group moves, and we follow it. We come to a fireline. Both sides are burned out. "Great," mutters Randy. "Look on the bright side," says Helitack Jack. "We can't burn out the wrong side by mistake." A hotshot crew marches up and down the line with propane flamethrowers. We sit down, pass the night in conversation, and heat some cans for ration coffee. Early in the morning we are brought back to camp. The fireline at Chews Ridge, we learn at the camp bulletin board, has been lost.

The next night we are taken to another line. There is still some daylight when we arrive. In addition to Sequoia Park Number One there is a hotshot crew somewhere and two SWFF crews. Safety regulations, however, require that personnel and tools be shipped in separate vehicles, and the predictable consequence is that the pickup with the SWFF crew tools becomes lost. To the forty Apaches Charlie donates his pulaski. Why we need handtools at all is not apparent: Cats have scraped off a fireline twenty yards wide. We are told to follow the dozer line and widen it. When we leave the SWFFs, they *are tossing dirt clods and taking turns throwing the pulaski against a tree.*

For two hours we dutifully whack apart chaparral from one side of the fireline and carry it to the other. The net difference in fireline width is nil, but at least it is something to do; it is something we understand; cutting, scraping, clearing—this is how we fight fire on the Rim. By midnight, however, the absurdity of the exercise overwhelms its charm. A D-4 Cat could scrape brush faster than we can walk, and we begin to hike down the line. Someone somewhere should be able to tell us something. Charlie continues to wear his ranger shirt, to which he has added a hard hat. In the distance we faintly hear the clank of bulldozers. Beyond that there is no sound except the tread of our boots. The night is dark, and smoke floods the valleys like a black glacier. All headlamps, however, point to the ground; so chewed up is the fireline from dozer blades, so lumpy with overturned rocks that it is hard to keep footing. Our march abruptly ends as Charlie points to a figure slumped against a tree.

We have seen no one for hours, and a premonition of some disaster hushes the crew. Stealthily Charlie approaches the body. "It's our sector boss!" he cries out. "What's-his-name from the Region Three strike team. He's asleep!" We spend the rest of the night following the fireline down the ridge.

It is, for all intents and purposes, our last shift on the Marble-Cone fire. We are on no shift pattern at all that anyone can discern. We wander around camp; we sleep in catnaps day and night; we know the location of every ice chest and candy cache in the mess tents. Randy has taken to hoarding first-aid supplies, Gatorade, and Kit Kats. He refuses to say why. As briefing time nears, the camp PA requests anyone with a plan to report to plans.

It is not a bad idea, I think. I have had some classroom training for plans chief, but no experience in the role. If we are not going on the line, I might as well request an assignment as a trainee. Charlie shrugs approval and indifferently returns to his card game. The plans tent seems grateful, if baffled, that anyone wishes to help. I learn that we are only one zone of several on the Marble-Cone fire, that each zone is being handled as a separate campaign fire, that one project fire team has already been dismissed, and that the fire boss for this—the second largest wildfire in recent California history—was also the fire boss for the largest fire. Some recommendation, I think.

For my first assignment they ask me to make up a master list of all the crews on the fire, and with stacks of sandwiches at our elbows the maps and records officer and I check the roster of crews ordered and crews on duty. The plans chief beams approval, until I point out that there is at least one crew on the fire for whom there is no record. "What? Impossible," he snaps. "Who is missing?" "Sequoia Park Number One," I reply. He fumbles through some old papers. "No, no, they were released from the fire two days ago. They're back home." "No," I stammer. "They are right here. Sequoia Park Number One is my crew." Since reality must reflect the official records, there is nothing to do now but send us home. We leave the next morning, shipped to a general staging area at Modesto. There we are feted to grilled steaks, which Randy converts into an enormous steak sandwich. I notice him pilfering a bottle of Gatorade and surreptitiously chewing Kit Kats. The following day a small charter plane flies us back to the South Rim. When we reach the North Rim on 210, it is dinnertime.

Everyone crowds the table in 176. We have been gone for two weeks, the longest duty tour away from the North Rim that anyone can remember. The stories of the great California fires are in all the newspapers, on TV screens, on the lips of every fire guard in the region. The Forest Service sent two engines, one from Big Springs and one from Jacob Lake. It seems fantastic that the Longshots have actually performed on a national stage. No one says a word. Every eye, every ear wait for us to narrate our adventures. Randy fumbles through the refrigerator, rifles the cupboards, shuffles the table. He mutters and shakes his head. "If you're gonna fight big fires, you gotta Bulk Up," he says to no one in particular. A Snickers bar, a banana, a quart of Kool-Aid, carrots, half a loaf of Roman Meal bread, a jar of peanut butter—a small midden of miscellaneous foods, the typical fare of 176—are gathered on the table.

"Now how, I ask, can you make a decent sandwich out of this crap?"

WHAT DANA AND I SEE FROM THE ROAD TO FREDONIA

The road to the Monument never seems to get shorter. We drop off the repaired pumper and attach a note for Riffey, who has gone with *Pogo,* then head back to the North Rim. Afternoon storms have been forecast.

Dana fumbles with the truck's AM radio. We catch snatches of music and news from broadcasts out of Vegas and Cedar City, but there is more static than information. We pass a road grader—the Monument's—that Riffey has parked next to an obviously trouble-some mudhole. Dana recalls a Riffey story that Sonja has heard from some archaeology friends who left their excavations on Mount Emma for a weekend at the North Rim. The story is that Riffey had just plowed his pickup over the sixty miles of marginal road at night through a ferocious thunderstorm, fighting mud, rain, and wind all the way. When the shaly soil gets wet, it becomes gummy, nearly impassable, and twice he had to winch himself out of jellied sludge. At last Riffey reached the paved highway near Pipe Spring and stopped to wipe off his windshield. A tourist drove up in an over-stuffed Winnebago and leaned out the driver's window. "Hey, ranger—yeah, you!" he shouted to Riffey above the wind. "That road you came over, that dirt road to—what's it called?—Grand Canyon Monument? Is it worth it?" Riffey looked up from wiping the headlights and replied quietly, "Only if you think it is, mister. Only if you think it is."

As we approach Fredonia, the highway closes onto brilliant red cliffs, outliers to the Great Rock Staircase, the staggered terraces that terminate the High Plateaus to the north. The Kaibab Plateau rises gradually on the southern horizon, nearly overwhelmed by lengthen-ing shadows. The Staircase flares with color and texture. It is one of the great geologic facades of the West, and out of it are excavated two of the scenic marvels of the Colorado Plateau: Zion and Bryce canyons. They are popular parks, whose scale comforts and whose sculpturing pleases tourists. Farther east, carved out of the lowest strata, there is Johnson Canyon, famous as a Hollywood movie ranch. The Kaibab, by comparison, appears to be little more than a geographic swell in a sea of sagebrush. There is no indication that anything like the Rim or Canyon exists within it. Instead, one's eyes follow the red, buff, and pink cliffs of the staircase that rise like a colossal ziggurat out of the valley floor. Over the Kaibab some thunderheads tower upward into miniature smoke columns and momentarily, ephemerally, capture the dying fire of the sunset.

At Fredonia we stop for dinner at Nedra's Café. By the time we finish, it is dark, and we turn on our headlights, tiny pencil points of light, and head south across the vast rock plains. Back to the Rim. The night sky is a galaxy of embers.

CHAPTER EIGHT

Point Sublime

BY SEPTEMBER the changes cannot be denied. We notice it first in the sky: the days shorten, and sunlight slanting through the trees is bright but cool. Autumn cold fronts, driven and hard, replace the serendipitous storms of summer. Clouds no longer build up in lazy white blossoms but race across the sky in dark streaks. Blustering westerlies replace the tidal flow of winds between Plateau and Canyon. Local circumstances are overwhelmed by larger events.

It is the beginning of the end of fire season. The very large fuels are as dry as they will get, and the canopies reach a moisture minimum as they prepare for dormancy. Grasses and herbaceous species cure. The aspen gradually change to oranges and yellows, the ponderosa lighten as they prepare for needle cast, and mixed conifer are dappled with color. Except in the wettest of years, the fuels can still burn; but the burning periods become briefer, and the sources of ignition more remote. The fire crew, too, breaks up. The onset of school sends some collegians back for fall semester and, by reducing Park visitation, dwindles the overall pool of seasonal reserves. The first departures, in August, are absorbed with little shock; but by September the losses mount, and the more crewmen who leave, the more who want to leave. Like a waterdog in the sun, hope begins to dissipate. Possibilities have become, to varying degrees, realities.

Yet the aspen display, the subsidence of a delicate Indian summer, the daily emergencies that keep a reduced work force comfortably busy—all make for a rewarding tour. And it has not yet ended. These are not preparations for winter, since no one stays, but a prolongation

246

of summer for as long as it can endure, which means for as long as there are fires. We find new projects and close out old ones, haul firewood by the truckload, bustle about the cache, and prepare for a round of prescribed burns. There are still fires to come. There can always be more fires.

The storm starts on Friday afternoon and continues for two days.

There is nothing to do but busy ourselves in the fire cache and drink coffee in the Fire Pit. This is no afternoon shower, but a full-blown storm system; thunder, hail, lightning, rain crowd us day and night. Cold and damp, everyone bundles in jackets. This late in the year we doubt that the forest can dry out completely again. Yet there is reason to hope that a smoke or two will survive.

We move the coffeepot from the Pit to the cache. Somewhat on a whim a few weeks earlier I had ordered a set of fire training films from the regional office. All day Saturday we watch films in the cache. We eat popcorn and lie on paper sleeping bags and think what a miserable way this is to end fire season. The rumble of wet thunder, an empty promise, punctuates the film's sound tracks.

Late Sunday afternoon there is a smoke report.

POINT SUBLIME: SUNRISE

Thumper and I take the pumper quickly through the slats of shadow and cool sunlight, down the unnamed valley in which the Sublime Road, dry and clear of debris, makes its final run. We left the cache early in order to rendezvous with some South Rim brass who wanted to land at a little-used helispot near the prescribed fire plot, but they radioed to say they would be delayed for at least another hour. So we drive on, our windows up and the heater on. Suddenly the narrowing valley opens. The Canyon is thrust upon us. The Canyon is everywhere. The road to the overlook, another mile away, veers upward to a spiny desert peninsula that will take us to Point Sublime.

Everyone has a favorite viewpoint, but Sublime, by consensus, is special. I park the pumper. There is no one else around and no evidence that anyone has been here for weeks. Thump leads as we walk down to the point and sit on a rock shelf that dangles over the brink. The cliff below our feet drops instantly to the Redwall, where another peninsula extends a further mile or so toward the River. The lower peninsula echoes the upper, and it creates one of the miracles of Sublime: you have the feeling that you are watching the viewpoint that you are watching from. At Point Sublime—midway in the Canyon—you can see everything.

Every other viewpoint is inevitably compared with the perspective at Point Sublime, and every other viewpoint is found wanting. Each has its special signature, and many are better than Sublime for this effect or that. But Sublime has everything, and it has it all the time. It is the universal Canyon overlook. So effective is it at orchestrating Canyon scenery that it almost loses its own identity, and that may be its unique attribute. At Sublime the Kaibab becomes vanishingly small. The Rim is reduced to an infinitesimal presence, like a mathematical point. You see the Canyon as though suspended over the brink. The sweep of the Canyon matches the sweep of the sky. At sunrise it appears as a great lake of shadows that breaks up into shafts of sunlight and glowing rock. At noon it is clear and still and sunburned with Canyon colors. At sunset it presents two panoramas from a common vantage point, one with the sunset and the other against it, as shadows sweep like ether around butte and gorge, and the sun and moon move in a minuet of light and space. At Point Sublime, there is only the Canyon, and a Beyond—an enormous tableland that stretches to mountains that appear blue and purple along empty horizons beneath an endless sky.

The supreme Canyon vantage point, Sublime is best viewed alone. Bring too many people here at one time, and they become distracted, restless. Send a crew to Sublime for lunch and they will start tossing pebbles over the brink, then larger stones, and end up rolling off boulders. The Point is barren of any but very small and very large rocks.

As a geographic presence Point Sublime encompasses a vast sphere of influence. To say of something that it is "near Sublime" can mean anywhere from Tiyo to Swamp Point. The power of Sublime is such that the Park will not deny access to it by visitors. It means that

the Sublime Road will not be considered a mere fireroad, that it will
not be abandoned (even if it cannot be maintained), and this demands
that the whole Sublime region must be denied wilderness status.
Sublime has equally influenced Canyon history, for Clarence Dutton
set the climax to his *Tertiary History* at the Point and communicated a
view from the Kaibab that no one since has ever approached. If you
want to experience the Canyon, go to Point Sublime.

Thump and I watch the sun bring the buttes to life, like breath on
glowing coals. We barely know our own presence, hushed by the
supreme stillness of a Canyon sunrise. Then our reverie snaps. The
Park radio crackles, "Seven-two-six, this is 210. I'm lifting off the
South Rim for Site S-1, near Point Sublime. ETA fifteen minutes."
The watch is over. We have just enough time to rendezvous at the
helispot.

*The smoke—faint and camouflaged among packs of waterdogs—is
reported by Scenic Airlines as somewhere north of Swamp Point. Tom
and I start the blue pumper toward the Shinumo Gate as the storm
reluctantly begins to clear. The sky swirls with great white and black
chunks of cloud pierced here and there by patches of blue.*

*The smoke is north of Castle Canyon, just inside the Park bound-
ary. We can see streamers of smoke on the ridge. Grass Canyon is
heavy with cold fog; waterdogs move like squirrels among the trees;
the grass is coated with dampness, and wet pine needles glisten in
reds and oranges. By the time we reach the boundary we are soaked.
Brushing against tree branches shakes down cascades of suspended
rainwater. I have a poncho, Tom does not. Our boots are saturated.*

*The fire is small, wholly contained within the lightning scar of a
green ponderosa. We need only drop the tree so that the part of the
twisting scar which actually contains the fire faces the sky. Hidden,
the fire will build up heat and gradually worm through the log and
enter the surrounding, drying landscape, but exposed, the fire will go
out. The work goes quickly.*

*Tom is at the end of his rookie year. He arrived with tie-dyed bell-
bottom pants, floppy hair, sandals, and a belief that firefighting was a
team sport, but without cheerleaders, like soccer. But he has learned
quickly, the SWFFs like him, and he is a natural athlete. He will*

return next season. Before we hike back to the pumper, I cut holes in a
plastic garbage bag for arms and head and have Tom wear the bag as
a raincoat.

The sky clears, and the night, frosted with stars, turns cold as
quartz. The main haul road takes us near the Conoco station in V. T.
Park, and we stop for a snack. Tom chews a candy bar and grips a
coffee cup while the Milky Way arches over us like a plume.

SMOKECHASING WITH BONE

Bone spots a faint drift of smoke.

He stops the pumper, gets out to check the wind direction—light
from the southwest—and points the pumper in that direction. The
pine forest is open, if rocky, and the old fireroad to Cape Final is
irrelevant. Bone steers through and around some outcrops, bypasses
a large downed ponderosa, and, with supreme indifference, passes
over the trace of the old road. His net draws closer. Cape Final is the
conclusion to a blunt peninsula, and there is no escape. "Get out and
swamp," he tells the fern feeler with him. He is met with bewilder-
ment and orders the fern feeler to take the wheel—"Drive like you're
walking on eggs," he says with disgust—and seizes a pulaski. What
I wouldn't give for a Longshot, he thinks, but everyone else is on a
fire, or on his way to a fire. He pauses and scans the forested horizon,
then treads, light as a long hunter, through the woods. He will track
the smoke to Chuar Butte if necessary.

The fire, of course, is the easy part. Hot-spotting is just common
sense, and even line construction is obvious—drudgery disguised by
adrenaline. The early fire is the fun part of being a Longshot. Spot the
flames and smoke through tall timber. Scout pine and fir reproduction
as they flare like blowtorches. Watch the snags belch smoke and
embers and bellow with hollow growls. Call for help. Spray dirt with
shovels; crash through half-rotted logs with pulaskis; scrape against
rock and soil with McLeods and shovels. Slap down a flame here.
Scratch a line there. Burn out over here. Listen to the rumble of an
unseen air tanker just above the trees, and watch as the slurry
descends in a pink cloud or a spray or a clump to coat, wash, or

smash through the scene. Chain-saw through thickets, over logs, into snags. Cry out alarms and insults, cough through clouds of smoke, and gasp for breath in the foul air and against the tug of pack straps. Move; move on; and move again, while the air is frantic with shouts and the noise of flames, aircraft, chain saws, pumps, clanging tools, and dull slaps of dirt. Anyone can like that. Almost everyone can suppress a fire with a little training; even tourists put out campfires daily. And after smokechasing and hot-spotting are done, fires belong to hotshots and big shots, not Longshots.

What takes instinct, and what shows character, are smokechasing and mop-up. What makes a Longshot is knowing how to get to fires and how to leave them. That can't be taught. It is learned by example. It is learned by doing and by perseverance. Nothing can happen until there are fires and the fires are found; that is the most important lesson a Longshot can learn. Finding your fire may take hours, maybe days. Sometimes it seems to take years.

Bone turns down the volume of his radio and smiles. The bust is insane. Leo and John-Boy are cautiously feeling their way through the Asbestos Forest, stumbling over downed timber, with rolls of flagging in their teeth and another mile, at least, to go. Pferd and Dean from Mars have rushed their attack, missed their fire altogether, and hauled themselves up a distant empty ridge; now Pferd is climbing a tree to see where they are. Rich and Kenny are executing a bizarre mating dance with Recon 1, neither able to see, only to hear, the other, and now recon has apparently lost not only the two smoke-chasers but their smoke as well, and vapidly flaps its wings over Walhalla. Charlie and Dash are incommunicado—or just plain lost, their radio 10-7 somewhere in the Forest. But he, Bone, and this miserable fern feeler have spotted smoke.

His senses alert—eyes darting for a patch of grey, nose sensitized to the acrid odor of woodsmoke, ears poised for a telltale crack or hiss—Bone waves to the fern feeler to shut off the engine and wait. Gripping his pulaski like a rifle, he stalks on.

The forest dries, and lost smokes clamor for attention.
Early Tuesday morning a smoke is reported along E-1, atop the high ridge that segregates E-1 from Fuller Canyon. Mac and B. Gray

*park the blue pumper along the entrance road and begin the brutal
hike in, first along the open meadows, then up the tangled forest
floors, still wet and slippery, that mantle the monstrous ridges. The
smoke column spirals up like incense, above the ridges, and they can
see it from the road. Mac is convinced that they should be able to hike
directly to it by sight. But once into the woods, they can see nothing.
They return to the pumper, take a bearing on the smoke, and compass
blindly into the burn. B. Gray mutters under his breath and trudges
mindlessly on—a fire drone, soon to depart the Rim forever.*

*The fire consists of a flaming, gigantic ponderosa. Fire entered it,
however, from an adjacent, lightning-shattered aspen, and not until
the fire smoldered away from the aspen and entered the pine was there
anything to see. With the ground wet, the fire will not spread easily, so
Mac prepares to drop the snag along its lean. An ember, however,
floats into B. Gray's eye, and Mac requests help. It takes a small corps
to transport B. Gray, temporarily sightless, back to the Area, and Wil
remains with Mac on the fire. Already the smoke is fast disappearing
in the damp air.*

*Shortly after lunch another smoke is reported in the vicinity of
Uncle Jim Point. Duane and Uncle Jimmy set out on the trail.
Meanwhile, I take a compass bearing from TT-1; then E.B. and I
drive to the Lodge parking lot, where there is a small nature shelter.
There I take another bearing. The parking lot is full of people, who
happily ignore us and the smoke. The Lodge and ranger station are
far enough apart, and Uncle Jim Point is close enough, that the two
sightings can be crossed with some accuracy. The fire, we estimate, is
about a quarter mile north from the point. I radio that information to
Duane and Uncle Jimmy, who quickly locate the Avuncular fire. The
source tree, it seems, long ago tumbled over and burned to ash—
patches of white powder with bony chunks of charcoal scattered in a
feeble outline like a rudely barbecued skeleton.*

*The days are warm and dry, and the Rim, shaking off the massive
storm, edges into Indian summer. We spend Wednesday checking the
two fires and reconditioning our gear. The rangers, too, are roused to
life. Two hikers have failed to close out their hiking permit to Thunder
River. The rangers tentatively organize for a search and want to know*

if they can use Recon 1. The hikers' vehicle, Recon 1 reports, is at the trailhead. The hikers are still in the Thunder River area.

In midafternoon, Recon 1 sights two smokes, both within the Park, in the vicinity of the Saddle Mountain Burn. The two fires are within an air mile of each other, and we send two crews. One fire is possibly accessible by pumper; the other, only by foot. But Recon 1, impatient with our progress and eager to search the Rim for yet more smokes, confuses the two crews and the two fires. Uncle Jimmy and E.B.— their fire maps spread over the hood of the pumper—are given directions for a hike into the Iron Triangle, while Wil and I are told to drive the Three-quarter Ton a hundred yards into a fire that is in fact a mile and a half away. By the time the confusion is recognized, by the time we each return to our vehicles and start over, hours have passed. Uncle Jimmy and E.B. drop the source snag, hose down the ground fire, clear away some brush, and depart in good conscience. Wil and I, however, discover a large, long-smoldering burn in mixed conifer in which fire has crept extensively around the moist forest floor. There are active flames only on the large logs, and small branch wood carries the fire down into the deeper layers of duff; but mop-up will take hours. It may take all night. Sometime around midnight, unre-quested but welcome, Uncle Jimmy and E.B. follow our trail of flags into the fire to help mop up.

Shortly after dawn Thursday, Scenic Airlines reports a smoke on Swamp Ridge. The Kid and Duane hike south from the Swamp Point road on a casual compass bearing suggested by Recon 1 before they arrived. When they reach the Rim and find nothing, they invite Recon 1 to try again. Contact is difficult. They try to locate each other by sound, then with a smoke grenade, then with the compass as a signal mirror. Finally they move to an outcrop projecting onto the Rim itself. This time they are marched back another half mile to a knoll of mature ponderosa flooded with a messy understory of white fir. There a few logs burn, while a huge smoking snag reaches to the sky like a colossal, supplicating hand sculpted out of black granite.

There are more smokes on the Rim; we know it in our bones.

The Thunder River search gears up incrementally. The rangers have designated some ground parties to hike the trail and request 210 for aerial observation. There is not much more we can do to help. The similarities between a search and a fire are superficial, all in the area of logistics. There is a rhythm to firefighting, a sequence of steps from first report to extinction, that is not true of a search. It is hard to say when a search starts and when it concludes. Even as it begins, a "missing" hiker may have already reappeared home, or taken a detour and forgotten to close out a permit, or be dead. A search can end instantly—or never. The missing person may never be found. A fire does not know it is being searched for.

On the Rim, fire is endemic, persistent, natural; the smokes from the Labor Day storm are pursued—make themselves available for pursuit—because they are evolutionary and ecological survivors. We come and go, we are found and lost; but the fires are eternal, and each fire creates the circumstances for more fires. Lost persons are, almost by definition, not native to the area. They are visitors and transients, usually lost in the Canyon, who must relate to the River, not the Rim. They look for water, not fire. Steadily the rangers gear up. We lend them canteens, batteries, assorted supplies. No one in the hikers' families has heard from them.

At midmorning on Friday another smoke is sighted, in the great wasteland north of The Basin and west of Lindbergh Hill. There is no obvious access, not even a helispot. Eric and Dana pause for a minute by the W-1 junction. If they drive to Lindbergh Hill, they will have an easy route in—all downhill. But they will have an equally difficult hike out, and they will have to depend on sophisticated compassing and flagging. There is no shortcut. They decide to take the long walk across The Basin to Robber's Roost Spring; from there they can call upon Recon 1 for a compass bearing, and they can use the spring to fill up fedcos. Still, they will require several hours just to reach the fire, another hour to drop the snag, many more hours to mop up even if the duff is wet. They place frozen rib steaks in their firepacks. Deep in the Plateau they will rely on the surface drainages, however deranged, to position themselves. When they get hungry, they will build a fire and roast their steaks—the Ribsteak fire. They can follow the drainages back, even at night.

The search moves into high gear. The Park brings in dogs and trackers, flies the Esplanade with two helos, and fields half a dozen ground teams. One party discovers a track; another, an empty can-teen. The searchers locate a pack, with a note pinned to it that reads "Keep looking. Please." The signs, the presumed track across the red rock, appear to be heading for the springs. The field parties use channel 2, avoiding the Park repeater, so we hear nothing of what transpires. The lead party locates a second pack. The helos and ground teams and dogs converge south of Monument Point. Then a smoke is reported "near Point Sublime."

The fire is pinpointed by Recon 1 in the northeast quarter of the northwest quarter of Section 29. It is not only adjacent to the Sublime Road, within sight of the Rim, but inside an old burn. Wil and I take the blue pumper and locate the fire—an archetypal snag fire—without difficulty. Everything around it is burned out. The scene is surreal, as though from some ancient, fire-swept world. The source tree is a green ponderosa with a huge catface at the base, probably a result of the previous burn. There are no surface fuels to spread the fire, which sizzles within the lightning scar like a suppressed scream. If the smoke were anywhere else, we might have taken days to find it. The Dream fire.

Wil cranks up the slip-on and hoses down the burning cavities as I prepare to fell the snag. McLaren, acting as an aerial observer in 210, flies over our position. Do we need any assistance? he asks kindly. No, we reply, we have located the fire. "We found those two hikers," he continues, impassive and calm. "They were both dead."

As the crews return, we gather at the cache. There is much to do. Our firepacks and the pumpers are half empty; old tools and disassembled saws cry out for repair; and the crew, fatigued from long nights, is starting to show wear. The spare ration bin is cleaned out. Every sleeping bag is dirty. Ranger King stops by to return some borrowed quart canteens and headlamps. Compulsively, helplessly, he talks about the search.

The hikers, it seems, tried everything. They even ignited some signal fires—clumps of bunch grass, a pinyon. But they were outside the fire regimes of the Rim, and it would have required an incredible coincidence for the pulse of smoke to have been sighted. No one saw anything, and the two hikers knew it. They apparently died from falls sustained during a desperate attempt to scramble down the Redwall to the water they saw but could not reach. They were probably dead before the search began.

When I close my eyes that night, I see the Dream fire. I see a bright small flame along the Rim. On one side is Canyon, dark and bottomless, and on the other, a fire-gutted forest.

POINT SUBLIME: NOON

Sublime is empty.

The atmosphere is ideal—clear and dry, too warm for a jacket and too cool to strip off a fireshirt. A few stray cumuli drift across the Canyon, but otherwise the scene is an aching, royal blue. Jack and I take our sack lunches from the pumper, grab a canteen, and proceed to a pinyon, on the west side of the Point, which has shaded generations of Longshots. We hang the canteen from a broken limb. In the noon sunlight, even at this time of year, everything is bleached and distinct in the cloudless sky. We munch on some cans of ration crackers salvaged from the recent fires. After a while it becomes a trifle cool under the shaded pinyon, and we want to see the rest of Sublime, so we shuffle over to the very tip of the Point. Heat radiates from the limestone rocks. We lean against some large boulders. When I look down, I have the sensation that I am soaring.

The mind drifts.

The revelation of the Canyon began when Captain Cardenas of the Coronado Expedition visited the South Rim, probably near Desert View, in 1540 and tried to reach the River. He was followed by the Franciscan missionary Father Garcés, who inspected the Havasupai Indians in the 1770s while en route to the Hopi mesas. But nothing permanent came of either visit.

Stories were propagated by American trappers, however, about a "Big Canyon" on the Colorado River of the West, and during the Utah War of 1857–58 the Army Corps of Topographical Engineers sponsored an expedition up the Colorado River that crashed a steamboat at Black Canyon, traveled down Diamond Creek into the gorge of the western Grand Canyon, then visited the Havasupais and exited along the South Rim. The Ives Expedition, whose report was published in 1861, communicated the first images of the Canyon—mostly those of the inner gorge—to Western civilization. Further exploration was thwarted by the Civil War.

Then came John Wesley Powell. A former major under Grant, Powell piloted a handful of wooden dories down the Colorado from Green River, Wyoming, to Pierce's Ferry, Nevada, in 1869. His was the first authenticated descent through what Powell called the "Grand Canyon," and his account of the adventure, *Exploration of the Colorado River of the West,* made Powell's reputation, catapulted him into national prominence as a scientific administrator, and established a genre of river writing that has never been surpassed. On the basis of his exploits, Powell organized the Geographical and Geological Survey of the Rocky Mountain Region. Not to be outdone, the peacetime Army tried to recapture its glory days by sponsoring the Geographical and Geological Survey West of the Hundredth Meridian under Lieutenant George Wheeler. Wheeler confronted Powell head-on in 1871 by trying to take small boats up the gorges of the Colorado, much in the manner of Ives, and succeeded in getting some of his party to Diamond Creek. There Wheeler's explorers exited, carrying away visions of Army glory along with their baggage train.

The future lay with Powell. Within a year he organized a second trip down the River. This time, buffeted by high spring floods, the party departed the western Canyon at Kanab Creek. Powell subsequently established a base camp at Kanab and inaugurated the scientific inventory of the region. Most of the creators of the Grand Canyon as a cultural phenomenon—as an exemplar of geology, as romantic earth biography, as an icon of American nationalism—were associated with Powell or his survey or its institutional successor, the U.S. Geological Survey. Through them the Canyon was introduced to, and preserved by, American intellectual culture. Photographers like Timothy O'Sullivan, E. O. Beaman, William Henry Jackson, and Jack Hillers; artists like Thomas Moran, fresh from his glorious canvasses of the Yellowstone, and William Henry Holmes, a genius in the metamorphosis of topographic illustration into art; cartographers, like Amon Thompson; geologists, like Clarence Dutton, on loan from the Army, and G. K. Gilbert, willingly shanghaied from the Wheeler Survey; artist-historians, like Frederick

Dellenbaugh—all contributed; and their collective masterpiece, *Tertiary History of the Grand Canyon District,* did for the genre of Rim writing what Powell's *Exploration* did for the genre of river writing.

The climax of the book was set at Point Sublime. There Dutton summarized the geologic evolution of the Canyon and traced the evolution of a scenic day. When intellectuals traveled to the Grand Canyon, however, they generally went to the North Rim. The North Rim brought the Grand Canyon into high culture. Later visitors, like the quietly influential Charles Walcott, also followed Powell's directions to the North Rim—in Walcott's case, to the Nankoweap Basin. Collectively they established the parameters of our understanding of Rim, River, and Canyon.

What has changed since then is the relative importance of high culture and popular culture and the significance of North Rim and South. Originally the Rim (and Canyon) were more accessible through the Mormon settlements of Utah than through an Arizona populated largely by hostile Indians. The Colorado River did not join the two rims but segregated them, and until the 1890s, the North Rim was the more prominent. Then came the transcontinental railroads. With the construction of the Atchison, Topeka & Santa Fe Railroad through Flagstaff, the tourist connection to the Canyon rapidly shifted from the North Rim to the South; Baedeker advised tourists to take the railroad to Flagstaff, then a stage to the South Rim; even Powell and Gilbert directed the 1894 International Geological Congress, on tour of the United States, to the South Rim, along rail lines. When Moran returned to make the Canyon a central icon of his landscape art, he did so under commission from the Santa Fe Railroad and he painted from the South Rim. When President Teddy Roosevelt in 1903 proclaimed the Canyon a national treasure, "the one great sight every American should see," he did so on the steps of the luxury hotel the El Tovar, positioned between the Rim and a new railroad terminus at Grand Canyon Village. Paved highways followed the railroad routes. Not until the late 1920s, after the construction of Rainbow Bridge, was it possible to drive from South Rim to North without crossing the Colorado River by ferry. During the 1920s, too, under the See America First campaign, the National Park Service actively promoted automobile traffic to the parks. Automobile tourism massed at the South Rim, and Park politics, then as now, followed the visitor. The process of intellectual assimilation began on the River and on the North Rim, but popular culture clustered on the macadamized roads and overlooks of the South. There the Park established its headquarters.

The geomorphic differences between the two rims are pronounced. The bulk of the Kaibab Plateau lies to the north of the River, and most of the Canyon's expansion comes from its erosion. The South Rim is folded into gentle waves; the North Rim is gouged into retreating peninsulas that leave in their wake strings of decaying buttes and mesas. The difference in elevation between Bright Angel Point on the North Rim and Grand Canyon Village on the South is over twelve hundred feet. But here geography fails as a guide to bureaucracy. Politically, it is the South Rim that looks down upon the North. The superintendent of Grand Canyon is, in reality, the CEO of the South Rim.

On the north side, there is simply too much Rim and too few tourists. It is too removed from major thoroughfares, its entrance a dead-end road, not a side street on the way to Los Angeles or Las Vegas. With the exception of Cape Royal, the North Rim's grand overlooks are too remote for heavy tourist visitation. There is too little Canyon, too little River, and too few people. While Point Sublime is open to the public, its perspective is, as Dutton made clear, to an intellectual Canyon.

The advent of the wilderness movement altered the balance of power within the Park, but not to the advantage of the North Rim. Joseph Wood Krutch's book *Grand Canyon: Today and All Its Yesterdays* (1958) reestablished the liaison between Canyon and a vigorous intellectual culture for the first time since Dutton and Powell. By appealing to the concept of wilderness, Krutch redefined the place of the Canyon in the moral geography of American civilization. The new associations were needed to make up for the old ones that had been lost. The Canyon's status as an exemplar of earth science had eroded badly as new conceptions of geologic time evolved, as new theories like plate tectonics directed scientific attention to other phenomena, and as a new era of exploration returned images of Antarctica, the deep oceans, the outer planets and their moons.

Symbolically, the publication of Krutch's book coincided with the International Geophysical Year, which effectively announced that new era of exploration and planetary science.

When high culture and popular culture converged again on the Canyon, as they did during the dam controversies of the 1960s, the River, not the Rim, became the object of attention, and the Canyon became synonymous with the River. By then the Park bureaucracy was firmly ensconced on the South Rim, and what made the River important was not its idea—its wilderness penumbra—but the phenomenal explosion of tourists attracted to it, the advent of mass tourism by raft, and the promulgation of popular literature, movies, and television images. The dialogue between North and South became a trilogue among North Rim, South Rim, and River. South Rim and River grew at the expense of the North Rim.

We as Longshots know the intellectual Canyon poorly, but we are encouraged by the example of Dutton—Dutton of the North Rim. He knew that the Canyon did not have to be transcribed into words but only interpreted. He knew that to be understood, it had to be absorbed into American civilization and that intellectuals would have to do that job because the folk—the usual frontier pioneers—were not present. He knew that appreciation would have to be cultivated by linkages with the literary, scientific, artistic, and esthetic canons of the day. This was done. The Canyon became an icon of American civilization, and its discovery a major event in cultural history. When in the mid-twentieth century linkages to the universe of Herbert Spencer, Alexander von Humboldt, and Captain Clarence Dutton became irrelevant, new linkages had to be forged, and with often dramatic effect they were.

Yet all this was, finally, an agenda for tourists and intellectual transients. It was a means by which to communicate understanding to those who did not live there—by which a civilization with its origins elsewhere in very different times and places could relate to the Canyon. Idea had to substitute for experience. As it became vulgarized, image—mass-produced and industrially uniform—substituted for idea. But we live on the Rim. We see the Canyon daily, not as an exotic spectacle but as a reference point, an informing presence. We know it by its sensory impressions.

We know it through fire, and we understand fire in such elemental terms as dirt, water, winds, needles, trees, rocks, sod, duff, punk, sun, clouds. We talk about fires in terms of very mundane natural phenomena and unencumbered human relationships. We know the lunar cycle because it governs the caliber of evening light. We know storm patterns because they bring lightning and rain. We know tree types and biotas and soils, all of which control what kind of fire burns and what kind of mop-up is demanded. We know that the forest cover shields fires from the wind, because we hear the wind in the canopy and don't feel it on the ground. We know that the ponderosa pine enjoys a peculiar symbiosis with fire, because we find most of our fires among the pines. We know about the strange hydrology of the Kaibab because we have to carry water to drink and to put out fires. We understand the differential between Rim and River because River trips, not Strip trips, are used as rewards. We appreciate the distinction between Rims, because we live on one and are governed by the other. We know the Canyon through its fires and its influence on Rim fires, and we know from painful experience that Plateau and Canyon don't mix. Smokey's Third Rule (Canyon corollary): Keep your fire on the Rim. It is good firefighting but bad politics.

You don't have to know very much to be a Longshot. Most of the crew have some college education, and a few possess advanced degrees; but they leave their academic learning at the entrance station. The chief mental requirement for a good firefighter is resourcefulness; the chief physical attribute, stamina. Two or three seasons are enough to master the basic lore of firefighting. Good fires have ample dirt, easily scraped duff, clean-burning needles, simple access, working saws and radios, unrotted snags. Bad fires do not. In their detail and particularities, fires are infinite, and as a scientific problem, tremendously complex and abstruse. But there is a difference between knowing and doing. While fire in the abstract is not easily knowable, firefighting on the North Rim is. While the North Rim may not be easily assimilated by intellectual systems, it is completely livable. While the Canyon cannot perhaps be described, it can be experienced. We understand the idea of wilderness because it affects the way we fight fire. We experience the particulars and know the generalities through them. Like the Canyon, those ideas are not always seen but are always there.

We know why artists and scientists were drawn to Point Sublime, because we are, too. Point Sublime is to the Canyon what The Basin is to the Plateau. Ironically, it is hostile to the most important contemporary idea about the Canyon—wilderness. Sublime's road denies the western Rim legal status as wilderness, and there is no direct connection from the Point to the all-defining River. You can see Boucher Rapids from Point Sublime, but there are no trails to the River from the Point. Point Sublime is not on the way to anywhere else. You have to go to Sublime for itself.

Point Sublime is the ultimate overlook, the ideal and most challenging vantage point for a Canyon tourist. But for someone who lives on the Rim, it offers an incomplete experience. The Canyon needs sense as well as ideation. The scene needs shadows and clouds and smoke as well as sunlight. Sublime is a place to visit, and we come often; it is not a place to live. We want instead that restless, tidal tension. Sublime can be too idealized. Sublime in the noonday sun blinds and bleaches. We want a place with fire. We want the Rim.

Jack and I startle awake.

Perhaps there has been chatter on the radio, or some biological clock has sounded an alarm that lunch is over, or we unconsciously hear the whine of a distant tourist flight through Muav Saddle. We blink in the sunlight. Jack points skyward. Overhead three turkey vultures circle lazily in the thermals. We gather our trash and, stiff-legged, walk back to the pumper.

The smoke is sighted early Saturday morning—a big smoke, near Tiyo. Barbara Red Butte gives a 15 degree azimuth. Recon 1 will be delayed, so we quickly sharpen some spare saw chains, fill some extra canteens with oil, toss a few extra handtools onto the pumpers, and replenish the slip-on tanks. As Recon 1 lifts off, we head for Tiyo.

Everyone goes. Recon 1 reports that the fire is near the junction of W-1D and the old W-1D-B. It is about three acres in size and spreading steadily. I take Uncle Jimmy, and outfitted with packs and handtools we start out on a loose compass bearing for the fire. Dana will follow and flag a proper route. The fire is only a couple of hundred yards distant, and with a little saw work we should be able to bring in the pumpers. For now we hot-spot and scout the fire. We'll need help.

I request some reserves and the water truck. McLaren informs us that there is an air tanker at Prescott, and we take the hint. "Send it." Dana arrives with the rest of the regulars. We organize into two small squads and begin putting in scratch lines around the fastest-spreading heads. In places the needles and duff are too thick to scrape with a McLeod, so we trench with shovels. When the air tanker arrives, I have it split its load into two parts, one along each of the two most active fronts. Good drops; between the retardant and the scratch line we contain the fire. The cost of control, however—deferred for the moment—is that mop-up will be crummy, an unsavory mix of dense duff and slurry. We complete the scratch lines; then I send one squad back for the pumpers while the other improves the fireline, bucks up some heavy logs, and drops two burning snags. When controlled, the fire is about five acres in size, the biggest of the bust.

The reserves arrive later that morning, and I start them on line patrol and mop-up along the perimeter while we break for lunch. Most of us have not eaten today. There are signs of fatigue as the afternoon grades into an endless round of bottomless mop-up. For some it is time to end not only the bust but the season. The fire smolders uncontrollably just beneath the surface crust of retardant; its spread is marked by tiny vents of smoke, like fumaroles in the Valley of Ten Thousand Smokes, as though hundreds of cigarettes were buried within the needles. I release the reserves before dinner, and we continue to mop up until we exhaust the water in both our slip-ons and the water truck, then pack it in for the night. We reach the fire cache about 2100 hours and fill up the slip-ons and water truck before heading off to Skid Row. One slip-on is decommissioned with a broken drive belt.

When we depart the cache early the next day, maintenance insists that one of its operators drive the water truck—easy overtime for a Sunday—and we agree. Ross has some fire experience. No amount of OT, however, will tempt the Park mechanic to search through his supply of fan belts for the other slip-on. No matter, only one pumper crew will go early. The others we leave behind to recondition equip-

ment and make a quick inventory of the fire cache; they can join us at the Tiyo fire in a couple of hours. The fire itself is a landscape of small smokes—loose, disorganized, smoldering. Wil scrapes together enough embers and branches for a small campfire and heats some water for coffee.

Mop-up continues with what might be termed professional resignation. It has to be done, and even as the morning sun heats the ground, the smokes diminish. It is with some surprise, then, that we hear from Barbara Red Butte around noon that she has a smoke in sight at approximately 14 degrees azimuth. McLaren interrupts to observe that this is probably the Tiyo fire. An hour later, as the smoke grows, Red Butte wants to know how much smoke our fire is putting up. We can't see a flame anywhere and are only a couple of hours away from complete extinguishment. Not much, we tell Red Butte. "Then you have another fire," she announces.

McLaren sees it as soon as he lifts off the helipad at the South Rim. The fire is burning on the long peninsula, flanked by Rim on both sides, that ultimately converges at Point Sublime. We leave Ross on the Tiyo fire, request that someone be sent to help him baby-sit the final embers, and take off with a roar. Phlegmatic, imperturbable McLaren has found an edge to his voice. He calls for an air tanker, but the nearest available ship is in Boise and cannot arrive for several hours. I mention the busted fan belt on the slip-on. "Tell me what size you want, and I'll get it from the South Rim," he says. Lookouts from Kendricks Peak to Dry Park call in the smoke. We request Forest Service assistance, and the North Kaibab mobilizes two engine crews. We request all the North Rim reserves that can be rounded up. McLaren drops a fan belt to us from the helicopter as we pause near a clearing on the Sublime Road. This, I think in a glow of adrenaline, this is what it is all about. And it is about all we are good for.

The fire is about fifteen acres, burning parallel with a ridgetop, and it has already started a one-acre spot fire perhaps one hundred fifty feet ahead of the flaming front. The ridge—steep and rocky on its southern exposure—trends southwest to northeast. By the time we make a quick reconnaissance the Forest Service has arrived. Red Butte must have reported the smoke on the Forest radio net to its dispatcher, and the crews probably started toward the Park before we officially requested them. We divide the fire into two sectors. Park crews will work the south; Forest crews, the north. There is not much to do but cut line where it can be most easily done, then burn out. More reserves will arrive within an hour. The air tanker should arrive within two.

I flag a proposed line, then double back past the Park crew and begin burning out with a fusee. McLaren hovers overhead in 210, injecting a note of calmness and curiosity. The burnout along the flanks proceeds well. The Park crews pull back from the Sublime fire; our line is relatively straight, short, and rapid through pockets of light fuel. The Forest crews work much closer. They crowd the fire's flank, putting in a line on the steep shoulder of the ridge. There will be problems with rolling firebrands later, I think; better if they sacrificed some acres and put the fireline on the other side of a shallow draw to the north; the draw would act as a ditch to catch even rolling logs. But it is too late now. Burning out along the head of the fire is touchy. Trees torch, and we finesse the burnout by backing the fire against strong, dry winds. Several spot fires flare up, but at last we tie our lines together. We let our backfire and the wildfire burn into each other and watch for new spots. When the two fires meet, there is a rush of wind. The Kid finds one spot, and Uncle Jimmy another. Yet we are winning. Then we hear the roar.

The air tanker, a B-17—not expected for another hour: it appears that BIFC dispatchers have forgotten again that Arizona stays on mountain standard time—is sighted through the trees. We have no communications with it whatsoever. We expect that it will make a dry run, establish contact, then return for a precision drop. Instead, the slurry spills out of the fuselage, and we hit the ground. The retardant atomizes and settles over the fire in a pink fog. It knocks out our backfire. Then, as suddenly as it appeared, the plane vanishes. It is too late for another drop today, and the plane heads for Cedar City.

We improve our lines, complete some burnout, and note danger spots. There are a couple of snags on the northeast corner that are too broken to fell safely. The BI arrives, and we send him to where he can watch the burning snags. Finally we break for dinner. The fire is contained. We estimate its size at sixty to seventy acres; the perimeter fireline is more than a mile long.

Most of the reserves want to return to the Area. Stay for a couple more hours, I plead, then we will release you. Reluctantly they agree. The Forest Service wants to remain as long as possible. Someone remembers the BI, and we find him asleep by the snags and send him home with the reserves. As regulars, of course, we will remain all night—some on patrol, the rest to sleep. Around midnight we release the Forest Service.

For the next three days we mop up the Sublime fire. For a while we think we have discovered a way to get pumpers to the fireline, but we dent one vehicle and abandon the scheme. Instead, we lay hose up the ridge from the Sublime Road. We request reserves to assist with mop-up—so vast is the fire—and we get some. There is even a hot meal from the Lodge. Each night after the first we leave a couple of Longshots on the fire, while the rest of us return to the Area. Our exhilaration fades. We are exhausted; our equipment is a mess; the cache is almost unusable; one slip-on is dented, and the other disabled; we are down to two cases of C rations. But we need only one more day to finish the Sublime fire and wrap up the season. The fire and accident reports should keep us busy for the rest of the month. Uncle Jimmy reminds us that we have yet to recheck the old fires. But we are thinking about big paychecks and big replacement orders. The fire will allow us to restock the cache over the winter.

It is time to think beyond this season.

Mopping Up; or, Tell Me Again When It Is *Really* Over

Uncle Jimmy has a fedco, and Eric a shovel. Eric digs up a chunk of duff, and Uncle Jimmy sprays it, while Eric flips the duff over, chops it into pieces, and mixes it with dirt. Then he digs up another chunk, and Uncle Jimmy sprays that. Wil has only a shovel. He pushes it into the ground with his boot—good, well-drained soil here—bends over to lift up the shovel head, turns it over, and chops with it as though he were churning butter. A small smoke spirals upward from the pile. He repeats his actions, then he digs the shovel into the ground exactly adjacent to it and begins all over again. Tim attempts, with negligible success, to do the same thing with a pulaski, using the grub end to lift and the ax and grub ends alternately to chop and stir. With shovels Duane and I scrape smoldering leaders of fire from unburned duff—in effect, installing scores of small, internal firelines within the general perimeter of the fire. The smoldering sections are piled, then spaded into holes. "Dirt," Wil yells, "is better than water." Uncle Jimmy answers back that "water is better than dirt." But Dana can stand no more of either. With a shout he masses a hundred square feet of smoking duff into a great mound and ignites the pile with a fusee. The pile refuses to flame. Instead, it billows in great puffs of acrid smoke that spread over the fire like smog.

The hardest part of controlling a snag fire is finding it, but the hardest part of suppressing a fire is mopping it up. It is one thing to know how to get to a fire, and something else to know how and when to leave it. Only a small fraction of a fire burns within the flaming front; most of a forest's fuels are consumed by a disorganized medley of flaming and smoldering combustion after the front has passed. A fire is not out until the fire in the duff is out. It is not a lesson anyone wants to hear, and one only a small minority learn.

There are some places where the surface fuels are light and burnout is more or less complete; grass and brush are like this. Almost universally, however, the North Rim has a heavy mat of semidecomposed humus, fresh needles, and windfallen branches, even whole trees that can burn for days. There are places, too, where standards for mop-up are lax, where the dull, meticulous labors of mopping up acres of smokes are superseded by a loosely conducted "patrol." The South Rim favors this approach and flaunts it before North Rimmers. But the consequences of leaving unburned fuels and pockets of combustion untouched are generally unpleasant. It may mean continual observation or incessant, casual mop-up for a crew; it may mean that those who return to inspect the fire must mop up for those who first abandoned it; or it may mean that the fire flares up or even escapes. On the North Rim our standards are simple: we mop up to the last smoke, and we return twenty-four hours after the last smoke to check the burn before officially calling the fire out.

As a result, we know the duff better than any other part of the Rim forest. The humid understory of the spruce-fir forest has the worst duff. Short needles refuse to fluff into deep, porous fuelbeds so that sustained flaming combustion is replaced by a malingering, creeping process of glowing combustion. Recently cast needles are covered with a cobweb of fine branches. Underneath they do not rest upon mineral soil but intercalate with rocks and the stringy lignin residue of largely decomposed trees; organic soil replaces mineral soil. Fires tend to be large in area and low in intensity—a hundred square feet of flame and four acres of mop-up. The real fuelbed in spruce-fir is the tree canopy, and high-intensity fires are invariably crown fires. Without copious quantities of water, mop-up in spruce-fir, or in most mixed conifer, is interminable.

By contrast, ponderosa pine has deeper, more sharply defined fuelbeds of long needles that support flaming combustion. The deep duff, moreover, is layered. The boundary between duff and mineral soil is sometimes sharply drawn, but above the soil there is a shallow layer of finely ground needles, an organic powder that can, improbably, carry glowing combustion. Then come several layers of needles, progressively decomposing and compacting like the transformation of snow into firn. Near the surface, small branches interweave with the duff, and on the surface are windfall and fresh needle cast. Each of these layers has a different fuel moisture, and each may burn out of sync with the others. The ways in which wet and dry fuels may combine to burn are endless. Only during intense droughts is the entire duff equally dry.

There are many techniques for extinguishing all smokes, but a good strategy is to begin with the large fuels and work down. Drop any burning snags and protect dead, as-yet-unburned snags by scraping a fireline around them. Break up the big burning logs into small pieces, chop out fire and embers, cool each piece with dirt or water, and toss it into a cleared zone, a boneyard. That sweeps the fire of everything but duff. Isolate the burned from the unburned duff. Then mix the burned duff with equal parts of dirt, water, and sweat. Spade it over, spray it, dump, chop, and mix; then begin again; and again. Divide the fire into sectors, and force crewmen to stay in their sector until every smoke is extinguished. For prolonged mop-up, bring in extra crewmen. Wait twenty minutes from the last smoke until you abandon the fire. Typically, some canteens or a fedco and a few handtools are left behind. Then return twenty-four hours later to inspect the burn, remove the remaining tools, and pull the flagging. When you return, write up the fire report: draw a map, code the fire behavior data, narrate the events. The fire is not over until its report has been filed. The pen is mightier than the pulaski.

In practice, everyone has his own favorite technique. The simplest and most direct approach is usually, in the long run, the surest. But one way or another, mop-up has to be done. That may take a long time. It takes patience to outwait fire. Duff is deep and complex, like memory. You just can't abandon a fire after hot-spotting or lining it. Worst of all is to bury it. Better to let a fire flame on and watch it in casual patrol, or indifferently tinker with this smoking duff pile or that, than to bury it and leave. A fire can smolder under dirt or retardant or wet needles for days. It can smolder for years.

Dana, Eric, Duane, Tim, Wil, Uncle Jimmy, and I have been mopping up for three days now, and each day has been slower than the last. Rather than fall back on basics, we are inspired by the tedium into innovations in the theory and practice of mop-up. We are becoming smoke-happy. When we close our eyes, we see tiny spirals of smoke. There are smokes everywhere; they emanate from tree trunks; they appear in our firepacks, sleeping bags, pumpers; they spiral insidiously out of every tiny mound of needles. We are haunted by infinitesimal smokes for which there is no escape and no limit.

Dana pounds his smoking mound with a shovel, and Eric joins him, while both scream incoherently. Uncle Jimmy's fedco leaks so badly his pants are soaked and become caked with ash, but when he looks down at his boots, he thinks he can see small smokes emerging from the eyelets. Wil sits down at the boneyard and stares toward the sun. If there are smokes in his sector, they will catch the light and be quickly apparent. One rises from the rotted log; another appears in a small hole where he had stirred dirt and duff. He sighs and drags himself to his feet. That night, as we bed down, the stars appear like white embers in a cosmic duff.

Dana is sure he sees a smoke emerging from Cassiopeia.

This should be our last day on the Sublime fire. Some pockets of duff remain on the far side, but with extra hose we hope to get close enough at least to fill up fedcos from the pumper without the half hour walk that has crippled us so far. Then the Park dispatcher reports that Scenic Airlines has sighted a smoke near Swamp Point. It seems impossible.

Its location is uncannily close to the site of the Back fire. Before we abandon the Sublime fire completely, we request that two reserves be sent out to watch; then we take the pumpers up the Sublime Road to W-4 and onto the Swamp Point road; we request Forest Service assistance; we order an air tanker; and we suggest to the BI—then, as always, back in the Area—that he order a hot meal from the Lodge. When we stop, our vehicles are next to the flagging of the Back fire, and the bearing that Recon 1 gives us to the Swamp fire is so close to the old route that we decide to follow the flags in. The Swamp fire is, in fact, exactly adjacent to the Back fire. A reburn or an independent start—we can't say. There is too much fire on the scene to worry at present about causes. Dispatch informs us that a C-119J will arrive within thirty minutes.

With saws we clear away a swath ahead of the active north flank— a volatile medley of snags, heavy fir reproduction, thick needles, and downed logs—then wait for the tanker. I tell the pilot to split his load four ways, one drop to each side of the fire. Then we back well off. After each load I rush in, assess the accuracy of the drop, inform the pilot where I want the next, and retreat. Each drop is exactly on target. The fire is contained. The slurry and heavy fuels will make for messy mop-up, but we are too fatigued—too high on adrenaline and momentum—to care much about the next day or even the coming night. It is enough that the fire is stopped. Two Forest Service engine crews arrive, and we cut line together. Before darkness deepens further, we drop a few snags and buck up some burning logs near the line. Tom locates some large pockets of soil along the fireline, and we excavate them for dirt and recycle them as boneyards. Several of the holes are knee-deep.

Then we retire to our packs—what passes for a fire camp—and to some food. There isn't much. We have a few spare cans of crackers and miscellaneous fruitcakes and nut rolls. The Forest Service crews share their rations, and we promise them a hot meal later. It has been a crazy, extraordinary bust, and we have gone far beyond our sup-

plies, beyond what any of us has experienced before, beyond what any of us could have believed possible. In our exhaustion we begin to believe that we can go on—that we can extemporize—forever.

The Forest crews want to know more about the bust. Nothing so extensive has occurred in the Forest. Uncle Jimmy assumes patrol duties around the fireline. The conversation soon deteriorates into BI stories. We forget, for an instant, about the smoke in our headlamps, the cold wind and our aching, lifeless legs. The Forest crews cannot get enough, and they contribute some new stories. Neither side will concede the last word, so the pace of outrageous stories accelerates. In the distance we hear the scrape of tools as Uncle Jimmy methodically digs in one of the boneyards and throws dirt on a burning limb. The Forest crews want to know how Big Bob could have become an FMO, how the Park plans to build a future fire program. Fossey tells them the future can take care of itself and proceeds with another BI story. The laughter is infectious. Then we hear footsteps and see headlamps, and out of the smoke step the BI and a maintenance man with trays of hot food. Embarrassment hangs over the scene like smoke trapped under a morning inversion. "Thanks," Duane says meekly. The BI has already eaten, of course, so we suggest to him that he patrol the fireline. "Sure," he nods, his lower lip curled. "Right away." The food slacks our hunger, but not our sense of guilt. A few minutes later, some twenty yards away, we see the BI's headlamp disappear, accompanied by a shout, into one of the boneyard holes in the fireline. He never returns to camp.

There is nothing left but tedious mop-up, brutalizing in its simplicity, and it is pointless to keep a full crew all night. Without water, mop-up will be difficult, and this time we will have to stay with the fire to the last smoke. Yet we also need to rework the cache and recheck the other fires. All we require tonight is for someone to stay with the Swamp fire. Uncle Jimmy reappears and promptly volunteers.

He is the oldest of the Longshots and the least known beyond his life on the Rim. Wiry, indefatigable, compulsively enthusiastic, Uncle Jimmy seems to be in a state of suspended animation, growing older without aging. He is excitable and meticulous, ruthless in exercise, a good Longshot. He despises Big Bob. If he has plans for the winter, he has kept them to himself. He has told The Kid something about traveling around and maybe working part-time on the Forest and maybe learning a trade like carpentry. He once confided to Duane that he might have been better off to stay with the Army (he was a paratrooper), that his sergeant had told him he would never make it in civilian life. He was the first recruit this season, arriving in April, he will probably hang on as long as the fire account holds out this fall, and he has indicated that he can report next spring as soon as we can pay. Now he appears before us like some kind of fire gnome—haloed by a week's growth of beard grimy with ash and dirt, thick stringers of black hair tied with a bandanna around his forehead, bright eyes in a gaunt face. He has a sad, fanatical look. Like most of us, Uncle Jimmy does not want the bust to end. Unlike many, he cannot afford to have it end.

It is decided that the rest of us will retire to the Area, put the slip-ons and our gear in shape, and return to the Swamp fire in the morning. Even if we rise early, however, so many things need to be reconditioned and so much time must be expended in the drive that we probably won't reappear until midmorning or later. That bothers Uncle Jimmy not in the slightest. He is poor with reports but good in the field. He obliterates a fire with meticulous attention, until nothing is left, because he knows there will always be—there have to be— more fires, another season. Besides, I remember, tomorrow is his lieu day. Overtime. The longer our delay, the larger his paycheck. When we leave we see Uncle Jimmy scrounging through the campsite, bustling like a shrew, hoarding unused ration cans.

We reach the fire cache shortly before midnight. For the next two days we recheck old fires and continue to dry-mop at Swamp. The days shorten and the nights turn cold with frost.

The bust is over.

POINT SUBLIME: SUNSET

The Tiyo fire, the Dream fire, the Sublime fire—we check them all, and there are no lingering smokes. Not enough of the workday remains to return to the cache before 1700 hours, but there is enough daylight left to drive to Sublime and watch the sunset. "Oh, hell," says Donnie. "Let's do it. Our time."

The afternoon clouds are breaking up, and a twilight wedge, still large and diffuse, begins to take shape. The wedge is more distinct in the autumn than in the summer because the air is cooler and more stable, and the refracted light is broken into strata. Our eyes rove restlessly over the panorama. Too often our view of sunsets away from the Area is compromised by our need to exploit every minute of sunlight to locate a fire or fell a snag—everything is refracted through the prism of fire. But now the fires are extinguished. Now we have the time to watch.

It is a complex and dynamic scene. The sunset is doubled: there is one to the east, with the sun, and one to the west, against it. Their effects are utterly different. One accents Canyon and light; the other, shadow and sky. The drama repeats daily, with the timeless play of dusty pale light on butte and mesa and gorge, with shadows washing through the Canyon like a tide. The rocks dull in intensity and brighten in color. The sky condenses from diffuse pastels into a brilliant wedge, compressed by an encroaching spectrum of blues— light blue at the horizon, and above that an immensely soothing royal blue, and finally a navy blue salted with early stars. Distant mountains are silhouetted in lavender, then blue.

We study both views, looking equally to past and to future. It is easier, however, to look back on a season, when everything that must happen has happened, than to stare at the sunlight with only hope to shield the eyes, and increasingly we look back. The Canyon fades before a murky, indistinct grey—the first in a sequence of shadow landscapes. Shadows sweep over the Canyon in wave upon wave, each layer darker than the last, until the gorge is swallowed in blackness, and the final drama transfers to the sky. The darkness grows; the wedge shrinks. Orange fades to lemon along the sharpened horizon, and as the sun meets horizon, it flares defiantly into orange and blood red, like a muted fire, before vanishing.

Yet there is more. There is not one process at work but two—not only the tidal sunset but the breakup of a storm. Light plays not just, as with the sunset, against rock sculptures—immobile, the dynamism of the scene set by the sinking, refracting lights; it plays also against the clouds. Here they tower into pinks and magentas, there they furrow into purples, blues, yellows, and greys, and everywhere virga shimmers downward like colored veils. Sunset and storm combine into a fugue of colors and shapes and motions. The storm breaks apart, the clouds shred and darken into black ink spots that interrupt and silhouette the enveloping twilight wedge before they shrivel away with the dying sun.

It is the supreme Canyon spectacle. Neither sunset nor storm alone but their interplay makes the scene Sublime; the Grand Ensemble, as Dutton called it, is put into complex motion. It could only be improved with a little smoke. It is an attribute of woodsmoke that the bulk of its particulates have diameters roughly comparable with the wavelengths of white light. In daylight smoke can obscure and lessen Canyon scenery. But at sunset, when the particulates magnify and scatter the refraction of sunlight, the scene is dramatically enhanced. Smoke intensifies the color and highlights the texture of sky and earth. Add a little fire, and the scene could be not merely viewed but lived.

Yet the power of the view resides equally in the viewer. The Point captures two analogous motions in the lives of its observers—one seasonal and one secular. The experience is not just of a place or a time or an event but of the whole lot in a crazy, incongruous mix. It is the North Rim and youth and fire. It is falling trees and hot-spotting and growing up and SWFFs and walking through blue night winds and flaming trees and C rations and moonlight on Canyon clouds. It is Saddle Mountain and Powell and The Dragon and Walhalla. It is the endlessly recycled summers and the irreversible storm of youth in dynamic counterpoint. It is fire on the Rim.

A few flakes of ink-black cloud drift by. The darkness arcs downward; stars and moon create a new sky; moonlight reverses the pattern of light and shadow. Warm winds from the Canyon mix with cool air from the Plateau. The future has become past.

Suddenly we feel the cold. The Point is wholly exposed. From everywhere there is the sound of distant, rushing winds.

CHAPTER NINE

Walhalla

INDIAN SUMMER erodes into the blustery edge of winter. The sun creeps low through trees and sets hastily across towering rims. It is dry enough and windy enough for fires, but the night suppresses them with cold. The smell of snow replaces the smell of smoke.

The landscape takes on a used, shabby appearance. Pines become brownish and shed large portions of needles. Spruce and fir seem endlessly dreary. Aspen alone give fire to the scene. Day by day their display of colors evolves as leaves change from a shiny to a flat green, then to a lime, then to fluorescent yellow and peach, with scattered flecks of international orange. In a deciduous forest the colors would be considered modest, and their variety slight, but here they introduce a stunning contrast. Hillsides of drab spruce become speckled with fluffy yellows and stabbing oranges, set against yellow-brown meadows and a royal blue sky. In places—the sites of old, intense fires—aspen dominate the forest, and the hillsides smolder with color. By the end of September the display is at its climax. After that, although new leaves enter the display, old ones fall away completely. By October the forest is littered with aspen leaves tumbling like gold coins before the wind. There is decay everywhere. The Rim, preparing for snow, returns to the raw appearance of spring; fallen leaves become grey and mottled like soot.

The Area, too, empties of summer life. After Labor Day visitation falls off, and by October even trailer caravans of seniors are gone. The store, the Lodge, the entrance station, the campground—all shut down. Skid Row is but half occupied. Most of the fire crew have left.

275

Those who remain begin the workday huddled around the heater in the Fire Pit with steaming coffee cups in hand, then reverse the processes by which the fire cache was opened. Tools, batteries, and rations are stored in the root cellar; slip-on units are removed from pumpers, drained, and pickled; crewmen check out. Still, there are many odd jobs, and the days have a quiet bustle.

The fires, too, are different in character—no longer wild but scheduled. Our big project is to haul firewood for the Office and select ranger fireplaces. It is too cold now for evening campfires, and we crowd around oil heaters instead; even the fires are moving indoors. The exception is prescribed burns. The fall—late September, early October—is prime season for controlled burning. But while prescribed fires give a flush of color and activity, they cannot reverse the inexorable approach of winter. Almost by definition scheduled burning occurs outside the natural fire season. It cannot be sustained indefinitely. Fire season must end.

High clouds make the sky ashen grey. Mice return to the cabins. Coyotes slink around the Area at dawn and dusk. Ravens gurgle loudly in the crystalline air, and owls cry in eerie harmony with the night wind.

It is early and cool when we gather at the site. A party of administrators—the Park's tribal elders—will arrive from the South Rim by helicopter later. We pace around our firelines, inspect the pumpers, and set up a small blackboard easel. Benson, the research biologist, cynically suggests that we ought to hang bunting and parade past a reviewing stand. It is his show, however; we are eager for fire of any kind, curious about how the prescribed burn will evolve and happy to participate in anything that the Park apparently values.

The plot encompasses a hectare of ponderosa forest along the Sublime Road, one of a series of burns projected under an expensive research program aimed at reintroducing fire to the North Rim. Earlier in the summer we cut fireline—SWFFs to one side, FCAs to the other in jeering rivalry. The plot sits within a small swale, and because of the open forest, you can see from one line to another. The fireline has a somewhat larger perimeter than the plot, and we have strengthened it by dropping a few snags and encircling a couple of others with bare soil. It is an interesting exercise. In some respects the problems of ignition and control are identical to controlling a wildfire; in important ways, however, they differ. Above all, the two fires differ in their politics.

We commence firing shortly after 0800 hours. Benson refuses to enter into any "management decisions." He is there only to research, he reiterates. Anything we do is equally useful to him; he is a scientist; and this is an operational matter. We ignite the whole plot more or less simultaneously.

There is not much to see at first. Fusees do not put down a lot of fire. Each spot requires time to build up, and more time must pass before the whole suite of spot fires merges. After the first flush of curiosity, both firing and control crews become bored. The morning is cool, the fine fuels unrecovered from the evening rise in relative humidity. This we sense and observe, but no one has calculated the fire-danger rating for the site because Benson has chosen to ignore the national rating systems for a multiple regression formula of his own devising—referred to as a "Y value"—which he has not bothered to explain to any of us. Our job is not to understand the fire but to start it and keep it from spreading beyond our prepared firelines.

Within an hour the fire builds up and coalesces into pockets of intense burning. A few trees torch. An immense green ponderosa acquires and holds fire in its crown. It becomes necessary to start up the pumpers and hose down portions of the perimeter. The Park elders and Benson retire up the ridge and out of the smoke. The fire in the big pine will not go out, so we fell it outside the line, against its lean. The tree costs us nearly a dozen wooden wedges; the smoke is acrid and dense, and our noses run with thick black mucus. Alston points out that we will not receive a penny of hazard pay for this because, technically, the fire has been controlled from the onset. By noon the Park elders and Benson have departed. The major thermal pulse of the fire is spent. Plenty of flame and smoke persist, but not as a dynamic system. Only the fire crew remains to watch.

Originally we planned to return day after day until the fire naturally extinguished itself. But when do you leave such a fire? Who decides it is "out"? What is the equivalent of mop-up? There is no one to answer such questions, and it becomes apparent that patrol will require weeks. The burn is pronounced a great success—and as a political statement it is. Not a word is ever published, yet it helps publicize a major restructuring of Park fire policy and programs. Subsequent patrol is nominal, and we spend most of our lunch periods at Point Sublime. The research program has three additional sites along the Sublime Road, each larger than Site A.

The research will continue for many years.

EVALUATING THE SEASON: WHAT DONNIE DOESN'T SAY

Donnie hands over a sheath of forms and asks, "What next?"

I look through the checklist. Close of business—COB—is our last official act as Park seasonals, and it is closely monitored. Every stage is prescribed. The fiscal office double-checks that there are no outstanding charges against the terminating employee, and it is our last chance to correct errors in overtime, hazard pay, holiday pay, or annual leave. Maintenance inspects quarters. Property ensures that each article of government equipment is returned, from driver's license to compass to radio to keys, though somehow or other a fireshirt usually seems to escape. The essence of the entire process, however, is the evaluation of seasonal performance, which determines whether the employee will be granted preferential hiring for the next year.

The review is designed to create the impression of equality. The Park evaluates the seasonal, and the seasonal is allowed comments in return. There should be no violation of due process or unjust discrimination. The reality is more complex. The Park so controls the process that the seasonal is nothing more than a migrant worker—in theory, seasonal employees are entirely dispensable and interchangeable. In reality, the Park cannot function well without experienced seasonals, so that the seasonal needs to be allowed to return and the Park needs to have him or her return. At one time seasonal employment was a kind of farm system for the Park Service by which prospective applicants would be evaluated for provisional acceptance into permanent ranks. This equilibrium is upset by the simultaneous advent of federal hiring freezes, the politics of affirmative action, and the sheer numbers of the baby boom.

Returning seasonals become a burden on the Park Service. There are too many applicants and not enough jobs, and recidivist seasonals lessen the size of the annual pool open to new hires. The Park Service removes the initial screening process from the parks and creates a national office to review applications. It also instigates a new category on the seasonal evaluation form (10-180)—"recommended for rehire in competition"—which, in theory, means that the seasonal is neither preferred nor discriminated against but must take his or her chances equally with the other applicants in next year's job lottery. The Park Service also dismisses any implied claim or right inherent in a "highly recommended" evaluation. It insists that it can select from the applicant pool whomever it wants for whatever reasons. What was designed as a means to limit political patronage is thus retrofitted to support a different form of preference, and the reformation in fire policy is matched by a reformation in employment policy. Once, when Captain Zero returns to the North Rim from his promoted post in the Western Regional Office, he announces baldly, grandly that the Park Service does not plan to hire any more white males as permanents in the foreseeable future. The seasonal evaluation form becomes unbearably complex, all for the unstated purpose of encouraging fewer rehires. The uncertainties of seasonal life are multiplied.

In fact, fewer people want to return. Not only is seasonal experience less useful as an entrée into a permanent career with the Park Service, but fire management in particular is a dead end. For anyone with ambitions in the Park Service, to remain a seasonal firefighter is a species of double jeopardy. The evaluation process reminds us forcefully that we live in a bureaucratic environment, not solely a natural environment; that the fiscal cycle is as powerful a determinant in fire management as the monsoon; that civil service regulations, not simply the laws of fire behavior, govern our conduct. The season begins when the Park hires and it ends when the Park terminates, and our EOD and COB dates may or may not coincide with the dynamics of fuel and weather that shape the arrival and recession of fires. Yet the agency cannot control the fire program completely because it cannot control lightning and forests. It cannot abolish fire by fiat, and that is why we remain.

We live within a crack—an incomplete weld—that joins an industrial society to a natural landscape. The two worlds, natural and bureaucratic, are at odds. Our lives as individual Longshots contradict our life as a fire crew. Even as we grow as individuals, we are put down as a crew. The evaluation process symbolizes this schizophrenia. Those who return do so for intensely personal reasons, almost in defiance of Park values, a decision that only reinforces our progressive alienation. I hand Donnie his forms and a copy of his seasonal evaluation. "Highly recommended for rehire."

"So what next?" Donnie repeats. "Get out of here," I tell him with a laugh. "Yeah," he says. "I'm packed."

That's the way to do it, I think. Just leave. Once there is no longer any connection to the fire crew, get out. Stay on the job as late as possible, then leave the day you COB. As you drive out, wave at the cache; honk at the pumper crew filling up the slip-on at the hydrant; shout at the sawyers bucking firewood for the Office. Next year there will be more fires.

I don't ask Donnie if he plans to return. That is his decision. He has no desire to join the Park Service, so he won't be compromised by returning as a Longshot. By the same token, there is no reason to stay in fire when that is not his career. He is an odd case. Adaptable, well liked, a natural athlete, he has learned the job as quickly as any rookie ever has. He was apparently recruited by the Park Service under a minority hiring program in the mistaken belief that, as the starting shortstop on the Howard University baseball team, he was black.

If he plans to return, Donnie will mail in an application form over the winter. He will not jeopardize his rating now by saying one way or the other, or if he says anything, he will say he is probably returning. If he does not, he knows that we will mail to him the nameplate that now hangs over his firepack.

There is no way to get a pumper safely to Site B without some major felling, so we pack in fedcos instead. In contrast with Site A, Site B is on a ridgetop, even more open and arid. Benson has upgraded his operation to include an Army-surplus communications module, which resembles a heavy-duty camper, in which he can keep his computer and radios. Within it he can calculate his Y value and monitor the burn. The module is parked at a pullout on the Sublime Road. Now that the day for ignition has arrived, he retires to his trailer, and we await his forecasts.

The Y value for the Site A burn was calculated at 6–7. We do not want a fire any hotter than that. Weather forecasts call for a warm, dry day. Benson figures the current Y value at 4.55 and predicts it will reach 8–9 by midafternoon. Does he wish us to proceed with the burn? "That," he snaps back on the radio, weary with endless reiterations, "is your decision, not mine." One burn is as good as another to him. It is all science. The decision to light up and burn is ours. We look at one another. The only reason we are here—the only justification for hauling our asses up this ridge during the summer to cut line—is to serve the research program. None of the permanent rangers, none of the Park elders, not even McLaren, will commit to a decision. They all look to me, a seasonal foreman, and I look to the crew. Benson returns on the Park radio. "Expected Y values will probably exceed nine," he says. There is a touch of anxiety in his voice. I compare that figure with the values at Site A; they don't register. Whatever the fuel moisture at the module, the duff here is still fresh with moisture from a recent storm. McLaren picks up a handful of needles and squeezes some water out of them. "Hell, let's burn," I say with a shrug. "It is your decision," says Benson. If the fire is lost, he means, it will be our responsibility.

Ignition is a disaster. With considerable labor we succeed in torching a few mounds of the fluffier needles. We send back to the pumpers for another case of fusees and a flamethrower. Whatever the fusees touch they char. When they are removed, the flame expires. Tom and The Kid begin piling up loose branches into small slash piles. Dave and Ralph rake up mounds of needles with McLeods. The heat from the flamethrower drives everyone away, but after the residual mix is burned, the fire dies out. The Kid removes the lid from the flamethrower and pours the mix onto some stacked piles, then ignites them. The fire hesitates and holds. Benson calls on the radio. His tone is urgent, wolfish. "Predicted Y values will exceed the prescription," he warns. "Does that mean we shouldn't burn?" I ask. "That is your decision," he insists.

The Fiasco fire. Now that we have begun we must continue: we can't mop up the small patches of fire that exist without destroying the plots. We take a coffee break, then an early lunch. We send a vehicle back for twenty gallons of torch mix. By early afternoon enough drying has occurred to sustain some continuous flame across the upper crust of needles, and by the end of the day most of the plot has been subjected to a degree of surface charring. The Park elders have long since departed. Benson shows up at the scene before lunch, muttering under his breath that we are trying to sabotage his research and vowing that it won't work, that his way is the future. There is no reason to leave anyone at the site that evening.

At our morning briefing in the Fire Pit we discuss the burn. Benson's trailer is the object of derision. Tom picks up an empty wastebasket and speaks into it with great, hollowing tones. "Pay no attention to the man behind the curtain!" There is nothing left but to patrol and hope the fire burns out soon. Duane, anxious to finish a long novel, volunteers.

Each day, however, is warmer and drier than the one previous; the fire smolders, then, after a couple of days, shows intermittent flame. On the fourth day there is an urgent message from Duane and Wil as they make their first morning tour of the fireline: the Site B burn has escaped its perimeter and supports nearly half an acre of wildfire. Response is instantaneous. We corral the fire, lay in some hoses for mop-up, and track down the source of the breakout to a creeping duff fire that entered the catface of a green ponderosa near the fireline, burned in the cavity until there was not enough heartwood left to support the tree, then flared over the trunk after it tumbled across the fireline. We have a lot to learn about prescribed burning.

FIRES OF SPRING

Dave flails at the outbuilding of the old camp with a sledge. Joe and I gather loose boards and pile them nearby. It would probably be easiest to attach chains to what is left of the main structure and pull the walls down with the pumpers or winch, as we did with the Sheep Shed, but there are so many nails around the site that we hesitate to drive very far off the road. If, however, we dismantle the main buildings with sledges and crowbars, as we are doing with the outbuilding, the project will take weeks. I elect to crush the major structures by felling nearby trees on them. The falls will smash the walls and floor, and needles and branches will add kindling. Besides, Joe reasons, the trees have grown up since the structure was abandoned and crown scorch would probably kill anything nearby when we light the pyre.

We pause before the largest structure, an elevated floor with broken walls. It is hard to believe that this site once supported a CCC camp, more than a hundred men strong. Now the old camp has been declared a pollutant in the wilderness, and we have been ordered to destroy it as part of a general housecleaning of the backcountry. In the fall, after a snow, the piles will be torched.

The presence of the CCC is manifest everywhere. There were two full companies on the North Rim each summer; during the winter one company relocated to Phantom Ranch, and the other to the South Rim. CCC enrollees built the camp at the Shinumo Gate to support their fence project, and they probably constructed (or improved) Tipover Spring as a water source. There was another major camp below Neal Spring. There they dammed water into a small pond, ran a pipe from the reservoir to a large wooden tank down the valley, and laid out a full camp in the meadow. Fireroad E-3 traveled to the site. A third camp—the main one—was in the Area. There the CCC constructed nearly every Park Service building; even Mission 66 failed to rework the Area, and more contemporary Park construction has tended to retrofit CCC buildings or introduce trailers to supplement the CCC legacy. The enrollees themselves lived in a tent camp by the heliport. Officers lived in the small wood frame houses along Skid Row. The structural fire cache and ambulance now occupy the old CCC fire cache; the Fire Pit thrives in a niche of a CCC warehouse; the fire cache claims an old CCC road storage shed; the ranger station is a refurbished CCC mess hall; the concessionaire's mule barns and the Park's long-term storage sheds are housed within former CCC structures located on what has become known as CCC Hill.

They restructured the backcountry, too. Many springs were outfitted with pipes and troughs made from hollowed logs—Fuller Canyon Spring, Robber's Roost, Basin, Kanabownits, Bright Angel, Tipover, and Harvey. You have to know they are there in order to find them; you can see the present entrance road and fireroads from the springs, but not the springs from the roads. The CCC also made, or improved, small impoundments at Greenland Lake and Basin Spring. It protected with aspen fences the Rim's natural ponds—those flooded sinkholes like Swamp Lake—and it erected aspen corrals at nearly all surface water holes. Although part of the justification for creating tanks was wildlife enhancement, the greater reason was fire protection.

Almost single-handedly the CCC created a physical plant for fire control on the North Rim. Enrollees moved one metal lookout tower—North Rim tower—to its present location and constructed a second metal tower at Kanabownits, erected cabins for both, and joined them with telephone wires. They established the tree tower network; they laid out the fireroad system; they put in a communications system, a ground return telephone net; they placed metal sheds with handtools at key locations in the woods; they laid out surface trails, some of which we uncover during the construction of the Bawgd Pass trail; they obsessively swept roadsides clean of dead and downed wood, partly for esthetics and partly as a fire prevention measure. The CCC built the first—the enduring—boundary fence. It built the original fire cache. And it fought fire.

It is impossible for us to see the CCC boys as anything but the original Longshots—an enormous crew of immense comradery, with a ceaseless parade of big projects and big fires. The era is imagined as a golden age, and every relic is treasured. Marooned for a day on the South Rim, Wil and I pawed through the Park archives for photos of the old camps. Our favorite is a picture of the original fire cache, circa 1936. Three enrollees stand admiringly beside a forest fire pumper and a structural fire truck, while a park ranger, overweight, stares vacantly upward. When we return we duplicate the scene with our modern vehicles. The two photos, side by side, go into the FCA Musuem.

It is a quixotic gesture, however. What the CCC built up, we are ordered to tear down. The revision in Park Service policy that established the foundations for a new fire program also decreed that all traces of human presence in the backcountry must be eradicated. We cease to man either North Rim or Kanabownits tower; the tree towers are condemned; the old fire cache is transferred to the rangers; the metal toolsheds are forgotten; CCC Hill subsides into a state of dilapidation; the aspen corrals are razed; the fireroads are abandoned, one after another. Mobile trailer homes overtake CCC cabins as preferred quarters. The ranger station is refurbished into an office, shedding almost all allusions to its origins; then one winter it is gutted by fire and replaced by trailer modules. We even pull up and pack out some nine miles of old telephone wire that once connected Kanabownits to North Rim tower. What is not ripped up or burned is simply abandoned or retrofitted to new purposes, and we quit informing the Park where corrals and spring troughs can be found and note with perverse pleasure the endurance of the western CCC-built boundary fence. We marvel, too, that the Park will make heroic efforts to preserve at Greenland Lake a "salt cabin" putatively erected by sheep and cattle herders in prepark days yet destroy with fanatical obsession every vestige of CCC edifices outside the Area. The salt cabin, however, stands next to a pullout on the scenic drive and provides an "interpretive opportunity," a visitor connection, which the CCC structures, remote in the woods, do not.

Lunch is over, and Joe and Dave toss some miscellaneous boards onto the pyre, while I wander along the faint trace of W-4C as it approaches the Fence. Just across the boundary the Forest Service has been logging heavily, and slash piles sprout like mushrooms; they will be fired in the autumn along with the other prescribed burns. When the old camp is torched, no one will notice another smoke among the general pall.

Site C has a little of everything.
Of special interest are a north-facing ravine, a ridge, and some thickets of white fir—precisely the target for a prescribed fire program aimed at restoring the natural ponderosa regime. The perimeter

of the site nearly abuts the Sublime Road, and we set up a camp across from it. Alarmed that tourists might happen upon the scene, the BI has us rout out a sign that reads: ENVIRONMENTAL BURN. IN PROGRESS. *He continues—as he has for several years—to refer to the fire as a "proscribed burn." "Maybe he knows something we don't," Wil reminds us. As Duane plants the sign along the Sublime Road, a tourist in a pickup slows down, studies the sign, and asks quizzically what fire is not an "environmental burn"? Duane has no answer.*

There are no dignitaries this time, only fire and research personnel and the new North Rim manager, Gonzo Gilliam. The ritual begins with the usual mating dance about who will be responsible for the decision to ignite. Benson calculates his Y value and makes his predictions, for which he is well paid and which we ignore in favor of the National Fire-Danger Rating System nomographs. But this time our question to him concerns ignition strategies. And again, we are informed, research is indifferent; one ignition pattern is as good as another; the decision to burn, and the choice of technique, are ours and ours alone. Patiently Gonzo, who has some legitimate fire experience and has shrewdly parlayed it into project fire positions, tries to explain to Benson that the procedures we adopt will dramatically affect the outcome. Benson reiterates, as to a child, that there is only fire, that all fires are equally usable to him.

While these queries rage, the Longshots stand in the ravine with the Park fire officer. McLaren, so far quiet, picks up some needles. More and more often he has been on the losing side of Park politics; a man of immense practical experience and unflappable in the face of emergencies, he discovers that his career, once moving briskly upward, has halted and he is condemned, perhaps forever, to be the assistant chief ranger at Grand Canyon. To the Park Service—to the new era of professional managers and information specialists—he is a relic who treats a helicopter as if it were a horse, who believes that all problems, even intensely technical ones, are really by and about people. Increasingly, he simply withdraws from political fights, from public appearances with Benson, Gonzo, and the others of the new regime, and leaves the fire crew to itself. We hear from him only during fires, and then we are reminded how much real fire experience he has. Usually bareheaded, he appears strange to us now in a hard hat. In a low voice to the crew he announces that the duff won't burn. Gonzo and Benson are now eye to eye over the issue of who should control the fire, or rather who should have the privilege of not directing the fire, and Gonzo is not only exasperated but excited. "OK, we burn from the bottom up!" he bellows.

For the next two hours we weave a tapestry of charred lines and rings across the slope. Nothing will hold a flame. By late morning we have reached the ridgetop. We bring out fusees, drip torches, and a flamethrower. Under Gonzo's roars and Benson's indifferent stare, we lay down strips of fire, each of which burns into the other while the first strips are still flaming; unobtrusively McLaren dampens some of the excess fire-starting, but there is plenty, and the effect is awesome. Within half an hour the ridgetop is a maelstrom of fire. A smoke column churns upward. In flashes we sight a large firewhirl embedded within the densest smoke. Tree after tree—mature ponderosa all, some over four feet in diameter—swell into flaming torches. When the great outburst subsides, it is discovered that the slope, heavily loaded with fuel and thick with fir reproduction, is practically unscarred, while the open, mature ponderosa forest has been gutted. Great trees now bear deep catfaces; they will topple over the road within a few days. Other trees suffer colossal crown scorch and will not survive the winter. "I thought," says Wil out loud, "that the purpose of this burn was to make the slope look like the ridgetop." McLaren's lips are pursed, and he looks unnaturally old in his orange hard hat. "Hey," says Eric, "anybody got a buck I can pass?"

Wil drives Benson, Gonzo, and McLaren to a helispot along the Sublime Road, and they depart in midafternoon. McLaren refuses to be drawn into a discussion about the fire, which the daily report proclaims another success of the prescribed burn program. The rest of us remain at camp and prepare dinner, a medley of barbecued entrées—every man his own chef. From rations come the desserts, crackers, fruit. Duane, however, refuses to eat his hamburger after it is caught in a grease flare-up and chars deeply. "It's carcinogenic," he insists.

Evaluating Seasonals: Life After the 10-180

With seasonal evaluations approaching, I arrange to meet with everyone for a brief conference so that the final day will hold no surprises. I suggest to Priest that he seems to be half-stepping his way through the end of the season and ask if he wants to return. "Yes, there is a problem," he admits; then he seizes high ground and announces that he cannot in good conscience extinguish any more fires on the North Rim. As an educated biologist he understands the ecology of the forest. "This is a dying forest," he declares. "It needs fire." "We all need fire," I reply. "Do you wish to resign?" "Oh, no," he says, shaking his head. He has discussed this with the BI. He wants to stay on; he has to stay on. He will reform the system from within.

We have different reasons for joining the Longshots, and we have different reasons for leaving. For some of us summer means adventure, a paying job, a chance to grow up in special circumstances. Others see the fire crew as an opportunity for career advancement. You can't remain in the first group unless you like fire. But if you want to make real money, you transfer to maintenance or to a construction contractor as E.B. and Randy do; if you want to get into the Park Service permanently, you become a ranger or a fern feeler or even a fee collector as Tom and Pferd and Bryan and Dave do; and if you want to work in the woods, you sign on with the Forest Service as Tim does. If you want to be a white-collar professional, you return to school and accept the mores of dentists and lawyers as do Duane, Ralph, and Wil. Even if you continue to remain a de facto migrant worker, you will eventually become bored with the Rim or disgusted with the bureaucracy and go elsewhere.

The issue is not whether you leave: you have to leave since your appointment is limited to a maximum of one hundred eighty days. Ours is a seasonal existence, circumscribed not only by the cycle of fires at the North Rim but by the seasons of our own lives. You can't be younger than eighteen, and you can't be too old—not only because the job will break you down physically but because you will have other obligations and will have been inducted into other institutions like families and careers. Even a true, aging migrant will think twice about seasonal work in fire because other jobs pay better and the special esprit of a fire crew will be lost on him. You have to be young for the magic to work. You have to believe that the North Rim is the greatest of places and the fire crew the most wonderful of groups. You have to live in that violent geography—that peculiar season—between adolescence and adulthood. It can last only so long.

But as a North Rim Longshot you are caught in another transition— suspended between two eras of philosophy about fire management. Firefighting becomes profoundly ambivalent, compromised. The Park loses interest, and reflects this indifference by an absence of leadership; fire management seems to belong somewhere west of safety management in the geography of its priorities. Only the persistence of fires ensures our continued existence.

The strategy behind the new era of fire management is that prescribed fire will ultimately supersede wildfire, and prescribed burning, firefighting. It intends to reorient fire programs from simple protection into the advancement of biocentric objectives, into support for wilderness values. To reduce the damage of suppression, prescribed fire programs will substitute information for prime movers, and research, for field operations. And it is a great era nationally for fire research. From our standpoint, the critical facts are two: fire remains on the Rim, and the Park will support a prescribed fire program. Unfortunately information does not equal knowledge, and it can't substitute for decisions and commitment. The exchange of controlled fire for wildfire, if it ever comes, will not occur at Grand Canyon within our seasonal lifetimes. Instead, we stand on the brink of two eras, each in disarray and both incommensurable.

Rich is nonplussed. "Look," he says, holding up a cardboard trap. "It gets us out of the Area and the BI likes it. He's a sort of entomologist, you know." "Yeah," says Randy, "but gypsy moths? Does anyone here even know what a gypsy moth looks like?" "Of course not," says Rich patiently. "That's why we have to trap the buggers. We have traps installed at all the overlooks and parking lots. It's part of our new resource management mission. The Department of Agriculture guy even gave BI these cloth patches. Look, 'Gypsy Moths.' Cute, huh? We can put them on our hats." "Yeah, you bet," says Randy.

They stop at Point Imperial. The trap has a spider, a mite, some pine needles and bark, a dozen mosquitoes, and a wad of pink chewing gum. "Nice," says Randy. "I hope you brought a lunch," says Rich. "We'll be doing this all day."

The control lines for Site D have been laid out several years in advance, and this time Gonzo will direct the operations from the start. A mature ponderosa forest is thoroughly invaded by white fir, and fuel loads in all categories are heavy. On one side the site is bordered by the Sublime Road. We place our camp on the opposite side of the road along a ridge.

Again there is a debate among ourselves concerning how we ought to light up. Uncle Jimmy suggests that we torch off a snag and let the fire spread from there. "It's more natural." Dana suggests that we offer a sacrificial victim, and Eric volunteers Dana, who allows himself to be strapped to a snag while others rake up branches and needles around the base. Gonzo orders the firing to begin—loudly, authoritatively, over the Park radio—but never decides how ignition should be conducted.

Since it is our choice by default, we elect to begin firing at the top of the ridge and burn down into draws on the north and south flanks. Benson arrives late and refuses to be involved in any decisions. We torch off a snag, then ignite concentric circles around it. Flame builds up slowly but steadily; only when the fire enters thickets of fir reproduction is there flaring, and then there is a rush to the scene with cameras and notebooks. Most of the fire is quiet, almost retarded. Dan worries, however, about the patches of young conifer. "I don't like all this fir repercussion," he says. "Yeah," Rich agrees. "It's pretty serious."

Perhaps a third of the seventy-acre site is burned the first day. The following two days, while the remainder is fired, we are pretty much on our own. We lay down parallel strip fires around the perimeter, back the fire down the south slope with contoured strips, and on the north slope burn a chevron pattern, a straight line from top to bottom that fans out as it progresses downhill, until it is apparent that there is too much fire, that another two days of drying and a heavy concentration of drip torches are too intense. There is one spot fire, possibly from radiant heat, that appears in a punky log located embar-

rassingly close to our camp. Otherwise for the next three days we patrol. No one else from the Park shows up.

As the fire ends, however, interest rekindles. Before Gonzo will allow us to depart, he insists that we fly the fire perimeter with him in a helicopter. The pilot, Joe Ugly, cruises the burn in fast, tight circles, better suited to a stock car race than a fire recon. Wisps of smoke rise everywhere in the burn, but there are no flames. The next day the BI, who at the time of ignition had conveniently retired to his house on the South Rim, tramps around portions of the fireline and denounces the entire operation as unprofessional and unnecessary. Benson informs the superintendent that the Sublime burns are complete and that the North Rim is ready to go operational with a full-scale prescribed fire program aimed at massive reconversion of fir understories to open ponderosa.

The early-morning smoke report a day later thus comes as a surprise. There have been no storms, and it is too long since the last round of lightning for it to be a sleeper. Recon 1 pinpoints the fire at Site D. A fire has indeed escaped—half a dozen logs, many aspen, lying in a meadow across the Sublime Road from the burn. The fire burns from log to interlocking log, the interstitial grass too green and wet to carry any combustion. The cause of the fire is a mystery, for there is no obvious connection to the Site D burn—no toppled trees across the road, no reservoir of punky wood that would be receptive to a firebrand, no source of radiant heat. There is only the fire, which we extinguish in a few minutes with pumpers. Back in the Area the BI gloats and struts. And back in the cache we admit that we don't understand prescribed burning.

Wil suggests that maybe the BI has been right all along. "It looks like a proscribed fire to me," he says.

Fires of Autumn

The heat drives us back. Dean from Mars is flabbergasted—both alarmed and thrilled—by the amount of heat the flamethrower has generated, but quickly fires off another burst against the boulders, and another. The air has a sickly smell of diesel and soot. The limestone appears to burn as the residual fuels coat it and flame. "OK, OK," says Pferd. "Enough. Let someone else have a turn." Dean says he wishes all our training courses were this much fun. "Just mix diesel and gasoline, pump, and shoot," he marvels. "No," says Pferd, ever cautious. "Fire doesn't work that way. It's not the mix of gas and diesel in the torch that matters; it's the mix of fire and fuel in the woods." "Yeah," Dan agrees. "There's no fuel like an old fool."

Enthusiasm for prescribed fire is everywhere, and it is almost everywhere justified. The fire crew needs a prescribed fire program, and we know it. It is clear that the Park Service will withdraw from classic fire suppression; our only salvation is another fire program to which it will commit. Prescribed fire is clearly the informing genius of the new era, and there are many selfish reasons for us to welcome it. It could extend our duty season into the fall, stabilize summer project work, and improve fire skills. It could allow us to jump on a Park Service bandwagon and recover some status within the agency. Any kind of fire is better than no fire; any project work, even line construction, is better than none at all; and to conduct prescribed burns, we have to learn about a lot of tools and techniques—such as firing out—that we would otherwise not know.

The problem is that Grand Canyon's superintendent has determined that no program will go operational until Benson completes his research. That will take years. Research is not being asked to supply vital information but to stall. Simultaneously, fire expertise within the Park Service is being supplanted. Whatever the outcome of Benson's research, the smart money says that there will not be a program because there will be no one knowledgeable enough about fire to translate a philosophy of prescribed burning into field operations. By the time the research is completed, evaluated, and translated into projects, no one presently in the Park will be around to assume responsibility for it. As a result, Grand Canyon can muster no more than the parody of a prescribed fire program.

There is little understanding of fire, marginal enthusiasm for a full-scale fire suppression program, and no mechanism for a genuine reconstruction based on prescribed fire. Instead, prescribed burning—especially the prospect for "prescribed natural fire"—becomes a convenient rationale for the Park to disinvest from fire management altogether. The Park wants a minimal organization, just enough to keep fire from becoming a public embarrassment, and it appeals to the convincing philosophy of prescribed fire to reduce its overall fire management obligations. It does not replace a program of fire suppression with a program of fire management; it simply guts the suppression component.

A bona fide fire management program centered on the concept of prescribed fire demands a heavy investment of agency time, resources, and personnel. It originates out of the belief that the positive reintroduction of fire into natural systems is essential for wilderness management. It requires a sustained commitment, a political will. No administrator at Grand Canyon wants any of this. On the contrary, the Park would be delighted if fire would simply vanish and leave the Canyon to people. That way rangers alone could run the Park, and the Park Service could keep a direct liaison with its constituencies. The reality is that resource management follows tourism, and the visitor is on the River. The Park's real research thrust is on the River with him.

The Park Service takes pleasure in declaring that its management philosophy for natural areas—announced by the Leopold Report in 1963 and encoded into administrative handbooks in 1968—pioneered the practice of wilderness fire management. There is some truth in that claim, but it is limited to particular individuals and particular parks. Nationally the Park Service simply lacked the system-wide technical expertise to manage fire. Only after its inexperience became a source of public notoriety, especially after a natural fire escaped and threatened a community outside Rocky Mountain National Park in 1978, did the Park Service establish a Branch of Fire Management and begin promulgating more methodical guidelines and standards for training. With few exceptions, the Service did not see prescribed fire as an opportunity to change its management philosophy or its mission; it did not see the concept as a means by which to promote positive programs of wilderness management. Its values lay elsewhere. That some parks do succeed in establishing prescribed fire is a testimony to local genius. There is none at Grand Canyon.

Yet, in the end, what did it really matter to the average Longshot?

Almost none of us stay for enough seasons to feel the decline. We have no personal memory of the past. Meanwhile, preparing fire-lines, setting up camps, firing off blocks—all are good jobs, certainly preferable to the Fence. The status of fire management in the Park becomes unbearable if and when there are not enough fires. Only when fires fail must we rely on the agency for sustenance, and only then does the inequality in our relationship—that the Park matters more to us than we do to the Park—become demoralizing. Whatever its wishes, however, the Park cannot ban fire from the Rim. And fire is our one indispensable requirement—snag fires by the score, prescribed fires wise and foolish, and big fires, the kind that start and end worlds.

Pferd explains that he prefers the fusee because it puts the least fire down with the greatest control. He remembers his hotshot days when he watched burning crews plaster hillsides with fire, the backfires worse than the originating one. But most of us like the drip torch, and Dean studies the flamethrower longingly. "It's not the tool," Pferd continues pedantically. "It's how you use it. You have to understand fire behavior. You have to pattern your ignition. You have to get your timing right. You hearing this, Dean?" "Sure, sure," says Dean from Mars, lost in unfamiliar abstractions.

"You know," he says slowly, "I think we can forget about Mr. Benson's Y value. With enough of these things we could burn down the fucking country."

The site is fine; the timing is dismal. Spring burns are the treatment of choice where the primary fuel is grass. The Walhalla site, however, is veneered with needles, and under the fresh needle cast are layers of wet duff and mulch—disastrous for a fire aimed at reducing fuels. No matter that we can ignite only the upper epidermis of needles. What matters is that the Park does not want to burn when everyone else in the Southwest burns—in the late fall—because that would mean extending the seasonal employment pattern. That would mean more money and a longer-lasting, if not larger, fire crew. If there is going to be a prescribed fire program, the Park decides it must occur during the regular fire season. That is the prescription that counts.

Early in the morning the fire will barely sustain a flame. We force ignition; we broadcast fire with drip torches as though we were spraying to control some malevolent insect. Meanwhile, the environmental conditions change. The air desiccates the forest floor, and southwest winds rush by straight out of the Sonora Desert, strengthened by Canyon updrafts. By late morning the fuelbed crust flashes into flame. Fire spreads quickly, more like a gas fire than a solid fire. Soon firewhirls form behind trees, flames rush up the bark of huge ponderosa, islands of pine reproduction blast into flame; crown scorch is devastating. By lunch we refuse to light any more, and by evening the fire is virtually out.

Only the top quarter inch, or in places the upper half inch, of duff has been consumed. Virtually no large logs have burned. Reproduction has been torched into naked stems, and the crowns of mature pine wilt into yellowed palsy. A few pockets of duff continue to smolder; left alone, without precipitation from storms, they might succeed in creeping across much of the site. But they will not be left—cannot be. They will have to be mopped up. In time the tree kills will cause the total fuel load of the site to increase dramatically.

ON THE FIELDS OF WALHALLA

There are many signs that announce the entry to Walhalla, but the one that matters to us is the extraordinary ponderosa that declares the hidden entrance to E-4, the first of the Walhalla fireroads. Lightning has split the tree in half longitudinally, and nothing is left but the enormous bole, its exposed heartwood glistening in the sun like burnished steel, rising swordlike out of the ground. A hundred feet beyond, overgrown with fir, is E-4. Jonathan steers the engine down the road, and a second pumper, driven by Leo, follows.

Once you reach E-4, the dominant character of Walhalla is quickly established. Walhalla Plateau is a gigantic mesa, almost completely isolated from the rest of the Rim by the transcanyon Bright Angel fault. In geologic times to come, Walhalla will be in fact segregated from the rest of the Kaibab, but for the present it is grafted by a narrow isthmus through which the scenic drive corkscrews up and around. Most of the North Rim resembles a hand that reaches down, its peninsulas—such as Sublime and Tiyo and The Dragon—like fingers that are slightly curled and separated. But Walhalla is divorced from the overall curvature of the Kaibab, a nearly level mesa, with fingered peninsulas of its own. It tilts slightly from north to south and from east to west. Its interior resembles a gently rolling plain, a great forested field unlike the rest of the Rim. Ponderosa pine dominates the biota, though it grades into dense mixed conifer to the north and into open grassy glades to the south. It is a good place for fire.

The western flank of Walhalla is one of the hottest sites for lightning fires on the Rim. As we drive down the road, the memory of old fires flashes past: the Knoll fire, nearly lost along the Rim; the Reunion fire, where Dave returned from the South Rim to assist his old crewmates with an unheard-of initial attack by pumper; the Hippolyta fire, nearly escaping control when it surged into fir reproduction until slurry drops cooled the fire down and Forest Service engines arrived; the Mariah, the Rookie, the Star fires; innumerable snag fires along the points—Matthes, Ariel, Obi, Komo. We hold the last day of fire school on Walhalla; here we induct recruits into the reality of field operations and the etiquette of firecamps. And now there are prescribed burns.

Walhalla is attractive as a natural fire province. Within its boundaries lightning fires could be left to behave in their natural state, subject only to surveillance. But the plateau is not truly isolated, and it must be sealed off or be made capable of sealing off a fire should one move into the isthmus. That calls for some fuel modifications. More compelling for management, however, is the argument that fifty years of fire suppression have so distorted the fuel complex that some prescribed burning is essential to reestablish a suitable base level. In particular, the white fir beneath the mature pine must be removed. This was, in fact, the rationale behind the fire ecology research program. The errors of the past must be purged by fire. To that end it is proposed to construct, through prescribed burning, a great arc of reduced fuels along the scenic drive and hence to protect the isthmus that leads into and out of Walhalla.

The prescribed fire, however, has prerequisites of its own. Along E-4 the fir must be thinned if the fireroad is to act as a fireline. That brings us and a complement of four chain saws to E-4. We climb into our web gear, now equipped for sawing, and debate tactics. Originally we cut a swath of reproduction and dragged it from the interior of the burn across the road. This was not only laborious but possibly dangerous since a spark or even radiant heat could conceivably ignite the drying piles. So we adopt a technique from Jonathan, formerly with the Flagstaff Hotshots, and dice up the young trees where they lie. Lop-'em-and-leave-'em. That requires a change in equipment as well as tactics, and so it goes, an endless regression.

The fact of the matter is that it is the Park bureaucracy, not the forest, that needs preburn preparations. The Park archaeologist delays a prescribed fire program for months and threatens to suspend it indefinitely until he can survey all the ruins in the region, clumps of rocks that have burned dozens of times since their abandonment in the thirteenth century. There are turf issues between the North Rim manager and the Park fire officer over who controls the operation, although neither particularly cares about what happens in the field, caring only about what happens in budget and staff meetings. There are questions about financing a prescribed fire with accounts and crews that were dedicated by line budgets to the suppression of wildfire. More seriously, as the Park proposes to put in the field what has been safely kept as philosophy—as the Park attempts to make operational what has previously been experimental ("scientific")—it denies itself the bureaucratic equivalent of protective firelines. It has to assume responsibility. Be it suppressed fire or prescribed fire, the Park has to commit to fire.

Each saw coughs and roars out of phase with the others, but the medley is delicious. We cut inward from E-4 for about twenty feet. The roads should introduce some real economies of scale. We can patrol the line with Park Service pumpers and Forest Service engines rather than with handcrews. The size of the Vista burn is increased substantially, but our capacity to control it, we believe, will be improved. Firing will begin along the perimeter, and we propose to burn out the interior by aerial ignition from the helicopter. When the fire concludes, those of us who are still on tour will COB. Jonathan comes across a surface ruin. Down at the Glades there are also terraces, once used for farming. There are ruins everywhere on Walhalla. Why the Indians abruptly left is unexplained.

"I think," says Dash, "that this will be one helluva way to close out the season."

When the time comes to fire the Vista burn, nothing remains of the plan except its grandiloquent scale. Instead of aerial ignition throughout the interior of the block, firing will be limited to the roads, and the interior will have to burn out on its own. Instead of the expected prescription, based on forecast fire behavior, the ignition will be determined according to a fixed calendar date driven by the programmed budgets of seasonal hiring. Instead of envisioning the Vista burn as the first in a cycle of restoration burns, this will be a one-time affair, the Ragnarok of fire management on the North Rim.

When the Forest Service engines arrive, we divide into squads. One group will hold the line, operating with engines; the other will ignite, and to improve its efficiency, we outfit the stake truck as a rolling arsenal of incendiarism. With the prevailing winds out of the southwest, we plan to begin near Vista Encantadora and burn south against the wind along the scenic drive. Rangers will ferry visitors through the smokey regions by convoy. Then, with the wind behind us, we will burn out along E-4. We will complete the circuit along the southern matrix of fireroads. The southwesterly flow should drive the fire away from the control lines; only along the paved highway, where pumpers can freely operate, should it be necessary to back the fire against the wind. Ignition is scheduled for early morning, when the winds are expected to be relatively calm.

It all starts slowly. The morning air is cool and moist. The understory near the Vista is thick with fir, and this makes for a poorer fuelbed and damper microclimate. Burns are spotty. As the morning progresses, as the sun dries the land, and as the forest continues to open up, ignition improves. The burning crews lay down arcs of fire a hundred feet from the road, then follow with more fire adjacent to the road. The idea is to stoke enough distant fire that it will create a draft which will suck the roadside fire into it and against the freshening winds; in general, the tactic works. There are some impressive flare-ups. Where pine and fir intermingle, the fuelbed extends unbroken from surface to canopy, and fire follows the fine fuels from ground to crown. But to clean out the insidious fir invasion is, after all, the

*announced purpose of the burn, and if the fires get hot, that, too, is
natural. That is how the Walhalla Glades, which the tourists now find
so attractive, were created in the first place.*

*As the burning approaches the Glades, however, the incidence of
torchings increases and the overall intensity of the fire mounts. I try to
dampen the firing crews, to string them out, but there is little opportunity for disengagement. Near the Glades several acres are virtually
incinerated. The earth swells with fire, a mounting smoke column
swallows the sky and the sun, and the roar and the stabbing flames are
finally too much even for the firing crews. Awed by the violence and
magnificence of the scene, they retreat to the road. The firelines hold.*

*We relocate to E-4, break for lunch, and review the proceedings.
The ferocity of the burn is in some ways more apparent than real, and
now the ambient winds will be with us; they should carry the fire away
from the fireroad without the necessity of stoking hot fires toward the
interior. Then, unaccountably, the winds shift. Intermittent breezes
from the east cause us to reinstate the strategy of establishing hot fires
away from the road. With denser fuels and without a broad, paved
road as a firebreak, however, it is more difficult to hold the line. Spot
fires spring up across E-4, and a degree of euphoria and pandemonium sets in.*

*The apparent chaos in the fire is nothing compared with the chaos
of its management. The BI, nominally the plans chief, sits under a tree
to pout. As fire boss, Gonzo—psyched up by the action—wants it to
continue. The Longshots want to slow down the operation, wait out
the winds, and perhaps burn through the night. The issue, however, is
decided on the South Rim.*

*There are visitor inquiries about the large smoke on the North Rim;
fern feelers on nature walks stop short in consternation, and pump
operators at Roaring Springs clog the radio with irritated queries; a
woman telephones a complaint to her congressman. With unintended
irony the Vista burn coincides with appeals to the Secretary of the
Interior from major environmental groups to deny permits for the
construction of coal-fired power plants in the Warner Valley region on
the ground that it will cause a deterioration of air quality in the
southern Utah parks and the Grand Canyon. But no industrial smoke
plume could match the convective column that rises from the ironically*

named Vista burn. For the remainder of the afternoon, its smoke hangs over Walhalla in a sun-obscuring pall before wafting toward the coal-fired power plants at Page. The superintendent orders the firing to stop.

The order is not to implement an alternative plan; it is simply to stop burning. We are not allowed to complete the burnout of untouched fuels or to suppress the fire. The Vista burn is left to smolder and flame on a huge scale. We patrol until sunset and then leave. That evening we watch from the Lodge as the smoke—a silver flood tide in the moonlight—spills into Bright Angel Canyon like a slow waterfall. Every night thereafter, as the evening inversion forms, the scene is repeated. There are complaints from Park personnel in the Canyon; there are complaints from visitors; there is another congressional inquiry. If the Park wants the fire to end, we can call the burn a wildfire and suppress it, or we can quickly complete the burnout—sacrifice a few days of heavier smoke for fewer days of smoke. The Park will order neither.

For a couple of days we patrol the perimeter with engines, then the Park proceeds to terminate us until only Charlie remains. Steadily the Vista burn fingers across the interior. Daily the smoke rises, and nightly it sinks into the Canyon like a cosmic tide. The unburned road is breached once, then twice. Hurriedly assembled crews of mainte- nance workers and seasonal rangers rush to contain the slop-overs. Eventually the superintendent orders that the fire be suppressed but with the stipulation that there be no additional crews or costs. Fire and Canyon are incompatible. Until he terminates in mid-October, Charlie daily drives a pumper down E-4 and sprays water in the direction of the smoking wreckage. The fire continues to wax and wane until the snows extinguish it.

The prescribed fire program—the fire program at the North Rim— is a shambles.

Ashes and Embers

The "Beef, Canned" in the rations is inedible. It is just as well, I think, that the light is too poor to see it. I put the can aside and open the crackers and fruit.

Gilbert patrols the burn—a "management" fire along the Sublime Road, between the road and the Rim, opposite Site C. It is a dark October night, cold and windy; clouds race across the stars like ink blots. There are flames everywhere, but the fire is remarkably docile and burnout in heavy fuels will be good. Our camp is by the road, near where it touches the Rim, and we have most of the comforts of the fire cache. I add some branches to our campfire. Somewhat to everyone's surprise this has been a successful burn. Tomorrow a storm is expected, and if it snows, as predicted, it will probably extinguish the fire. Timing is everything.

This is my last night; tomorrow I terminate. Gilbert will hang on as long as the money lasts, not long if it snows. Everyone else has departed: Dana to marriage and schooling at Berkeley, then to a divorce and a career in civil engineering; Wil to law school; Williams to the phone company; Randy to stockbrokering; The Ape to the Navy, then to urban forestry jobs in the San Francisco area. Gummer and Booby join the Park Service, get stuck on the cannonball circuit, and quit; Gummer goes to work for the Forest Service in Oregon, and Booby gets a job as a hospital administrator in Salt Lake City. Uncle Jimmy drifts on—a seasonal campground ranger at Sequoia-Kings Canyon, hotshot crewman in Washington, seasonal carpenter at Yellowstone. Bone moves to seasonal rangering jobs at Joshua Tree and God-knows-where-else. Jonathan smokejumps for a couple of seasons in Idaho before becoming a computer specialist with the Department of Defense. Tim cruises timber for the Forest Service. Lenny takes over the Longshots, then gets a permanent job as a fiscal clerk on the South Rim. "It's a way to get in," he explains; he later moves to a technician position at Everglades. Kenny replaces him as foreman, then clerks for the North Kaibab and goes to Desert View as a patrol ranger. Swifter is a district ranger at Denali National Park in Alaska. Alston goes to grad school in economics, works for Xerox in Los Angeles, quits to run rafts for the Park Service at Dinosaur, becomes a concessions specialist at Yellowstone and Alaska and a park superintendent in Colorado. Kent joins a hotshot crew and rises to assistant fire officer in the Apache-Sitgreaves and Coconino national forests. Charlie enlists with the rangers, seeks out the action at Lake Powell, and ends up with the Border Patrol in Nogales. Rich

attends grad school at Wyoming and gets a job with the Fish and
Wildlife Service. Abner acquires a national reputation as a writer of
novels and nature essays. Stiegelmeyer transfers to the South Rim,
becomes a permanent ranger, and goes to Grand Coulee; when he
returns to the North Rim for one season as a ranger, he is struck by
lightning. Dean disappears on his motorcycle in his infinite quest for
new hot springs. Achterman becomes a p.e. teacher and coach at a
Bend, Oregon, high school; Duane, a dentist; Fran, a Park groupie on
the South Rim; The Kid, manager of a ranch and ski resort in New
Mexico. Earl moves to the winter fire scene at Everglades, then to
whatever; Pferd, to seasonal rangering and the Tucson Fire Department. Donnie is a Marine; Scot, a sixth grade teacher; Jim, a personnel clerk on the South Rim; Priest, a biologist with the Forest Service
and USDA; E.B., a permanent maintenance man at Zion; Jack, a
county officer in New York state. Dan returns to New Hampshire, to
landscaping and a silver recovery business. Gilbert makes it to the
Tetons, becomes a seasonal ranger at North Cascades, and then a
technician at the Rocky Mountain Experiment Station. Sonja and I
marry. Of the rest—Gray, Stone, Roberts, Draper, Reed, Hardison,
Kieffer, Dawson, Harding, Halvorson, Crumrine, Johnson, Stovall,
Olivas, Wright, Depringer—no one knows. When we leave the Rim,
we leave each other.

I've eaten everything except the "Beef, Canned." The Canyon is a
cold black hole. There are more clouds. The stars look like snow-
flakes. I return to the burn, a chilly palimpsest of campfires. Something is wrong with the meat. I carry the ration can to the truck, turn
on the headlights, and inspect the inside. The meat is webbed with
heavy, sinewy fibers and whitish veins, and there is a huge white
artery on one side. I squint in the light. "Hey, Gilbert," I ask. "You
ever see anything like this?" In his clipped western Massachusetts
accent he replies that you never know what you'll find in these things.
Then he peers inside. "Good God!" he cries, drawing back. "It's the
damned heart." I dump it out on the fire.

The next morning I claim a day of annual leave, COB early, and
drive off the Rim. The snow is already heavy by the time I reach
Jacob Lake.

Part
Three

COB

STAY LATE.

There are great snowbanks in Little Park, and small rivulets meander among buried sinkholes. The winter snows have been above average; there will be no spring fire season. I stop the car. It is too early to man the entrance station, too early for tourists. The dry, cold air floods through me. Sonja watches wistfully. I put Lydia, now only a year and a half old, on my shoulders and point out the sights: the ponds, now iced and snowy; the forest, grim in its olive drab; the chilled and crystal sky. The large ponderosa snag that guards the entrance to the Sublime Road—so anomalous amid the spruce-fir, so queerly malformed into half a dozen trunks—has fallen. Everything else is submerged under snow.

The one exception is the entrance road, still under construction, which makes a muddy gravel scar through the scene. We drive to the Area, and the snow thins as we approach the Rim. In the Area the snows are sparse, crowded under shadows and the shaded north walls of buildings. We move into Building 177, next door to and nearly identical with 176 except for the large picture window overlooking Transept Canyon, which Walter, the carpenter, put in when he lived there. Through scattered trees we watch the sun set.

Surely this year there will be good fires.

We scramble around the Rim, hopping from outcrop to outcrop like goats, but we can find nothing. When Kenny finally sees stringers of smoke, they emerge from far below us. The fire is deep in the upper divide of Nankoweap Canyon, and we cannot see it directly from the Rim. We request an air tanker and bushwhack down perhaps seven hundred feet through dense spruce and fir, choked with heavy logs, that mantle the north-facing slopes. A DC-6 arrives and makes a pass, well below our field of vision. We request Alpine, a Park Service–sponsored IR crew stationed temporarily in the Park. Eventually we climb onto a limestone column that thrusts boldly up and away from the cliffs. The fire is probably another thousand feet below us.

It is a classic Canyon-Rim fire. It cannot be attacked directly, and it cannot be ignored. The best we can hope for is to contain it below the Rim, and there is some hope that we will be able to do that. The fire burns within an inverted triangle with its apex in the Canyon and its sides roughly defined by two rock ribs, one of which we stand upon. We could build fireline from each rib to the Rim, transforming the triangle into a diamond, though the cost would be enormous and the project would require a Class II fire team. If the fire escapes this perimeter, however, there is nothing to stop it: it could burn to Point Imperial; it could burn out the entire north-facing slope of Nankoweap Canyon; it could invade and even reburn the Saddle Mountain region. If the fire reaches the Rim, it will burn until the monsoon rains extinguish it.

I decide, for the moment, to lay down a retardant line. The DC-6 raises its flight path and shingles the slopes with slurry. When it releases its load, the tanker jolts upward, and it passes almost directly over our position on the rock column. The Doppler roar of the engines is exhilarating. The retardant may be enough to halt the fire.

But it may not. This is forest, not desert brush and grass. We talk with Butch and Lynn, the FMOs for the Park and Forest respectively. Lynn notes that there is a Class II fire team, for which he is fire boss, available from the Kaibab National Forest; we agree to request it if the need arises. Butch reminds us that the decisions are ours to make. Meanwhile, the whole crew drives to the Turnaround at Saddle Mountain, where the fire spreads before us, across the colossal side canyon, in magnificent panorama. Behind us stretches the Saddle Mountain Burn. We discuss strategy and watch. For the next two days the Emperor fire burns below the retardant line.

Then the line is breached, and I request a helo for a close recon-
naissance. The chief ranger and the Park's administrative officer, who
are on board for other purposes, join the ride. It is apparent that the
retardant alone cannot halt the spread of the fire; the surface fuelbed
is too thick, and the large logs are too dry; the fire simply creeps
underneath the veneer of slurry. A fire weather forecast calls for more
of the same—warm and dry. I decide to mobilize. The chief ranger
and administrative officer are silently dubious. I request the Kaibab's
Class II fire team.

Within minutes the team is mobilized, fire orders are placed
through the Forest dispatcher for crews, hoses, a caterer, ancillary
overhead, equipment—nearly all of it drafted out of Forest Service
fire caches. The Kaibab helitack crew assumes helo duties. Since the
Park radio is ineffective in the Saddle Mountain area, the Forest
dispatcher takes over radio traffic. We establish a camp near the
Turnaround, on Forest lands. The Park agrees to supply two of the four
requested crews: Alpine and a pickup crew of reserves, many from the
South Rim, for which Longshots will serve as crew and squad bosses.
I function as Park liaison with the fire team.

Lynn rendezvouses with me at the Turnaround while we wait; a full
mobilization will require about two hours. Already Forest crews
prepare the camp, and Longshots ready the fire cache and supervise
the organization of the pickup crew. Then we watch as a nearly
isolated cloud over Point Imperial matures into a thunderhead; watch
while it spreads; watch while over the entire Nankoweap Basin and
Saddle Mountain region a light rain falls. More thunderheads boil
upward, and a particularly heavy cell passes directly over the
Emperor fire and drenches it. Within half an hour a second cell
repeats the cycle. Between the two, the camp receives probably an
inch of rain. Heavy strata of clouds limn the north slope, streaking
across the burn. When the sun once more appears, steam hisses off
the exposed Canyon rocks. There is not a wisp of smoke anywhere.
Within an hour the mobilization of the Emperor fire will be completed.

It is easy to fight fire when a fire rages; it is less obvious what to do
when a fire apparently vanishes. But whether the fire has been extin-
guished or has passed into hibernation, we cannot say. Two, maybe
three wisps of smoke rise from the lower reaches of the burn—no

doubt smoldering logs. There is no way to predict the future of the fire. A competition exists between the logs, which are dry enough to keep the fire from going out, and the fine fuels, which are too wet to allow the fire to spread. If the logs burn out before the fine fuels dry, the fire is over. If not, the fire may propagate. We elect to proceed with the planned control lines, and they are constructed, with extraordinary labor, over the following day. That afternoon, without warning, the superintendent and his staff fly over the scene. They are appalled, and they demand that the fire be demobilized as quickly as possible.

Before we release them, the line boss has the hotshot crews attempt to blackline—burn out—the perimeter. But the fuels are too wet, and even as the hotshots depart, the Longshots and Alpine are busy mopping up the abortive burnout. No one else from the Park visits the site. Since there is no direct radio contact on the Park net, I must drive to the entrance station (or the Area) each time I wish to communicate. Quietly we reopen E-1A from Point Imperial, set up a portable tank along the Rim, lay out a complex hydraulic system to get water from the Rim to the fire, and shuttle pumpers between the tank and the Area. The Longshots supervise the hydraulics, and Alpine oversees the mop-up. I position Kenny at the Turnaround with binoculars as a precautionary lookout. All in all we have almost no contact with the Park. We have nothing new to report, and we have nothing to report that anyone wants to hear. We just do what we know best, while deep in the Canyon the Emperor fire continues to smolder in logs and burrows of deep duff.

Two days later, as we are about to abandon the burn, Kenny jumps on the radio to inform us that the fire is acting up. Within seconds a loud whoosh echoes off Saddle Mountain; a roar of winds seems to reverberate throughout the Nankoweap Basin; the Alpine crew boss, Larsen, shouts to his crew to get out of the burn. The long-anticipated, much-doubted blowup of the Emperor fire has begun.

There is no way that the fireline by itself or handcrews, even with hoses, can hold the fire if it continues its rush up the slope. We will have to burn out the line. I request Forest Service assistance, and the Forest sends two engines; it can supply a handcrew in the morning. We will have to burn out on our own. I request a spot weather forecast from the fire weather service in Phoenix, try out test fires, distribute belt weather kits. The test fires burn well. The forecast predicts normal downslope evening winds, which should, theoretically, push our backfires away from our lines. We fire out the south flank within two hours, a crisp, clean burn. "We ought to call this the Backwards fire," a bemused Alpine squad boss tells Leo. "First we mop it up, then we burn it out." "Yeah," Leo replies. "Welcome to the North Rim."

If the winds hold, we should have the north flank burned out by midnight. But the winds shift. Burnout slows—an exercise in tedium, full of torching trees, searches in green timber for spot fires, constantly finessed backfires. Not until the early light of dawn do we reach the rock outcrop that terminates the line.

There is not much more we can do. The fire will continue—it will in fact accelerate—its run. There has been virtually no humidity recovery over the night. The Forest handcrew arrives shortly after burnout, and we use them to protect the much extended blackline with hoses. We will try to swat out spot fires as they appear on the Rim. We can reinforce threatened sectors with slurry. The Longshots have worked in shifts during the night so we would have some reasonably alert firefighters the next day, but I am utterly drained. It is an axiom of fire supervision that fatigue leads to bad judgments. The textbook solution is for me to delegate responsibility to someone else, drive back to the Area, have a shower, get a hot meal, take a short nap, and return. Jonathan assumes control over the fire.

And he is there—in charge—when the Emperor fire roars out of the Canyon with all the fury of which it is capable. The devastation is total. What had been a dense forest is now a gutted debris of sticks and white ash. As the flames dance wildly near the Rim, Jonathan requests retardant to dampen them. The slurry is probably ineffective, and after a few drops it is abandoned. Alpine attacks several spot fires, and thanks to the evening burnout the line holds. The superintendent, however, is furious. He is playing softball—pitching, of course—when the air tanker flies over the field. Immediately, right there on the mound, he seizes his radio and demands to know what is happening in his *park. "I* run *Grand Canyon!" he screams, quivering.*

Butch calls me. "I don't know what's happening," I reply, "but the

*guys on the fire know what to do." It is difficult to determine whether
the problem is that the Park does not know what is happening or that
no one from the usual administrative ranks is in charge. Who's the fire
boss? I am asked. "Jonathan . . . I am . . . we're all sort of in
charge," I reply. I should never have left the scene, I realize, whether I
had any special contribution to make or not. So much for textbook
solutions. The only book that matters is the one we write.*

*The next day the saga of the Emperor fire is noted on the national
fire situation report from BIFC. The crew is euphoric. The superintendent orders a board of review.*

*The fire team is reassembled from the Kaibab, and each of the
major Park divisions contributes reviewers. We meet in the conference
room of the administration building—the Big House, as it is called—
on the South Rim. I relate the events of the fire and the decisions
taken. For those not on the scene, for those not familiar with fire, the
special character of the Emperor fire is difficult to accept. The BI
seizes the floor. "The fire should never have been unmanned," he
insists. He pounds his fist for emphasis. "You have to stay with a big
fire like this one." The Park administrative officer worries about the
cost of air support. A South Rim ranger notes that the fire was not
properly "managed" to advance the red cards—that is, the career
goals—of permanent Park staff. As fire boss, Lynn explains that there
was not much room for maneuvering. The fire couldn't be attacked
directly, and it couldn't be abandoned. "It's a special case," he
argues. Twice I go to the blackboard and recapitulate the sequence of
fire behaviors and suppression responses. Butch mutters out loud that
the superintendent should really have come to the meeting. "The
superintendent," he avers, "really needs to hear all of this." A
maintenance man expresses another cause of unhappiness. "No one,"
he complains, "knew what was happening." The play-by-play had not
been broadcast over the Park radio. The decision to switch to the
Forest net had deprived the whole Park—from fee collectors to the
superintendent—of a chance to participate vicariously. While, from
our perception, we have been abandoned by the Park, the Park's
perception is that we have unfairly hoarded a precious resource and
denied others a romp into voyeurism.*

When the session ends, inconclusively, I am exhausted and wired.

The superintendent wishes the Emperor fire to remain as a festering reminder that he and he alone runs Grand Canyon. No one from the Park Service hierarchy thanks the Forest Service for its help. The members of the fire team disappear to their duty stations in Fredonia and Williams. I fly back to the North Rim.

A few days later at the Turnaround the Longshots conduct our own review. It is a bright day, and sunlight sweeps across the collage of white and black that is the Emperor burn. I stand in front of the crew, with my back to the fire site, and try to review events while we eat lunch. The crew stares past me. Beyond the Emperor fire they can see Point Imperial, the Nankoweap Basin, the gorge of the Little Colorado, the Painted Desert, Desert View, the San Francisco Peaks. The Emperor fire is only a prelude, a foreground vanishing point. Discussion is impossible. They wave me aside. "You're blocking the view," says Rich.

"Hell," Bone says happily. "This was one hell of a fire."

My days are spent with the crew.

The Longshots have been reduced to six seasonals. The SWFFs have long since exited the program. The past couple of years have been slow fire seasons throughout the Southwest, and the feeble fire loads enhance our bureaucratic isolation, for fire alone justifies a fire program. A new superintendent transfers the BI to a staff position in resource management on the South Rim, responsible for Park fire planning but without line authority. The South Rim fire crew gives up fire to operate the heliport full-time. Gonzo transfers to a California park. McLaren retires. His replacement, a ranger from Yosemite, has little experience with fire and little interest in it; Butch explains that he will let us run the fire show for the Park, that we will be the Park's fire crew. The reduction in fire organization, the Park believes, will mean a reduction in fire problems. We suppress fires because there is no alternative. There is no prescribed fire program because the superintendent has decreed that there can be no smoke in the Canyon, that any plot ignited must be mopped up by the close of business each day. The Park's real obsession on the North Rim is the new entrance road, which, after years of fitful construction, is about to open. The road chips are defective, however, and when the final miles of asphalt are laid down, they are put down in a snowstorm; within a year portions of the road will begin to crumble.

The Longshots are once more lean and mean. Kenny, Jonathan, Bone, Rich, Leo, myself—all are veterans. We stage fire school for the reserves. We open the roads without incident and rendezvous at Tipover to enter another year by our names. I argue, successfully, to relocate the Park's Affirms computer to the Fire Pit so we can enter directly our situation reports and daily weather readings into the national network. We obtain from the Forest Service some crystals with its frequency to use on a spare channel in our hand radios and erect an antenna so that we can communicate directly with its dispatcher from a surplus base set it has lent us. We secure a one-ton pickup with double-rear tires and outfit it with a slip-on—probably the first vehicle since the old powerwagons that is equipped to do the job demanded of it. We fight fires in the Canyon, along the Rim, and deep in the Plateau.

As long as fires continue, we cannot be dismissed, but we cannot be dealt with directly and routinely. We hear rumors that the Park Service is serious about reconstituting its fire presence nationally, that new programs will better integrate the Service with other agencies, better control the fire accounts, improve fire planning and credentialing. But it is all heat lightning to us. We see none of the promised reforms, and if they do come, they will belong to another time than ours. No matter. The project work is good, the fires continue, the Longshot logo spreads from T-shirts to insignias, and the idea of the Longshots shrugs off the legacy of poor years. When two smokes are reported a few hours before the saloon has scheduled its season opening—a vital ritual—Rich downs the rest of his beer, struggles into his fireshirt as he jogs to the cache, and assures us in his New Hampshire twang that "sacrifices must be made."

The Longshots we have become.

Lenny calls for assistance. The fire is burning below the Rim on very steep terrain south of Point Imperial. "I could use a couple more guys to help trench a line and mop up," he says. The duff is thick, and large logs litter the slope, lodged precariously against standing trees. With no other smokes on the Rim, we all go.

There is a shout of approval as we arrive under darkening skies. Lenny briefs us about the fire. Jonathan and Kenny go to work with saws; Bone and I, with pulaskis. The Canyon fills with mist. The trench below the fire has to be deep enough to catch rolling debris, yet it must be free of combustibles. Needles, cones, twigs, duff—they all have to go. The trench becomes an excavation.

Fire smolders over a large area, flaring in hot spots. The sky starts to drizzle as Jonathan yells for help. He has donned a poncho, and the log he is cutting has jackknifed and rolled down onto the poncho, trapping him. We use pulaskis and a shovel handle as crowbars and lift the log off him. The bucked logs we rotate perpendicular to the slope so they can't roll downhill. Sometimes we scrape a small trench of dirt for them to lie in. The rains fall harder. We are soaked; but the fire burns briskly, and as long as it continues, we can stay.

We complete the fireline and break for lunch. Nothing but spruce-fir around here, trunks that bristle with branches, branches that drag on the ground—no real shelter anywhere. We sit beside a rock outcrop and open C rats. The rain drips off our hard hats, jackets, and ponchos. Lenny decides to name it the Wetrats fire.

Even with the rain, mop-up takes hours. Still, we are all together, a shovel of Longshots. Jokes fly with every toss of dirt and duff. "You know," says Lenny, "you just can't keep a good fire down."

My evenings are spent with my family, and the family schedule is dictated by the needs of Lydia.

The cabin is all we require for quarters. Packing a summer's worth of gear for three people (including crib and wooden high chair) into a compact car discourages materialism. We bathe Lydia in the kitchen sink. On sunny days she plays in a small inflatable swimming pool in the grass by the Rim. She knows the deer and ravens. She picks grass for the mules to eat, and the evening walk to the corral is a happy ritual. She helps sweep the porch. At night sometimes I carry her in a backpack to the fire cache. She knows "canyon" and nods sagely when we say the word.

When I arrive for the summer, I am nursing a chronic but not debilitating lower back pain, the product of an old athletic injury. The condition worsens, and after the Emperor fire, I am incapacitated by it. For a while I travel to Cedar City for workouts on a traction machine, which helps. In a few weeks I return to work, reaggravate the condition, and start the cycle over again. I am thirty-three years old; my tenure as a seasonal firefighter is rapidly coming to an end.

We walk Lydia to the heliport. Sonja and I were to be married here one May 14, but the snow—a freak storm in a drought year—started late on May 13 and did not stop until late on the fourteenth after eight miserable inches of white slush. The snow closed the North Rim; the unit manager's house became a makeshift wedding chapel; the Office was cleared into a reception room. That night the snow sloughed from the roofs like wet icing off a cake. The next day the sun returned, and by afternoon, when we walked to the heliport for wedding pictures, there was only bare, drab earth. Specks of snow could be found only on the shaded north slopes of Transept.

The sky is clear overhead, but to the west—toward Sublime and The Dragon, toward the boldly setting sun—the horizon is draped with virga tinted in yellows, oranges, and reds. Lightning flashes rhythmically. There is not much rain striking the ground, no more than a brush of moisture. Although strange in the types of fires, it has been an average fire year in numbers, and there is no reason to think the display will lead to a fire bust. The underside of the cloud deck darkens into furrows of grey and orange; the horizon is a broad wash of yellow and orange; sheets of virga darken and reflect the light. Sonja watches with a connoisseur's eye, but Lydia is frightened. We point to the west; Lydia looks only with reluctance. The lightning continues. Occasionally a faint rumble of thunder can be heard. She wants to be held, and only then will she look.

Together we watch the sunset, an almost operatic fugue of lightning, colors, and motion.

As 210 lifts off the pad, the ship points us to The Dragon.

The tempo of the fire bust has been perfect; day after day, one smoke is reported in the morning, another at night. We pull a crew from one fire and ship it directly to another. In two instances, where the smokes are more than snag fires and the mop-up more involved, we replace regular fire crew with reserves. Smokey's Fourth Rule of

Firefighting: Use your reserves for mop-up, and save your fire crew regulars for initial attack.

The fire on The Dragon is something of a mystery. Only two days ago we shipped Bone and John-Boy from a fire on The Dragon to one along the abandoned fireroad W-1E. The Balls fire on The Dragon was distinguished by its helispot—a limestone column, like a gargoyle, that rested against the Rim only a hundred feet or so from the fire. The surface was choppy with chert fossils and scalloped limestone and crowded with a large snag. When 210 first used it, it landed on one skid, and Bone and John-Boy exited with saws and pulaskis while the helo flew off and hovered. They dropped the large snag and cleaned out several shrubs before 210 returned for a proper landing. Bone was so enamored of the spot that he slept on it that night. Two South Rimmers, both red-carded, then replaced them on the Balls fire when they went to a fire on Crystal Ridge. Yesterday, with the fire declared out, the reservists departed the scene. Now Scenic Airlines has reported a smoke on The Dragon.

There is a good smoke column, a fire of several acres. As we circle the fire, it is obvious that this is the Balls fire reincarnated, yet nowhere can I see any firelines. We land and hustle to the scene. The fire is spreading evenly in all directions; the fire burns briskly, has already invaded several snags, and threatens to spill over the Rim. We scratch a line along the Rim and request more firefighters and a box of fusees. Then we begin to encircle the fire with a line. My back still plagues me a little, so Kenny chops and scrapes a scratch line with the McLeod. I flag a route, picking the easiest fuels and the shortest path of line construction, then double back to burn out the intervening fuels with fusees from my firepack. We will probably increase the present size of the fire by 50 percent, but there is no real alternative. When Lenny arrives with the next group of reinforcements, the line is quickly completed, and he and Kenny begin felling snags. Lenny maneuvers the big Stihl saw skillfully, and Kenny, flamboyant in a red Longshot cruiser vest, watches for widowmakers and drives in wooden wedges with a pulaski, slamming it lengthwise like a pile driver.

Some clouds develop, and the site is partially shadowed and cooled. With the flaming front stopped, the poorly vented fire sim-

mers, smothering the ground with a blanket of smoke. I try to unravel the story. We locate the old fireline, only to discover that the South Rimmers had painstakingly rolled the berm of duff back into the line before they departed. They mopped up not a foot of fire. It will burn out soon, they reasoned—just as on the South Rim. I learn later, too, that the BI, anxious that The Dragon not be subjected to the scars of firefighting, took the South Rimmers aside before their arrival and instructed them to return everything to its "natural" state. Instead, the unmopped Balls fire smoldered, erupted into flame, and crossed the now-obliterated fireline to become the Recapitulation fire.

Whatever confusion exists in the Park, there is none for us. We have our own standards, and we know how to control fire. A second helo flight brings in cubitainers and fedcos. We mop up for a while in the heavy fuels and snags; then I release Lenny and the others; Kenny and I will remain for the night. Before the close of business for the day I radio our plans. Nominally I am talking to the Fire Pit, but the broadcast sweeps over the entire Park. For perhaps ten minutes I monopolize Park radio traffic, and I narrate the whole sorry sequence of events: the rolled berm, the abandoned mop-up, the excruciating saga of careless, witless firefighting. After furious debate the South Rim decides that it does not want the fire mopped up rigorously, just "secured." We improve the line and mop up the hottest spots along the perimeter, then call it quits for the day. Since the fire is located about midway on The Dragon, we decide to walk to the neck.

The sky has cleared, and the sun bathes everything in yellow. In another day I will COB. We watch the sun set over the Canyon. The Dragon is situated in the middle of the Hindu Amphitheater. The view to the west is shielded by the Sublime peninsula, and to the east by the Tiyo peninsula. The sunset, though compelling, has a remote quality. For the sunset we are spectators; for the fire, participants. As the sun drops, we are drawn back to the fire.

Only patches of daylight remain when we reach our camp. We set up our sleeping bags, locate our headlamps, and look for a campfire to cook rations and coffee. One of the snags felled earlier is burning quietly along a lightning scar, now red with embers. The scar faces to the sky, and we can place ration cans there for cooking. The stump we *use for a table. Sunset winds can be heard rushing along the Rim, perhaps one hundred feet away. Smoke hangs low to the ground.*

Kenny is the youngest member of the Longshots, a second-year man; last year he saw few fires. This is a good crew, one of the best, and it has been a good fire season, better than most. We make coffee cups out of fruit cans and boil water. We sit up late and drink ration coffee and talk about old crews and old fires. I tell Kenny about The Ape and Gummer and The Kid. I tell him about the fires on The Dragon. I talk about the Sublime fire and the Dutton fire and the Regeneration fire. I tell him about the Sure fire, the Miss fire, the Smoker fire; the Scorcher, Hippolyta, Honeymoon, Charlemagne, Sunrise, Odoriferous, Poltergeist, Twilight fires. Tomorrow we will fly back to the cache; the cabin must be cleaned for inspection; my gear must be checked in, papers signed and completed—without a written report the fire is not finished. Tomorrow I COB. But tonight we are at a fire on The Dragon.

Stars glimmer through the trees. Smoke catches the light of flames and transports it—a diffuse glow—into the darkness. Embers pop. Our laughter flickers through the black shadows of trees, and the evening air settles on the fire like a soft blanket.

The October darkness comes early.

Thickening clouds shut off the sunset, and some break free and settle in the Canyon, obscuring most of Transept. By the time the car is loaded, snow begins to fall. At Lindbergh Hill it is snowing heavily. If I can make it to Jacob, I'll be fine. Fire season is over.

At Little Park winds whip the snow into whirls and clouds. For an instant—a blink of the mind—I blank into reverie. The snow turns to smoke; the car headlights, to headlamps. There is a clamor of shouts; the rasp of a chain saw; the thunk and scraping of pulaskis and shovels; the snap of falling branches; the rush of flames. Through the smoke and noise I see a fire.

It is a fire I will always carry within me.

Final Report

WHILE THESE STORIES have their origins in actual events, the names of participants have been altered, episodes are combinations of several incidents, and some events attributed to one person happened, in fact, to someone else. A few fires have suffered a change in name, and others a change of timing. What I experienced is not identical to what others experienced. Anyone who needs to know why these alterations have been made will not be satisfied with any explanation I can give, but to those who were even circumstantially participants, I offer as an apology an appeal to the prerogative of someone who remains at heart a crew foreman, compulsorily plotting out each day's agenda, while expecting—hoping—that it will be interrupted by a smoke report. Promise ends; hope does not.

Those who participated in the adventure know my debt to them, even if now, as then, they resent the jobs assigned them or their position on the dispatch chart. A few deserve special acknowledgments: Paul, Joe, Dan, Bruce, Jonathan, Ralph, Tom, Mike, Jack, Dana, Eric, Jim, Rich and Richard, and, yes, Pete, who made it worthwhile and good; Lenny, Kenny, and Kent, who carry the tradition on. To Sonja, a sincere thanks—yet again. To Lydia, a remembrance. To Molly, a promise. To my dad, gratitude that comes too late.

To all of you, and the others, too, I hope I got most of it. But good or bad, the story is as right as I can make it.

S.J.P.
Glendale, Arizona

Glossary

Affirms   Computer-based national network for accessing fire-weather data and calculating fire-danger ratings.

Air tanker   Fixed-wing aircraft used to drop fire retardant, or slurry, on fires. Also known as a "slurry bomber."

Area   Developed Park Service area in the vicinity of Bright Angel Point on the North Rim.

BI   Burning Index; an integrated fire-danger rating parameter that estimates the intensity of a spreading fire.

Big Mac   Any one of several gear-drive McCulloch saws, principally models 890 and 895.

CCC   Civilian Conservation Corps; a conservation program created during the Depression.

COB   Close Of Business; final termination of a seasonal employee.

Engine   Forest-fire vehicle with water-spraying capabilities, by analogy to urban fire engines. Older term is "pumper."

EOD   Enter On Duty; the onset of hiring for a seasonal employee.

FCA   Fire Control Aid; a seasonal employee whose principal duty is firefighting. Commonly abbreviated to "fire aid." Older terms include "smokechaser" and "fire guard." Replaced by "Longshot."

Fern feeler   Ranger–naturalist or interpreter.

Fire cache   Forest-fire term for the firehouse or fire station.

Fire guard   Old term for FCA.

Fire map   Special map issued to fire crews; includes cadastral system and fireroads and trails; Chartex used for backing, and clear plastic for overlay.

Fire Pit   Office used by the fire crew foreman for dispatching and paperwork.

Fireline   Interruption in the fuels surrounding a fire, usually made by scraping combustibles away. Other variants: wet line (water), retardant line (fire retardant), hot line (flaming), handline (made with hand tools), catline (made by bulldozer).

Firepack   Individual smokechaser packs, outfitted with rations, small tools, maps, flagging, etc.

Fireshirt   Workshirt made of Nomex, a flame-resistant cotton material. Originally orange in color, later changed to yellow.

FMO   Fire Management Officer; the principal line officer on a district or administrative unit with fire responsibilities.

HDP   Hazard Duty Pay; a form of premium pay equal to 25 percent of base pay awarded for fireline work.

Helo   Slang term for helicopter. The Park helicopter is generally known by its radio call number, 210.

Hotshot   Common sobriquet applied to members of interregional (IR) fire-suppression crews.

Hot-spot   To attack the most critical portions of a fire as part of the initial attack.

Initial attack   First actions on a fire; sometimes abbreviated IA.

Inn   North Rim Inn, a more proletarian version of the Lodge; situated near the campground; converted to a store and recreation room.

IR   Interregional; used as an abbreviation for Interregional Fire Suppression Crew.

Line   Fireline; an interruption in the fuels surrounding a fire.

Lodge   Grand Lodge, located at Bright Angel Point; the main facility for tourist accommodations and dining.

Longshot   Term adopted by the North Rim fire crew to describe themselves; self-deprecating variant of "Hotshot."

Maintenance   Maintenance Division, one of four major administrative divisions in the National Park Service. Maintenance is responsible for everything connected with the physical plant of the Park; consists of two subdivisions: Roads and Trails, and Buildings and Utilities.

Mark III   Portable pump, about fifty pounds in weight.

McLeod   Special fire rake with large tynes and a flat, sharpened top.

Monument   Grand Canyon National Monument; eventually absorbed into Grand Canyon National Park and renamed Tuweep.

Mop-up   Final stages of a fire suppression, during which the fire is extinguished. Standards vary.

National Fire Danger Rating System   Algorithms established for calculating fire danger in several parameters; abbreviated NFDRS; uses the Affirms network for data input and output.

Nurse tanker   Water truck that supplies water to smaller pumpers.

T'óó baa'ih   Navajo expression for "no good" or "dirty."

OT   Overtime; a much sought-after form of premium pay.

Overhead   Fireline supervisors, especially members of project fire teams.

Permanent   Full-time careerist with the National Park Service, as distinguished from a seasonal, who works part-time.

Prescribed fire   Controlled ignition that seeks to advance some objectives of the land management agency, in this case the Park Service—commonly, but not exclusively, fuel reduction.

Project fire team   Organized cadre of specialists who direct large project, or campaign, fires. Also known as "overhead."

Pulaski   Firefighting tool that combines a grub hoe and an ax.

Pumper   Forest-fire vehicle with water-spraying capabilities. More current term is engine.

Ranger station   Main administrative building on the North Rim; also known as "the Office."

Recon 1   Radio call number for the Park fire-reconnaissance aircraft; sometimes known as "211."

Regular   Local term used to identify fire crew members, as distinguished from reserves.

Rehire   Status granted to seasonals during final evaluation; gives recipients priority consideration during the next year's hiring.

Reserve   Personnel used to back up the regular fire crew during large fires. While reserves have some training, fire is not their primary responsibility.

Seasonal   Temporary employee hired by the Park, with a maximum annual duty tour of 180 days, as distinguished from a permanent.

Slip-on   Pump and water-tank assembly that can be attached to the bed of a pickup truck to convert it into a pumper or engine.

Slurry   Fire retardant dropped from air tankers. At the North Rim, diammonium phosphate is usually used.

Smokechaser   Early term for a forest firefighter. Later replaced by "FCA" and "Longshot."

Snag   Dead tree. Sometimes generalized to any single tree that is burning.

SWFF   Southwest Forest Firefighter (also SWFFF); an experienced but temporary firefighter, usually Indian or Hispanic.

210   Radio call number for the Park helicopter.

211   Radio call number for the Park fire-reconnaissance aircraft; replaced by "Recon 1."

Three-quarter Ton   Chevy pickup with three-quarter-ton load capability, used by fire crews.

Tour of duty   Basic administrative unit of hiring and pay; a two-week period.

Widowmaker   Dead branch on a tree that can break loose and injure a sawyer.